MISSING RELATIVES
AND
LOST FRIENDS

MISSING RELATIVES
AND
LOST FRIENDS

by

Robert W. Barnes

CLEARFIELD

Printed for
Clearfield Company by
Genealogical Publishing Co.
Baltimore, Maryland
2008

ISBN-13: 978-0-8063-5368-5
ISBN-10: 0-8063-5368-6

Made in the United States of America

To Annette K. Burgert

Contents

Introduction

I dedicate this book to Annette K. Burgert, whose work in tracing the overseas origins of German settlers to America is unparalleled. Her painstaking research has brought her the distinction of being a Fellow of the American Society of Genealogists, but her gracious manner has earned her the title of *gnadige frau*.[1] Where possible I have cross-referenced many of the entries in ths book to her publications.

When I was a boy I used to listen to a radio program called "Mr. Keene, Tracer of Lost Persons." Now, like other family historians, I am tracing lost persons. When the family has stayed in one area for several generations, acquired property, gone to church, and taken part in community activities, the job can be quite easy. When family members don't stay put, the job gets harder. I hope this book will help to make some researchers' jobs easier.

This book contains advertisements for missing relatives and lost Friends from 18th and early 19th century newspapers. The notices taken primarily from newspapers in Maryland, Pennsylvania, Virginia, Delaware, a few in New York, and the District of Columbia chronicle the appearances, and disappearances of 1325 (Change number as needed) individuals. I have chosen 1719 as the starting date because 1719 is the year the *American Weekly Mercury* began publication in Philadelphia.

The 1332 notices chronicle the appearances and disappearances of 1566 individuals. This number includes an appendix containing items taken from the letters (published in the *Maryland Historical Magazine*) of Dr. Charles Carroll of Annapolis, who often instituted inquiries for individuals at the request of others.

Although the newspapers used were from a limited geographical area, the searches covered a wide geographical area. Sometimes I have been able to enhance notices with additional information on what happened to the individuals who were sought. I did not include runaway wives, servants, or slaves in this work as these categories are large enough for separate volume.

Statistics of my findings to date show that some 806 ads gave places of origin more specific than just the country. Relatives of the missing individual were named in 804 of the advertisements. Indentured servants were mentioned in 80 of the ads, while convicts were mentioned in another 25. Veterans of the Revolution were named in 41 of the notices (or in additional research notes). Ethnic origins were tabulated and the people sought included 341 Germans, 288 English, 241 Irish, 66 Scots, and 89 "Other," including 17 French, 16 Swiss, 13 Dutch, 7 Welsh, 2 African Americans. Missing children were the subjects of 72 ads. Native-born people were mentioned in 128 ads.

---

[1] Gracious lady.

Most ads contain the phrase (or some variation) "may hear of something to his (or her) advantage," which probably indicates there is a legacy waiting for the lost heir. Some indicate that family members are seeking a lost relative who as been separated. Other notices indicate that someone has a legal obligation to fill. Some items illustrate events in the history of our country.

An appendix contains entries taken from the letters of Dr. Charles Carroll of Annapolis, who often instituted inquiries for individuals at the request of others. These letters were originally published in the *Maryland Historical Magazine.*

Some items contain quite a bit of specific biographical and genealogical data. One of the longest ads was seeking the whereabouts of Montague Cope Austin. Two separate notices concerning Elizabeth Dring and Thomas Dring complement each other. Two ads for John Bayes also add to our knowledge of that family. One of the most startling notices was for the children or next of kin of Governor Samuel Ogle. His family has been well researched, but this ad spoke of a legacy in Dublin. Sometimes, strict proof of identification was required. See the notice for William Ellis, 1791.The ad seeking Betsy Sargeant, 1811, is an example of an ad for abducted children.

So, gentle reader, this book is offered in the hope that it may assist you in the never-ending attempt to create as complete a family history as possible.

A note about the arrangement: all names starting with Mac, Mack, and Mc, are filed as if they were spelled Mc. Thus Mayer will come before the Mc's.

Acknowledgments

I have found many clues in the works of Annette Burgert, Peter Wilson Coldham, David Dobson, Robert K. Headley, Edward Hocker, Kenneth Scott, and F. Edward Wright. On-line sources include the *Pennsylvania Gazette*, 1728-1800 (available from American Archives), and America's Historic Newspapers (News Bank, Inc.).

I must thank Judith Roach and the staff members of the Local History and Genealogy Reading Room at the Library of Congress, Michael McCormick, Director of Reference and Research at the Maryland State Archives, and my colleagues in that department. They have all provided encouragement and technical advice.

Patricia Dockman Anderson, Editor of the *Maryland Historical Magazine.* Francis P. O'Neill and the staff of the Maryland Historical Society Library have also been extremely helpful.

Unusual Advertisements

In the course of my research I found some advertisements, not for individuals, but for whole groups of people.

Andrew Dewees, & Co., of Dugan's Wharf, advertised for any person, or the heirs of any person that served on the frigate *South Carolina* during the Revolutionary War, to call on him, as they may hear of something to their advantage (*Republican Star or Eastern Shore General Advertiser* 22 March 1808).

New York, May 21, 1763: Those Persons who came from North Britain, into the Province of New York, in the Years 1738, 1739, or 1740, with Captain Laughlin Campbell, and are now residents in any of the neighboring governments, or the descendants of such of them as are now dead, are hereby desired to take notice, that there is a meeting proposed to be had at the House of Neil Shaw in the City of New York, on the first day of July next, at which the said persons are requested, by some of their fellow emigrants, to attend, either personally or by others in their behalf (*Pa. Gaz.* 21 May 1763).

Bibliography

Periodicals and Newspapers On Line

America's Historical Newspapers (subscription). Posted by NewsBank [verify data]. The newspapers used from this site are listed below.

Accessible Archives Inc., <www.accessible.com>. (subscription)[Contains free index to eighteenth-century *Pennsylvania Gazette.*] Scanned Text; searchable; at Library of Congress

Early English Journals.< http://www.bodley.ox.ac.uk/ilej/> [Contains searchable index to The Gentleman's Magazine, Notes and Queries, Blackwood's Edinburgh Magazine, and Philosophical Transactions of the Royal Society

Early Maryland Newspapers on Line, at www.mdsa.net (free) (Go to Archives of Maryland; All Volumes; Early State Records/Newspapers. Newspapers scanned as PDFs to date include: Annapolis *Maryland Gazette, 1727-1839* (with a few gaps) Baltimore *American and Commercial Daily Advertiser,* 4 Sep 1802- 31 Dec 1807; Baltimore *Whig,* 2 July 1810 – 31 Dec 1810; Cambridge *Chronicle* 25 Dec 1830 – 13 June 1845, 3 Jan 1846 – 30 Dec 1857; Cecil *Whig* Aug 1870-Aug 1874; Centreville *Observer* June 1871 – Oct 1918; Ellicott City *Times* Sep 1870 – Dec 1879, Jan 1892 – Dec 1895, Jan 1898 – Dec 1899; Kent County *News* Jan-June 1965; *Maryland* Journal Jan 1889 – Dec 1889; *Maryland Republican* June – Dec 1809; *Montgomery County Sentinel* Jan 1860 – Dec 1872; *Queenstown News* Jan 1888 - July 1903; *Republican Star, or, Eastern Shore General Advertiser* Sep 1802 – Dec 1803.

Historic American Newspapers; ProQuest; Searchable Text; available at Baltimore Co. Public Library. <www.bcplonline.org> Go to History on Pull Down menu, Free at Baltimore Co. Public Libraries or to BCPL card holders. Includes The New York *Times* (all published); Washington *Post* (all published); Baltimore *Sun* (last ten years only); *The Wall Street Journal* and *The Christian Science Monitor.*

Past Portal: Colonial Williamsburg's Portal to American History, www.pastportal.com> (free). [Contains a free index to eighteenth-century *Virginia Gazette.*] PDFs; on Internet

Individual Newspapers of Delaware, The District of Columbia, Maryland, New York, and Virginia

Aberdeen Journal (Scotland); *Alexandria Advertiser* (VA); *Alexandria Expositor* (VA); *Alexandria Gazette (and Daily advertiser)* (VA); *Alexandria Herald* (VA); *Alexandria Times* (VA); *American Beacon (and Commercial Diary)* (VA); *American Beacon and (Norfolk and) Portsmouth Daily Advertiser* (VA); *American Farmer* (MD); *American Star* (PA); *American Star* (VA); *American Telegraph* (PA); *American Watchman* (DE); *American Weekly Mercury* (PA); *Amerikanischer Beobachter* (PA); Annapolis *Maryland Gazette* (MD); *Apollo* (MD); *Aurora General Advertiser:* (PA).

Missing Relatives and Lost Friends

Baltimore Daily Intelligencer (MD); *Baltimore Evening Post* (MD); *Baltimore Patriot (& Mercantile Advertiser)* (MD); *Baltimore Price-Current* (MD); *Bartgis's Maryland Gazette and Frederick-town Weekly Advertiser* (MD); *Bradford's New York Gazette* (NY).

Carey's United States' Recorder (PA); *Carlisle Gazette (Kline's)* (PA); *Carlisle Gazette and the Western Repository of Knowledge* (PA); *Carlisle Republican* (PA); *Centinel of Liberty* (DC); *City of Washington Gazette* (DC); *Columbian Chronicle* (DC); *Courier* (DC); *Chesnuthiller Wochenschrift* (PA); *Chronicle* (PA); *Claypoole's American Daily Advertiser;* (PA); *Columbian Advertiser* (VA); *Commercial Register* (VA); *Constitutional Diary* (PA); *Courier de l'Amerique* (PA).

Daily National Intelligencer (DC); *Delaware Gazette* (DE); *Democratic Republican* (MD); *Democratic Republican* (PA); *Dunlap's Pennsylvania Packet and General Advertiser* (PA); *Dunlap's American Daily Advertiser* (PA).

Easton Gazette and Eastern Shore Intelligencer (MD); *Edward's Baltimore Daily Advertiser* (MD); *Enquirer* (VA).

Farmers' Register (PA); *Federal Gazette* (PA); *Federal Gazette and Baltimore Daily Advertiser* (MD); *Federal Intelligencer and Baltimore Daily Gazette* (MD); *Federal Republican* (DC); *Federal Republican* (MD); *Fincastle Weekly Advertiser* (VA); *Finlay's American Naval and Commercial Register* (PA); *Frederick Town Herald* (MD); *Freeman's Journal or The North American Intelligencer* (PA).

Gazette of the United States (PA); *General Advertiser* (PA); *General Staatsbothe* (MD); *Genius of Liberty* (VA); *Germantauner Zeitung* (PA); *Gleaner* (PA); *Greensburgh & Indiana Register* (PA); *Grotjan's Philadelphia Public-Sale Report* (PA).

Hagers-town Gazette (MD); *Herald of Gospel Liberty* (PA); *Herald of Liberty* (PA); *Hornet or Republican Advocate* (MD).

Independent American (DC); *Independent Gazetteer* (PA); *Independent Whig* (PA).

Lancaster Journal(PA); *Library* (PA).

Mail (PA); *Maryland Chronicle, or Universal Advertiser* (MD); *Maryland Gazette and Baltimore Advertiser* (MD); *Maryland Gazette and Frederick Town Weekly Advertiser* (MD); *Maryland Herald and Elizabeth Town Advertiser* (MD); *Maryland Journal and Baltimore Advertiser* (MD); *Mechanic's Gazette; and Merchants Daily Advertiser* (MD); *Metropolitan* (DC); *Monitor* (DC).

National Gazette (PA); *National Intelligencer (and Washington Advertiser)* (DC); *National Messenger* (DC); *New York Evening Post* (NY); *New York Mercury* (NY); *New York Post Boy* (NY); *Newport Herald* (PA); *Norfolk Herald and Public Advertiser* (VA); *North Carolina Gazette* (NC).

Olio (DC); *Oracle of Dauphin* (PA).

Pa. Gaz. Pennsylvania Gazette (PA); *Palladium of Liberty* (VA); *Pennsylvania Chronicle (and Universal Advertiser)* (PA); *Pennsylvania Chronicle* (PA): *Pennsylvania Correspondent* (PA): *Pennsylvania Evening Herald (and the American Monitor* (PA): *Pennsylvania Evening Post* (PA): *Pennsylvania Herald* (PA): *Pennsylvania Journal* (PA): *Pennsylvania Ledger: or the VA, MD, PA, and NJ Weekly Advertiser* (PA): *Pennsylvania Mercury (and Universal Advertiser)* (PA): *Pennsylvania Packet and Daily Advertiser* (PA): *Pennsylvania Packet and General Advertiser* (PA): *Pennsylvanische Berichte* (PA): *Penn-sylvanische Geschichts-Schreiber* (PA): *Pennsylvanische Staatsbote* (PA): *Petersburg Daily Courier* (VA); *Philadelphia Evening Post* (95 issues); *Philadelphia Gazette (& Universal Daily Advertiser)* (PA): *Philadelphia Literary Reporter* (PA): *Philadelphia Minerva* (PA): *Philadelphia Repository* (PA): *Philadelphische Correpondenz* (PA): *Pinkney's Virginia Gazette* (VA): *Political Censor* (VA); *Political Mirror* (VA); *Porcupine's Gazette* (PA): *Poulson's American Daily Advertiser* (PA): Purdie, Clarkson, and Davis' *Virginia Gazette* (VA).

Republican (MD); *Republican Star or (Eastern Shore) General Advertiser* (MD): *Richmond Enquirer* (VA); Rind's *Virginia Gazette* (VA): *Royal Pennsylvania Gazette* (PA).

Scott's Philadelphia Price-Current (PA); Senator (DC); *Sower's Newsspaper* (PA): *Spirit of 'Seventy-Six* (DC); *Spirit of the Press* (PA): *Spirit of the Times* (Carlisle) (PA): *Star of Freedom* (PA): *Staunton Spy* (VA); *Temple of Reason* (PA).

The New York Gazette and Weekly Mercury (NY); *The Times and District of Columbia Daily Advertiser* (DC); *Tickler* (PA): *True American* (PA).

United States' Gazette (PA).

Village Record or Chester and Delaware Federalist (PA): *Virginia Chronicle* (VA); *Virginia Chronicle and Norfolk and Portsmouth General Advertiser*(VA); *Virginia Gazette* (VA): *Virginia Gazette and Alexandria Advertiser* (VA); *Virginia Gazette and American Advertiser* (VA); *Virginia Gazette and General Advertiser* (VA); *Virginia Gazette and Richmond and Manchester Advertiser* (VA); *Virginia Gazette and Weekly Advertiser* (VA); *Virginia Gazette or Norfolk Intelligencer* (VA); *Virginia Herald and Fredericksburg Advertiser* (VA); *Virginia Independent Chronicle* (VA); *Virginia Journal* (VA); *Virginia Journal and Alexandria Advertiser* (VA); *Voice of the Nation* (PA).

Washington City Weekly Gazette (DC); *Washington Expositor* (DC); *Washington Federalist* (DC); *Washington Spy* (Hagerstown) (MD); *Weekly Advertiser* (PA); *Welt Bothe* (PA): *Whig Chronicle* (PA): *Wochentlicher Pennsylvanischer Staatsbote* (PA).

Newspaper Abstracts

Barnes1: Robert Barnes. *Marriages and Deaths from the Maryland Gazette, 1727-1839.* Baltimore: Genealogical Publishing Co., Inc., 1973.
Barnes2: Robert Barnes. *Gleanings from Maryland Newspapers, 1727-1795.* 4 vols.
Bates, Marlene, and Martha Reamy. *Abstracts of Carroll County Newspapers, 1831-1846.* Westminster: Family Line Publications, 1988.

Dixon: Joan M. Dixon. *National Intelligencer and Washington Advertiser Newspaper Abstracts, 1800-1805/* Bowie: Heritage Books, 1996.

Dobson, David. *American Data from the Aberdeen Journal, 1748-1783.* Baltimore: Clearfield Co., 1998.

Eyster: Anita L. Eyster. "Notices of German and Swiss settlers Seeking Information on Members of Their Families .... 1742 –1761, 1762-1779." *Pennsylvania German Folklore Society* 3:1-41.

GAVN: See Headley.

Headley: Robert K. Headley, Jr., *Genealogical Abstracts from 18th Century Virginia Newspapers.* Baltimore: Genealogical Publishing Co., 1987.

Hocker: Edward W. Hocker. *Genealogical Data Relating to the German Settlers of Pennsylvania and Adjacent Territory. From Advertisements in German Newspapers Published in Philadelphia and Germantown, 1743-1800.* Baltimore: Genealogical Publishing Co., 1981.

Schlegel: Donald M. Schlegel. *Irish Genealogical Abstracts from the Londonderry Journal, 1772-1784.* Baltimore: Printed for Clearfield Co., by the Genealogical Publishing Co., Inc., 1990.

Scott 1: Kenneth Scott. *Abstracts of Franklin's Pennsylvania Gazette, 1728-1748.* GPC, 1977, and checked Scott1 through p. 69 (beginning of 1733)

Scott 2: -------. *Abstracts of Franklin's Pennsylvania Gazette, 1748-1754.* Baltimore: Genealogical Publishing Co.

Scott 3: -------. *Genealogical Data from Colonial New York Newspapers.* (1977). Repr. Baltimore: Genealogical Publishing Co., Inc., for Clearfield Co., 2000.

Scott 4: ------- and Rosanne Conway. *Genealogical Data from Colonial New Haven Newspapers.* (1979). Repr.: Baltimore: Genealogical Publishing Co., Inc., for Clearfield Co., 1999.

Scott 5: -------. *Genealogical Data from the New York Post Boy, 1743-1773.* Washington: The National Genealogical Society (Special Publication No. 35), 1980.

-------. *Genealogical Abstracts from the American Weekly Mercury, 1719-1746.* Baltimore: Genealogical Publishing Co., 1974.

Wright: F. Edward Wright. *Abstracts of the Newspapers of Georgetown and the Federal City, 1789-1799.* Silver Spring: Family Line Publications, 1986.

-------. *Abstracts of South Central Pennsylvania Newspapers, 1785-1800.* 3 vols. Silver Spring: Family Line Publications, 1988.

-------. *Newspaper Abstracts of Allegany and Washington Counties, 1811-1815.* Silver Spring: Family Line Publications, no date.

-------. *Newspaper Abstracts of Frederick County, 1811-1815.* Westminster: Family Line Publications, 1992.

-------. *Western Maryland Newspaper Abstracts, 1786-1798.* Westminster: Family Line Publications

-------. *Western Maryland Newspaper Abstracts, 1799-1805.* Westminster: Family Line Publications.

Primary Sources And Abstracts

1790MD: Heads of Families at the First Census of the United States, Taken in the Year 1790: Maryland Washington: Government Printing Office.

1790PA: Heads of Families at the First Census of the United States, Taken in the Year 1790: Pennsylvania. Washington: Government Printing Office. 1908.

1820 Pension List. Repr. Baltimore: Genealogical Publishing Co.

AA Co.: Anne Arundel County, Maryland.

AACR: F. Edward Wright. *Anne Arundel County Church Records of the Seventeenth and Eighteenth Centuries.* Westminster: Family Line Publications, 1989.

AAWB: ANNE ARUNDEL CO., MD, REGISTER OF WILLS (Wills), MSA C153.

AIS 1790 Census Index: 1790 U. S. Federal Census Index AIS. Ancestry CD SKU:2362.

AIS Census Index: Pre 1790. Ancestry CD SKU:2362

ARMD: The Archives of Maryland. Vol. 1 - . Baltimore: The Maryland Historical Society, 1883-

ARNJ: The Archives of New Jersey.

AWAP: Peter Wilson Coldham. *American Wills and Administrations of the Prerogative Court of Canterbury.* Baltimore: Genealogical Publishing Co., 1989.

BA Co.: Baltimore County, Maryland.

BAAB: BALTIMORE CO. REGISTER OF WILLS (Administration Bonds), MSA C264.

BAJA: Bill and Martha Reamy. *St. James [of My Lady's Manor, Baltimore Co.], Parish Register, 1787-1815.* Westminster: Family Line Publications.

BALR: BALTIMORE COUNTY, MD, COURT (Land Records), MSA C352.

BAPA: Bill and Martha Reamy. *Records of St. Paul's Parish.* 2 vols. Westminster: Family Line Publications, 1988. © by Martha Reamy. [Baltimore City and Lower Baltimore County].

Barnes, Robert W. *British Roots of Maryland Families.* 2 vols. Baltimore: Genealogical Publishing Co.

-------. *Maryland Marriages 1634-1777.* Baltimore: Genealogical Publishing Co., Inc., 1975.

-------. *Maryland Marriages, 1778-1800.* Baltimore: Genealogical Publishing Co., Inc., 1978.

BARP: See Henry C. Peden, Jr. *Revolutionary Patriots of Baltimore Town and County, 1775-1783.* Westminster: Family Line Publications.

BAWB: BALTIMORE CO., MD, REGISTER OF WILLS (Wills), 1666-1851, MSA C 435.

BCMR: Henry C. Peden, Jr. *Methodist Records of Baltimore City, 1799-1839. 2 vols.* Westminster: Family Line Publications, 1994.

BDML: Edward C. Papenfuse et al. *Biographical Dictionary of the Maryland Legislature, 1635-1789.* 2 vols. New York: The Johns Hopkins University Press, 1985.

Berks Births John T. Humphrey. *Pennsylvania Births: Berks County.* Washington: The Author, 1997.

Berks Churches. Wright, F. Edward. *Berks County Church Records of the 18th Century.* 4 vols. Westminster: Family Line Publications, 1993-1994. See FTM CD#512.

Berks Wills. Wright, F. Edward. Abstracts Berks County [PA] Wills. Based on the work of Jacob Martin and John P. Smith. Westminster: Family Line Publications, 1993-1997. Vol. 1. Vol. 2, 1752-1785. Vol. 3, 1785-1800. Vol. 4, 1800-1825.

BFD: PREROGATIVE COURT (Balance Books), 1751-1776, MSA S533. See also Debby Moxey and C. L. Skinner, Jr. *Abstracts of the Balance Books of the Prerogative Court of Maryland.* 7 volumes in 5. Westminster: Family Line Publications.

Bockstruck, Lloyd Dewitt. *Denizations and Naturalizations in the British Colonies in America. 1607-1775.* Baltimore: Genealogical Publishing Co., 2005.

BOCP: BALTIMORE COUNTY, MD, REGISTER OF WILLS (Orphans Court Proceedings), 1777-1851, MSA C396.

Boyer: Carl Boyer, 3rd. *Ship Passenger Lists: Pennsylvania and Delaware, 1641-1825.*
Repr.: Westminster: Family Line Publications, 1992. Beg. 3/1/04: checked A-Z.*

Boyer2: Carl Boyer, 3rd. *Ship Passenger Lists: The South (1328-1825).* Westminster: Family
Line Publications, (c) 1979 by Carl Boyer, 3rd. Beg. 3/20/04 checked A*, E*, J*, R*

Brumbaugh, Gaius Marcus. *Maryland Records: Colonial, Revolutionary, county, and
Church, from Original Sources* 2 vols. (1915-1928). Repr.: Baltimore:
Genealogical Publishing Co., 1967.

Bucks Churches: Bucks County, Pennsylvania Church Records of the 17th and 18th Centuries.
3 vols. Westminster: Family Line Publications. See FTM CD#512.

Bucks Churches 4: Wright, F. Edward. *Bucks County, Pennsylvania Church Records of the
17th and 18th Centuries. Volumes 4.* Lewes [DE]: Colonial Roots, © 2003.

Bucks Co. Wills. Abstracts of Bucks County, Pennsylvania, Wills, 1685-1785. Westminster:
Family Line Publications.

Burgert's *Alsace:* Burgert, Annette K. *Eighteenth Century Emigrants from Northern Alsace
to America.* The Pennsylvania German Society, Vol. 26, 1992.

Burgert's *Gimbsheim:* Annette K. Burgert. *Brethren from Gimbsheim in the Palatinate to
Ephrata and Bermudian in Pennsylvania.* Myerstown: AKB Publications, 1994.

Burgert's *Northern Kraichgau:* Annette K. Burgert. *Eighteenth Century Emigrants from
German Speaking Lands to North America. Volume I, The Northern Kreichgau.*
Breinigsville: The Pennsylvania German Society, Vol. 16, 1983.

Burgert's *Palatine Ancestors:* Burgert, Annette K. *Palatine Origins of Some Pennsylvania
Pioneers.* Myerstown, AKB Publications, 2000.

Burgert's *Western Palatinate:* Burgert, Annette K., *Eighteenth Century Emigrants from
German-Speaking Lands to North America: Volume II: The Western Palatinate.*
Birdsboro: The Pennsylvania German Society, Vol. 19, 1985.

CBEB. Peter Wilson Coldham. *Complete Book of Emigrants in Bondage.* Baltimore:
Genealogical Publishing Co. Reissued on FTM CD#350 Complete Book of
Emigrants, 1607-1776.

CBE2: Peter Wilson Coldham. *Complete Book of Emigrants, 1661-1699.* Baltimore:
Genealogical Publishing Co., 1990. Reissued on FTM CD#350 Complete Book of
Emigrants, 1607-1776.

CBE4: Peter Wilson Coldham. *Complete Book of Emigrants, 1751-1776.* Baltimore:
Genealogical Publishing Co., 1993. Reissued on FTM CD#350 Complete Book of
Emigrants, 1607-1776.

CELR: CECIL COUNTY, MD, COURT (Land Records). 1674-1792. MSA C 626. See also
June D. Brown. *Abstracts of Cecil County Land Records, 1673-1753.* 2 vols.
Westminster: Family Line Publications, 1998-9.

CH Co.: Charles County, Maryland.

Chester Wills: Wills of Chester County, Pennsylvania. Westminster: Family Line
Publications. [Based on the work of Joseph Martin].

CMN: Jeffrey A. Wyand and Florence L. Wyand. *Colonial Maryland Naturalizations.*
Baltimore: Genealogical Publishing Co., 1975.

CMSP: Black: Calendar of Maryland State Papers: The Black Books. (1943). Repr.:
Baltimore: Genealogical Publishing Co., 1967.

Coldham, Peter Wilson. *American Migrations, 1765-1799.* Baltimore: Genealogical Publishing Co., 2000.

-------. *British Emigrants in Bondage.* Baltimore: Genealogical Publishing Co., 2005. CD.

Crozier, William Armstrong. *Spotsylvania County Records.* See his *Virginia County Records.* 10 vols. (1905-1913). Repr.: Baltimore: Genealogical Publishing Co., 1965-1973.

CVRP: See *RPCV.*

DCC: "Extracts from the Account and Letter Books of Dr. Charles Carrroll, of Annapolis," beginning serially in the *Maryland Historical Magazine,* vol. 18.

DIEN: David Dobson. *Irish Emigrants in North America.* Six parts, varying dates. Baltimore: Genealogical Publishing Co.,

Dobson, David. *American Data from the Aberdeen Journal,1748-1783.* (1998). Repr. by the Genealogical Publishing Co. for Clearfield Co.

-------. *The Original Scots Colonists in Early America, 1612-1783.* Baltimore: Genealogical Publishing Co., 1989.

DOJA: -------. *The Jacobites of Angus, 1689-1746. In Two Parts.* Baltimore: Genealogical Publishing Co., 1997.

DSBA: -------. *Directory of Scots Banished to the American Plantations, 1650-1775.* Baltimore: Genealogical Publishing Co., 1983.

DSSA: -------. -------. *Directory of Scottish Settlers in North America, 1625-1825.* Volume I. Baltimore: Genealogical Publishing Co., 1984.

DSSB: -------. -------. Volume II. Baltimore: Genealogical Publishing Co., 1984.

DSSC: -------. -------. Volume III. Baltimore: Genealogical Publishing Co., 1984.

DSSD: -------. -------. Volume IV. Baltimore: Genealogical Publishing Co., 1985.

DSSE: -------. -------. Volume V. Baltimore: Genealogical Publishing Co., 1985.

DSSF: -------. -------. Volume VI. Baltimore: Genealogical Publishing Co., 1986.

DSSG: -------. -------. Volume VII. Baltimore: Genealogical Publishing Co., 1993.

Early Church Records of New Castle Co., Delaware. Westminster: Family Line Publications.

Egle's Notes and Queries.

EMH: [Easton] *Maryland Herald.*

ESVR: F. Edward Wright. *Maryland Eastern Shore Vital Records, 1648-1825.* 5 vols. Westminster: Family Line Publications, 1982-1986.

Eustace: P. Beryl Eustace. Ed. *Registry of Deeds: Dublin: Abstracts of Wills. Vol. 1 1708-1745. Vol. II, 1746-1785.* (1956), Repr. Baltimore: Clearfield Co., Inc., 1996.

Faust 2: Albert Bernhardt Faust and Gaius Marcus Brumbaugh. *Lists of Swiss Emigrants in the Eighteenth Century to the American Colonies. Volume II, From the State Archives of Bern and Basel, Switzerland.* Washington: The National Genealogical Society, 1925.

Fothergill. Gerald. *Emigrants from England, 1773-1776.* (1913). Repr.: Baltimore: Genealogical Publishing Co.., 1992

FRLR: FREDERICK CO., MD, COURT (Land Records), 1748-1847, MSA C 814.

FTM CD#19: *Egle's Notes and Queries of Pennsylvania.*

FTM CD#133: Maryland and Delaware Revolutionary Patriots, 1775-1783; beg. 25 Feb 2004 checked: K

FTM CD#178: Maryland and Delaware Church Records; beginning 3/1/04: checked A-Z*

FTM CD#195: Maryland Genealogies and Marriages.

FTM CD#206: Maryland Probate Records, 1634-1777.

FTM CD#209: Pennsylvania Wills, 1682-1834: beg. 19 Feb 2004: checked K*

FTM CD#350: Complete Book of Emigrants: beg. 15 Feb 2004: checked A-Z*

FTM CD#521: Maryland Settlers and Soldiers. Beg. 25 Feb 2004 checked:

Grogaard and Warfield. Hans Grogaard and Mary Warfield. *Burials in Pro-Cathedral and Cathedral Cemeteries, Baltimore, Maryland, 1791-1874.* Westminster: Willow Bend Books, 2004.

Gwathmey, John H.. *Historical Register of Virginians, Soldiers, Sailors, Marines, 1775-1783 in the Revolution.* Richmond, 1938.

Harris, Ruth Ann M., and Daniel M. Jacobs. *The Search for Missing Friends: Irish Immigrant Advertisements Placed in the Boston Pilot.* 7 vols., 1831-1876. Boston, New England Historic Genealogical Society, 1989-.

IGI: International Genealogical Index, <www.familysearch.org>.

Irish. PGM. Irish, Donna. *Pennsylvania German Marriages.* Baltimore: Genealogical Publishing Co. 1982.

KEWB: KENT CO. REGISTER OF WILLS (Wills), 1669-1798. MSA C1107. See also Christos Chritou, Jr., and John Anthony Banhouser. *Abstracts of Kent County, Maryland, Wills.* 2 vols., 1777-1867, Westminster: Family Line Publications.

KPMV: Peter Wilson Coldham. *The King's Passengers to Maryland and Virginia.* Westminster: Family Line Publications.

Lancaster Churches. Wright, F. Edward. *Lancaster County, Pennsylvania Church Records of the 18th Century.* 4 vols. Westminster: Family Line Publications.

Lancaster Journal. See Rita Schive Mowrer, "Genealogical Gleanings from the Lancaster Journal," in *Pennsylvania Vital Records* (Baltimore: Genealogical Publishing Co.), 2:548-644.

Lancaster Wills. F. Edward Wright. *Abstracts of Lancaster County, Pennsylvania Wills, 1732-1785.* Westminster: Family Line Publications.

Lebanon Churches. F. Edward Wright. *Early Church Records of Lebanon County, Pennsylvania.* Westminster: Family Line Publications. 1995.

LEMK: Jack and Marion Kaminkow. *List of Emigrants to America, 1718-1759.* Repr. Baltimore: Genealogical Publishing Co., 1989.

MCHR: CHANCERY COURT, MD (Chancery Record), 1668-1852, MSA S 517. See also Debbie Hooper. *Abstracts of Chancery Court Records of Maryland, 1669-1782.* Westminster: Family Line Publications, 1996.

MDAD: PREROGATIVE COURT, MD (Accounts), 1718-1777, MSA S 531. See also V. L. Skinner, Jr. *Abstracts of the Administration Accounts of the Prerogative Court of Maryland.* Westminster: Family Line Publications.

Memoirs: Martha Reamy and Marlene Bates. *Memoirs of the Dead and the Tomb's Remembrancer* (1806). Published by the transcribers and by Westminster: Family Line Publications, 1989.

MHM: Maryland Historical Magazine:

MINV: PREROGATIVE COURT, MD (Inventories), 1718-1777. MSA S 534. See also V. L. Skinner. *Abstracts of the Inventories of the Prerogative Court of Maryland.* Westminster: Family Line Publications

MNA: Robert Andrew Oszakiewski. *Maryland Naturalization Abstracts: Volume 1: Baltimore County and Baltimore City: 1784-1851.* Westminster: Family Line Publications, 1995.

Montgomery Wills: F. Edward Wright. *Abstracts of Montgomery County, Pennsylvania Wills and Administrations, 1784-1823.* Westminster: Family Line Publications, 1998.

Montgomery's *Berks.* Morton L. Montgomery. *Historical and Biographical Annals of Berks County, Pennsylvania* 2 vols. Chicago: J. H. Beers Co., 1909.

MPL: LAND OFFICE (Patent Record) MSA S 11, SM 2. (See Peter Wilson Coldham. *Settlers of Maryland, 1679-1783. Consolidated Edition.* Baltimore: Genealogical Publishing Co., 2002; Carson Gibb. *Supplement to [Skordas'] Early Settlers of Maryland.* Electronic data base located on the Maryland State Archives web site; and Gust Skordas. *Early Settlers of Maryland, 1633-1680.* Baltimore: Genealogical Publishing Co., 1979..

MSA: Maryland State Archives, Annapolis, Maryland. When used with C, CM, S, SE, or SM, denotes a specific county or state record series, either original, digital, or on microfilm.

MWB: PREROGATIVE COURT, MD (Wills), 1635-1777, MSA S 538. See also Jane Baldwin (and Roberta B. Henry). *Maryland Calendar of Wills From 1635 to 1743.* 8 vols. (1908). Repr.: Baltimore: Genealogical Publishing Co., 1968. *Maryland Calendar of Wills.* Vols. 9-16. Westminster: Family Line Publications. See also Carson Gibb. *Abstracts of the Prerogative Court Wills.* Libers 23-31. Go to ww.mdsa.net and click on "Reference and Research." Then click on "Probate (Estate) Records." and you will see Abstracts of wills.....

Names of Foreigners Who Took the Oath of Allegiance to the Province and State of Pennsylvania, 1726-1775, With the Foreign Arrivals, 1786-1808. Edited by William Henry Egle. (Originally Published as the *Pennsylvania Archives,* Volume XVII, Second Series, Harrisburg, 1890). Repr.: Baltimore: Clearfield Co., 2002.

Nelson, William. *New Jersey Marriage Records, 1685-1800.* (1900). Repr.: Baltimore: Genealogical Publishing Co.,

New Castle Co., DE, Wills. Colonial Dames of Delaware. *A calendar of Delaware Wills. Newcastle County, 1628-1800.* (1911). Repr.: Baltimore: Genealogical Publishing Co... 1969.

Newman, Harry Wright. *Maryland Revoutionary Records.* (1938) Repr.: Baltimore: Genealogical Publishing Co., 1993.

NGSQ: National Genealogical Society Quarterly.

Northampton Births: John T. Humphrey. *Pennsylvania Births: Northampton County, 1733-1800.* Baltimore: Gateway Press, 1991.

Peden, Henry C., Jr. *Revolutionary Patriots of Baltimore Town and County, 1775-1783.* Westminster: Family Line Publications.

-------. *Revolutionary Patriots of Cecil County.* Westminster: Family Line Publications.

-------. *Revolutionary Patriots of Frederick County, Maryland, 1775-1783.* Westminster: Family Line Publications.

-------. *Revolutionary Patriots of Prince George's County, Maryland.* Westminster: Family Line Publications.

Pennsylvania Evening Post. See Elizabeth Parker Fitler. "Genealogical Gleanings from the *Pennsylvania Evening Post, 1775," "-------, 1776," "-----, 1777,"in Pennsylvania Vital Records* (Baltimore: Genealogical Publishing Co.) 2:349-402.

PGCR: Pennsylvania German Church Records. *3 vols. Baltimore: Genealogical Publishing Co.* Reissued on GPC CD#7130.

PGLR: PG CO. COURT (Land Records) MSA C 1237, CM 782. (See Elise Greenup Jourdan. *Prince George's Co. Land Records, 1702-1743.* 6 vols. Westminster, Family Line Publications, 1990).

PGML: PRINCE GEORGE'S, MD, COURT (Marriage Licenses), 1777-1851, MDSA C 1260. See also Helen W. Brown. *Index of Marriage Licenses of Prince George's County, Maryland, 1777-1886.* GPC, 1973.

PGP: Ralph Beaver Strassburger and William John Hincke. *Pennsylvania German Pioneers.* 2 vols. (1934) Repr.: Baltimore: Genealogical Publishing Co., 2002.

PGQA: Queen Anne's Parish, PG Co. MSA SC 2667.

PGS: Indentures. "Record of Indentures of Individuals Bound Out as Apprentices, Servants, etc., and of Germans and Other Redemptioners in the Office of the Mayor of the City of Philadelphia, October 3, 1771 to October 5, 1773." *The Pennsylvania German Society Proceedings and Addresses, 1905, vol. 16. (Repr.) Baltimore: Genealogical Publishing Co., 1973.*

Philadelphia. Wills. F. Edward Wright. *Abstracts of Philadelphia County Wills.* 10 vols. Westminster: Family Line Publications, 1995-1998.

Phillimore, W. P. W. *Indexes to Irish Wills.* (1909-1920). Repr. Baltimore: Genealogical Publishing Co., Inc., 1997

PIET: Piet, Mary A., and Stanley G. *Early Catholic Church Records in Maryland, 1782 through 1800.* Westminster: Family Line Publications, 1989.

PVR: Pennsylvania Vital Records. 3 vols. Baltimore: Genealogical Publishing Co. Reissued on CD#7172.

QRNM: Henry C. Peden, Jr. *Quaker Records of Northern Maryland.* Westminster, Md.: Family Line Publications.

QRSM: Henry C. Peden, Jr., *Quaker Records of Southern Maryland.* Westminster, Md.: Family Line Publications, 1992.

Records of Holy Trinity (Old Swedes) Church, Wilmington, Delaware, from 1797 to 1773. 1909.

RPCV: Henry C. Peden, Jr. *Revolutionary Patriots of Calvert Co., Maryland.* Westminster: Family Line Publications. See FTM CD#133, above.

RPMO: Henry C. Peden, Jr. *Revolutionary Patriots of Montgomery Co., Maryland.* Westminster: Family Line Publications. See FTM CD#133, above.

RPPG: -------. *Revolutionary Patriots of Prince George's County, Maryland.* Westminster: Family Line Publications. See FTM CD#133, above.

Rupp: J. Daniel Rupp. *A Collection of Upwards of Thirty Thousand Names of German, Swiss, Dutch, French and Other immigrants to Pennsylvania from 1727 to 1776.* (1876). Repr.: Baltimore: Genealogical Publishing Co., 2006.

SJSG: St. John's and St. George's Parish, BA and HA Counties; MSA SC 1642. (See Henry C. Peden, Jr., *St. John's and St. George's Parish Register, Baltimore and Harford County, Maryland, 1696-1851.* Westminster, Md.: Family Line Publications, 1987). (Page numbers are to the Lucy Harrison transcription at the Maryland Historical Society). See also Henry C. Peden. *A Closer Look at St. John's Parish registers, 1701-1801.* Westminster: Willow Bend Books, 2003.

SOCD: David Dobson. *Scots on the Chesapeake, 1607-1830.* Baltimore: Genealogical Publishing Co., 1992.

TAG: The American Genealogist.

TALR: TALBOT CO., MD. COURT (Land Records), 1662-1851. MSA C 1880. See also R. Bernice Leonard. *Talbot County, Maryland Land Records.* St. Michael's: the Author

Tepper, Michael. ed. *Emigrants to Pennsylvania, 1641-1819: A Consolidation of Ship Passenger Lists from the Pennsylvania Magazine of History and Biography.* Baltimore: Genealogical Publishing Co., 1979.

Thrift, Gertrude. *Indexes to Irish Wills.* (London:1913) Repr.: Baltimore: Genealogical Publishing Co.

Vicars, Arthur. *The Index to the Prerogative Wills of Ireland,1536-1810.* (1897). Repr: Baltimore: Genealogical Publishing Co., 1997.

Virginia Land Records, Baltimore: Genealogical Publishing Co.,

Weisiger, Benjamin B., III. *Chesterfield Co. Wills, 1749-1774.* 1979,

Wright, F. Edward. *Early Records of the First Reformed Church of Philadelphia.* Westminster: Family Line Publications, 1994.

YCLR: York County Land Records. See also: Mary Marshall Brewer. *Land Records of York County, Pennsylvania. 1764-1771.* Westminster: Family Line Publications, 2002.

Yoder's *PGI.* Don Yoder, ed. *Pennsylvania German Iimmigrants. 1709-1786.* Baltimore: Genealogical Publishing Co., 1984.

York Churches. Marlene Strawser Bates and F. Edward Wright. *Church Records of York County, Pennsylvania of the 18ᵗʰ Century.* 4 vols. Westminster: Family Line Publications, 1991.

Web Sites

Accessible Archives Inc.: www.accessible.com. [Contains free index to eighteenth-century *Pennsylvania Gazette.*]

Boston Pilot "Missing Irish Friends" column http://infowanted.bc.edu

English Immigrants Project, http://immigrants.byu.edu

Family Search: www.familysearch.org

International Genealogical Index, <www.familysearch.org>.

Internet Library of Early Journals, http://www.bodley.ox.ac.uk/ilej

Old Bailey Criminal Records: <www.oldbaileyonline.org>

Past Portal: Colonial Williamsburg's Portal to American History, www.pastportal.com>. [Contains free index to eighteenth-century *Virginia Gazette.*]

Port Cities, <www.portcities.org.uk>.

Virtual Jamestown: www.virtualjamestown.org

ACKERIN, ANNA CATHERINE, came to America about five years ago with her sister Dorothea Ackerin, who is now with Henrich Schenck, and who is now seeking information about Anna Catherine (*Hocker:* 83 cites the *Pennsylvanische Geschichts-Schreiber* 15 Feb 1760).

ACKROYD, JOHN, of Halifax, Old England, is lately deceased. His grandchildren or heirs should apply to Capt. Roberts of the ship *Grange* or to Jere. Warder, Parker and Co., to hear of something greatly to their advantage (*The Pennsylvania Packet and Daily Advertiser* 26 April 1790).

In 1790 a John Ackroyd was head of a family in Christiana Hundred, New Castle Co., DE (*AIS 1790 Census Index*).

ADAMS, JAMES, late of King William Co., VA, was a son of Philip Adams who died, leaving Philip Mallory as his administrator. Mallory advises James, if living, to apply immediately for the legacy left him by his grandmother Davis (*GAVN:* 2 cites *The Virginia Gazette* 7 April 1781).

ADAMS, THOMAS, and Frederick Mayer were both in the same company in the Continental Army commanded by Capt. Alexander Kirkpatrick. Adams deserted and left them at Old Cumberland Court House in VA. Adams told Mayer that his father lived in Nansemond Co, VA. Mayer, a Dutchman, came to Savanna, GA, early in 1782, and died on 1 Jan 1790. He devised all his estate, amounting about 3000 pounds current money, to Adams. If Adams is living he should apply to Thomas Hughes, Savanna (*Pennsylvania Mercury and Universal Advertiser* 24 April 1790).

AGEMAN, THOMAS, a man of about 80 years of age, late of Burlington in the western division of the province of New Jersey, has been missing ever since last 30 March, his son William and most of his neighbors are suspicious that he may have been murdered. Anyone with information should communicate with his son William, or by directing his or her letters to George Eyre, Esq., in Burlington (*Pa. Gaz.* 6 Feb 1753).

In 1732 Thomas Ageman was a debtor to the estate of Enoch Fenton of Burlington (*ARNJ* 30:173).

Thomas Ageman had at least one son: WILLIAM.

AITKEN, HUGH, *als* **AIKEN, HUGH,** son of William Aitken of Learne, Co. Antrim, arrived in PA two or three years ago. He will learn something to his advantage if he applies to one of several persons (*GAVN* 3 cites *The Virginia Gazette*, 20 Aug 1772).

AKERS, GEORGE, tinman, from London, brother of Elizabeth Gross of George Yard, Shoreditch, left England 14 or 15 years ago, and in the year 1761 was at Princetown, NJ, and in 1766 was heard of at Lancaster, PA. Since then he has not been heard of. If he is living and will apply to Capt. Spain, commander of the snow *Sally,* in Philadelphia, he will hear of something to his advantage (*Pennsylvania Journal* 22 Sep 1768).

ALBRECHT, JACOB, son of Johannes and Margretha Albrecht, of York Twp., over the Susquehanna, was indentured with English people in the Welsh Twp., Philadelphia Co. (Lower Merion or Gwynedd Twp., Montgomery Co.). Johannes Albrecht has died and the mother is seeking her son (*Hocker:*84 cites the *Pennsylvanische Geschichts-Schreiber* 24 April 1760).

ALBRECHT, JOHANNES DAVID, stocking weaver, arrived in America last year and left his wife, who was in confinement. Now he cannot be found. Information should be sent to Peter Schneider, Rock hill Twp., Bucks Co. (*Hocker:*37 cites the *Pennsylvanische Geschichts-Schreiber* 1 Dec 1752).

ALEXANDER, HUGH, and his wife **ELIZABETH ALEXANDER,** with three children, named **MARTHA, MARY** and **WILLIAM ALEXANDER,** left Ireland, from the County of Tarone [Tyrone?], and Town of Balamana, within one mile of Cookes Town, some years ago. If all, or any of them, be alive, and will apply to Mr. William Carson, peruke maker, in Front St., Philadelphia, may hear of something to their Advantages (*Pa. Gaz.* 24 July 1760).

     He may be the Hugh Alexander of Tyrone Twp., Cumberland Co., who advertised for the return of a runaway Irish servant (*Pa. Gaz.* 24 Aug 1774).

ALLBROOK, ROBERT, became a servant to Mr. Butterworth c1718. In 1721 he was a servant to Mr. Robert Clark. In 1723 he was a servant to George Rigdon, all living near Baltimore. In 1728 he hired himself to Cornelius Carmack of the Principio Company in Cecil Co., MD. If he is still living he should apply to Edmund Hough of Snow Hill, Worcester Co. for news of a legacy in England (Annapolis *Maryland Gazette* 8 July 1746). He was advertised for again in 1753 (Annapolis *Maryland Gazette* 5 July 1753)

     On 18 Aug 1734 Allbrook was listed as a creditor of the estate of Joseph Young of Cecil Co., MD. (MDAD 12:487). He was still in Cecil Co. on 4 Sep 1739 when he witnessed the will of John Johnson of Cecil Co. (MWB 21:537).

ALLEN, Mrs., widow of Thomas Allen, left Savannah with her two daughters in July 1812, and arrived here in the brig *Lucy.* If she is still living and in Baltimore she will hear something to her advantage by calling at the *Patriot* office (*Baltimore Patriot* 29 July 1828).

ALLEN, DAVID, went from Aberdeen some 15 or 10 years ago, and died in Antigua. If his nearest relations will apply to John Durno, advocate in Aberdeen, they will hear something to their advantage (Dobson *Aberdeen Journal* 11 Dec 1759, issue # 1144).

     David Allan, son of Peter Allan, was born 9 Aug 1718 at New Machar,

Aberdeenshire, where he resided until 1749 when he went to Antigua. He died in June 1759 at St. John Antigua (David Dobson, *The Original Scots Colonists in Early America, 1612-1783*. Baltimore: Genealogical Publishing Co., 1989, p. 5, cites the Aberdeen Propinquity Books).

ALLEN, JOHN, of Bloom's Grove, Worcestershire, wire drawer, about seven years ago sailed for America, with his son John, and resided for some years with a Mr. Wells, a planter in New York City, and then became an Anabaptist preacher in the eastern part of MA, and was last heard from at Kennebec [ME]. His father, John Allen, of Bury St. James, Esq., has died leaving him £300. He is asked to apply to the only surviving executor, Matthew Yetman of Percy St., London, apothecary (*Scott* 3:211 cites *The New York Gazette and Weekly Mercury* 10 Nov 1777).

ALLEN, ROBERT CAMPBELL, from New York, was in Richmond or its vicinity in the spring of 1826. If Allen is alive and will come to New York, and will apply to John Allen, 509 Pearl St., he will hear something to his advantage (Richmond *Enquirer* 15 May 1829).

ALLEN, THOMAS, late belonging to His Majesty's Fireship *The Infernal*, died at Chichester, Sussex, Eng., in Jan 1781. By his last will and testament dated 24 Aug 1779, he left divers legacies or sums of money to several persons named in his will, and then gave or bequeathed the residue of all the money he should died with, both prize money and wages to be divided equally among the children of his three sisters, Jane, Mary, and Ann, residing in Pennsylvania. He appointed Thomas Allen of Burr St., Wapping, Middlesex, and Edward Ommaney of American Square, London, as executors. The children of the said Jane, Mary, and Ann are entitled to a distributive share of the residue of the testator's effects. They are requested to transmit to the executors the registers of their respective baptisms, attested and authenticated as the law requires, to prove that they are the only lawful and legitimate children of the testator's sisters (*Pa. Gaz.* 4 June 1783).

ALLERTON, ROBERT, blacksmith, born in England, was supposed to have lived in Annapolis since about Feb 1771. He should apply to the printer (*Maryland Gazette or Baltimore General Advertiser* 24 April 1787).
  Robert Allerton, felon, of Yorkshire, was reprieved and sentenced to transportation for 14 years for stealing a sheep at Hampnell (*CBEB*). He was to be transported from Bristol in Dec 1770 by the *Trenton*, Joseph Blickenden, Capt., and registered in Baltimore Co., MD. There was a notation that he "had escaped in London" (*KPMV*: 218).

ALLIOD, JACK, a joiner of Oley, Berks Co., arrived in this country two years ago, and his daughter, Charlotte, 22 years old was indentured. Now he is seeking her (*Hocker*:51 cites the *Pennsylvanische Geschichts-Schreiber* 1 Aug 1755).

ALLISON, FRANCIS, son of Robert and Mary, of MD in North America, served his apprenticeship to a coach maker in Philadelphia. He left that place about 12 years ago, and has not been heard of since. If he is alive he is asked to apply to Mr. Ferguson McIlvaine, merchant in Philadelphia, to Messrs. Parnther and Druce, solicitors in

London, and he will hear of something greatly to his advantage. If he is dead, anyone who can give make that fact appear, is asked to give notice thereof (*Pa. Gaz.* 19 May 1784).

ALLKINS, ELIZABETH, arrived in Baltimore last fall as an indentured servant, from Dublin. She is urged to apply to the printer (*Maryland Journal and Baltimore Advertiser* 9 Nov 1784).

ALLMAN, SOLOMON, late of Lower Penn's Neck, Salem Co., died leaving an estate in the hands of Joseph Copner, who desires his heirs, if any are living, to come and prove their [right to the] property (*Pa. Gaz.* 9 April 1779).
    A Solomon Allman, son of Joseph, was born c1694, and bapt. at Christiana, DE, on 15 July 1722. He died at Lower Penn's Neck, Salem Co., NJ, early in 1768. He married Jane [-?-], who was granted administration of his estate on 9 March 1768 (*ARNJ* 30:262, 33:51, 440; *Records of Holy Trinity (Old Swedes) Church, Wilmington, Delaware, from 1797 to 1773.* 1909, p. 272).

ALSTON, JOSEPH, left Wilmington, DE, for Charleston, SC, some time in 1784, and left his daughter in the care of James Knowles. His daughter would like to hear from him. She has been told that her father was falsely informed that she was dead. Anyone with information is asked to contact Mrs. Polly Jones near London, Madison Co., OH (*The Daily National Intelligencer* 1 Dec 1815).

AMES, WILLIAMS, was born c1727 at Deal, Kent, and about 1750 he married Thomasine Frithers or Fivers, by whom he had one dau., Elizabeth, who lived with her aunt, Mrs. Sanderson at Yarmouth, in Norfolk, until the latter died, and the daughter now has also died. About 1758 William Ames went on a voyage and is now reported in England, to be living in New York City, and to be employed in trading from New York City to the West Indies in partnership with one Ward. If Ames is still living, he is asked to contact Messrs. Geldard and Gimingham in Staple Inn, Holborn, London. If he is dead, anyone with knowledge of his death is asked to give information to Charles McEvers in New York City, or to Messrs. Geldard and Gimingham (*Scott* 3:149 cites *The New York Gazette and Weekly Mercury* 12 Nov 1770).

ANDERSON, JAMES, son of John Anderson, cooper, formerly of the Loudon Co., if living, is asked to apply to Mr. J. Fox, South Third St., corner of Church Alley. No. 11, Philadelphia, one of the executors of James Anderson's uncle, William Anderson, or to his brother John Anderson on Licking Creek, Washington Co., MD, he will hear of something greatly to his advantage (Elizabeth Town *The Maryland Herald and Elizabeth Town Advertiser* 17 Feb 1802).

ANDERSON, WILLIAM, late of Portanonoe, Ireland, is said to be living in Philadelphia Co. This is to inform him that he has been sent, care of John Porter, a suit of clothes, which he may receive by applying to the said Porter, or to John Wallace in the

Horseshoe Road, Earl Twp., Lancaster Co., four miles from Windsor Forge (*Pa. Gaz.* 13 July 1769).

ANSTETT (or ANSTERT), JOHANNES, was sought by his brother-in-law Martin Schroeter (*Hocker:* 19 cites the *Pennsylvanische Geschichts-Schreiber* 1 June 1750). For more on the An(g)stett Family, see Burgert's *Alsace:* 29.

APPELLEE, WILLIAM, a native of Old England, was living in this city about ten years ago. He is urged to contact Daniel Offley where he may be informed of something to his advantage (*Pa. Gaz.* 19 July 1775).

ARAHSMITH, HENRY, *alias* **HENRY SMITH,** aged about 40, of a swarthy complexion, with black eyes and black hair. He served his time with a captain that sailed out of Philadelphia in the Jamaica trade before the war, and served on a British man of war at the beginning of the disturbances in America. If he is alive, he is asked to apply to the printer, or to Russel and Clap in Court St., Boston, where he may hear of something greatly to his advantage (*The Independent Gazetteer* 25 June 1787; *Newport Herald* 28 June 1787).

ARCHBALD, EBENEZER, son of the Rev. Robert Archbald, minister of the Gospel at Hadington, North Britain, should apply to William Archbald, shoemaker, Front St., Southwark, Philadelphia, and he shall hear of something to his advantage (*The Independent Gazetteer* 27 Nov 1784).

In 1790 an Ebenezer Archibald [*sic*] was head of a family in Cecil Co., MD (*AIS 1790 Census Index*).

ARMSTRONG, NANCY, formerly lived in Philadelphia about three years ago. If she will apply to Joseph Morebane, 398 North Third St., she will hear of something to her advantage ([D.C.] *Washington Federalist* 15 April 1801).

ARNDT, HERMAN, arrived in this country 19 years ago from Hanau, with his three sons, **PETER, MICHEL,** and **JACOB,** and a daughter **ANNA MARGARETHA ARNDT.** His son Heinrich, a stocking weaver, living near the Reformed Church in Philadelphia, arrived this year, and   is seeking the others (*Hocker*:29 cites the *Pennsylvanische Geschichts-Schreiber* 1 Nov 1751).

ARNOLD, JOH. NICLAS, came here seven years ago, and now is sought by his brother-in-law Joh. Leonhard Gottman, from Kirch-Brunnbach in Odenwald, who came here this summer, and is very sick on the ship *Union*, Capt. Bryson. (*Hocker*:126, and *Eyster:*33 cite the *Pennsylvanische Staatsbote* 19 Oct 1773).

Joh. Nicolaus Arnold arrived on the ship *Chance* on 23 Oct 1766 (*Eyster:*33).

ARNOLD, PHILIP, arrived in this country two years ago last autumn, with his brother Nicolaus, of Maxatawny, Berks Co., near Jacob Levan, who was indentured for three years. Nicolaus is seeking news of Philip (*Hocker*:56 cites the *Pennsylvanische Geschichts-Schreiber* 16 June 1756).

Johan Nichlaus Arnoldt arrived on the *Two Brothers*, Capt. Thomas Arnot, from Rotterdam, and qualified on 28 Sep 1753 (*PGP* 1:565).

In 1790 a Philip Arnold was head of a family in Upper Milford Twp., Northampton Co., PA (*AIS 1790 Census Index*).

ARUNDEL, HANNAH, advertised that her husband John Arundel of Philadelphia, left her during the prevailing fever in that City, and may have come to Baltimore (Baltimore *Daily Intelligencer* 30 June 1794).

ASHBURN, EDWARD, was born in Whitehaven [Cumberland, Eng.], bred a shipwright, and worked in Jamaica, and then went to Georgia c1776/8. His brother **GEORGE ASHBURN** was bred a mariner and resided for some years in Liverpool. About 1779 or 1780 he sailed from New York to the Windward Islands and has not been heard from since. These two men would be about 60. George has a family in Liverpool. They may hear something to their advantage by applying to George Venable, merchant in Liverpool (*GAVN:*11 cites *The Virginia Gazette and General Advertiser* 2 May 1792).

ASHMAN, JOHN, printer, left New York about 12 months ago. If he is still alive and will inform Thomas Bridges of 32 Oak St., New York, of his residence, he will hear of something very much to his advantage (*The Daily National Intelligencer* 24 Nov 1819).

ASMUSSEN, MATTHIAS, son of a merchant of that name in Gondern, Duchy of Sleswick, a Province of the King of Denmark, in 1805, at the age of 15, went from Copenhagen to Norway, and then to London. His two sisters, Mariana Hoyer and Maria Asmussen, have not heard from him since, and think it probable that he has gone to the United States, since he had always expressed a strong desire to visit foreign countries. Anyone with information should contact Henry G. Jacobsen, Danish Vice Consul, Baltimore (*Baltimore Patriot* 20 April 1822).

ATHERTON, JOSHUA, late of Lancashire, Great Britain, came into this Province. He should apply to Stead Lowe, Christopher Lowndes, or Benjamin Young (Annapolis *Maryland Gazette* 18 Feb 1762).

　　　　Joshua Atherton witnessed the will of Nehemiah Hicks of Baltimore Co., MD, on 7 April 1769 (MWB 37:348).

　　　　Atherton died by 29 June 1774 when admin. bond was posted by admx. Ruth Atherton with Stephen Price and Wm. Price as securities (BAAB 1:13).

　　　　His estate was appraised on 4 July 1774 by John Daughaday and Thomas Cole and valued at £15.7.7; his inventory was filed by the admx. Ruth Atherton on 22 Oct [1774?]; Joshua Atherton and Samuel Atherton were mentioned. Stephen Price and William Price signed as next of kin (MINV 121:161).

ATKINSON, ELIZABETH, niece of Henry Inman of Burneston, near Bedal [*sic*], Yorkshire, came to this country about 1770, and is supposed to have married a man named Court. She is urged to contact the printer (*Baltimore Daily Intelligencer* 14 June 1794).

ATKINSON, HENRY, son of Michael Atkinson, late of Manor Twp., Lancaster Co., PA, if living, is asked to apply to Joseph Hughes in Emmitsburg, and he will hear of something favorable (*Fredericktown Herald* 22 July 1815).

ATWOOD, ELIJAH, late a private in the Army of the Revolution, applied for a pension under the Act of Congress. He is hereby notified that if he will call upon Ziba Pyle, Attorney-at-Law of West Chester, PA, he will hear of something to his advantage (*Village Record or Chester and Delaware Federalist* 21 April 1829).

Elijah Atwood, private in the Connecticut Line, was placed on the pension roll of Pennsylvania under the Law of 18 March 1818 (*1820 Pension List*. Baltimore: Genealogical Publishing Co., p 494).

AUCHTERLONEY, JOHN, son of Alexander Auchterloney, merchant of Dundee, was living in MD in 1740. If he or any of his children are alive, they should contact the printer, to hear something greatly to their advantage (Annapolis *Maryland Gazette* 23 Aug 1764).

AUSTIN, MONTAGUE COPE, was the son of attorney at Peterborough, Northants, and was born there. He first went to school with a clergyman named Lloyd at Islington, Middlesex, and from thence to Charter House. In the year 1776 or 1777 he entered as a common sailor on board a merchant ship then lying in the river Thames, and bound for the West Indies. Previous to his going to sea, when of the age of 15 years or thereabouts, resided at Durham, and it is supposed that about the year 1783 he lived in the area of James River, America. In pursuance of a Decree of H.M. Court of Exchequer, dated 3 July 1804, in a case in which James Raven was plaintiff and Daniel Sutton and others were defendants, it was referred to Abel Moysey, Esq., the deputy to H.M. Remembrancers of the said court, to inquire whether the said Mordecai Cope Austin was living or dead, and if he survived the age of 21 years, then who was his heir at law. If the said Austin is alive, he is requested to give notice to the said Moysey at his chambers in the Exchequer, in the Inner Temple, and if Austin is alive, and will apply to Thomas and Amos Ladd, he may get further information on the above subject and may also hear of something to his advantage (*The Enquirer* 8 Dec 1804).

BACON, SARAH, dau. of George and Sarah Bacon, of Bristol, Eng., some time in or about 1734, came from Bristol to Philadelphia, where she lived for some time. Her friends would be glad to hear from her, and if she will apply to Mr. Edmund Beach, cooper, in Front St., at the corner of Race, she will hear something to her advantage (*Pa. Gaz.*, 7 March 1765).

BADER, PETER, and **MATHEUS BADER,** are sought by their brother, Hansz Adam, at Gottschalk's Mill, Skippack, Montgomery Co.; they all came into this country last year (*Hocker:* 12 cites the *Pennsylvanische Geschichts-Schreiber* 1 Dec 1748).

Peter Bader married Susanna Marg. Kron on 8 Dec 1761 at the First Reformed Congregation in Lancaster, PA. (*Lancaster Churches.* Vol. 2.).

Peter Beader (signed Bader), made a will on 13 Nov 1778. He named his wife Susanna Beader. Cassel Bayer was the exec. (*Lancaster Churches.* Vol. 2.).

Peter and Susanna were the parents of (*Lancaster Churches*. Vol. 2.): ELIZABETH, b. 1 Sep 1767, bapt. 11 Oct 1767 at First Reformed Congregation at Lancaster (sp. were Henry Schweitzer and Susanna). In 1790 Matheus Bader was head of a family in Richmond Twp., Berks Co., PA (*AIS 1790 Census Index*).

BAIDMAN, JOHANN HEINRICH, a cooper and beer brewer, born in the Rhine Grafschaft Daun, who came to America and was apprenticed to [-?-] Frick, brewer, in Lancaster, is sought by his brother, Simon Peter Baidman, a cooper living with Isaac Paris, Stone Arabia, on the Mohawk River, in the Province of NY. Address any information to Peter Paris, merchant, Philadelphia, or his brother Isaac Paris, Stone Arabia (*Hocker:* 123 cites the *Wochentlicher Pennsylvanischer Staatsbote* 15 June 1773).

Simon Peter Baidman arrived on the *Boston* on 10 Nov 1764. Joh. Heinrich Baidman arrived on the *Hamilton* on 6 Oct 1767 (*Eyster:*31).

BAILEY, ARCHIBALD, a native of Cork, Ireland, some time ago lived in Swanzey, Newport, RI. If he will apply to the printer he may hear of something very much to his advantage (*The Freeman's Journal or The North American Intelligencer* 2 June 1784).

BAILEY, JOHN, a sailor, left Lancaster Co., VA, shipping as a steward, and was last heard of in Oct 1816. If he is alive he will something to his advantage by applying to William Callahan and John Gresham, administrators of William Chowning of Lancaster Co., VA (*Baltimore Patriot* 3 Feb 1822).

BAKER, JOHN, son of Charles Baker, late of Cove Lane, Cork, Ireland, arrived in America about 10 years ago. He is asked to contact Mrs. Anne Baker at Mrs. Smith's in Broad St., New York City. A letter concerning John Baker may be directed to Godfrey Baker, Esq., at Cork (*The New York Gazette and Weekly Mercury* 26 July 1773).

BAKER, JOHN, aged about 40 years, left his residence in Cheltenham Twp., near Germantown, about ten weeks ago, and has not been heard of since. Any information regarding him will be thankfully received by his wife Mary Baker, at Daniel Rush's, in Kensington, near the Black Horse on Frankford Road (*Poulson's American Daily Advertiser* 27 May 1814).

BAKER, MARIA CATHERINE *als.* **STRETER**, came from Germany with her father, Hans Baker, and her brother Henry Baker in 1744. In December 1760, Henry Streter, *als.* Baker was living in Greenwich Twp., Sussex Co., NJ, when he advertised for his sister, who at age nine had been bound to Mary Tomlinson, after her arrival and not been heard from since (*Pa. Gaz.* 4 Dec 1760).

In May 1761 Maria Catherine advertised that she was living in Market St., Philadelphia, and was married to Jacob Stuckke, stocking weaver, and that she would be glad to see her brother (*Pa. Gaz.* 14 May 1761).

BALL, ELIZABETH, was carried off by the Indians in June 1756 from a place near Mr. Brownmill [Mr. Brown's mill?], in Conococheague. She wishes to inform her parents, Thomas and Catherine Ball (who formerly lived on Thomas Owen's plantation), or her uncle James Ball (now or lately living at Marsh Creek), or her mother's relations, named Harrison, in Maryland, that she is at present, at a convent at Montreal, Canada, and that if her parents or other relations will please inform William Allen, of Philadelphia, of their place of residence, and their desire of having the said Elizabeth return to them, he will forward such notice to General Gage, Governor of Canada (*Pa. Gaz.* 2 July 1761).

BALLANTINE, HAMILTON, acquaints Mr. Alexander Ballantine, lately from Co. Tyrone, Ireland, that he [Hamilton] is now in New Castle on Delaware, where the said Alexander is requested to bring or send the goods, letters, etc., sent by him from Ireland; in ten days from now he is directed to direct the letters for me in Fairfield, New England. In doing so he will oblige his friend and cousin (*Pa. Gaz.* 18 June 1772).

In July 1769 Benjamin Craige of New York, advertised for the return of a certain Hamilton Ballantine, age about 22 or 23, very talkative, who bragged of his learning, and was a noted liar, and who professed to be a schoolmaster. He is likely to have gone to Pennsylvania, where he had taught school (*Pa. Gaz.* 27 July 1769). Ballantine replied by stating that he resided in Duck Creek Hundred, Kent Co. [DE], where he will abide any actions – civil or criminal - that the said Craige can begin against him. Moreover Ballantine believed that "Craige" is a fictitious name, and that the advertisement was maliciously published with a design to prejudice [blacken] his character. He had been employed by the Government in the West Indies, and most recently has resided in Kennett, Chester Co. Finally, he offered a reward of twenty dollars [*sic*] top anyone who could bring him the name of the subscriber (*Pa. Gaz.* 14 Sep 1769).

In 1778, Attorney Hamilton Ballantine, "late of the Island of Jamaica," announced that he planned to settle in NC and expected to establish a legal practice in the state. Ballantine advertised that the "laws now being opened in their full latitude," he would travel around to the various superior court sessions. His desires were quite modest, for he wished only such encouragement as "his integrity to his clients and the justice of their cause merits" (*North Carolina Gazette* 9 Jan 1778).

It should be noted that a Col. Hamilton Ballendine [*sic*] was hanged at Charleston, SC, on 5 March 1780, for making a drawing of the town and fortifications (*The New York Gazette and Weekly Mercury* 24 April 1780).

BALSTER, WILLIAM, bleacher of linen, lately from England, is asked to call on Reuben Haines, where he will hear of something to his advantage (*Pa. Gaz.* 13 Sep 1770).

BANT, RICHARD, who left England about 13 years ago, and is supposed to have sailed in a merchant ship from Boston, or New York City, is asked to apply to Speakman and Carter, chemists in Philadelphia, to learn something to his advantage (*Scott* 3:174 cites *The New York Gazette and the Weekly Mercury* 14 June 1773).

BARKER, JAMES, of or near Birmingham, Warwickshire, has been some time in North America, and is supposed to be living in New York. He is asked to contact John Rawlins of Baltimore to hear of a handsome sum of money left him by relations in England (*GAVN:*19 cites *The Virginia Journal and Alexandria Advertiser.* 1 Sep 1785; *Maryland Journal and Baltimore Advertiser* 9 Aug 1785).

BARNARD, WILLIAM, who at one time resided in Canada, is sought by the Post-Master of Baltimore, who has something interesting to communicate (*Baltimore Patriot & Mercantile Advertiser* 23 Nov 1818).

BARNES, HENRY, aged about 40, in 1736 or 1737 left England, intending for VA. He arrived there and remained until 1740 when he write to friends in England, that any letters sent to him should be left with William Davis, near Onoquan Ferry on Potomack; there is information that Barnes went on the expedition against Cartagena [Carthagena], An estate has descended to him in England. He is to apply to John Ross, attorney-at-law in Philadelphia, who is seeking news of Barnes (*Scott* 1:525 cites the *Pa. Gaz.* 26 Sep 1745).

BARNET, JOSEPH. was born in Ireland, from whence he removed to the Island of Antigua, and lastly to Jamaica, in the year 1741, where he died some years past, having, as it is said, a brother, who formerly lived in or near New Castle County, on Delaware. These, at the request of a friend to that family, are to inform the said Mr. Barnet (whose Christian name is unknown) if living, or his heirs, if dead, that on application to Edmund Kearny, of the City of Philadelphia, he or they may hear of something considerable to their advantage (*Pa. Gaz.* 14 Dec 1758).

BARNET, WILLIAM, some years ago removed to Chatham Co, NC; if he is living and will apply to James Early of Orange Co., VA, who is executor of James Barnet, dec., William may receive the estate left by his father (*GAVN:*19 cites *The Virginia Gazette and General Advertiser* 16 Aug 1799).

BARNS, MARTHA, left England three or four years ago in the character of a cook for John Morton Jordan, Esq., and came to MD. If she will apply to Levi Hollingsworth she will hear something to her advantage (*Pa. Gaz.* 1 Sep 1773).

BARR, CHARLES, came from Ireland with John McKirgen. He is sought by his brother, John Barr, who came from Ireland last year, and has heard of his brother, Charles. Charles Barr is asked to come, or send a letter to his brother, care of Rev. Robert Smith at Pequea, Lancaster Co. (*Pa. Gaz.* 8 May 1760).

A John Barr married Elizabeth [-?-]. They were the parents of (*Lancaster Churches* MARGARET, b. 16 June 1758, bapt. 27 June 1758 at First Reformed Congregation, Lancaster (sp.: Christopher Graffort and wife).

BARR, WILLIAM, formerly of Juniata Settlement, PA, is asked to apply to Robert Hill, at the corner of Chesnut and Front St., Philadelphia, as he will hear of something to his advantage (*The Philadelphia Gazette & Universal Daily Advertiser* 24 Nov 1797).

BARRAS, JOHN, a native of England, left the neighborhood of New Castle upon Tyne in the 1773, aged about 30 years of age, in the capacity of a seaman. He arrived at Norfolk, VA, and from thence proceeded to Portsmouth, NH, from which place he addressed a letter, dated 8 July 1773, to his mother requesting her to write to him, care pf Capt. John Bettenham of that place. If the said John Barras will apply to Samuel Spackman, merchant, of Philadelphia, he will hear something very much to his advantage ([DC] *Daily National Intelligencer*9 May 1820).

In 1790 a John Barras was head of a family in Cheshire Co., NH (*AIS 1790 Census Index*).

BARROM, FIELDING, who was a soldier in Col. Harrison's Regiment of Artillery, is due a considerable legacy from his late father, Peter Barrom of Charles City Co., VA. Lawrence Egmon, Peter Barrom's executor, so advises (*GAVN:*20 cites *The Virginia Gazette or American Advertiser* 4 Dec 1784).

BASSTONE, EDWARD, hosier, was born in Three Tun Alley, London, which he left some 50 years ago. He landed in VA and was sold to one Shepherd of Gloucester Co. for the payment of his passage. If he is living he is to apply to O'Connor M'Crammuck to learn something greatly to his advantage (*GAVN:*21 cites *Pinkney's Virginia Gazette* 1 June 1775).

BATTERTON, JOSEPH, a free Negro from the Island of Nevis, embarked on the sloop *Sally* for MD on 30 Aug 1768. His mother, Elizabeth, wants news of his whereabouts (*GAVN:* 22 cites Rind's *Virginia Gazette* 29 June 1769).

BAUER, JOHANN DEWALD, came from Gauersheim, five miles from Worms, to PA four years ago with his sister, Maria Elizabeth, and his "Basze," (aunt or cousin), Anna Barbara Babin. His father, Johannes Bauer, seeks information about him (*Hocker:*9 cites the *Pennsylvanische Geschichts-Schreiber* 16 Nov 1747).

BAUER, LUDWIG, from Oderdrunn, Alsace, linen weaver, arrived in America several years ago, and is believed to be in or near Philadelphia. Information about him is sought (*Hocker:*117 cites the *Wochentlicher Pennsylvanischer Staatsbote* 11 Aug 1772).
Ludwig Baur arrived on 13 Aug 1750 on the *Edinburgh* (*Eyster:* 27).

BAUER, MICHAEL, linen-weaver, was born at Liebenstadt, near Heilbrun, in Wurtemberg, and **MATTHIAS BAYER,** "Kaercher," believed to be in Philadelphia, came to America thirty years ago. They are sought by Philip Bayer, with William Jones, two miles from Philadelphia (*Hocker:*172 cites the *Philadelphische Correspondenz* 14 Dec 1784).

BAYER, MAGDALENE, came into this country last fall with her husband Erhard Bayer and her brother Hans Sax. She was sick, and sent with others to the House provided for the sick, and during the time of her confinement there, the merchant's cruelty was so great as to sell her husband from her, but she cannot find out to whet part of this or the neighboring provinces. After her recovery, she was sold, big with child, to John Ray, living in Alloway Creek Precinct, near the Glass House, West New Jersey. If anyone knows anything about her husband or brother, they are asked to communicate with Richard Wistar in Philadelphia (*Pa. Gaz.* 11 July 1765).

BAYES, JOHN, from Northamptonshire, who formerly lived with a farmer in Patapsco Neck near Baltimore, or John's son **WILLIAM BAYES,** should apply to Ebenezer Mackie (*Maryland Journal and Baltimore Advertiser* 9 Oct 1789; *Maryland Gazette or Baltimore General Advertiser* 16 Oct 1789).

This notice seems to have given more data: John Bayes, formerly from Northamptonshire, lately lived with a farmer at Patapsco Neck near Baltimore. His son William lived with Robert Robertson, tavern-keeper, Bedminster Twp., Pennsylvania. If either of them are living and will send an account of themselves to Samuel Elam of Newport, RI, they will hear of something to their advantage (*The Pennsylvania Packet and Daily Advertiser* 15 Oct 1789).

BEALL, JOHN BRADLEY, son of Josias Beall, late of PG Co., dec., is notified that if that if he will apply to either of his bros. in Montgomery Co., or Prince George's Co., he will hear of something to his advantage (*Washington Federalist* 19 Dec 1803).

BECKER, CHRISTIAN HEINRICH, or any branch of his family now in this country, should apply to E. C. Boyson, at 118 South Second St., as they may hear of something greatly to their advantage. Anyone who can provide information will confer a great obligation on his aged mother, and a respectable family in Germany (*The Philadelphia Gazette & Universal Daily Advertiser* 25 June 1796).

BECKER, PHILIP JACOB, and **GEORG JACOB BECKER,** father and son, from Pfortzheim in Baden-Durlach, are sought by Ernst Ludwig Baisch (*Eyster:*40 cites the *Pennsylvanische Staatsbote* 26 Nov 1776).
　　A Philip Becker was in Philadelphia Co., PA, in 1737, 1752, and 1754 (*AIS Census Index Pre-1790*; no source given).

BEDFORD, JONAS resided on Roanoke Island about 40 miles from Salisbury, NC, and was in England in 1785. He is asked to apply to Cumberland Wilson, merchant at Dumfries, VA, or to the British Consul at Norfolk to hear something to his advantage (*GAVN:*23 cites *The Virginia Chronicle and Norfolk and Portsmouth General Advertiser* 23 Feb 1793).
　　In 1790 Jonas Bedford was listed in the Census of Rutherford Co., NC, p. 118 (*AIS 1790 Census Index*).

BEHRINGER, JOH. GEORG, of Fluhr in Saxony, near Merganthal, is sought by Joh. Georg Fischer, master tailor and Beadle in Heilbrun (*Eyster:*27 cites the *Pennsylvanische Staatsbote* 28 July 1772).

BELL, ADAM, is supposed to have come to VA in 1769 with his wife and two children. A carpenter on a King's ship in the late war, he has been left a legacy of £1500 by his messmate John Mears, a gunner in the navy (*GAVN:*24 cites the *Va. Gaz.* 15 Oct 1772).

BELL, JOHN, son of Robert and Mary Bell, late of London, dec., came to America about 10 years ago. He is asked to apply to Samuel Franklin in New York City or to John Franklin of Philadelphia, to hear something to his advantage (*The New York Gazette and Weekly Mercury* 28 Jan 1782).

BELL, ROBERT, who came from Co. Down, Ireland, and kept a public house at Brooklyn Ferry in 1780, will hear something to his advantage of he applies to Hugh and Alexander Wallace of New York City, merchants (*The New York Gazette and Weekly Mercury* 19 May 1783).

He might be the Robert Bell who emigrated from Belfast to Philadelphia in May 1771, and who arrived at Delaware Bay on 4 July 1771 (DIEN 2:1).

BELL, THOMAS, a house carpenter or joiner, left Frederick Co., about two years ago and is supposed to be in Baltimore. He will hear of something to his advantage by calling at the office of *The Patriot* (*Baltimore Patriot* 10 Feb 1810).

BENDERIN, MARIA JOHANNA, widow, arrived in America, five years ago, with three daughters, **MARIA MARGRETHA, APPOLONIA,** and **CHRISTINA,** who have served their time. Maria, who is with Henrich Zimmerman, Conestoga, Lancaster Co., PA, is seeking her mother (*Hocker:*36 cites the *Pennsylvanische Geschichts-Schreiber* 1 Nov 1752).

BENER, PETER, about 18 years ago, when he was 14, came into this country, and served seven years with one Peter Not, living in the Jerseys, about 60 miles from Philadelphia. His sister, Elizabeth Bener, has not heard from him, and wants to hear from him. He may write to her, living about eight miles from Neilson's Ferry on Susquehanna, or to Neal Toner, living in Queen's Town in York Co., to the care of John Shaw of the same place (*Pa. Gaz.* 10 July 1760).

Peter Bener of Rockhill Twp., Bucks Co., PA, appeared in a newspaper notice (*Hocker:* 89).

A Peter Bener married Catherine [-?-]. They were the parents of (First Reformed Church of Lancaster, PA, in *PGCR* 1:242, 248): JOHN, b. 4 Nov., bapt. 9 Dec 1753; and JOHN FREDERICK, b. 16 Oct, bapt. 15 Nov 1756.

BENNETT, SAMUEL, an Englishman who once taught school in the Province, should apply to the printer (Annapolis *Maryland Gazette* 15 Aug 1750)

He may have been the convict of that name from Cornwall who in 1718 was transported to MD for 7 years (QALR IKA: 208). Another Samuel Bennett, husbandman, of black complexion, was transported from London in October 1720 on the *Gilbert,* and given a landing certificate in Maryland in May 1721 (*CBEB*).

On 16 Aug 1735 Bennett was listed as a creditor to the estate of James Thomas of Kent Co. (MDAD 13:249).

Samuel Bennett of Kent Co. died by 25 July 1749, when Margaret Bennett filed an inventory appraised by John Gleaves and George Medford at £318.12.5 (MINV 41:81).

Another Samuel Bennett, of Kent Co. died by 29 April 1751, when his estate was appraised by Pa. Whichcote and George Griffith, and valued at £296.10.7. No creditors listed. Sarah Chapman signed as next of kin. William Absley, (surviving) administrator, filed the inventory on 2 May 1751 (MINV 60:483).

Samuel and Margaret Bennett had the following children born in St. Paul's Parish, KE Co (*ESVR* 2:18): WILLIAM, b. Feb ---; SAMUEL, b. 19 Dec ---; TEMPERANCE, and [-?-], dau., b. ----.

BENHAM, JOSEPH, a boy aged about 12, left John Hamer's on Tuesday afternoon, without permission and without means of subsistence. The same night he lodged at the Washington Inn in Germantown, and early the next morning directed his course towards Reading. As his mother lives in Northumberland [Co.] he will doubtless try to go there. Any information concerning him may be left at the Bull's Head, N. Third St., at the Tiger, corner of Vine and Fourth, at the Reading stage office on Race St., or sent through the Post Office (*Poulson's American Daily Advertiser* 28 April 1820).

BENWITZ, FREDERICK, a native of Danzig, left that city in 1790 for Baltimore, and since that time has not been heard of. Charles F. Mayer, corner of Church and Charles Sts., requests any information on behalf of the relatives (*Baltimore Patriot* 9 Jan 1824).

BERCKMEYERIN, ANNA GERTRAUT, from the Maesenheim Region, is sought by her brother Georg, who is serving with Melchoir Baser in Macungie, Lehigh County, and will be free in the autumn. Georg and Anna Gertraut arrived in this country three years ago last autumn (*Hocker:*69 cites the *Pennsylvanische Geschichts-Schreiber* 4 March 1758).

Hans Georg Berckmeyer arrived on the *John & Elizabeth* on 7 Nov 1754 (*Eyster:*16).

BERINGER, URSULA, from Heilbrun, came to America seven years ago, with her mother Catharina Beringer or Berlinger, and her sister Catharina, who are now seeking Ursula. They may be contacted at care of Ludwig Stein, Lancaster (*Hocker:*85 cites the *Pennsylvanische Geschichts-Schreiber* 6 June 1760; *Eyster:*20 cites the *Pennsylvanische Berichte* 5 June 1760).

BERLEN, JOHANN CASPER, came to America in 1750 from Steinheim am der Murr, and left three children in NY: Justinia Magdalena who married Seckler Falckenhan, Sophia Catharine, who married Dreher Wohlhaupt, and a son Johann Casper, who was a shoemaker. The father's sister Eva Agnes Durstin, died in 1774. Jacob Geiger, living with Nicolaus Weber, Third St., Philadelphia is seeking information about Johann Casper (*Hocker* 148 cites the *Wochentlicher Pennsylvanischer Staatsbote* 5 Dec 1775).

BERLET, HANS WOLFF, miller, arrived in this country seventeen years ago. His brothers, Johann Conrad, papermaker, at Oley, Berks Co., with Mr. Womelsdorf, and Paul, a carpenter, have now arrived and are seeking him (*Hocker:*16 cites the *Pennsylvanische Geschichts-Schreiber* 16 Dec 1749).

John Wolf Berlet was naturalized in New York on 3 July 1759 (Bockstruck: 22).

BERNAHT, JOHN ULRICH, a native of Dehingen, is sought by his brother, John Jacob, who wants to know if his brother is alive. They came to Philadelphia from their native country about thirteen years ago, but were soon separated. John Jacob has heard nothing from his brother since then, and invites him to come to him or send word to him at Mt. Holly, NJ (*Pa. Gaz.* 22 March 1764).

Hans Jacob Bernaht and Ulrich Bernhart [*sic*] both arrived 25 Aug 1751 on the *Anderson*, Hugh Campbell, master, from Rotterdam, last from Cowes (*PGP* 1:451).

BERO(TH), FRANTZ and his wife **SUSANNA** are being sought by Abraham Reiber of Sandhofen, and his wife Anna Margretha, daughter of Hansz Jacob Reuther of Ophau. Abraham and Susanna arrived in PA last autumn and are at Hans Bauer's house in Goshenhoppen, Montgomery Co., PA (*Hocker:*19 cites the *Pennsylvanische Geschichts-Schreiber* 1 May 1750).

Frantz Ludwick Berot [*sic*] of York Co., PA, was naturalized on 11 April 1761 (Bockstruck: 22).

BERRIMAN, JOHN, by trade a carpenter, lived at the corner of Second St., Philadelphia. He had a daughter who was bound to the wife of a Mr. John Thomas, who left the city in Dec 1794, bound for England, after sailed for Kingston, Jamaica. Mrs. Thomas died in May 1795, after which Mr. Thomas put this little girl in the Parish House, and then took his passage to England. The daughter, now 8 or 9 years old, and a promising child, now lives with Mrs. Bartram, learning the millinery business, and wants very much to hear of her mother, who she believes married a Mr. Wise, by trade a rope maker (*The Philadelphia Gazette & Universal Daily Advertiser* 5 Aug 1796).

BESSERER, JOHANNES, from Doffingen, Wurtemburg is sought by Ernest Ludwig Baisch (*Eyster:*27 cites the *Pennsylvanische Staatsbote* 28 July 1772).

BESTIN, CHRISTINA, and her five children, arrived at Philadelphia in 1754. They are sought by her son Johann Georg Best, from Nurnberg, serving with James Horner in Allen Twp., nine miles from Bethlehem, (*Hocker:*63 cites the *Pennsylvanische Geschichts-Schreiber* 25 June 1757).

Johann George Best arrived on the *Halifax*, Capt. Thomas Coatam, from Rotterdam, took the Oath of Fidelity on 2 Oct 1754 (*PGP* 1:653).

BEYERFALCK, JOHANN MICHAEL, and his wife and one daughter, came to Pennsylvania about 40 years ago from Zweibrucken, and settled near Georgetown in the Holz Schwamm. The daughter married a European. Information is sought about their whereabouts (*Hocker:*162 cites the *Philadelphische Correspondenz* June 1781).

For more on the Beyerfalck Family, see Burgert's *Alsace* 57.

BEYMUELLER, HANSZ MICHEL, of Schoen-Eich, wrote to Germany five years ago, urging his wife's relatives to come to America. Maria Catharina Braunin, from Schoen-Eich, has arrived, and is with Matheus Kaiser, Germantown. She is seeking her brother, Hansz Michel, Beymueller (*Hocker:*30 cites the *Pennsylvanische Geschichts-Schreiber* 16 Dec 1751).

BICKEL, FRIEDRICH, married the sister of Michael Mueller's wife. Georg Adam Schmaltzhof is seeking Bickel (*Hocker:*117 cites the *Wochentlicher Pennsylvanischer Staatsbote* 29 Sep 1772).

BIDENER, MARIA SOPHIA, is the wife of Johann Gottlieb Klingener who is hereby informed that his wife is on board the ship *Condide*, which recently arrived at Philadelphia from Amsterdam (*Hocker:*176 cites the *Philadelphische Correspondenz* 5 Sep 1786).

BIGGS, BENJAMIN, lived in this city [Philadelphia] in 1788. If he will apply at the office of the *American Daily Advertiser* he will hear of something to his advantage (*Poulson's American Daily Advertiser* 12 March 1818).

BILDMAN, CHRISTOPH SAMUEL, from Bietigheim, five hours below Stuttgart, arrived two years ago. His brother Jacob asks him to write to him. Jacob also announces that he is going to Germany, and if anyone wishes him to take commissions, he can be found at Michael Ege's in Philadelphia (*Eyster:*13 cites the *Pennsylvanische Berichte* 16 Nov 1752).

Christoph Samuel Bildman arrived on the *Eliot* on 24 Aug 1749. Jacob Bildman arrived on the Edinburgh on 19 Sep 1752 (*Eyster:*13).

BIRAM, ELIZABETH, of Lancashire is presumed to be in America. Anyone knowing her address should leave it at the office so that she may obtain information that may be of service to her (*Baltimore Patriot* 20 March 1821).

BIRCKERT, LUDWIG FREDERICK, son of Maria Juliana Birckert, came to Philadelphia in 1754 with Capt. Cottam, when he was only eleven years old and was bound as a servant to a man whose name the mother has forgotten. She has not been heard of him since then. Anyone with information can give it to Frederick Stuber, barber, in Walnut St., Philadelphia, or to Mr. [Wagdor?] King, tavern keeper in York Co. near Conewago, on the Maryland Road (*Pa. Gaz.* 5 Sep 1765).

BISCHOFF, GEORG, alias Dichan Albrecht, from Alsace, is sought. He lived in the Whitemarsh Twp., Philadelphia County (now Montgomery Co.), up to the end of 1759 (*Hocker:*84 cites the *Pennsylvanische Geschichts-Schreiber* 23 May 1760).

For more on the Bischoff Family, see Burgert's *Northern Kraichgau:* 65.

BLACK, JOHN, son of James Black of Middletown Twp., Chester Co., PA, dec., if living, is asked to apply to James M'Minn or Robert Miller, exec., for news of a considerable legacy. The said John left his father 14 years ago and was said to be a Captain in Col. Washington's Legion of Light Horse (*GAVN:*28 cites *The Virginia Gazette and American Advertiser* 12 Nov 1785).

BLACK, ROBERT, bricklayer, some time ago left Philadelphia, and may be living at a place called Rock Bridge. If he will apply to the printer he will hear something greatly to his advantage (*GAVN:*28 cites *The Virginia Gazette and General Advertiser* 15 May 1793).

BLACKBURN(E), Capt. WILLIAM, of Great Brook St., Hanover Square, London, came to VA c1754/5 and lived for some years with Maj. William Talliafero of King and Queen Co. His friends have not heard from him and wish to know if he is alive and well (*GAVN:*29 cites the *Virginia Gazette*, and Rind's *Virginia Gazette* 20 Sep 1770).

A William Blackburn appears on a 1782 Tax List of Powhatan Co., VA. Another William appears in Hampshire Co., VA in 1782 (*AIS Census Index: Pre-1790*, gives no other documentation)

BLAIR, PATRICK, came to PA from Newtown-Stuart, Co. Tyrone, Ireland, some years ago. If he applies to Thomas Lucas at Pequea, Lancaster Co., he will hear of something to his advantage (*Scott* 2:302 cites the *Pa. Gaz.* 29 Aug 1754).

BLUMIN, ANNA CHRISTINA, and her children, who arrived ten or eleven years ago; her [their?] father Johann George Blum died on the voyage. Her sister's son, Johannes Wickel, from Eyershausen, Nassau-Dillenburg, now a schoolmaster in Vincent Twp., Chester Co., is seeking her (*Hocker:*136 cites the *Wochentlicher Pennsylvanischer Staatsbote* 18 Oct 1774).

Johann Heinrich Krum, tailor, Byberry Twp., Philadelphia Co., in replying to the advertisement of Johannes Wickel, states that Anna Christina Blumin is his mother-in-law, and she lives in Virginia, one mile from Straffordtoen [Stafford Town?](*Hocker:*136 cites the *Wochentlicher Pennsylvanischer Staatsbote* 25 Oct 1774).

BOAKE, HENRY, left Cork, Ireland about seven years ago, and came to Philadelphia. If he is living, and will apply to the printer, he may hear of something greatly to his advantage (*Pennsylvania Packet and General Advertiser* 4 Oct 1773).

BOARDMAN, FRANCIS, son of Samuel Boardman of Gorton, Lancs., came to MD several years ago, married and had children. He has inherited a considerable estate in England and should apply to John Eden of SM Co. (Annapolis *Maryland Gazette* 14 July 1768).

For the English Ancestry of Francis Boardman see this author's *British Roots of Maryland Families II*, Baltimore: Genealogical Publishing Co., 2002.

BOLLERE, JOHN, came into this country some time ago from Bordeaux and is of the Family "Clauzel," is urges to apply to the Governor for some things much to his satisfaction (*GAVN:*31 cites the *Virginia Gazette* 11 May 1739).

BONTHRON, HENRY, is the brother of John Bonthron, late of the City of Charleston, South Carolina, grocer, a native of Edinburgh, Scotland. John died in June 1817, and in his will left a specific bequest and share in the residue of his estate to his brother Henry. Since the death of John, his executors have made diligent enquiry, both in Edinburgh and elsewhere to locate Henry. Anyone with information about him is asked to contact Robert Walker of Charleston or William Walker, Writer to the Signet, in Edinburgh (*Daily National Intelligencer* 2 Nov 1820).

John Bonthron, son of James Bonthron, builder in Edinburgh, died in Charleston, South Carolina on 20 June 1817 (*DSSC* 3:13 cites *Blackwood's Edinburgh Magazine* 1:617).

BOOTH, ELIAS, served his time with an eminent wool comber in Norwich, went abroad, returned c1725/6 and then returned to VA, where he married a dau. of [-?-] Demissy, and had a son William, who may be living near Williamsburg. If any of them apply to Samuel Metcalfe of King and Queen Co., they will hear something to their advantage (*GAVN:*33 cites the *Va. Gaz.* 23 May 1766).

On 10 Oct 1726 the following were bound to serve Elias Booth in VA: James Murray and Richard Blancourt Mayleigh (*CBE2*).

BOTT, Mr. [-?-], master smith, from Stoeckenoeth, Amt Idstein, is sought by his friend Philip Conrad Christ, son of Johann Philip Christ, who arrived in America last autumn to visit him (*Hocker:*114 cites the *Wochentlicher Pennsylvanischer Staatsbote* 21 April 1772).

BOURNE, THOMAS, came into this country from Great Britain about the year 1670, and as it was supposed resided for some time in Pennsylvania. He was possessed of considerable estate and effects, and died without returning to England. Anyone who can give an account of Thomas Bourne, or where he died, or where he left his effects, they will be suitably rewarded if they contact Benjamin and Samuel Shoemaker of Philadelphia (*Pa. Gaz.* 5 May 1748).

BOWDEN, JOHN, born in the Parish of Topsham, Devonshire, left the parental roof some years ago, to the great grief of his friends. If he will return to his family he will of something to his advantage, and restore peace to the bosom of an affectionate mother (*The American Beacon and Commercial Diary* 3 March 1818).

BOWS, JOHN, and his brother **HENRY BOWS**, natives of Newcastle upon Tyne, are sought by G.S. & J.P. Oldfield, 24 S. Charles St. who have something to their advantage to impart (*Baltimore Patriot* 26 June 1826).

BOYD, WILLIAM, came from Scotland to MD as a schoolmaster some 50 years ago. He should apply to Walter Boyd in Prince [William?] Co., VA (Annapolis *Maryland Gazette* 2 April 1767).

He may be the William Boyd who on 22 Sep 1730 was listed on as a creditor of the estate of John Falconer of QA Co. (MDAD 10:514). William Boyd witnessed the will of James Countess of QA Co. on 29 Dec 1731 (MWB 20:412).

A William Boyd took the Oath of Fidelity in Washington Co., MD in 1778 (*AIS Census Index: Pre-1790* gives no other documentation).

BOYD FAMILY: Any members of the name Boyd descended from the Family of Trockbridge, Ayrshire, will hear something to their advantage by applying to Thomas Macudie, of Fredericksburg (*GAVN*:35 cites the *Va. Gaz.* 17 July 1752).

BRABAND, JACOB, is in this land, having come from Zweibericken in 1743, and is sought by his brother, Henrich Braband, a Swiss, who was captured by the Spaniards two years ago, but was soon released. Henrich Braband asks anyone with knowledge to contact Jacob Bauman of Germantown (*Hocker*:8 cites the *Pennsylvanische Geschichts-Schreiber* 16 May 1747).

BRACKET, JOHN, stone cutter, late passenger in the *Faithful Stewart*, is asked to apply to William Young, bookseller, corner of Second and Chestnut Sts., Philadelphia, where he will receive assistance at the desire of his brother in Scotland (*The Pennsylvania Packet and Daily Advertiser* 5 Aug 1785).

BRADLEY, POLLY, aged about 15, and **CATHERINE BRADLEY**, aged about 13, were orphan children when they were separated about eleven years ago, and have not seen each other since. The sisters are supposed to reside in Baltimore, or in some part of Maryland. They are sought by their brother Thomas Wilson Bradley of Gettysburg, Adams Co., OPA (*Baltimore Patriot* 28 March 1828).

BRADNER, WILLIAM, or his son, or any other near relation, should speedily apply to the printer, to hear of something very much to their advantage (Philadelphia *American Weekly Mercury* 12-19 Aug 1742).

BRAEUNISCHOLTZER, HANSZ ADAM, was indentured to a German named Jacob Frey, who cannot now be found. His mother Anna Barbara Brauenischoltzerin, at the Great Swamp, near Michel Eberhart, came to America with her son, and is seeking information about him (*Hocker:*35 cites the *Pennsylvanische Geschichts-Schreiber* 16 Sep 1752).

BRATTAN (or BRITTAN), HORACE, son of George Brattan of Tullybroom, Co. Tyrone, Ireland, Gent., dec., left Ireland about 30 years ago and came to Philadelphia. If he or any of his children are alive, they will hear something to their advantage by informing Kenelon [Kenelm?] Chandler and John McCord, of the City of Quebec, executors of the last will and testament of Robert Britain [*sic*], dec., by letter of their names, ages, and places of abode, and by sending proper certificates thereof to them. In the mean time, Mr. Samuel Purviance of Philadelphia, will give them directions how to act ("Quebec, 1 Aug 1765," *Pa. Gaz.* 16 Jan 1766).

BRATTEN, EDWARD, who recently resided in Myer's Town, Dauphin Co., is urged to contact his brother James Bratten who has recently arrived from Ireland. Bratten should apply to John Reily, Esq., Atty. at Law in Myer's Town, or William Wray, Esq., in Harrisburg (Kline's *Carlisle Weekly Gazette*10 Jan 1798).

BRAUN, HANSZ ADAM, a year and a half ago was indentured off the ship, but received no papers. Anna Margaretha Braunin, his mother, is seeking the boy's master (*Hocker:*55 cites the *Pennsylvanische Geschichts-Schreiber* 1 March 1756).

BRAUTIGAM, JEDEL aged 7, and **DOROTHEA BRAUTIGAM,** aged 5, were taken by their mother, Margaretha Elizabeth, four years ago. Their father, Joachim Brautigam, of Colebrookdale Twp., Berks Co., at the old Potts Furnace, is seeking them (*Hocker:*91 cites the *Pennsylvanische Geschichts-Schreiber* 3 July 1761).

Joachim Andreas Brautigam arrived on the *Queen of Denmark,* George Parish, commander, from Hamburgh. When he took the Oath of Fidelity on 3 Nov 1752 he made his mark (*PGP* 1:505).

BRAY, JAMES, born in Co. Tipperary, Ireland, who came to North America about 17 years ago, and lived with a gentleman named Karney in either NY or NJ, is asked to get in touch with Hugh Wallace, merchant in New York City (*The New York Mercury* 30 Sep 1765).

James' brother, now in New York City, advertised for news of his brother (*The New York Mercury* 1 Sep 1766).

BRAY, WILLIAM GEORGE, formerly of Berkeley Co., VA, in 1819 was living at Boston, MA. If he is living he is asked to apply to F. C. Grey, Esq., at Boston, where he will learn something to his advantage (*The Daily National Intelligencer* 13 Oct 1819).

BREMNER, JAMES, aged about 15, son of a widowed mother, left Baltimore on 8 July 1822 with Philip Roach (*q.v.*), and has not been heard of since. Any information concerning him should be sent to Samuel Russell, near Pratt St. Bridge (*Baltimore Patriot* 6 Sep 1822).

BRENNEN, JAMES, block maker of Annapolis, thought to still be in Maryland, is sought by Thomas Fleming, who has a message for him (Annapolis *Maryland Gazette* 18 Feb 1746).

On 4 July 1730, James Brennan [*sic*], of Alhallow's Staining, was indicted for stealing two silver candlesticks, value £0.8.l, a pair of silver snuffers, &c. in the dwelling house of Henry Vand, Brennan's master, last 25 April. Brennan tried to sell them to Mr. Bundel or Blundel, a silversmith, who was suspicious of how Brennan came by the objects. Blundel had him arrested, and at his trial, the jury found him guilty to the value of 39 s. Brennan was sentenced to transportation to the colonies (www.oldbailey-online.org).

A James Brennan [*sic*] of London was sentenced to transportation and was transported in Oct 1730 on the *Forward* and given a landing certificate at Potowmack in Jan 1731 (*CBEB*).

BRIDEN, JOHN, WILLIAM BRIDEN, and **GRIZALD BRIDEN,** of Scotland, were left legacies by Robert Briden, son of John Briden, who was born at Wainfrey, within four miles of Moffat, Scotland. John went to VA and married the widow of a planter, by whom he had a son: Robert, who died c1745. Robert left his estate to his relations in Scotland, William, John, and Grizald Briden. Mr. Bell of Dumfries has offered each of them £100 each for their shares of the estate. It is believed that Capt. James Johnson, born near Moffatt and in the employ of Mr. Luttwidge of Whitehaven was left trustee of the estate by Robert Briden's will. Johnson also died in VA. Information on the estate, believed to be on the James River, is requested . . . (*GAVN*:38 cites the *Va. Gaz.* 26 Sep 1755).

BRIDGE, DANIEL, born in Ross, Herefordshire, is supposed to be living in Maryland. Thomas Wharton, Jr., of Philadelphia, has a letter for him (*GAVN*:38 cites *The Pennsylvania Chronicle* 10 Oct 1768).

BRINDLEY, NICHOLAS, and **WILLIAM BRINDLEY,** sons of George Brindley of Cut-purse-row, London, shoemaker, have inherited property from Robert Shimin, merchant, late of Dublin, Ireland, who died in May 1766. Knowledge of these sons or their issue is sought by William Lamber of Prospect, Co. Wicklow, Ireland (*Pennsylvania Chronicle* 15 Jan 1770).

BROCAS, RICHARD, who left England about 17 years ago, and lived at Wilmington in or about 1776, and who was known to a family named Quince in Brunswick Co., is asked to apply to John Beckley in Richmond, to hear something to his advantage (*GAVN*:39 cites the *Va. Gaz., or American Advertiser* 16 Oct 1784).

In 1784 a Richard Brocas was in Sampson Co., NC (*AIS Census Index: Pre-1790* gives no other documentation).

BROOKS, PHILIPS, book-binder, native of Dublin, came to Philadelphia in 1773 and left New York City in 1780. Information about him is sought (*Scott* 3:242 cites *The New York*

Gazette and Weekly Mercury 3 Nov 1783).

A Philips Brooks arrived in Philadelphia in 1771 as an indentured servant (*AIS Census Index: Pre-1790* gives no other documentation).

BROOKS, THOMAS, took ship at Larne and left Ireland in 1783. His father and all his family now reside at Susquehanna, Cecil Co., and would be glad to see him (*Maryland Journal and Baltimore Advertiser* 12 Aug 1791).

BROWN, JAMES, left his parents in the parish of Chapel of Carrioch, Aberdeenshire, eight years ago, and should apply to "J. G.," c/o Messrs. Thomas Williams and Co. (Annapolis *Maryland Gazette* 24 Oct 1771).

BROWN, JEAN, a native of Aberdeen, or somewhere thereabouts, lately [died] at St. Croix in America. She went first to Philadelphia, and then to Barbados, and from thence to St,. Croix, where she married one Aspinall, a carpenter, who is likewise lately dead. Whoever can prove herself her relations may be out in the way of recovering her effects by applying to the publisher of this paper (Dobson, *Aberdeen Journal* 16 Oct 1759, issue # 613).

Jean Brown was a daughter of John Brown and Jean Westland of Midmar. She went to Philadelphia in 1743, then to Barbados, and in 1749 went to St. Croix. She married Daniel Aspinall, a carpenter, and died in 1758 (*DSSC* 1:20 cites the Aberdeen Propinquity Books).

BROWN, MARY, is the wife of Richard Brown, formerly of Northampton Twp., Burlington Co., NJ. If she, or her husband, or any of her legal heirs are living, they should apply to Benjamin Jones of Northampton, they will receive information of they property to which their have become entitled, by the decease of her father. /s/ Benjamin Jones, administrator of Hezekiah Jones, dec. (*Spirit of the Press* 1 June 1807).

BROWN, WILLIAM, was born at Bently, Derbyshire, and is said to have come to VA with a son and family some time before 1716. He left several brothers and sisters in England, and he or his descendants may hear something to their advantage from Ben Waller of Williamsburg (*GAVN:*43 cites the *Virginia Gazette* 29 Nov 1770).

BRUNSKIL, Rev. Mr., a native of Westmorland, Eng., about 1775 lived in a parish in Amelia Co. He will hear something to his advantage by applying to the printers (*GAVN:*45 cites the *Va. Gaz. and Alexandria Advertiser* 11 Nov 1790).

BRUNT, GEORGE, from the west of England, came into this Province some time ago. He should apply to James Ruth or Reith of Annapolis (Annapolis *Maryland Gazette* 4 June 1767).

He may be the George Brunt who was sentenced to transportation for shooting with intent to rob at Lent. He was reprieved for transportation for 14 years in the summer of 1765, from Staffordshire (*CBEB*).

A George Brunt appears in the 1772 and 1777 Rent Rolls of Berkeley District, VA (*AIS Census Index: Pre-1790* gives no other documentation).

BRYAN, ANDREW, of New Castle Co., Delaware, has been absent for some years, and no one has heard from him. Any person knowing of his being dead or alive is asked to contact George Read, Esq., of New Castle, or Nathaniel Bryan in the said county (*Pa. Gaz.* 9 April 1783).

Andrew Bryan, perhaps the father of the missing Andrew, was of New Castle Co., and died leaving a will dated 26 Aug 1777 and proved 1 Dec 1777. He named his sons Nathaniel and Andrew, and his daughters, Mary, Rebecca, Lydia, and Agnes. Son Nathaniel and John Crawford were named executors (New Castle Co., DE, Wills L:5).

Andrew Bryan married Emy [-?-]. They were the parents of at least one child: MARY SARAH CATHERINE, born 21 Feb., bapt. 18 June 1775 at the Old Swedes Church (*Early Church Records of New Castle Co., Delaware.* Westminster: Family Line Publications, 2:167).

BRYANT, JOHN, mariner, and son to Mrs. Ann Gow, dec., is asked to apply to Duncan McDonald and James Ker of Norfolk, where he will find something very much to his interest (*GAVN:*45 cites *The Norfolk Herald and Public Advertiser* 6 Nov 1797 and the *American Gazette and General Advertiser* 7 Nov 1797).

Mrs. Ann Gow died. James Ker of Norfolk advertised he would settle her estate (*GAVN:* 139 cites *The Norfolk Herald and Public Advertiser* 16 Nov 1797).

BRYDON, JAMES, a Scotchman, possibly a shoemaker, resided near Richmond, VA, (poss. at a place called Elliebank) about 40 years ago. If there are any legal heirs living in America, they may hear of something of considerable advantage to them by applying to William Russell, watchmaker, of Columbus, GA (*Richmond Enquirer* 16 Aug 1831).

BULL, HENRY, came to the Eastern Shore of Maryland some 30 years ago with Capt. Billings from Liverpool, as an indented servant. If he or his family are living, they should apply to Capt. Lowndes for important news (Annapolis *Maryland Gazette* 13 Oct 1757).

BULTEEL, RACHEL, or her son **HENRY BULTEEL,** from Co. Cavan, Ireland, are supposed to live in some part of Delaware or Maryland. If they will apply to Dr. Robert Stafford in Philadelphia, they will hear of something very much to their advantage (*Poulson's American Daily Advertiser* 25 Dec 1805).

BURDON, WILLIAM, of Great Farrington, Co. Devon, mercer, in 1756 went to New York City as a factor and lived for a time with Mr. Johnscourt at the Meal Market, and age c36. Charles Burdon, near Hatherly, Devon, wants news of him (*Scott* 3:166 cites *The New York Gazette and Weekly Mercury* 12 Oct 1772).

BURK, MARY, wife of Francis Burk, and mother of Hannah Burk, who was taken prisoner by the Shawanese [Shawnee] Indians but was relieved from them about three years ago. Hannah is now living at Fort Pitt and is married to Robert Rosebrock. She has heard that her mother is living on Hogan's Creek, Orange Co., NC, and would like any information on her mother's current whereabouts (*GAVN:*48 cites *Pinkney's Virginia Gazette* 22 Dec 1774).

BURKE, PATRICK, lived in Baltimore in 1805. If he is still living and will apply at this office he will hear something to his advantage (*Baltimore Patriot* 25 Sep 1819).

BURL, THOMAS, came over from Ireland to Baltimore in 1792 in the ship *Norfolk,* Capt. [Willow?]. For some time he was a cattle drover, and is then supposed to have gone to the Federal City. His father is supposed to have taken one of the daughters of Kitty McDonald (*q.v.*) to Patterson Town and then to Philadelphia. [She?] is the one who wishes information about Thomas Burl and her mother Kitty McDonald. She lives at 167 South Second St., Philadelphia (Wash., D.C. *Centinel of Liberty* 5 Feb 1799).

BURNEY, EDWARD, came to America as a surgeon several years ago. He was the son of Mrs. Anne Burney of Wrexham, England. If he will apply to Richard Peters, Jr., in Philadelphia, he will hear something to his advantage (*Pa. Gaz.* 14 Dec 1769).

BURNEY, WILLIAM, came from Co. Tyrone, Ireland, about 30 years ago. Formerly of Horsham Twp., Philadelphia Co., but lately of Warminster, Bucks Co., he has died leaving a considerable estate, but he had no wife, child, or heir. Any person claiming to be the heir, and properly proving themselves to be such, should apply to Oliver O'Haughan, administrator (*Pa. Gaz.* 7 May 1772).

BURNS, ANNE, came to Philadelphia from Bristol on the ship *Four Friends* last May. If she will apply to Jesse and Robert Waln she will receive some very agreeable and interesting information (*GAVN*:48 cites *The Virginia Gazette and General Advertiser* 11 Jan 1797).

BURNS, WILLIAM R., saddle and harness maker, came from Ireland, and in 1831 was about 20 years old, 6" tall, and of handsome face. About 15 months ago he left Baltimore, and went to PA, where he is believed to be living in Lancaster Co. If he is alive and sees this notice, he is asked to write immediately to Margaret Burns, his widowed mother, who has recently arrived in Baltimore (*Baltimore Patriot* 31 Aug 1831).

BURRIDGE, THOMAS, of the City of Gloucester, came to New York with one Capt. Totterdel of Bristol in 1713, and is said to be married and living in some part of Pennsylvania or the Jerseys. If he will come or send to Obadiah Hunt of NY, he may be informed of an estate fallen to him, and also of a legacy to a sister of his, who came over some time after him (*Archives of NJ* 11:62 cites the *American Weekly Mercury* 10 May 1772).

BURROUGH, ROBERT, carver, resided in the Parish of St. Mary's, Rotherhithe, Surrey, son of Richard Burrough, bookseller of London who died c1728. Robert Burrough went to live at Cheyne, Bucks in 1731, and from thence to Jamaica or some other part of America. He is asked to apply to various agents in England and VA to hear something to his advantage (*GAVN*:49 cites the *Va. Gaz.* 11 April 1766).

BURTON, THOMAS, is supposed to be living in Pennsylvania. If he will give notice where he may be spoken with, to Mr. Samuel Soumaine, Goldsmith, in Philadelphia, or to James Richard, in Baltimore County, Maryland, he will hear of something much to his advantage, and the subscriber will immediately wait upon him. James Richard. (*Pa. Gaz.* 20 June 1765).

He may be the Thomas Burton who was living in Philadelphia when he advertised for the return of a runaway mulatto boy (*Pa. Gaz.* 12 Oct 1774).

In 1790 a Thomas Burton was head of a family in the Northern Liberties of Philadelphia, p. 206 (*AIS 1790 Census Index*).

BUTLER, Mrs. ANNE, if still living, will hear something to her advantage, and something about her husband, if she applies to Capt. Daniel Cheston in Philadelphia (*Pa. Gaz.* 13 July 1738)

BUTLER, Mrs. ANN, whose maiden name was Routh, and who lived at Risby, Brunswick Co., VA, c1773, or either of the sons of David Routh who is supposed to have lived near New Mill Creek, in Norfolk Co., VA, will hear something to their advantage by applying to Mrs. Elizabeth Routh of Kirklington, near Boroughbridge, Yorkshire (*GAVN:*51 cites the *Virginia Gazette or American Advertiser* 25 Oct 1783).

BUTZE, TRAUGOTT, apothecary, was born in Saxony and came to America seventeen years ago. B. Bohlen, 7 North Water St., Philadelphia, is inquiring for him (*Hocker:*189 cites the *Philadelphische Correspondenz* 24 Nov 1791).

BYRNES, JOHN, bricklayer of Maryland, is asked to call immediately on his friend J. M. of Philadelphia, in order to hear of something to his advantage (*Pa. Gaz.* 6 Nov 1776).

CADDEN, JUDY, otherwise SUSANNA, dau. of Charles Cadden of Clougher, Co. Tyrone, Province of Ulster, came to Philadelphia about 16 years ago, with one Robert Wallace. If she is alive, she is asked to write to her brother Philip Cadden, Corporal in Capt. Butler's Company in Halifax, and to Daniel O'Murphey, living on Maquire's Bridge, near Linasgay in Farmanagh, Ireland. If said Judy is deceased and Robert Wallace knows when and where she died, whether she was married or not, and in what circumstances, he is asked to transmit an account to the above persons (*Pa. Gaz.* 29 Jan 1767).

CAHOON, GEORGE, aged 15 or 16, son of George Cahoon, was taken with three brothers and three sisters from Cumberland Co, VA, about ten years ago by French and Iroquois Indians. He was later bought by a French officer. He arrived in New York from New Orleans in the brig *Africa* on his way to Trois Rivieres, Canada, attending on the two sons of the Surveyor General of Canada (*New York Post Boy* 30 July 1767).

CALBFUS, HENRY, from Pirmssaens[?], Germany, a tanner by trade, came to America about eight years since. He may hear of something to his advantage by applying to Ross and Vaughan, of Philadelphia, or to Reedy and Thuringer, merchants in Nantes (*Pennsylvania Packet and Daily Advertiser* 8 April 1785).

CALDER, WILLIAM, and **ROBERT CALDER,** brothers of Alexander Calder of Asswanlie, Parish of Glass, Lordship of Huntly, Sheriffdom of Aberdeen, are supposed to have gone to America and were alive when Alexander died in 1768, and to have left families. If any of their descendants can distinctly make out their propinquity to Alexander Calder, they will hear something to their advantage by applying personally or by letter to Thomas C. Amory, Esq., of Boston, James Lenox, Esq., of New York, to John Maybin, merchant of Philadelphia, Alexander Mundell, Esq., No. 3, Fludyer St., London, or to Mr. Thomas Cranstoun, Writer to the Signet, 23 N. Castle St., Edinburgh (*Gazette of the United States* 13 Feb 1804).

CALDWELL, JOHN, son of Thomas Caldwell, near Baylimoney, Co. Antrim, Ireland, came to this country in 1771. If he will apply to Robert Knox in Southwark Dist., Philadelphia, administrator of William Caldwell, dec., he may hear of something considerably to his advantage (*Dunlap's Pennsylvania Packet or the General Advertiser* 5 Dec 1770).

CALL (or COLL), TIMOTHY, and **JAMES CALL,** of the Parish of Doe, Co. Donegal, left Ireland about 56 years ago, and they and/or their children resided in BA Co. for a number of years. They were brothers of Andrew, Hugh, and Neal Call of the above Parish. Anyone who can give information about them should contact Peter Call at John McFadon's, mill stone maker, Lexington St., Baltimore (*Federal Gazette and Baltimore Daily Advertiser* 8 Dec 1801, 18 Dec 1801).

CALLAGHAN, PATRICK is supposed to have come into this Province from Cork, Ireland, as an indentured servant for four years. He was with one James Kenny, blacksmith in Salisbury Twp., Lancaster Co., PA. He is about 18 or 19 years old, 5'4" tall, by trade a weaver. He is asked to send a letter for Daniel Callaghan, directed to James Huston, at the Sign of the Highland Man and Bear, in Second Street, Philadelphia, between Market and Chestnut Sts. (*Pa. Gaz.* 28 Dec 1769).
    A Patrick Callahan was a private from Pennsylvania during the Revolutionary War. He was dead by about 4 May 1807 when the last payment on his pension was made (Murtie June Clark. *Index to U.S. Invalid Pension Records, 1801-1815*. Baltimore: Genealogical Publishing Co., 1991, p. 55). Another Patrick Callahan from Pennsylvania appeared on the U.S. Pension Roll of 1825 (*The Pension Roll of 1835: Indexed Edition*. Repr.: Baltimore: Genealogical Publishing Co., 1992, 2:609).

CALLAON, BARTLY, private, lately of the 7th Maryland Regiment, is asked to apply to John Welsh of Annapolis to hear of something to his advantage ((*The Pennsylvania Packet and Daily Advertiser* 15 Nov 1790).
    Barth'w Callahan, private, enlisted in the MD Line on 7 Dec 1776 and was discharged on 7 Dec 1779. He appeared at Annapolis on 25 April 1799 (*ARMD* 18:196).

CALLOW, ROBERT, of Hemlock, Devonshire, about nine years ago sailed to Philadelphia, and there lived with Owen Owen at the Sign of the Indian King in Philadelphia; later he removed to Bucks Co. If he will apply to Joseph Williams at Concord, Chester Co., he will hear something to his advantage (*Scott* 2:89 cites the *Pa. Gaz.* 5 July 1750).

CAMERON, JOHN, came from Ireland to PA, and was a peddler for ten or twelve years past, then went back to Ireland. He returned to PA. If he is alive he should contact the printers where he will hear of something greatly to his advantage (*Pa. Gaz.* 31 May 1775).

CAMPBELL, JOHN, came from Scotland some years ago and resided in New York City. He had an uncle in Scotland named David Campbell, and a sister Elizabeth, now wife of Robert Hill. Campbell is asked to get in touch with William Malcolm, merchant of New York City (*Scott* 5:109 cites the *New York Post Boy* 18 Sep 1766).

CAMPBELL, JOHN, arrived last fall from Liverpool in the ship *Three Sisters.* He should apply at once to the printers to hear of something greatly to his advantage (*Maryland Journal and Baltimore Advertiser* 24 May 1785).

CANNAR, WILLIAM, being unfortunately in a deranged state of mind, left his father's house some [time] last fall, and has not been heard of since. Anyone having information about him is asked to inform Sailes Cannar, living at Chancellor's Point Ferry, TA Co. (*Republican Star or Eastern Shore General Advertiser* 26 April 1803).

CAR, or KERR, ANN, came from Glasgow to Philadelphia in 1768 in a ship commanded by Capt. Robert Spear, and later paid some time to Thomas Cloudsdale of this city. Anyone with information about whether she is alive or dead, married or unmarried, in the city or county, is asked to communicate this information to Robert Aiken, bookseller and printer near the coffeehouse. (*Freeman's Journal or North American Intelligencer* 1 Oct 1783).

CARLILE, THOMAS, some time ago lived with Mr. Edmond Maws, in Annapolis. His brother William died last 9 Jan at the house of Mr. William Beats, Tullamore, King's Co., Ireland, and the said profits and rents have devolved to the said Thomas: profit rent of the freehold of Green Hills, or Killnomanagh, Co. of Dublin, amounting to £113 per annum, also three freehold leases in the Town of Tullamore, two of which are rented at £31.0.10 per annum; the other the said William held in his own possession, and built thereon a stated house, three stories high. Mr. Carlile is urged to return home. He may be informed of other matters by applying to R. M. at Mr. Philip Marchinton's, merchant, in Philadelphia (*Pa. Gaz.* 22 June 1774).

CARNMAGHAN, JOHN, came from Ireland and is thought to be in Philadelphia. His brother Alexander Lemen is now living in East Nottingham, Chester Co., and would be glad to hear from him. If he will apply to him in person, or by letter, he will hear something to his satisfaction (*Pa. Gaz.* 19 Oct 1769).

CARPENTER, RICHARD, born in the Town of Kidderminster, Worcestershire, 17 years of age, of fair complexion, a tinman, left London in Dec 1774. If he will apply to Mr. William Moore in Chesnut St., Philadelphia, he will hear something to his advantage (*Pennsylvania Evening Post* 7 March 1775).

CARRICK, JOHN, HUGH, and MARY, natives of Ireland, left there about 30 years ago, and then settled in Bucks or Chester County, about 40 miles from Philadelphia.. The last of them to die was Hugh Carrick, who died about two years, without issue. He made a will and appointed William Mathers and a Mr. Christy his executors. He is supposed to have died owning two valuable plantations in one of the aforesaid counties, which he left to his brother Francis Carrick, in Ireland. The executors, if living, are asked to write or appear personally to speak with Abraham Usher in Philadelphia, and inform him of the deceased persons and their affairs (*Pa. Gaz.* 1 Jan 1761).

A tract of land in the tenure of John Carrick of Londonderry Twp., Chester Co., containing 106 acres, with good improvements, is to be sold (*Pa. Gaz.* 30 May 1751).

CARSON, ISABELLA, JOHN [JOAN?] CARSON, WASHINGTON CARSON, NATHANIEL CARSON, and ELLEN CARSON, five children of Nathaniel Carson from Portaferry, Co. Down, Ireland, when last heard of, were living in Fells Point, Baltimore. If they will call upon Wm. & Thos. Adair, they will hear of a legacy left them (*Baltimore Patriot* 4 Oct 1834).

Nathaniel Carson married Eleanor Creaman by Baltimore Co. Marriage License dated 3 March 1791. Eleanor Carson, wife of Nathaniel, aged 32 years, died 25 May 1800 and was buried 26 May 1800 (Grogaard and Warfield:47). Nathaniel may be the Nathaniel who married Nancy Specknel in St. Paul's Parish on 16 April 1801 (*BAPA* 2:3).

In 1796 Nathaniel Carson, grocer, was listed at 32 Anne St., Fells Point. In 1807 he was listed as a storekeeper at 73 E. Aliseanna St. (Baltimore City Directories, 1796, 1807).

Nathaniel and Eleanor were the parents of (Piet:22): MARIA ISABELLA, b. 28 Nov 1791, bapt. 9 May 1793; JOAN GOULDING, b. 13 Dec 1795, bapt. 3 Oct 1797; JULIET, b. 10 Jan 1797, bapt. 17 April 1797, died 22 April 1798, aged 15 mos., and was buried 23 April in St. Peter's Church Yard (Grogaard and Warfield:47); GEORGE WASHINGTON, b. 19 Oct 1798, bapt. 10 Nov 1799; and MARY ELEANOR, b. 8 May 1800, bapt. 8 June 1800.

CARTER, GEORGE, aged about 40, was born in White Parish, 11 miles from New Sarum, Wilts. He was a baker, and about 1722 boarded a ship at Bristol for PA. He is asked to return to England or give notice of where he lives to John Atkinson at the Whyte Lyon Tavern on Cornhill, London, or to Israel Pemberton at Philadelphia. If he is deceased, information as to when and where he died, and knowledge of any children, is requested (*Pa. Gaz.* 18 Dec 1740; *American Weekly Mercury* 18 Dec 1740).

George Carter, baker of Annapolis, has a letter waiting for him from his sister Barbara Carter in Salisbury, Eng., waiting for him at the printer's (Annapolis *Maryland Gazette* 20 May 1756).

A George Carter took the Oath of Fidelity in Montgomery Co., MD, in 1778 (*AIS Census Index: Pre-1790* gives no other documentation).

CARY, S. See **CURLE, LOCKY.**

CASEY, MARK, sailor or shoemaker, bro. of Michael Casey, came from Co. Cork, Ireland, to PA some seven years ago. He is to apply to Jonathan Thomas, postmaster in Burlington, where he will hear something to his advantage (*Pa. Gaz.* 26 July 1750).

CASEY, MICHAEL, shoemaker, bro. of Mark Casey, came from Cork to PA some seven years ago. He is to apply to Jonathan Thomas, postmaster in Burlington, where he will hear something to his advantage (*Pa. Gaz.* 26 July 1750).

CASS, ANNE, dau. of Daniel Sharp of Wakefield, Yorkshire, some years ago was sold as a servant to John Page of Williamsburg, and then sold again by him to Mr. Penman, who sold her again. It is believed she may live somewhere in NC. If she, or her master (if she is still a servant), will make known her place of residence to the Hon. William Fairfax of VA, he will make the required satisfaction and give the said Anne an account of some proposals for her benefit (*GAVN:* 60 cites *The Virginia Gazette* 6 June 1755).

Anne Cass of Yorkshire was transported in 1749 (Coldham. *British Emigrants in Bondage:* 186).

CATER, JOSEPH, served his apprenticeship in London, with a silk thrower, and later married a daughter of Mr. Viller of Coventry. If he is in these parts and will apply to John Rhea, near the London Coffee House, Philadelphia, he may hear of something to his advantage (*Pa. Gaz.* 26 Jan 1751).

CAUGHLIN, WILLIAM, supposedly resides in or near Town. He should apply to the Printing Office to hear something to his advantage (Baltimore *Evening Post* 9 Oct 1792).

CHAMPNESS, JAMES, came to this town in 1774, in the *Ashton Hall*, and was sold to Walters and Gettrell. He is now about 28 years old, and is a hairdresser. He should apply to the printer (*Maryland Journal and Baltimore Advertiser* 12 April 1785).

He may be the James "Champnis" who enlisted as a private on 6 May 1778. James "Champness" was at White Plains on 5 Sep 1778 (Peden, *Revolutionary Patriots of Frederick County, Maryland, 1775-1783:* 68).

CHAPMAN, GEORGE, left England in 1807 for America. If he will contact his brother at No. 45, The Minories, London, and let him know his address, he will hear of something much to his advantage (*Federal Republican* 3 March 1813).

CHAPMAN, THOMAS, born at Darby and brought up in London, has been absent from his friends for 20 years, and may be living in New England. He is urged to contact his brother Francis Chapman, Master of Shadwell Charity School near London to hear something to his advantage (Annapolis *Maryland Gazette* 7 June 1749).

He may be the Thomas Chapman who was sentenced in Aug 1724 in Middlesex, and transported October 1724 in the *Forward* and given a landing certificate at Annapolis in June 1725 (Coldham. *British Emigrants in Bondage* 193).

CHARLTON, JOHN M., is asked to inform his friends in Georgetown, DC, of his whereabouts. He will receive some information in which he is much interested (*The Daily National Intelligencer* 16 Dec 1815).

CHEER, JOHN, formerly of Reading in Berkshire, Eng., maltster, embarked from thence about 14 years ago, and by the best information landed in South Carolina, and lived there for some time, and then moved to Annapolis, MD, where he followed the mercantile business. A near relation of his is now living in Philadelphia, and wants to communicate to him something considerably to his advantage. He should contact Mary Cheer, now living with Samuel Pleasants, merchant, in Philadelphia (*Pa. Gaz.* 19 Feb 1764).

CHRISTMAN, GEORGE, a shoemaker, left the vicinity of Kaiserslautern, in the Palatinate, about twenty years ago. He is being sought by his brother, Michael Christman, who is at Martin Kirschner's mill on the Conococheague, six miles from Hagerstown, (*Hocker* 192 cites the *Philadelphische Correspondenz* 23 April 1793).

   In 1790 a George Christman was listed in the census of Windsor Twp., Berks Co., PA, p. 44 (*AIS 1790 U.S. Federal Census Index*).

CHRISTMAN, HENRICH, linen-weaver, from a place two hours from Traarbach, "aus dem Claeninger Kirchspiel," arrived in this country eight or nine years ago, with his family. This year his sister Anna Margaret and her husband, Anton Graber, a smith, arrived in Conestoga, on Cocalico Creek, Lancaster Co., where they are with Johan Nickel Zerrfasz, near the Ephrata Cloister, and they are seeking news of her brother Henrich Christman (*Hocker* 22 cites the *Pennsylvanische Geschichts-Schreiber* 16 Oct 1750).

   For more on this Christman Family, see Burgert's *Western Palatinate:* 75.

CLARK, GEORGE, died about twenty years ago (c1743). He had come to Province with two of his brothers, from the City of Gloucester or from Newent in Glos., Eng. The two brothers died before George. About eighteen years ago someone sent some of George's personal effects. His relations [in England] wish to know where to apply, and ask that any person who knew the said George Clark or his circumstances, leave a letter directed to William Clark at The New Printing Office (*Pa. Gaz.* 28 April 1763). .

CLARK, MARY, *als* **SUNDERLAND,** born at Stepney Parish, London [Mddx.], came to MD some eight or ten years ago. She should apply to Capt. Thomas Beare of the ship *Tryton* (Annapolis *Maryland Gazette* 13 April 1758).

CLARKE, L., last fall lived in Baltimore (possibly with a Mr. Clarke, an Englishman who had been some years in Baltimore), and was a teacher in a female academy, and more recently kept a grocery store. If he will call on the Post-Master, he will hear of something that may prove to be a source of satisfaction (*Baltimore Patriot and Mercantile Advertiser* 26 Aug 1818).

CLARK, WILLIAM, came to Virginia in 1724 and lived in Timber Neck Creek, James River. If he will apply to Mary Ellis in King William Co., he will hear further particulars of his brother Edward, of St. Peter's of Hungate, Norwich, Co. Norfolk, who is the only one of the family in England, without heirs (*GAVN:* 65 cites Rind's *Va. Gaz.* 1 June 1769).

CLEMENT, JO. HEINRICH. came to America six or seven years ago, and [settled] in York County, PA, and married a daughter of Lorenz Schweiszgut. He is bring sought by his sister Elizabeth Catharina Clement, now Artinin, who arrived in Philadelphia five weeks ago on the ship *Crawford*, Capt. Smith.. The brother and sister are from Mittelfischbach, in the Darmstadt region, in the Nieder Grafschaft Catzenellenbogen, and are children of Christoph Clement (*Hocker* 119 cites the *Wochentlicher Pennsylvanischer Staatsbote* 17 Nov 1772).

Johan Henrich Clement came to America on the *Betsy*, John Osman, commander, from Rotterdam, last from Cowes, the Oath on 19 Sep 1765 (*Names of Foreigners* 473).

CLEMENTS, RICHARD, supposed to live in some part of Maryland, should apply to the printer, where he may hear of something to his advantage (*Pa. Gaz.* 28 Aug 1732).

A Richard B. Clements was listed in the 1778 Census of Bryantown Hundred, CH Co., MD (*AIS Census Index: Pre-1790* gives no other documentation).

CLENDENNING, THOMAS, of Baltimore Town., died before Feb 1764 leaving Thomas Sligh as his executor. Thomas Wilson advertised that Sligh planned to make a speedy sale of Clendenning's houses and lots, and Wilson advised would be purchasers that Clendenning's wife was expected in the Province soon, to claim her thirds, and if anyone purchases the property they should make a reserve for the widow's thirds (Annapolis *Maryland Gazette* 23 Feb 1764).

Thomas Clindining [*sic*] of Baltimore Town, Gent., died leaving a will dated 5 Feb 1762 and proved 20 March 1762. He named his friend Sarah Palmer, wife, reputed widow of Abraham Palmer, shipwright, 20 pounds current money. Rebecca Stewart, dau. of Sarah Palmer and wife of John Stewart, tailor, and Sarah Palmer, dau. of Sarah Palmer, were each to have 10 pounds current money. Son John Clindining of Glasgow, if living, was to have the remainder of his estate. If he was deceased, the estate was to be divided between wife Margaret, dau. of George Wilson, writer [of the signet?] in Glasgow. Thomas Sligh and Abraham Wayne of Baltimore were named executors. Brian Philpot, William Askew and Thomas Rutter witnessed the will (MWB 31:570).

Thomas Sligh, exec., filed an account of Clendenning's estate on 16 May 1763. He cited an inventory of £87.15.9. and listed payments of £69.4.2 (MDAD 49:236).

CLOUGH, ROBERT, was born in Bradford, and came over to PA, where he settled about 1712. He died an old man. If anyone can give the printers information of his late residence he shall be handsomely rewarded (*Pa. Gaz.* 6 Aug 1783). Another notice states that he was born in the Parish of Great Horton, Yorkshire, and came to America about 1713. He is supposed to have died about 10 years ago. Anyone with any knowledge of him should inform the printer (*Maryland Gazette and Baltimore Advertiser* 12 Sep 1783).

CLOUGSTON, MARY, came about six or seven years ago from Antrim. Her brother has arrived in Philadelphia, and wants to see her. She should apply to Mr. Harper at the Drawbridge in Philadelphia (*Pa. Chronicle* 17 April 1769).

COBLANTZ, PETER, DAVID COBLANTZ, and **PHILIP COBLANTZ,** are said to be relations of Jacob Coblantz, late of Cheltenham Twp., Montgomery Co., Pennsylvania, who has died. They are supposed to reside in the State of Virginia. If they apply to Bartholomew Mather, within one year of this advertisement, they will hear of something to their advantage. Anyone indebted to his estate is requested to make immediate payment thereof to Bartholomew Mather, exec. (*Pa. Gaz.* 13 April 1785).

Jacob Coblantz was in Philadelphia Co., PA, in 1770 (*AIS Census Index: Pre-1790* gives no other documentation).

One Coblentz [*sic*] owned a valuable plantation of 23 acres, between four and five acres of watered meadow, located in Cheltenham Twp., with a good two-story stone dwelling, with a good spring of water in the cellar, a stone stable, and an orchard of good fruit (*Pa. Gaz.* 18 Jan 1786).

Philip Coblens [*sic*], a German from Frederick Co. was naturalized in St. Anne's Parish, Anne Arundel Co., MD, on 13 April 1763 (Provincial Court Judgments DD#3:125; Bockstruck erroneously says he was naturalized in Baltimore Co.).

COLBERT, MARY, child of Elizabeth Colbert, was given by her mother to some woman near Brandywine Meeting House, on the road leading from Philadelphia to Lancaster, to keep her until she was of age. Now Elizabeth is very uneasy as she did not take the name of the woman, and now she wants her daughter back. Whoever has the child is asked to bring her to the Overseers of the Poor in Philadelphia or to the child's mother (*Pa. Gaz.* 4 March 1756).

COLES, THOMAS, mariner, brother of William Coles, sailed from the Thames for Cork and from thence to Boston about the beginning of the late American War, and is supposed to have settled in some part of the Continent. He is asked to send word to Mr. Bradford, printer, in Philadelphia to hear something greatly to his advantage (*GAVN* 71 cites the *Va. Journal and Alexandria Advertiser* 13 July 1786; *Maryland Chronicle or Universal Advertiser* 2 Aug 1786).

COLLINS, SOLOMON, worked in this town some time ago as a mason. His father now lives in Cumberland County. Collins should apply to Tiggat and Hyndman (*Maryland Journal and Baltimore Advertiser* 14 July 1786).

A Solomon Collins was a private in Capt. Walter Alexander's Company, Cecil Co. Militia, on 27 July 1776 (Peden, *Rev. Patriots of Cecil County:* 22).

COLLISON, MARGARET, eldest dau. of Capt. Robert Collison of Dunbarton's Regt. by his wife Margaret Dugud (dau. of [-?-] Dugud of Achinhoove, Scotland), left England with her husband (whose name her family has forgotten) about 50 years ago. He is supposed to have been a sheriff in PA in or about 1715. Information is sought about Margaret or any of her family who may still be alive (*Pa. Gaz.* 20 June 1751).

COLTON, JAMES, age 21, about 5'7" tall, a gilder and looking glass maker, left Northampton, MA, on 20 Oct 1829, to seek employment in some place in the South or West. A few days later he was seen by an acquaintance in New York, and expected to leave that city for Philadelphia. Since then he has not been heard from. Anyone with information about him is asked to contact Samuel H. Colton at Worcester, MA (*Baltimore Patriot* 27 May 1831).

COMBES, Mr. |-?-| Is supposed to live somewhere in Bucks Co., PA. He is the eldest son of Elizabeth Combes, born in Beckington, in Somersetshire, whose father was a wine cooper in Bristol. Mr. Combs is urged to apply to Isaac Jones, living opposite to the George Inn, in Arch St., Philadelphia, where he will hear something to his advantage (*Pa. Gaz.* 19 July 1739).

Elizabeth Combs, at her house over the Draw Bridge, advertised that she had for sale all kinds of white and check linens, and other types of cloth, for ready money or short credit (*Pa. Gaz.* 11 Dec 1740).

COMBES, JAMES, who left London about five years ago to settle in VA, is hereby informed that his son Richard Combes is now at Mr. Wootton's in Hampton, and would be glad to know where he resides (*GAVN*: 72 cites Purdie, Clarkson and Davis' *Va. Gaz.* 1 May 1778).

In 1782 a Richard Combes was listed in a "continental census" of Richmond Co. VA (*AIS Census Index: Pre-1790* gives no other documentation).

CONEEN (or GRAHAM), CATHERINE, came about seven years ago from Limerick, Ireland, to Philadelphia. She has inherited a handsome estate in England (*Scott3*: 26 cites *Bradford's New York Gazette* 30 March 1747).

CONN, THOMAS, said to live in the lower parts of MD, should apply to Jonas Green to hear something to his advantage (Annapolis *Maryland Gazette* 5 Sep 1754).

Thomas Conn died in Frederick County leaving a will dated 15 July 1758 and proved 30 Jan 1760. He left his son Thomas lands after his mother should die. He left his personal estate to his wife Martha for her lifetime, and then to his son James and his several daughters. His wife and son Thomas were named executors. Andrew Heugh, William Tannehall, and Joseph Miles witnessed the will (MWB 31:137).

On 14 March 1760 Andrew Heugh and Josias Beall appraised Thomas Conn's personal estate at £313.16.10. George Conn, Sr., and George Conn signed as next of kin. Thomas Conn, executor, filed the inventory on 10 April 1760 (MINV 68:259).

CONRAD, JONATHAN, and **JOHN CONRAD**, sons of John M. Conrad, if living, may hear of something to their advantage by applying to Christiana Conrad in Middletown, Dauphin Co., PA (*The Pennsylvania Packet and Daily Advertiser* 17 June 1790).

CONREY, Capt. |-?-|, a citizen of the United States, lost his vessel near the Philippine Islands, afterwards arrived at Manilla, got the command of a vessel trading to Acapulco, and died on his return to the Marianne Islands. It is not known what vessel he commanded, or what part of the United States he was from. His heirs or representatives may hear of something to their advantage by applying to the Customs House, Baltimore. (*Baltimore Patriot & Mercantile Advertiser* 30 April 1818).

COOK, JOHN, is a son of John Cook, carpenter and joiner of the Parish of St. Mary Magdalen in the Borough of Southwark, by Sarah his wife. He is also a grandson of Moses Bywater of the same place, potter, all of whom are deceased. If Cook is living, he will hear something to his advantage if he applies to Hewes and Anthony of Philadelphia

Daniel McCormick of New York, or Patrick Jeffrey of Boston. (*Pa. Gaz.* 26 March 1788).

COOKE, JAMES, a wright, lived a good many years ago in the West Indian Islands and died about 8 months ago. If his nearest relation, or heirs at law will apply to the printer, they will hear of a person who will put them in the way to obtain some money left them by the said Cooke (Dobson, *Aberdeen Journal* Sep 1777: issue 1549).

COOKE, RICHARD, brother of Anna Cooke who died in 1775, was born in Rotterdam, and has been married and settled for some years in America, and is believed to exercise the trade of surgeon or apothecary in Maryland. He or any of his lawful heirs should apply to the printer to hear something to his or their advantage (*The Pennsylvania Packet* 28 Jan 1778).

A Richard Cooke was listed in 1758 as a resident of St. Mary's Co., MD (*AIS Census Index: Pre-1790* gives no other documentation).

COON, ANN, taken on the Delaware, and other children, are now at the State House in Philadelphia. During the war they had been taken captive by the Indians from several parts of the Province, and have been lately released by General Amherst. They are to be returned to their parents or other relations, who are desired to come forthwith and receive them (*Pa. Gaz.* 2 July 1761).

COOPER, JAMES, son of John Cooper of the Parish of Bangor, Co. Down, came to this country in 1771. Daniel Rabb, living at William McKeown's five miles from Charles Town, Cecil County, Maryland, asks the said Cooper to come to him, where he may have some things to his advantage (*Pa. Gaz.* 11 Nov 1772)

COOPER, JOHN, left England about 20 years ago. He is urged to contact his daughter Mary Cooper, now in Baltimore (*Maryland Journal and Baltimore Advertiser* 9 Jan 1775).

Some time between 7 and 14 Feb 1773, Mary Cooper, aged 29, girt maker, an indentured servant, of London, embarked on the *Letitia* for Maryland (Fothergill 1913: 32).

CORFIELD, JOHN, if living, should apply to John Pemberton in Philadelphia, where he may be informed of something to his advantage. If is with the Army, as is supposed, in New York Government, and cannot have liberty to come himself, he is desired to send a letter to Pemberton or to his last Master in Philadelphia (*Pa. Gaz.* 29 Oct 1761).

CORRY, ELIZABETH, of Dunory or Chew Magna, Somerset, came to America, and is supposed to have been given an account of by Edward Cook, a cooper, living with John Strand, cooper of Brandywine hundred in New-Castle Co. If she goes to the printer, she may be sent home to her friends (Philadelphia *American Weekly Mercury* 3 Dec 1730).

CORRY, MARTIN, born in the town and parish of Cong, came over from Ireland a good many years ago, sailing from Dublin. If he will apply to the printer, he may hear something greatly to his advantage (*Pennsylvania Packet and General Advertiser* 9 Nov 1772).

CORSE, THOMAS, formerly resided at the Head of Chester, Queen Anne's Co., MD. He will much oblige his relations by informing them where he is living. Any information concerning Thomas Corse, alive or dead, will be gratefully received at the Office of the *Federal Gazette* in Baltimore, by John Corse (*Gazette of the United States* 1 June 1803).

COSGROVE, ANDREW, cooper, recently arrived from Ireland. He advertised for his wife last summer. This is to inform her that she and her father, Michael Little (*q.v.*) are living in Baltimore County, within fifteen miles of the town, in the Forks of the Gunpowder, on part of Nicholas Lee Darnall's land, and are very desirous of his coming there (*Pa. Gaz.* 26 June 1766).

In 1790 a Michael Cosgrove was listed in the census of Cecil Co., MD, p. 46 (*AIS 1790 U.S. Federal Census Index*).

COSSAR, JACOB, came into this Province about two years ago from Holland, and sold one of his children, named Margaret, to a person who said he lived about fifteen miles from Philadelphia. Cossar asks anyone who knows the whereabouts of his daughter to inform Caleb Wistar of her whereabouts (*Pa. Gaz.* 5 Sep 1751).

COTTON, WILLIAM, native of Ireland, was a sailor on the brigantine *Minerva,* Capt. William Sherman, from New Haven to St. Croix, from Feb to May 1767. He will hear something to his advantage if he applies to Adam Babcock, in New Haven (*Pa. Chron.* 20 March 1769).

COWAN, JAMES, sailed from Dublin on 12 June 1806, for some port in the U.S.. He will hear something to his advantage by writing to Thomas S. Walsh, 42 Water St., New York (*Washington Federalist* 31 Oct 1807)

COX, JOHN, now about 32 years old, took his passage from Bristol on the Bristol Packet in the Brigantine *Bristol Packet,* Capt. Marshall, and landed in Philadelphia some time in the month of December 1761. Since then his friends in England have not heard from him. A near relation has died, and left him a legacy. He may receive the same by applying to Henry Drinker of Philadelphia, and hear further from his relations (*Pa. Gaz.* 11 July 1765).

COX, SAMUEL, came from Byfield in Northamptonshire, Eng., about three or four years ago and went to live with Thomas Messer in Chester Co. If he is alive, he is to apply to David Stratton in Evesham Twp., Burlington Co. in the Jerseys, where he may hear something to his advantage (*Scott* 2:299 cites the *Pa. Gaz.* 8 Aug 1754).

COYNE, JAMES, sailed from Dublin to New York on the *Draper* or *Dragon* on 13 May 1797. He will hear something to his advantage if he contacts the Rev. James Griffin in Alexandria. He was to settle at Richmond, Petersburg, or Warrenton, NC (*GAVN:* 78 cites *The Times and District of Columbia Daily Advertiser* 29 Oct 1799 and the *Va. Gaz. and General Advertiser* 10 Dec 1799).

CRAIG, ARCHIBALD, left Ireland some years ago, and went to PA, where he may have followed the business of a peddler. If he is still living, and will apply to the printer, he may hear something to his advantage. If anyone can inform the printer of whether he is still living, or of his whereabouts, it will be greatly appreciated (*Pa. Gaz.* 13 Jan 1763).

CRAIG, JOHN, brother of the late Sarah Allen of Carlisle, is said to have lived near Pittsburgh. If he will apply to the executors of the deceased, he may hear of something to his advantage (*The Carlisle Gazette and the Western Repository of Knowledge* 6 Aug 1794).

CRANLEY, JOHN, age about 40, upholsterer, formerly of the City of Winton, served his apprenticeship in London. Samuel Smith, draper, of Winchester, offers a reward of five guineas for information about his whereabouts (*Scott* 1:232 cites the *Pa. Gaz.* 27 April 1732).

CRAWFORD, JAMES, a native of PA, a distiller by trade, was taken prisoner at Fort Michilimackinac and left Detroit in the brig *Adams*. He landed at Buffalo the time she was destroyed by the Americans. His son-in-law John Penny, who is married to his daughter, Hannah Crawford, has not heard of him since. Penny came to Pittsburgh about the latter part of September, 1812, with Lieut. Darragh. If Crawford is still living, he will get information from His son-in-law and daughter by sending a letter to Penny or to Capt. A. Darragh at Pitsburgh (*The True American* 28 Sep 1814).

CRAYTON, |-?-|, a turner, was employed at the queensware manufactory in this city about 18 months or two years ago. If he will write to the printer of this paper, he may hear of something to his advantage (*Poulson's American Daily Advertiser* 24 June 1805).

CRIB, ELIZABETH, served her time with Benjamin Lownes in Springfield, Chester Co., and left that about four years ago, since when her friends have heard nothing from her, and she is asked to send an account of where she is to her friends or to come to John Smith's near Bachelor's Hall, where she may learn of her mother (*Pa. Gaz.* 4 June 1761).

CROSLAND, THOMAS, schoolmaster, lately died intestate at the house of Harman Umstadt, who administers the estate, in the Twp. of Skippack and Perkioming, Philadelphia Co., about 22 miles from the city. He left more property than would pay his just debts and funeral expenses, and it is said that Crosland had a wife in this or some other neighboring state. If she, or any other heirs, will apply as above, and provide the proper ad necessary proofs, they may receive the same (*Pa. Gaz.* 17 Dec 1783).

CULVERWELL, RICHARD, of Cheddar, Co. Somerset, was shipped to MD in May 1759 on the *Atlas* from the port of Bristol. He should apply to Capt. John McKerdy of the *Royal Charlotte* (Annapolis *Maryland Gazette* 6 June 1771).
    Richard Culverwell was sentenced to transportation for 14 years at the Somerset Quarter Sessions on Oct 1758. Transportation Bond was posted in May 1759 (*CBEB*).
    In 1790 a Richard Culverwell was head of a family in Anne Arundel Co., MD (*AIS 1790 Census Index*).

CUNLIFF, JOHN, said to reside in or near Christeen [*sic*], New Castle Co., upon Delaware, is sought by his nephew Dennis Ryley, late of Acrington, Lancs., but now of

New Hanover Twp., Burlington Co., West New Jersey (*American Weekly Mercury* 30 Nov 1727).

CUNNINGHAM, DAVID, second son of Sir John Cunningham of Robertland, Scotland, came to VA or MD about 22 years ago (c1729). He is asked to contact Robert Peter, merchant, or William Cunninghame, merchant, at the Falls of Rappahannock in VA, for good news (Annapolis *Maryland Gazette* 16 Oct 1751).

A William Cunningham died by Jan 1797 when his administrator, Elizabeth Cunningham of Norfolk advertised she would settle his estate (*GAVN* 82 cites *The Norfolk Herald and Public Advertiser* 5 Jan 1797).

CUNYNGHAM, JOHN JAMES, native of St. Eustatius, aged 36 years, embarked at that island on 15 June 1775, on the brigantine *Adventure*, John [Pontoslet?], master, bound for Amsterdam, where he arrived, and then proceeded to Magadore the December following on a brigantine belonging to New York, since which his friends have not heard from him. Anyone with information is asked to communicate with John Mease of Philadelphia. (*Pennsylvania Packet and Daily Advertiser* 23 Dec 1789).

CUPPLES, MOSES, native of Clough, near Ballymena, Co. Antrim, Ireland, in 1775, lived near the Red Lyon on the great road leading from Philadelphia to Lancaster, in Whitehead Twp., Chester Co., PA. He is asked to contact Daniel M'Cormick to hear something to his advantage (*Scott* 3:230 cites *The New York Gazette and Weekly Mercury* 28 May 1781).

The Index to the Prerogative Wills of Ireland, edited by Sir Arthur Vicars, lists two Samuel Cupples of Killyree, Co. Antrim, whose wills were [deposited?] 1780. One will was proved in 1771 and the other in 1779. A Moses Cupples of the same parish died in 1798 (p. 118).

CURAND, PAULUS Del, arrived in this country two years ago, is sought by his stepbrother, Philip Misze. Inquire of Conrad Weiser of Tulpehocken, Berks Co. (*Hocker:* 15 cites the *Pennsylvanische Geschichts-Schreiber* 1 Nov 1749).

CURLE, LOCKY, S. CARY (of in or near Williamsburg), and **SOLOMON NUNIS** (of Norfolk), are asked to give information of the residence and address to the editor of the Richmond *Enquirer*, they will hear of something greatly to their advantage (*Richmond Enquirer* 31 Jan 1833).

CUSHIN, ROBERT, son of John Cushin, formerly of Donoman, but afterwards of Rathkeale, Co. Limerick, embarked from Cork as a redemptioner in the ship *Anne*, Capt. Benjamin Edmondstone, on 16 June 1783, for Philadelphia. If he will enquire of the printer of this paper, or inform Mr. Paul Zantsinger at Lancaster, of his place of residence, he may be informed of something interesting of his friends (*Pa. Gaz.* 25 Oct 1786).

DALY, AENEAS, came from England to MD or VA some four or five years ago with Owen Griffin. Daly is now about 18 years old. He is urged to contact Joseph Royle, printer in Williamsburg (Annapolis *Maryland Gazette* 13 Oct 1763; *Pa. Gaz.* 27 Oct 1763).

DAM, PETER, for some years past resided sometimes in Philadelphia, and sometimes in NJ. He went out to sea this spring. If he would leave a letter with the printers, directed to his brother Andrew Dam, he will hear some agreeable news (*Pa. Gaz.* 31 May 1770).

DAMANT, WILLIAM, of Eye, Co. Suffolk, whitesmith, left England on the 3 Aug 1773, and arrived in America in the month of September following, in the *Isabella*, Capt. Smith. He is entitled to a considerable legacy by the death of his late uncle Thomas Cooper of Eye, Suffolk. He may lay claim to his legacy by directing a line to Mr. Meadows at Dis, in Norfolk, Old England, or to Mr. Hicks, bricklayer, Kees Alley, Philadelphia (*Pa. Gaz.* 2 June 1784).

William Damant married Ann Davy on 11 Feb 1766 at Eye, Suffolk (Undocumented statement in the IGI).

DANNER, JACOB, a wheelwright's son from Schaffhausen, arrived in this country last year. His brother Johann Georg Danner, arrived this year, now with Christian Benner, in Franconia Twp., Montgomery Co., and is seeking Jacob (*Hocker:* 23 cites the *Pennsylvanische Geschichts-Schreiber* 16 Dec 1750).

Jacob Tonner [sic] arrived on the *Lydia* on 19 Oct 1749 (*Eyster:* 10).

DARCK, CHRISTIAN, a native of Hanover, who formerly lived in Franconia Twp., Montgomery Co., left there last Feb with his wife and two daughters and two sons (*Hocker:* 88 cites the *Pennsylvanische Geschichts-Schreiber* 27 March 1761).

DARDIS, MICHAEL, came into this country from Dublin, some 5½ years ago and served his time with Capt. Flower, and worked last Branson's Iron-works. A mill-wright, he is supposed to have gone to York or Cumberland Co. with Arnold Pender, a German millwright. Dardis is sought by his wife Catherine, who has lately come over. Word of Dardis may be sent to Mr. Erwin's in Strawberry Alley (*Scott* 2:143 cites the *Pa. Gaz.* 22 Aug 1751).

Michael Dardie [sic], a servant from Ireland, was assigned by William Humphreys to William Branson of Philadelphia, for £24, merchant, for four years starting as of 5 June 1746 (Tepper, ed., *Emigrants to Pennsylvania, 1614-1819* 126).

DAUM, JOHANN LUDWIG, formerly a gamekeeper at Daaden, Sayn-Altenkirchen, in 1783 went to the United Netherlands and thence to Philadelphia. He is being sought (*Hocker:* 190 cites the *Philadelphische Correspondenz* 3 July 1792).

N.B.: The Following may not apply to Johann Ludwig Daum. John [sic] Daum and wife Anna Maria were the parents of (F. Edward Wright, *Early Records of the First Reformed Church of Philadelphia*. Westminster: Family Line Publications, 1994. Vols. 1, 2): SUSANNA, age 17 years, buried 13 Sep 1793; MARIA CATHERINE, b. 6 Dec 1780, bapt. 24 Dec 1780 (sp.: John Schreiber and Anna Maria); ELIZABETH, b. 29 Sep 1783, bapt. 19 Oct 1783 (sp.: Fred. Greiner and Elizabeth); MAGDALENA, 2 weeks old, bapt. 26 Nov 1786 by Rev. Casper Weyberg (sp.: Sam Kloethy and Cath. Kloethy), at 2 years, 6 mos., and 2 weeks was buried 22 April 1789.

DAVENPORT, JAMES, came from Ireland and taught school in Sudbury Twp., near Philadelphia. If he applies to Josiah F. Davenport in Front St. in Philadelphia, he will hear something to his advantage (*Pa. Chronicle* 18 Jan 1768).

Josiah F. Davenport advertised he would lease The Bunch of Grapes Inn in Third Street, between Market and Arch Sts., Philadelphia (*Pa. Gaz.* 30 May 1771).

DAVIS, DAVID, carpenter, son of Ellis Davis, dec., late of Horsham, Philadelphia Co., PA, left PA about ten or twelve years ago, and went to New England. If he applies to Thomas Fletcher of Abington in the same county, he may hear of something considerably to his advantage (*Pa. Gaz.* 6 Dec 1745).

DAVIS, MARGARET, is urged to apply to the printer if she is the sister of one Edward Davis who lately died in VA (*Pa. Gaz.* 9 May 1751).

DAVIS, SAMUEL, son of James, of the City of Gloucester, came from Bristol to Pennsylvania some 35 years ago as a servant. When his time had expired he married and settled in Bucks Co., and had children. If he, his wife, or children, are still alive, they will hear something to their advantage by applying to Thomas Williams in Frederickstown, Cecil Co., MD (*Pa. Gaz.* 29 Aug 1758).

DEAKIN, JOHN, about six years ago, sailed from Portsmouth in the man-of-war *Experiment,* and was in her at the attack on Sullivan's Island, SC, and later on the *Phoenix* and in hospital in New York City. He married a farmer's daughter on Long Island. If he will apply to the printer, he will hear something to his advantage (*Scott* 3:243 cites *The New York Gazette and Weekly Mercury* 28 July 1783).

DEAN, JOSEPH born in Dublin, a son of William Dean has a legacy waiting for him, and is asked to apply to Messrs. Hugh and Alexander Wallace, merchants in New York City (*Scott* 3:152 cites *The New York Gazette and Weekly Mercury* 18 March 1771).

DEAN, WILLIAM, was born at Gibraltar, and was a Sergeant in the Young Buffs. He was a son of William Dean who had formerly been a soldier of the XXIX Regt., and who has since lived near Gorey, Co. Wexford, Ireland. William (the son) was married at Warrington, Eng. He also has a legacy waiting him (*Scott* 3:153 cites *The New York Gazette and Weekly Mercury* 18 March 1771).

DEANE, or DEAN, JOHN, a native of the north of Scotland, is supposed to have died in MD or VA or SC about 1790 in affluent circumstances (Query posted by W. T. Deane in *Notes and Queries* 12 (316) 17 Nov 1855, p. 384).

He may be the John Dean, merchant of Glasgow, who sailed some time before 1757 and settled in Tappahannock, VA (Dobson *Scots on the Chesapeake* p. 38).

DECHAMP, HONORINE, a girl about 12, who speaks the French and English languages fluently, her face much marked with freckles, left her mother's house in New York and gone to the South with her uncle, Mr. Leon Perot, a married man, who may have taken her as he thought her mother was unable to support her. At one time he resided in Richmond, VA, and later was a segar [*sic*] maker at Baltimore. Anyone with information is asked to contact the French Consulate, 34 Reed St., NY (*The City of Washington Gazette* 5 Oct 1819).

DEETRICK, ABRAHAM, who came into this country about 18 years ago, is being sought by his brother Peter Deetrick, who came into this country last spring. Anyone knowing Abraham's whereabouts is asked to contact Peter, who is living in Lebanon Twp., Lancaster Co. (*Pa. Gaz.* 13 Dec 1764).

Peter Dietrich arrived on the ship *Polly,* Capt. Robert Porter, from Rotterdam, last from Cowes, and qualified on 19 Sep 1764 (*Names of Foreigners* 460).

DEGRAFFENREID, ISCHARNER, in 1764 was a Justice of the Peace in VA. George Meade of Philadelphia, want to know if he is living or dead, and if he is deceased, whether he left any children. "Philadelphia 19 Oct 1785" (*GAVN:* 89 cites *The Virginia Gazette or the American Advertiser* 3 Dec 1785).

Ischarner DeGraffenreid of Virginia was listed as a private with an annual stipend of 60.00, on the Pension List of 1813 (*Revolutionary Pensioners: A Transcript of the Pension List of the United states for 1813.* Repr.: Baltimore: Genealogical Publishing Co., 1994, p. 38).

DEHEAUME, ROLAND, ELIZABETH, and **ANN,** were natives of the Isle of France. If they will call on Joseph Anthony & Co., they will hear of something to their advantage (*Claypoole's American Daily Advertiser* 11 June 1799).

DEINHART, JOHANN WILHELM, and his sister, **CHRISTINE MAGDALENA DEINHARTIN,** were born at Gartsch, Wurtemberg. They came to America 34 years ago. Christina Margaretha married Peter Haller of York (*Hocker:* 202 cites the *Germantauner Zeitung* 12 Dec 1786).

DELAFORCE, JOSEPH, cabinet maker, was brought into this country as a convict over two years ago, in the ship consigned to Messrs. Davenport, Strather and Lane, merchants in Prince William Co., VA. News of his whereabouts is desired (Annapolis *Maryland Gazette* 9 Dec 1773).

Joseph Delaforce of Co. Middlesex was transported for life from London to MD on the *Scarsdale,* Capt. Christopher Reed, in July 1770 (*KPMV:* 216).

DEMPSEY, RICHARD, arrived in this country from near Barrymanock, Co. Antrim, Ireland, about 9 years ago, and is supposed to be in western PA. His brother John Dempsey is seeking information (*The National Intelligencer and Washington Advertiser* 20 Feb 1801).

DEIPIA, SEBASTIAN, age c17, left St. Augustine some months ago. If he will apply to the printer he may learn something to advantage (*New York Post-Boy* 31 May 1761).

DEREHAM, RICHARD, son of Sir Richard Dereham, who was sent to the West Indies about 20 years ago, and has been seen in MD and PA, has been left a legacy of £500 sterling (*American Weekly Mercury* 20 April 1732).

DERING, NICHOLAS, son of Henry Dering, late of New Hanover Twp., Philadelphia Co., is asked to apply or send to his brother Henry Dering at Lancaster (executor of Henry Dering, dec.) as he may hear of something to his advantage (*The Pennsylvania Packet or the General Advertiser* 4 Sep 1781).

DERRYMAN, MARY, who was at Tollard-Royal on 29 Sep 1727, wrote a letter to her son, Arthur Oliver, at Philadelphia. Her son is asked to claim the letter (*American Weekly Mercury* 6 Feb 1728).

DESAU. CHRISTIAN FRIEDRICH, who served with an English smith, five miles from the White Horse Inn, on the Lancaster Road, is sought by his step-brother, Johann Eberhard Bens, of Ringwood, Hunterdon Co., NJ (*Hocker:* 80 cites the *Pennsylvanische Geschichts-Schreiber* 28 Nov 1759).

DEUNSCHMAN, JACOB, born in Niedermerschbach, near Hochenburg, with Sebastian Schuechen, left Amsterdam on 29 May last for Philadelphia. Jacob Fischer. Reformed schoolmaster in the Stone Church, Bern Twp., Berks Co., PA, is seeking them (*Hocker:* 172 cites the *Philadelphische Correspondenz* 22 Feb 1785).

DICKS, RICHARD, ship carpenter, son of Edmund Dicks, formerly of Giminghham, Co. Norfolk, came to MD some 11 or 12 years ago. He or his widow or children should apply to the printers (Annapolis *Maryland Gazette* 9 Aug 1770).

Richard Dicks, carpenter, died in Baltimore Co., MD leaving a will dated 24 Jan 1781 and proved 12 Feb 1782. He left his wife Catherine, dau. of Elicksander Dean, 17 a. part Ensor's Inspection, 8 a. in Cecil Co., MD, and all his personal estate. She was named extx. James Maydwell, Abraham Ensor, and Sarah Wooflet or Wooflet witnessed the will (BAWB 3:455).

Catherine Dicks, extx., posted admin. bond on 12 Feb 1782, with James Maidwell and Abr. Ensor as sureties (BAAB 6:209).

DICKSON, DAVID, late of the Parish of Ballysullin, Co. Derry, Ireland, wheelwright, left his home in May 1783, and came to Philadelphia in the *Irish Volunteer.* After his arrival he went into the country. If he will apply to the printers, he may hear of something to his advantage (*The Pennsylvania Packet and Daily Advertiser* 24 June 1785).

DICKSON, MARGARET, the three-year-old daughter of James Dickson of Little Britain Twp., in Lancaster Co., has been missing from her father's house since last 26 Dec. It is suspected that she was stolen away. Anyone who can give intelligence of where she is should contact her father aforesaid. the Rev. Samuel Blair in Chester Co., or Mr. George Gibson in Lancaster Town (*Pa. Gaz.* 10 Feb 1743).

John Dickson of Lancaster Co., died leaving a will dated 17 Feb 1747 and proved 23 Nov 1748. He named children: James, Grizel, John and Robert. John McCown and James Dickson were named executors (*Lancaster Wills,* 1732-1785).

On 10 Aug 1753, by order of the Orphans court of Lancaster Co., James Dickson was appointed one of the guardians of Richard Dillworth, a lunatic, age 35 years old (Sophie Selden Rogers. "Genealogical Gleanings from the Orphans Court Records of Lancaster County, Pennsylvania." *PVR* 1:351).

DIEBUSCH, ALBERT, is sought by his brother's daughter, Christiana Diebuschin, who arrived last autumn and is now in NY (*Hocker* 135 cites the *Wochentlicher Pennsylvanischer Staatsbote* 20 Sep 1774).

DIMOCK, DAVID S., has been absent from his parents for a long time. If he will come home or write, so that his friends can send a letter to him, he will news that will be both pleasing and interesting to him. Anyone with information is asked to communicate with Asa Dimock, Esq,, Clifford, Luzerne Co., PA, or David Dimock in Exeter (*Gleaner and Luzerne Advertiser* 24 May 1811).

DISIUSIN, SUSANNA, widow, formerly of Schoharie, NY, is asked to communicate with Mr. Brunnholts, Philadelphia (*Hocker:* 32 cites the *Pennsylvanische Geschichts-Schreiber* 1 March 1752).

DINES, JAMES, about 5' tall, left home on 15 Aug, and had not been heard of. His wife fears that his mind was insane and that he may have destroyed himself. York Co. papers are requested to copy this notice (*Baltimore Patriot* 24 Aug 1830).

DOBBINS, JOHN BATEBY, came from England some years ago, and resided for some time at Washington (it not certain in what state). If he will call on or write to Samuel Spackman, 1 Bank Alley, Philadelphia, he will hear something very much to his advantage ([D.C.] *The National Intelligencer and Washington Advertiser* 31 Oct 1808).

DOBELBAUER, FRIEDRICH, son of Christoph Dobelbauer, a dyer, is sought by Jacob Keller, Jr., Cocalico Twp., Lancaster Co., PA (*Hocker:*169 cites the *Philadelphische Correspondenz* 9 March 1784).

DOBLEMAN, JOSHUA F., a German, left his brother at the German Hotel, Pratt St. Bridge last Sunday evening with the intention of turning home. It was thought he would very likely take the nearest road home by crossing the drawbridge. He has not been seen since. He was a man of sober and industrious habits, and has a wife and two children. It is supposed that he was murdered on the bridge and thrown over. Anyone with information is asked to contact his wife who lives in Thames St., two doors from Bond St. (*Baltimore Patriot* 8 Nov 1834).

DOCK, JOHANN ADAM, tailor, left Anweiler, near Landau, ten years ago. His sister Anna Margretha, with her second husband, Jacob Werth, arrived in this country two years ago, and she is seeking her brother (*Hocker* 29 cites the *Pennsylvanische Geschichts-Schreiber* 1 Oct 1751).

DODD, GABRIEL, was born in London, and served his apprenticeship with Anthony Joiner, ship-joiner in Philadelphia. He is said to have gone to South Carolina and died. His brother Thomas Dodd, near George Gray's Ferry, is seeking information (*Pa. Gaz.* 26 June 1740).

In Nov 1738 Gabriel Dodd or his wife had a letter waiting for them at the Philadelphia Post Office (*Pa. Gaz.* 2 Nov 1738).

DOIG, DAVID, late Deputy Provost Marshal of West Florida, should contact his friends in Scotland, who will inform of something very much to his advantage (*GAVN:* 103 cites *The Virginia Gazette* 2 July 1772).

DONNALL, SAMUEL, was born in Belfast, Ireland, and served his time with James Blow, printer in Belfast. He has lived with Hugh Gaine, printer in New York. He is requested to write to John M'Donnall, at the Sign of the White Swan, Head of Severn, Anne Arundel Co., MD (*Pennsylvania Chronicle* 29 Jan 1770).

DONOVAN, JAMES, shoemaker, in trade with a partner, resided in Baltimore about 20 years ago. He was married and has children. His wife married again and died in 1813. Any information about him should be addressed to A.S., and put in the Post Office or at No. 76 Wilkes St. (*Mechanics' Gazette and Merchants' Daily Advertiser* 8 May 1815).

A James Donovan and Mary Mehan were married 1 Feb 1795 in St. Paul's Parish, BA Co. (*BAPA* 1:85).

DORAN, HUGH, of Baltimore Co., MD, was living in 1761 when he employed Samuel Allinson to recover some debts due him in Burlington, NJ. At first unsuccessful, Allinson finally recovered the debt in 1764 and then heard that Doran was dead. In Dec 1766 he advertised for Doran's representatives to make themselves known to him so he could pay them the money he owed them (*Pa. Gaz.* 9 Jan 1766).

DORAT, Mr. DISNEMATIN, is sought by Mr. Tissier, who has just arrived from Martico, and who begs Mr. Dorat to let him know his direction. Anyone with information is asked to apply to Miss Fillette Amon, corner of Pine and South Second St., Philadelphia (*Poulson's American Daily Advertiser* 15 Sep 1807).

DORMER, Rev. Mr. JAMES, native of England, is supposed to be in some part of America, probably in SC; he has been away from his friends for about 25 years; any intelligence of this gentleman will be received by James Rivington of NY (*GAVN* 104 cites the *Virginia Gazette or American Advertiser* 30 Aug 1783).

DORMEYER, PETER, is being sought by his sister's husband, Leonhard Bauer. Dormeyer was born in Diemringer Amt, Dorf Deringer, in 1764 came to America, with his sister Carolina Christina, and her husband, and was indentured. Dormeyer is believed to be in the dry lands near Bethlehem. Notify Jacob Friesz, innkeeper, Salem Co., NJ (*Hocker:* 165 cites the *Philadelphische Correpondenz* 1 June 1783).

Peter Dormeyer was head of a family in Pennsylvania in 1790 (*AIS 1790 Census Index*).

For more on this family, see Burgert's *Alsace* 120-121.

DORN, PATRICK, an Irishman who came to the colonies about 12 year ago as an apprentice to an attorney, may contact his sister through the offices of the printer (*Scott* 4: 92 cites the *Connecticut Gazette* 1 Nov 1760).

DOUGHERTY, DENNIS, from near Londonderry, came to Philadelphia some time ago. He served his time with one McConnell in or near Middle Octerara. He should contact George Connelly, soap boiler, to receive some goods sent to him from Ireland (*Pa. Gaz.* 17 Nov 1768).

On 24 March 1763 Dennis Dougherty and James Byrne, executors, advertised they would settle the estate of Dudley Dougherty of Philadelphia (*Pa. Gaz.* 24 March 1763).

Dennis Dougherty and Margaret Murphy were married by license dated 23 Nov 1764 (*PVR* 1:689).

He may be the Dennis Dougherty of Philadelphia, who died by March 1785 when Margaret Dougherty, administrator, advertised she would settle the estate (*Pa. Gaz.* 15 March 1785).

DOUGHERTY, KEZIAH, granddau. of Ambrose Farmer, left Dublin about 10 years ago at the age of 13, aboard a ship commanded by James Stevenson of Dublin, bound for Philadelphia. She is asked to inquire of William Reynolds of Chester Co., PA, or others (*Pa. Gaz.* 9 Aug 1739).

DOUGHERTY (DAUGHERTY), ROBERT, from the Parish of Conner, Co. Antrim, should apply to Robert Smyth, hatter, in Market St., Philadelphia, or John Smyth, from Ireland, at Mr. Samuel Love's, in West Nottingham Twp., Chester Co., to hear of something to his advantage. The sooner application is made, the better, as John Smyth sails for Ireland at the first opportunity (*Pa. Gaz.* 7 June 1770).

A Robert Dougherty was head of a family in Pennsylvania in 1790 (*AIS 1790 Census Index*).

DOUGHERTY, WILLIAM and **JOHN DOUGHERTY**, came to PA from Belnascreen, Co. Derry, about nine years ago. They are being sought by their brother Robert, who lately arrived from Ireland, and is now living with Aaron Ashbridge in Goshen, Chester County,. He understands they lived some years ago in Foggs Manor (*Pa. Gaz.* 10 Oct 1771).

DOWDLE, RICHARD, is heir to Major John Dowdle, dec., who lately lived at Sassafrax River in Cecil Co., MD, and left an estate worth many thousand pounds. Richard Dowdle is asked to apply to the printer (*Pa. Gaz.* 17 April 1729).

In 1761 another notice appeared: "If Richard Dowdall [*sic*] heir of Major Dowdall of Chester River, be alive, he should apply to the printers to hear some good news" (Annapolis *Maryland Gazette* 30 April 1761).

DOWLING, JEREMIAH, formerly of Kildare, Ireland, lived in Baltimore Town some time ago, and now is said to keep school somewhere near Juniata, PA. He is urged to contact the printer (*Maryland Journal and Baltimore Advertiser* 18 May 1792).

DOWNEY, DENNIS, late Sgt. of the 3rd Maryland Regiment, is asked to apply to John Welsh of Annapolis to hear of something to his advantage (*The Pennsylvania Packet and Daily Advertiser* 15 Nov 1790).

Dennis Downey was a private in the MD Line on 13 March 1777, was made a sergeant on 10 Oct 1777, and discharged in April 1780; he had been left out of the December 1779 roll (*ARMD* 18:103, 199).

DOYLE, THOMAS, from Waterford, Ireland, brother of Stephen Doyle, of New Britain, Bucks Co., came to this country a few years ago from Dublin. Stephen Doyle is seeking news of his brother's whereabouts (*Pa. Gaz.* 13 Oct 1768).

DRAKE, THOMAS, was married in Baltimore about 28 March 1813 to Miss Martha Hynson and left the city the following 6 May, stating he to settle some business in the State of Ohio. He served his time with David Curry, hatter, Lexington, Northumberland Co., PA, and was last heard of at Chilicothe, OH, in the employ of Samuel M'Farren.

hatter. Any information about him should be sent by letter to John C. Hynson, near Rockhall, and will be considered an act of benevolence toward said Drake's distressed wife and helpless child (*Baltimore Patriot* 16 May 1815).

Thomas Drake and Martha Hynson were married 28 March 1813 by Rev. Joseph Fry (Henry C. Peden, Jr. *Records of the Methodist Church in Baltimore City, 1799-1829.* Westminster: Family Line Publications: 8).

John C. Hynson died 11 Sep last near Rock Hall, KE Co., aged 53, he left a widow and a number of children (*Baltimore Patriot* 22 Oct 1822). Hyson died leaving a will dated 7 Sep 1822 and proved 21 Sep 1822. His wife Martha was to have all his dwelling plantation and 20 a. of land in Skinner's Neck or Chestnut Neck, plus all his personal estate as long as she was his widow. Son John Carvill Hynson was to have all the real property devised to his wife after her death or remarriage. His personal property was to be equally distributed among his four daughters, Martha Henrietta, Sarah Ann, Harriet Matilda, and Laura Lavinia, who was not yet 16, and a fifth daughter 26 a. of land which she has already received plus $1.00. Wife Martha was to be extx. Thomas Hynson, Nicholas Spelman, and Charles R. Hynson witnessed the will (KEWB 10:281).

DRESCHER, PHILIP, and the **WIDOW of FRIEDRICH DRESCHER**, with several children, left Ellmendingen several years ago for Pennsylvania. They are the subject of an official inquiry from Pfortzheim in Baden-Durlach (*Hocker:* 137 cites the *Wochentlicher Pennsylvanischer Staatsbote* 1 Nov 1774).

In Oct 1761 Philip Drescher of the Long [Swamp?], Berks Co., warned all persons not to take an assignment of three bonds he had given Michael Schroeder until Schroder should given him an indisputable title to the land which Drescher had bought (*Pa. Gaz.* 29 Oct 1761).

Philip Drescher and wife were the parents of (*Berks Churches,* vol. 2): MARIA LISABET, bapt. 2 Oct 1765 at Longswamp Church (sp.: Joseph Bieri and wife).

DRESKY, JOHN, who came to America in 1776/7 with the Hesse Cassel Jaeger Corps, is sought (*Hocker* 177 cites the *Philadelphische Correspondenz* 10 Oct 1785).

DREWRY, WILLIAM, of Granville Co., NC, will hear of a considerable legacy, which was left to him, if he will apply to M. K. Goddard, printer, in Baltimore (*GAVN* 106 cites the *Virginia Gazette* 2 March 1779).

DRIETSCH, JOHANN PHILLIPP, from the Darmstadt region, arrived in America twelve months ago, with his son Johann Jacob. The son is in Anwell, NJ, with Justus Gansz, and seeks his father (*Hocker:* 41 cites the *Pennsylvanische Geschichts-Schreiber* 1 April 1754).

DRING, ELIZABETH, dau. of Jonathan Dring of Waterford, Herts., married Archibald Watson. If she is living or has children living, she will hear something to hear advantage by calling on Rev. Dr. Rogers in Philadelphia. Thomas Dring, of West Chester, Chester Co., asks her to call on him, or any of her heirs, to call on him, concerning the estate that comes to her by the death of her father. Thomas Dring plans to go to England at the end of the month.(*Pa. Gaz.* 14 Sep 1796; *GAVN:* 106 cites the *Virginia. Gazette and General Advertiser* 27 April 1796).

DRING, THOMAS, optician, of the town of Watford, Herefordshire, lived in Philadelphia for some years, if he is living, and will call on Dr. Rogers, No. 40, north Fourth St., he will hear of something to his advantage (*The Philadelphia Gazette & Universal Daily Advertiser* 21 July 1795).

DRISCOLL, Dr. MATTHEW, native of Baltimore, Co. Cork, Ireland, should apply to Messrs. Montgomery and Allen, merchants in Richmond, to hear something to his advantage (poss. concerning the estate of the late Cornelius Driscoll (*GAVN* 106 cites the *Virginia Gazette or the American Advertiser* 18 Dec 1784).

A Cornelius Driscoll of Crookhaven in the Diocese of Cork and Ross died leaving a will in 1770 (Phillimore, *Indexes to Irish Wills* 2:38).

DRUMMOND, JOHN, from Scotland, North Britain, came to this country as a soldier, in the 42nd Regiment in time of the war. He worked as a smith for some time as some foundry in the state of New Jersey. If he will apply soon to the office of this newspaper, he will hear of something to his advantage (*Finley's American Naval and Commercial Register* 5 Aug 1796).

DUCHALARD, Citizen JEAN, embarked from Havre, for the Scioto about the year 1790, at a period when several Frenchmen came over to the United States. It is believed that Duchalard drowned since his arrival. Anyone who could give the information relative to either, is asked to transmit it to he Minister or consuls of the French Republic. [The notice is repeated in French] ([PA] *Aurora General Advertiser* 20 Jan 1795).

DUERMGERN, Mrs. [-?-], arrived in this country last autumn, with her daughter Margaretha, and son-in-law, Adam Fichs. Margaretha is seeking them. She is at the Glass House (*Hocker:*26 cites the *Pennsylvanische Geschichts-Schreiber* 16 May 1751).

DUFFLE, EDWARD, has been absent from Philadelphia for twelve or thirteen years. If he is still alive, he should apply to Elizabeth Duffle of Burlington, NJ, where he may hear of something greatly to his advantage (*Pa. Gaz.* 7 May 1767).

DULL, JOHANN MICHAEL, was born at Neustadt, on the Aisch, near Nuremerg, and brought up a merchant, at Erlang. On 3 May 1764 he came by the way of Holland England to New York, and from thence, at the recommendation of Mr. Stephany, to Adam Simon Kuhn, in Lancaster. After a short stay there he came to Reading, where h pretended to be an apothecary and a doctor, and for certain reasons was obliged to stay there for two years. Afterwards he returned with Jacob Hoffman from Reading to New York, and was employed by Peter Hassenclever at the Iron Works. He remained there a short time and then went back to Pennsylvania, and since then has not been heard from. Now his brothers and sisters desire to receive an account concerning him, for the dividing their inheritance. For his own interest's sake, he should apply to Sebastian Stephany, chemist, in New York, or to Henry Miller, printer, in Race Street, Philadelphia (*Pa. Gaz.* 18 Nov 1772; *Hocker* 118 cites the *Wochentlicher Pennsylvanischer Staatsbote* 3 Nov 1772).

DUNBAR, WILLIAM, born in Portfoy, Banffshire, North Britain, came to Virginia about four years ago. He will hear something to his advantage if he applies to William Smith at the Eden Academy, Somerset Co., Maryland (Annapolis *Maryland Gazette* 13

April 1786; *GAVN* 108 cites the *Va. Gazette, or the American Advertiser* 7 Dec 1786; Dobson *Scots on the Chesapeake:*43).

DUNN, JACOB, left his house in Upper Providence Twp., Delaware Co., on the 17th of this instant somewhat deranged in mind. He is between 60 and 70 years of age, middle sized, and stoop shouldered. Anyone with information is asked to contact Thomas Dent, Weston School, Jacob Dunn, Jr., near the Centre engine House, Philadelphia, or James Paist, Providence, Delaware Co. (*Poulson's American Daily Advertiser* 14 Sep 1809).

DUSKINS, JOHN, waggoner, has been missing from his family for two weeks. He may have been murdered by a Negro who is now in gaol, but other reports have placed him in Baltimore. /s/ Ann Duskins, his wife, of Washington (*The National Intelligencer and Washington Advertiser* 5 June 1801).

DUSWA, JOHN, came into these parts from Stockholm, Sweden, about seven years ago. He should contact Mr. Leadman, Minister of the Swede's Church at Wiccaco, near Philadelphia, or Charles Springer at Christina Creek, for news of an inheritance (Annapolis *Maryland Gazette* 3-10 June 1729).

DWYER, MICHAEL, a native of Co. Tipperary, Ireland, was a teacher on the Eastern shore of Maryland. His wife Catherine is seeking information concerning him; the information can be sent to the office of the *Federal Republican* at Gay St., Balto. (*Baltimore Patriot* 31 July 1821).

An earlier Michael Dwyer, of Glinbawn, parish of Lattin, Co. Tipperary, died testate in 1794 (Gertrude Thrift, *Indexes to Irish Wills,* (London:1913) Repr. Baltimore: Genealogical Publishing Co., 3:10).

DYSON, JAMES, formerly lived in Blockly Twp., Philadelphia Co., and has been gone from there for almost two years. His brother Abraham has not heard from him in all that time, and asks James to send a letter to the New Printing Office, Philadelphia (*Pa. Gaz.* 12 June 1755).

EALES, THOMAS, left Henrico Co. in 1767. He should return and apply to Richard Cottrell, from whom he may hear of something to his advantage (*GAVN* 111 cites Rind's *Virginia Gazette* 23 June 1768).

EBELIN, STADIAN, a young man and son of a carpenter, from Deinheim, near Openheim, may have come to PA in 1744. He is known to have gotten as far as Rotterdam. His parents want to hear from him. Anyone knowing about him may leave information at Christopher Sauer's (*Eyster* 6 cites the *Pennsylvanische Berichte* of 16 Nov 1746; *Hocker* 8 cites the *Pennsylvanische Geschichts-Schreiber* 16 Nov 1747).

EBERHARD, SOLOMON, his wife [-?-], and his son GEORG, who sixteen years ago removed from the Makus River, above Albany, leaving behind the son Johannes and his twin brother Jeremias, is sought by Solomon's son Johannes, who is living sixteen miles above Esopus, on the North River, NY, with Abram Baer (*Hocker:*175 cites the *Philadelphische Correspondenz* 7 Feb 1786).

EBERHARTIN, CATHARINA, arrived in this country last autumn with her daughters, Maria and Anna. She was separated from her daughters and is now seeking them (*Hocker* 19 cites the *Pennsylvanische Geschichts-Schreiber* 1 May 1750).

ECHEW, JOHN, native of Ireland, is sought (Frederick *Bartgis' Republican Gazette* 25 Jan 1805).

ECKHARDT, GOTTFRIED, 12 years old, son of Anna Margretha Eckhardtin, widow, was indentured several years ago to Valentin Muckin, a German merchant in Bucks Co. Both have disappeared, and Anna Margretha is seeking information about them (*Hocker:*73 cites the *Pennsylvanische Geschichts-Schreiber* 14 Oct 1758).

ECKHARDT, JOHN PHILIP, of Hanau, in the Electorate of Hesse, embarked in the month of May 1791 at Amsterdam for Philadelphia., and is supposed to have been a clerk for a Mr. Waydemayer at Boston or Philadelphia. If he is still living in any part of the United States, he may hear of something to his advantage by applying by letter or otherwise of Mr. David Sears of Boston (*The United States Gazette* 1 Feb 1806).

EDMONDSON, WILLIAM, son of William Edmondson, late of Leeds, Yorkshire, Eng., jeweler, dec., a youth of about 18 years, left England in 1812 as a sea apprentice on the ship *Henry,* Capt. Dryden, on a voyage to the Island of St. Croix. The ship was captured by the privateer *Comet,* and carried into Baltimore. If the said William Edmondson will apply to William Wilson & Sons of Baltimore, he will hear of something to his advantage. Anyone who can give information about the said William Edmondson will be rewarded (*Baltimore Patriot* 17 Jan 1817).

EDWARDS, SANDFORD, and his children, some 13 years ago lived within 30 miles of Edenton, NC, near Perquimans River, probably in a county of the same name. If he or any of his children will contact Ben Edwards of Bardstown, KY, they will hear something very much to their advantage and will relieve an anxious and affectionate brother (*The National Intelligencer and Washington Advertiser* 20 Feb 1805).
    In 1790 Sanford Edwards was head of a family in Perquimans Co., NC (*AIDS 1790 Census Index*)

EGNEW, Dr. JOHN, native of Ireland, if living, is asked to send a line to the printer of this paper (The *Hornet* 22 Jan 1805).

EIGENBRODIN, SOPHIA ELISABETH, arrived in this country last year, and is sought by her brother, Johann Just Eigenbrod, living in Frederick Co., MD, on Monocacy Creek, understands that his sister, and he is seeking information about her (*Hocker 30* cites the *Pennsylvanische Geschichts-Schreiber* 1 Jan 1752).

ELDERTON, JOHN, born in the Parish of Bow, near London, will hear something to his advantage if he applies to the printer (*Scott* 1:138 cites the *Pa. Gaz.* 16 Sep 1736).

ELGERTIN, SUSANNA, who came to America from Wales in May 1751, with George May, and now is sought by her mother, Maria Eva Elgertin (*Hocker:* 133 cites the *Wochentlicher Pennsylvanischer Staatsbote* 31 May 1774).

ELKINTON, GEORGE, lived in Northampton, Burlington Co., NJ. If his heir or heirs are living, and will apply to the printer, they may hear of something greatly to their advantage (*Pa. Gaz.* 25 Sep 1740).

    See Arthur Adams, "The English Ancestry of the Elkinton Family of New Jersey," *TAG* 85 (1) (July 1945) 1-6.

ELLASON, JOHN, has died. If any of his offspring are living they may hear of something to their advantage by applying to Samuel Swann of Nansemond Co. or to John Swann of Cumberland Co. (*GAVN:* 113 cites *The Virginia Gazette* 7 Jan 1775).

ELLIS, TEMPEST, aged about 13, is in the care of James Seagrove, Superintendent of Indian Affairs at St. Mary's. She was taken by the Indians near the Cedar Shoals on the Oconee, from the house of a Mrs. Scarlet about seven years ago. Her friends are desired to take her away (*GAVN:* 114 cites the *Virginia Gazette and Weekly Advertiser* 20 Aug 1796).

ELLIS, WILLIAM, merchant of Leeds, Eng., came to America about 1728 or 1729 and lived, by last account, at or near Mr. Nathan Magruder on the Eastern Branch of the Potomac, in MD. He is desired apply to Mr. President Davies in Prince Town, NJ, who will give him an article of private news, in which he is interested. If he is dead, anyone who can provide legal attestation of his death will be satisfied for his trouble (*Pa. Gaz.* 28 Aug 1760).

    William Ellis, age 20, of Leeds, Yorkshire, cloth dresser, on 3 Dec 1729 bound himself to serve Peter Simpson of London for five years in MD (*LEMK:* 72).

ELLIS, WILLIAM, left the borough of Southwark, Co. Mddx., in Aug 1789. If he will send two certificates of his being living, with the place of his residence, certified by a minister, magistrate, or two well-known public officer, with Christian names of his mother or father, and place of abode, to John Waddington, Philadelphia, he will hear of something to his immediate advantage (*Dunlap's American Daily Advertiser* 16 Nov 1791).

ELLISON, AMOS, of Squan, East NJ, who for some time past has lived in or near Queen's Co., NC, is hereby informed that his father has died, and he is desired to return home to Squanas quickly as possible. /s/ Thomas Ellison (*Pa. Gaz.* 2 May 1771).

    Amos Ellison and Elizabeth Ellison, both of Burlington, were married by license dated 11 Nov 1760 (Nelson, *New Jersey Marriage Records, 1685-1800.* Baltimore: Genealogical Publishing Co., p. 125).

ELLISON, HENRY, Jr., brought up to the sea, left his native England, nine or ten years ago, and since then his immediate connections in Cumberland have not heard from him. He landed first in Virginia, but then removed northward, probably to Philadelphia, where it is said he had a wife and children, but that he had changed his name. If he or any of his family should see this advertisement, they should contact the editor of the paper (*Poulson's American Daily Advertiser* 8 June 1803).

ELLKINS, EDWARD, of Londonderry, north of Ireland, arrived at New Castle, DE, and is urged to contact Dr. Henry Stevenson of Baltimore. Town. The notice was placed by James Ellkins (Annapolis *Maryland Gazette* 26 March 1761).

EMMERY, JOHN, cabinet-maker, went from England in 1725 to the West Indies, and later to some of the northern colonies. He is urged to contact the printer to hear something to his advantage (*Scott* 1:44 cites the *Pa. Gaz.* 15 July 1731).

EMMOTT, WILLIAM, son of John Emmott, late of Dublin, Ireland, merchant, will hear something to his advantage by communicating with his brother John Emmott, care of William Dunlap of Philadelphia (*Scott* 3:101 cites *The New York Mercury* 30 April 1764).

William Emmott came from Ireland and went from New Castle to New York about twelve years ago. If he is living he will hear something to his advantage if he contacts John Emmott, care of Thomas Moore, shoemaker, living in Trenton, NJ (*Pa. Gaz.* 8 Dec 1763).

EMRICH, VALENTIN (married), **FRIEDRICH EMRICH** (single), **and their sister |-?-|**, are sought by their father, Nicolaus Emrich, of Allemangel, Albany Twp., Berks Co. (*Hocker:*79 cites the *Pennsylvanische Geschichte-Schreiber* 22 June 1759).

ENGEL, JOHANN JACOB, who arrived in this country ten years ago from Mandel, is sought by his sister Gertraut Engelin, who is living with Nicolaus Kern, at the Blue Mountains (*Hocker:*29 cites the *Pennsylvanische Geschichts-Schreiber* 1 Nov 1751).

In 1773 Johann Jacob Engel was in Philadelphia Co., PA (*AIS Census Index: Pre-1790* gives no other documentation).

ENNIS, MICHAEL LUCAS, a native of Ireland, a carpenter, left his home in 1801 to meet his brother Thomas Ennis, who was settled in Baltimore, in the grocery line. If the said M. L. Ennis will apply personally or by letter, to Pattison and Brother, in Philadelphia, he may hear something to his advantage (*Baltimore Patriot* 3 July 1817).

EPPLE, ANDREAS, who is said to be in Philadelphia, is sought by Jonas Epple of Leonberg, Wurtemberg (*Hocker:*116 cites the *Wochedntlicher Pennsylvanischer Staatsbote* 28 July 1772).

In 1790 an Andrew Epple was listed as head of a family in the census of Philadelphia, PA, p. 222 (*AIS 1790 U.S. Federal Census Index*).

ERDMAN, FREDERICK HENRY WILLIAM, arrived in Philadelphia from Oldenburg, Germany in 1784. From there he went to Frederick Town, MD, and his friends have not heard from him since. If he applies to B. J. Von Kapf, 202 Market St. in Baltimore, he will hear of something to his advantage (*Maryland Gazette and Frederick-Town Weekly Advertiser* 21 July 1796).

ESCH, JOHANN WILHELM, from Runckel, arrived in America a year and a half ago. His brother Henrich arrived last autumn and is serving with George Schmitt, opposite the printer in Germantown, and is seeking his brother (*Hocker:*48 cites the *Pennsylvanische Geschichts-Schreiber* 1 April 1755; *Eyster:* 14 cites the *Pennsylvanische Berichte* 1 April 1755).

Wilhelm Aschelman [*sic*] arrived on the *Brothers* on 30 Sep 1754; Henrich Esch arrived on the *Friendship* on 21 Oct 1754 (*Eyster* 14).

ETTER, CHRISTIAN, who was indentured in Philadelphia several years ago, to William Mueller, in the Jerseys, is sought by his father, George Etter, wheelwright, living in the White Oak Land, Rapho Twp., Lancaster Co., PA, (*Hocker:*41 cites the *Pennsylvanische Geschichts-Schreiber* 16 June 1754).

For more on the Etter family, see Burgert's *Alsace:* 150-151.

EVANS, JOHN, supposed to be at Mark Evans' Mill in the State of VA, is the eldest son of Methusela Evans of Upper Dublin Twp., Philadelphia Co. Methuselah died without making any mention of the said John in his last will and testament. John is supposed to have gone in the Continental service at the time of his father's decease. If he is living and will return to his former place of abode, he will hear of something greatly to his advantage; it is imagined he is best entitled to the estate of his deceased father. It would be proper for him to give his attendance as soon as possible as the deceased's estate is going to ruin very fast (*Pa. Gaz.* 28 Nov 1781).

EVANS, JOHN, some time in 1795 sailed in the *Polly* of Gloucester, Capt. Mayo (a south sea man), commander. If he will write to Mr. S. J. Lilley, of Peckham, near London, he will hear something to his advantage. Capt. Robert Cowper of Norfolk wants information about him (*GAVN:* 117 cites *The Norfolk Herald* 13 April 1799).

EVEREST, RICHARD, from England, about 10 years ago lived with a Mr. Hough, storekeeper in Loudon Co., VA. He has been left a considerable legacy and is asked to contact Edward Vidler of Annapolis (*GAVN:* 118 cites *The Virginia Journal and Alexandria Advertiser* 25 Aug 1785).

EVERTON, ELIZABETH, in about the year 1740 was bound by her mother, Elizabeth, to Edward Thomson, living at Fairfax in VA. Now the daughter Elizabeth is free and has come to East Caln in Chester County and taken great pains to find her mother, Elizabeth Everton, of Philadelphia, but to no effect. She asks her mother to let her know where she may be found, and if she is dead, Elizabeth would like to know (*Pa. Gaz.* 30 March 1758).

EWING, DAVID, late Master of the sloop *Friendship,* owned at Greenwich, near Cape May, is sought. Anyone with information as to his whereabouts will be suitable rewarded (*Gazette of the United States* 20 Jan 1804).

EYSSENLOHR, JOHN GEORGE, a minister's son of the City of Durlach, came to this country some time ago. If he is still living he should apply to John Roman of Market St., he will hear something to his advantage (*Pa. Gaz.* 10 Jan 1771; see also *Hocker:* 104 cites the *Wochentlicher Pennsylvanischer Staatsbote* 1 Jan 1771).

FACHSER, CHRISTIAN, from Doffingen, Wurtemburg, is sought by Ernst Ludwig Baisch (*Eyster:* 26 cites the *Pennsylvanische Berichte* 28 July 1772).

FALL, JOHN, mariner, late of Philadelphia, was born in MD, near the Wye River, and is now dec. If any of his friends be living and will apply to Joseph Graisbury, living in Philadelphia, they will hear of something to their Advantage. (*Pa. Gaz.* 27 May 1762) [See also John Tall].

FANER, HANSZ GEORG, is sought by his brother Jacob Faner, who is living near Dewald Scholas, over the Susquehanna, on Conewago Creek, York Co, PA (*Hocker:* 27 cites the *Pennsylvanische Geschichts-Schreiber* 16 June 1751).

FARGUSON (or FERGUSON), SARAH, came from England about six years ago, and served her time with Charles Lewis, now dec., on the Rappahannock. She will hear of something greatly to her advantage if she applies to the printer (Rind's *Virginia Gazette* 14 July 1774).

FAUCETT, JOHN, mariner, formerly of Liverpool, sailed some time ago in the ship *Mary Anne*, Capt. Priestman. He had been mate of a brig or schooner in Baltimore. He is urged to contact George Grundy (*Edward's Baltimore Daily Advertiser* 21 Dec 1793).

FAULKNER, THOMAS, and **LAURA FAULKNER** left Co. Donegal, Ireland, some time between 1724 and 1730. Any of their descendants will hear something to their advantage if they apply to Francis Hatfield, Bladensburg (*Maryland Gazette or Baltimore General Advertiser* 9 Jan 1776).

In Nov 1750 Thomas Faulkner of Bethlehem Twp, Bucks Co., PA advertised for the return of a runaway Irish servant, one Joannah Griffin, age c28 (*Pa. Gaz.* 15 Nov 1750).

Between the years 1724 and 1730 a Mr. and Mrs. Faulkner left Ireland to settle in PA and bought a parcel of land near Chester Creek. A few months after that, notice was received that Mr. and Mrs. Faulkner, otherwise Reynolds, were both dead. Mrs. Faulkner had a son soon after her arrival. About 15 years ago, word was received that the boy was grown up and living in PA. The Faulkners had left their eldest child in Ireland. Now Capt. Thomas Faulkner died on 15 Jan 1773 intestate leaving a freehold in Ireland. If any son of the above parents is living, he should apply to Joseph Cruttenden, Esq., Surgeon's Hall, London, where he may hear something to his advantage (*Pa. Gaz.* 8 March 1773).

FAULKNOR, [-?-], was employed at the queensware manufactory in this city about 18 months or two years ago. If he will write to the printer of this paper, he may hear of something to his advantage (*Poulson's American Daily Advertiser* 24 June 1805).

FELLENZERIN (or FELTENZER), JULIANA, of Creutzenach, came to America ten years ago, and was with Jacob Bauman in Germantown. She married a tailor named Wolff, and they went to the Blue Mountains. Her brother Johannes Feltzer [*sic*], arrived last year, and waits for news of her at Bastian Neff's – Schuh Bastel – at the Crown Tavern, outside Germantown (*Hocker:* 39 cites the *Pennsylvanische Geschichts-Schreiber* 16 Oct 1753).

Juliana Maria "Fellendser" and Johann Heinrich Wolff (Reformed) were married 17 July 1746 at St. Michael's and Zion Church in Philadelphia (*PGCR* 1:380).

Hans Feltz arrived on the *Halifax* on 9 Sep 1751 (*Eyster:*130.

FENESEY, JOHN, son of William, should get in touch with his father, who is anxious to hear from him. A letter addressed to the care of Samuel Cleland, at Big Pipe Creek Bridge, Frederick Co., MD, will be forwarded (Frederick *Maryland Chronicle or the Universal Advertiser* 30 Aug 1786).

On 16 Feb 1758 a John Fenessy was listed as a creditor of Elijah Sturgis of WO Co. (MINV 64:478).

John Fenessy was one of those who contributed to aid the sufferers of the Boston Fire, listed in the return of Rev. John Ross of All Hallows Parish, Worcester Co., dated June 1760 (*CMSP: Black Books,* item 1031).

He might be the John "Fenessey" [*sic*], who was listed as a creditor of Patrick Guttrey of Worcester Co, MD, on 1 Aug 1760. On 3 Sep 1762 "John Fneery" was a creditor of Angus McFadden of WO Co. (MDAD 44:334, 48:282).

FENN, JAMES, son of John Fenn, came into the Province about ten years ago. He is urged to apply to the James Wood, chief mate of the *William*, William Wood, captain, to hear something to his advantage. Fenn was a ship captain who served his time in London River and has worked in Annapolis and other places in the bay (Annapolis *Maryland Gazette* 15 June 1748).

James Fenn of Kent, Eng., was transported from London in the *Dorsetshire*, Capt. William Loney in Feb 1736 and registered in VA in Sep 1736 (*KPMV* 66).

FENNELL, DEBORAH, came to this place two or three years ago from Ireland. If she is alive, and will come to Captain William Haselton, living in this City, in Front street, over the Drawbridge, she will hear of something considerably to her Advantage (*Pa. Gaz.* 28 May 1767).

FENNER, THOMAS, of Swan's Point, advertised that a brother of his in London, wrote to him in January, but he has not yet received the letter (*Va. Gaz.* 3 June 1773).

FERNAND, JOST CHRISTIAN, has been a servant to one William Dyer, as appears by his *I*ndenture, and the term of his servitude being expired, he is desired to come (for his own benefit) to his [the subscribers?] father William Sill, living near the Yellow Spring, in Chester County. Any Christian friend or neighbor, who will be kind enough to acquaint said Fernand, if alive, with his father's request, will greatly oblige Adam Sill (*Pa. Gaz.* 24 Sep 1761).

FERRIS, JAMES, came into Maryland about five years ago with Capt. Darby Lux. He is urged to contact Capt. Lux (Annapolis *Maryland Gazette* 20-27 Sep 1734).

James Ferris of Mddx., Eng., was transported for 14 years from London on the *Patapsco Merchant* in March 1730 and registered at Annapolis in Sep 1730 (*KPMV:*44).

FESKIN, JAMES, weaver, sailed from Glasgow the latter end of last year or the beginning of this year. If he will apply to Peter Feskin of Williamsburg, he will hear of something to his advantage (*Va. Gaz.* 4 July 1771).

FICHS, ADAM, arrived in this country last autumn, with his sister Margaretha Duermgern, and Margaretha's mother. Margaretha is seeking them. She is at the Glass House (*Hocker:*26 cites the *Pennsylvanische Geschichts-Schreiber* 16 May 1751).

FICHTNER, JOSEPH, and HENRICH FICHTNER, brothers, have been in America for ten tears. Their sister Dorothea is concerned about them. Now Hansz Adam Neidig, of Brecknock Twp., Lancaster Co., PA, their brother-in-law, is seeking them (*Hocker:* 96 cites the *Pennsylvanische Geschichts-Schreiber* 20 Nov 1761).

FILE, JOHN, came from Germany about eight years ago, and served his time with Llewellin Davis, in Chester Co., PA, and has never heard from his Father, Mother, brother, or sisters during that time, these are therefore to desire anyone who has any knowledge of them, to acquaint the said John File, living in Charles Town, Chester County, and they shall be thankfully rewarded (*Pa. Gaz.* 16 Dec 1762).

In 1790 a John File was listed as head of a family in Harrisburg Twp., Dauphin co., PA (*AIS 1790 Census Index*).

FINCH, JOHN, formerly of Hothfield Parish, Co. Kent, Eng., came to MD in 1740, and may have moved to VA. He is urged to contact the printer (Annapolis *Maryland Gazette* 14 May 1772).

John Tunstall of Somerset Co. made his will on 7 Aug 1746, leaving 9 or 10 acres to the Visitors of the Public School of Somerset County, and mentioning the land lying near Princess Ann Town, which he had bought from John Finch (MWB 24:471).

On 4 Sep 1754 a John Finch was one of schoolmasters of SO Co. who had taken an Oath to the government (*CMSP Black Books* :#809).

John Finch of SO Co., MD, died leaving a will dated 11 March 1758 and proved 2 March 1758 [*sic*]. He named his wife Margaret, and children John and James, all of whom were named executors. William Brown, Isaac Giles, and George Twilley witnessed the will (MWB 30:483).

John and Margaret Finch of Somerset Co. were the parents of: JOHN; and JAMES.

FINNEY, GEORGE, the son of George Finney of Wolverhampton, is supposed to have been in this Country about seven years. If he will apply to William Vere of Philadelphia, or in his absence to Nicholas Steele in Trotters Alley, he may hear of something to his Advantage (*Pa. Gaz.* 28 Oct 1736).

On 12 Aug 1728, George Finney of Wolverhampton, Staffordshire, age 15, made his mark when he was bound to James Gerald for seven years in PA (*LEMK:*78).

On 19 Nov 1748 Finney again made his mark when he witnessed the will of George Jones of Philadelphia (Philadelphia Co. Will Book G:119).

FISCHER, MATTHES, is sought by his brother Gottlieb Fischer, care of Johannes Herr's Mill, Lampeter Twp., Lancaster Co., PA, who arrived in America six years ago (*Hocker:*78 cites the *Pennsylvanische Geschichts-Schreiber* 25 May 1759).

FISHER, JAMES, arrived at St. John's, Newfoundland, about two years ago from Co. Donegal, Ireland. He is supposed to be in some part of the United States, but has not been heard of in more than twenty months, at which time he following fishing out of St. John's. Any information concerning him should be directed to his father, John Fisher in Union St., Baltimore (*Baltimore Patriot* 3 Feb 1823).

FISHER, MARIA, servant girl, was sold to John Smith on 23 Sep 1742, for seven years. Anyone with information as to the whereabouts of Fisher or Smith, is asked to notify Daniel Stonemat in Second St., Philadelphia, or Maria's father, Melchoir Fisher, living near Nehsaminy Ferry. He or she will have a reasonable reward (*Pa. Gaz.* 1 Nov 1750).

FITZPATRICK, MARGARET, age 4 or 5, and **ANN FITZPATRICK,** age 13 or 14, were taken prisoner by the British at Fort Niagara and are now supposed to be at Genessee Co., NY, are sought by their father Edward (in the service of the U. S. at Boston), his son John (in the artillery corps at Buffalo), and Edward's dau. Mary, now living at Pittsburgh, are seeking information about Edward's daughters. Anyone with information is asked to contact his or her father at Boston or his or her sister at Pittsburgh (*The Daily National Intelligencer* 6 April 1815).

FITZSIMONS, FRANCIS, son of John Fitzsimons, late of Cavet, Co. Cavan, Ireland, if living, is asked to apply to Mr. John Welch at Mr. Abraham Morrow's, gunsmith, in Dock Street, Philadelphia, or at Mr. John Hog's in Harrisburg, North America, where he will hear of something very much to his advantage (*Pennsylvania Packet and Daily Advertiser* 14 Oct 1786).

FITZSYMONS, MAYNARD, (now residing, as 'tis believed, in some part of Pennsylvania) the son of Norris Fitzsymons of the Kingdom of Ireland, deceased, is given notice that upon applying to the Printer hereof, he will be directed to a Gentleman of this Place, who is desired by his Relations to enquire for him, and acquaint him that he is Heir to a considerable Estate in that Kingdom (*Pa. Gaz.* 7 Aug 1732).

FLEMING, SAMUEL, married Margaret Wethers of East Grinstead, Sussex, Eng. If he or his lawful representative will apply to Benjamin Johnston of Spotsylvaia Co., VA, he may hear something to his advantage (*Va. Gaz.* 18 July1766).

FLENNE, JOHANNES, JOHANN HEINRICH FLENNE, ELIZABETH MILLER, CATHERINE FLENNE, and **MARIA FLENNE,** are sought by their brother, Johann Jacob Flenne, that he lives in Cheltenham Twp., Montgomery Co., PA, and that he has heard nothing from then in ten years (Hocker:*170* cites the *Philadelphische Correspondenz* 6 July 1784).

FLIN, JAMES, is sought by his mother Ann Flin, who about twelve months since, was driven from her place of abode, among the Western Back Inhabitants of Pennsylvania, and was at that time parted from her son, James, at Wright's Ferry, on the Susquehannah,. Since then she has not received any intelligence from him that could be depended upon, she therefore takes this public method, to request the said James Flin, if living, to come to the Sign of the Turk's Head, in Goshen, Chester Co., where he may hear of her, and be directed to Her place of abode. The last imperfect account, which she received, was, that he was seen near Lancaster (*Pa. Gaz.* 27 Dec 1764).

FLOWERS, THOMAS, and MARIA MARGARETTA FLOWERS, or their heirs of legal pretensions [*sic*], are asked to apply to William Montgomery and Son, 1010 N. Front St., as they may hear of something much to their reciprocal advantage (*Poulson's American Daily Advertiser* 27 July 1815).

FLOYD, WILLIAM, came to this county, about three or four years ago, by the best account. He was from Birmingham, a mason by trade, and son of John Floyd, late of Staffordshire, in England; these are to inform said William, that he has a sister living at Mr. Almoney's, in Gunpowder Barrens, who was married to William Billings, of Open Park, in England. If the said William Floyd will apply to Mr. Slade, tavern keeper, in My Lady's Manor, in Baltimore County he will direct him to where she lives (*Pa. Gaz.* 24 Nov 1768).

FOERSTNER, or FORSTER, GEORG, was indentured, and is sought by his brother Thomas, born near Nurnberg, who arrived in America about 12 years ago, and is with Johannes Georger (or Geiger), Falckner Swamp, Montgomery Co., about one mile from Johannes Schneider (*Pennsylvanische Geschichts-Schreiber* 10 Dec 1757; *Eyster:*17 gives the name as Forster).

FORBES, JAMES, of Upper Isle of Wight Parish, son of Alexander Forbes who came to this colony many years ago, is asked to apply to William Montgomery of Yorktown, to learn of an estate left him in Britain (*Va. Gaz.* 10 April, 2 May 1752).

Dobson lists an Alexander Forbes, clergyman, who was educated at King's College, Aberdeen, in 1706 and settled to VA in 1709 (*SOCD:*50).

FORD, REYNOLDS, was bred to the Sea, and served his time on board a Ship called the *Heron,* and is supposed to be lately settled at Philadelphia, or New York. He is desired immediately to call upon Mr. Samuel Purviance, Jr., merchant, in Philadelphia, who will inform him of something greatly to his advantage. If any person can give information, to Mr. Purviance, concerning said Reynolds Ford, if gone to Sea or dead, it will be taken very kindly (*Pa. Gaz.* 16 June 1763).

FORSHAW, MARY, came into MD some time ago, and has lived with Samuel Gar-shard [Guishard?] near Herring Bay. She is urged to contact Capt. Hurt of the *Hart,* Frigate in Patapsco or the printer (Annapolis *Maryland Gazette* 15-22 July 1729).

FORSYTH, JOHN, and ELIJAH FORSYTH, brothers, left the county of Derry, and parish of Balteaugh, in the kingdom of Ireland, about twelve years ago, and have not been heard of these seven years past. Their brother William Forsyth came from Ireland last fall, and is seeking them; he intends in a short time to return home. If they or either of them be living, are earnestly desired, as soon as possible, to call on him at his lodgings, at Mr. Lewellin Davis's, in Charles Twp., Chester Co., near Valley Forge, where they may hear something of consequence respecting their friends at home, &c. by 30 July 1784 (*Pa. Gaz.* 4 Aug 1784).

In 1790 a John Forsyth was listed as head of a family in York Borough, York co., PA (*AIS 1790 Census Index*).

FOUASSIER, FRANCIS, came to Baltimore in 1781 in the ship *Marquis de la Fayette* and worked for some time in the cabinet trade. He is urged to contact the printers (*Maryland Journal and Baltimore Advertiser* 22 April 1791).

FOWLER, JOHN, son of John Fowler, late of Wapping St., London, sandman, left England as a servant some six or seven years ago, to go to some part of North America. If he will apply to Capt. David Ross, commander of the *Betsy* he will learn of matters greatly to his advantage (*Virginia Gazette or Norfolk Intelligencer* 23 Feb 1775).

FOWLER, PARKER, of Maryland, may be holding part of the estate of his nephew Joseph Fowler, whose mother married Peter Desain, and removed to Virginia. Joseph Fowler died in the American army in 1777, leaving a widow, Anne Fowler, the subscriber, and three children (Annapolis *Maryland Gazette* 4 Oct 1792).

FOWLER, THOMAS, a native of Kerry or Cork in Ireland, came to the coast of Labrador some time in 1774. He died last Nov at the house of John Tabb in Amelia Co. His legal representative may hear of something to his advantage by applying E. Meade of Amelia Co. (*GAVN:*127 cites the *Virginia Gazette and Richmond and Manchester Advertiser* 9 March 1795).

FOX, SAMUEL, was late a sergeant in Capt. Murray's Co., in the service of the United States at Natchez or New Orleans. If any of his heirs or legal representatives will call at this office, they will hear of something to their advantage (*Poulson's American Daily Advertiser* 24 Nov 1817).

FOY, the family of, arrived from Ireland about 40 years ago, and settled in Boston. Members of the family are asked to write to a close relative, Dennis Mahony, mariner, at the house of Capt. William Dobs, behind the English church in New York City (*Scott 3:* cites the *New York Mercury* 19 May 1760).

FRANCK, CHRISTOFFEL HENRICH, ANDREAS FRANCK, ANNA MARIA FRANCKIN, MARIA GERTRAUT MUELLERIN, MICHEL MUELLER, and **CHRISTIAN MUELLER,** brothers, sisters, and friends of Jacob Franck, late glazier of Lancaster and his wife, who have both died. They are asked to apply to the executors, Friedrich Dambach, Johannes Eberman, and Kraft Roesser, for their inheritance (*Pennsylvanische Geschichts-Schreiber* 19 Feb 1757).

FRANKLIN, GEORGE, who came lately from Ireland, should apply to Christopher Hughes. He will hear of something to his advantage (*Federal Gazette and Baltimore Daily Advertiser* 19 March 1799).

FRANKS, ISAAC, son of Benjamin Moses Franks, a native of New York, left there when our troops evacuated that city, and, by the last accounts of him, resided somewhere near Pecks Kill. If he will inform the printer hereof where he now is, or if any of his friends can give intelligence of him, it will be much to his advantage (*Pennsylvania Packet* 8 Sep 1778).
Benjamin M. Frank, a Jew, was naturalized in New York on 18 Oct 1748 (Bockstruck: 96).

FRASER, THOMAS, a native of the Island of Bermuda, and late was a seaman on board one of the ships of the United States' navy. If he is living and will apply to the British Consul at Norfolk, Philadelphia, New York, or Charleston, he will hear of something to his advantage (*American Beacon and Portsmouth Daily Advertiser* 20 July 1819).

FREEMAN, CAEZAR, lived about three years ago at Bedford or Ligonier, PA. If he will apply to the printer, he will hear of something to his advantage (*The Pennsylvania Ledger: or the Virginia, Maryland, Pennsylvania & New Jersey Weekly Advertiser* 9 Sep 1775).

FREEMAN, SAMUEL, a native of Younghall, Co. Cork, Ireland, emigrated to Baltimore some time since 1817. If he is living, he will hear something to his advantage by applying to Maurice P. Hore, Baltimore (*Republican Star and General Advertiser* 1 March 1825).

FRETZ, BURKHARD, has been in America for six or seven years. His mother, Margaretha Fretzin, living with Michael Kaeyser, by the fresh water, New York, is seeking her son (*Pennsylvanische Geschichts-Schreiber* 6 Nov 1761).

FREY, GEORGE, PETER FREY, and their sister **MARIA FREY,** arrived in this county six years ago last autumn, and were indentured in Conestoga, Lancaster Co., PA. Their sister Anna Margaretha Freyin is seeking them. Notify Jacob Weyermann, Hatfield Twp., Philadelphia Co. (now Montgomery Co.) (*Pennsylvanische Geschichts-Schreiber* 16 March 1748).

FRICKE, AUGUST JOHANNES, came to America as a cadet with the Brunswick troops in 1776, was captured in 1777, and in 1778 joined the American army. His relatives in Wolfenbuttel inquire for him (*Philadelphische Correspondenz* 2 Nov 1784).

FRIZZELL, JOHN and **WILLIAM FRIZZELL,** and Catherine Phillips (*q.v.*), all resided in Baltimore in 1808. If any of them are now living, they are requested to call at the Office of Wm. & Thos. Adair, 175 Baltimore St. (*Baltimore Patriot* 25 Aug 1834).

FROMSTONE, WILLIAM, came from North Wales some years ago, and is supposed to be settled in the Province of Pennsylvania, or some place adjacent. If he will send Broughton Reynolds of Elizabeth Town, NJ, with a line, to inform him of the place of his residence, it will be esteemed a particular favor (*Pa. Gaz.* 27 Feb 1766).

FRY, PETER, late of London, who came to Pennsylvania, will something to his advantage if he will apply to Christopher Marshall in Chesnut St., Philadelphia (*American Weekly Mercury* 13 Aug 1741).

FRY, WILLIAM, states that he was informed, that some time last Spring he was enquired for in one of the Pennsylvania Gazettes, but not having the paper in which the advertisement was, cannot be informed to whom he was directed to apply; and as he apprehends it is to some Gentleman living in Philadelphia, he hereby gives notice, that he now lives in the lower part of Kent County, in Maryland, and being informed that the Gentlemen, who enquired for him, advertised that he could inform him (Fry) of something to his advantage, should be much obliged to him to take the first opportunity of informing Fry to whom he must apply (*Pa. Gaz.* 5 Feb 1767).

In 1790 a William Fry was living in Kent Co., MD, with one white male over 16, five white males under 16, and two white females (*1790MD:*83, col. 1).

FUHRMAN, GEORG PHILIP, and **JULIANA FUHRMANIN,** arrived in this country 20 years ago from Muehlbach on the Necker, near Ober-Mimpffen, between Heilbun and Heidelberg. Their sister **CATHARINA FUHRMANIN** came three years later, and information about her is desired. Juliana is the wife of Johann Georg Baszel, Saucon, living two miles from Michel Bischoff (*Pennsylvanische Geschichts-Schreiber* 1 March 1758).

FULWIDER, HENRY, has died. His heirs are supposed to reside in the western country. Jacob Fulwider of Maryland, dec., devised an estate to those heirs. The heirs are asked to contact Jacob Koontz living twelve miles from Fredericktown, about four miles from Middletown, in Frederick Co., Maryland, as quickly as possible (*Alexandria Herald* 9 Sep 1812).

In Oct 1812 Henry Fulwider and Jacob Koontz advertised a sale of the real estate of Jacob Fulwider (*Fredericktown Herald* 17 Oct 1812). In Jan 1814 Richard Brooke, trustee, advertised a chancery sale of the real estate of Jacob Fulwiler [*sic*] of Middletown (*Bartgis' Republican Gazette* 15 Jan 1814).

FURNALD, WILLIAM, Jr., son of William Furnald, late of Portsmouth, NH, mariner, dec., if living, is asked to apply to Edward Sergeant and Samuel Hutchings, both of Portsmouth, executors to said William Furnald, as he may hear of something to his advantage (*Dunlap's American Daily Advertiser* 24 May 1792).

FYSON, WALTER, who formerly lived at Snailwell, near Barnwell, or New Market, and was a wool comber, should direct a letter to Samuel Berry of Bristol, for news of an estate worth £27,000 (Annapolis *Maryland Gazette* 30 June 1757).

Walter Fyson, son of John and Ann (Avey) Fyson, was bat. 17 Jan 1716 at Snailwell, Cambridge (*IGI*).

GACH, JOHANNES, came to America ten years ago with his cousin, Simon Ritter, and entered into service in New Jersey. Simon Ritter, who is now with Ludwig Lauman, Lancaster, is seeking information about Gach (*Pennsylvanische Geschichts-Schreiber* 23 May 1760).

GALLAGHER, FRANCIS, from Letterkenny, in Ireland, landed at New York last October. If he will apply to William Gallagher, in Second Street, Philadelphia, by letters, or in person, he will hear of something greatly to his advantage (*Pa. Gaz.* 7 July 1763).

GALLAUGHER, CATHERINE, has not been heard of for a number of years. If her brothers, John, Peter, or Patrick, or her sisters, Mary and Margaret, have any information about her, they are asked to give it to Hessel G. Freeland at the Post Office (*Poulson's American Daily Advertiser* 14 Oct 1806).

GALLOWAY, ANDREW, late of Top Mill, Co. Antrim, near Ballimony, in 1774, came to Philadelphia in the Ship *Hannah*, from Londonderry. He taught school for some time, and then went jobbing. When the War began he went to sea and was taken prisoner by the English. Afterwards he was taken by the Spanish and imprisoned for ten or twelve months. He returned to this city some time after that. His brother John Galloway is arrived from Ireland, and is anxious to see or hear from him, as it would be considerably to his advantage. Information concerning Andrew, be he alive or dead, should be sent by letter to Mr. James Hunter, merchant in Philadelphia, or the printers. John Galloway plans to return to Ireland (*Pa. Gaz.* 4 Sep 1784).

GANDER, AUGUSTINIUS and **CHRISTIAN GANDER,** came to America four years ago. They are sought by their brother Gottlieb Gander, from Lomersheim, Wurtemburg, linen weaver, who arrived in America six years ago, and is now in Frederick, MD. He is seeking his brothers Augustinius and Christian, who came to America four years ago (*Hocker*: 76 cites the *Pennsylvanische Geschichts-Schreiber* 2 March 1759).

GANNON, JOHN, a young man, a currier, son of Thomas Gannon of Back Lane, Dublin, left Dublin, Ireland in Aug 1815, and arrived in New York on or about Oct of the same year. He will hear something very much to his advantage if he applies to No. 118 Chatham St., New York (*Baltimore Patriot* 14 Dec 1822).

GANSLER, JOHN PHILIP, born at the Village of Nusloch, near Heidelberg, in the Palatinate, came to Pennsylvania about eleven years ago, when he was about ten years of age. At that time his mother was married to Andrew Wetstein, her second husband. She is now marred to Michael Munch, living at Brecknock Twp., Lancaster Co., at Philip Brondel's Mill. She would like to know if her son John Philip is still alive, and where he is living. He should apply to Henry Miller, printer, at Second St., Philadelphia, or to his mother (*Pa. Gaz.* 15 Aug 1765).

GANTLET, Capt. JOHN, late of the Brig *Augusta*, of Philadelphia, was cast away on last 1 May, on Cape Hatteras. He announced his intention of going to Dedham, where he was born. No information has been received from him, and Charles Pettit, President of the Insurance Company of North America, is asking for any information (*Poulson's American Daily Advertiser* 25 Jan 1806).

GARRET, JOHN, from Ballyknocken, Parish of Santfield, Co. Down, Ireland, came over in the *Friendship*, Capt. McCullock, from Belfast. If he is living, and will meet William Mills at the house of John Faris, in Second St., Philadelphia, on 27 Nov inst., he may hear something to his advantage. He is asked not to fail, as Mills intends to leave the Province about that time (*Pa. Gaz.* 10 Nov 1773).

A John Garrett came to Philadelphia in 1772 as an indentured servant (*AIS Census Index: Pre-1790* gives no other documentation).

GASKINS, DARIUS, left his father, Spencer Gaskins of Wicomico Church, VA, early last February, with the intention of procuring employment in either Alexandria or Georgetown as a cooper. He promised to write his father as soon as he should suit himself with an employer, but his father has not heard from him, and has serious fears for his safety. ([DC] *Metropolitan* 24 May 1820).

GASSER, PETER, from Gunters-Hoffen, Alsace, came here twelve years ago. Now Hans Peter Fischer and his wife Maria Elisabeth Gasserin, who arrived in this country last autumn, are seeking her brother. Fischer and his wife are in Heidelberg Twp., "an der Brunen Kehr," on Michel Schauer's place (*Hocker:* 21 cites the *Pennsylvanische Geschichts-Schreiber* 18 Aug 1750).

For more on this family, see Burgert's *Alsace* 188-189.

GAY, Capt. JOHN, late of the ship *Fair Phebe,* if he is living in any part of this State, the printers will inform him where he may hear of his brother Archibald (*GAVN:*133 cites *The Norfolk Herald* 9 March 1799).

He may be the Capt. Gay who married Miss E. Willoughby of this borough on Thursday evening (*GAVN:*133 cites *The Norfolk Herald and Public Advertiser* 31 Dec 1796).

GEBHARD, JOHANN WILHELM, shoemaker, arrived in this country three years ago. His parents arrived this year and they are seeking their son. Notify Pastor Handschuh at Germantown (*Hocker:*45 cites the *Pennsylvanische Geschichts-Schreiber* 1 Dec 1754).

GEHRUNG, GOTTLIEB, of Dusseldorf, Germany, left that place in 1794 at the age 18 years, in order to repair to Surinam, by way of Holland. The last letter received from him, by his sister, Helena Gehrung, widow of the late John Capff, merchant of Dusseldorf, was dated 12 April 1795, at Philadelphia. Since then his brothers and sisters have not had any account of him. Anyone with information is asked to communicate with A. Halback, of Philadelphia (*Poulson's American Daily Advertiser* 21 April 1819).

GEIGER, GEORGE, and **JOHN JACOB GEIGER,** or their heirs of legal pretensions, are asked to apply to William Montgomery and Son, 1010 N. Front St., as they may hear of something much to their reciprocal advantage (*Poulson's American Daily Advertiser* 27 July 1815).

GENARD, Citizen JEROME, aged 17, embarked from Havre, for the [Scioto?] about the year 1790, at a period when several Frenchmen came over to the United States. Anyone who could give the information relative to either, is asked to transmit it to he Minister or consuls of the French Republic. [The notice is repeated in French] ([PA] *Aurora General Advertiser* 20 Jan 1795).

GERST, MAGDALENA, married [-?-] Volkel. Her brother **MICHAEL GERST** arrived at Philadelphia seventeen years [ago?] from Oberhoffen, five hours from Strasburg, in Lower House. An inquiry is made for both Magdalena Gerst and Michael Gerst (*Hocker:* 185 cites the *Philadelphische Correspondenze* 26 May 1789).
For additional information on the Volkel Family, see Burgert's *Alsace:* 511-512.

GETZ, ANDREAS, formerly a doctor with the Anspach troops, and now believed to be in Canada, is sought by his sister Engel Christina Getzin (*Hocker:*192 cites the *Philadelhpische Correspondenz* 9 April 1793).

GIBBERT, RICHARD, was an apprentice in London to Mrs. Levethorpe, horner, and about four years ago he came as a servant to Philadelphia, where his time was bought by an Indian trader. He has inherited an estate yielding £100 annually plus houses and other money. He is urged to contact William Jones, merchant of Birmingham, Chester Co., PA (*Scott* 1:233 cites *Pa. Gaz.* 26 July 1739).

GIBBIN, MARCUS, youngest son of the Rev. John Gibbin of King's County, Ireland, came to the back settlements of Philadelphia about 25 years ago, and was a schoolmaster. If he is living, he is requested to write to Mrs. Martha Gibbin, Stephen St., Dublin. For further details, enquire of Marcus Gibbin, Chesterfield Co. (*GAVN:* 134 cites the *Virginia Gazette* 16 June 1774).
   A Rev. Marcus Gibbin died at Birch, near Colchester, Essex, 29 July 1752. (*Gentleman's Magazine.* No. 384).
   A Marcus Gibbin, born 1747, was a sergeant in the Revolutionary War in the 2nd and 6th Continental Lines (John H. Gwathmey. *Historical Register of Virginians. Soldiers, Sailors, Marines, 1775-1783 in the Revolution.* Richmond, 1938, p. 304).

GIBBS, JOHN, formerly of Hagedon, Essex, Eng., may be living in Virginia. If he is, he may be benefited by making himself known to Frances Corbin of Caroline Co., VA (*GAVN:*134 cites the *Virginia Gazette and General Advertiser* 29 Nov 1797).

GIBSON, HENRY, of Augusta Co., son of James Gibson, dec., late of Middlesex Co., Virginia, if living should apply to William Deane of Middlesex Co., where he will hear of something greatly to his advantage (*GAVN:* 134 cites *The Virginia Gazette* 18 Oct 1776).

GIBSON, JAMES, son of John Gibson, of Sligoe, in the Kingdom of Ireland, came into the Province of Maryland, in the year 1746. If he is yet alive, he is desired to go to George Gibson, of Lancaster, in the province of Pennsylvania, where he may be informed of something very considerable to his advantage. If any person will inform the said George Gibson where he may be found, it will be kindly taken "George Gibson, Lancaster, April 13, 1753" (*Pa. Gaz.* 19 April 1753).

GILBERT, Mrs. ALEXANDER, is lately arrived from Maryland from Scotland and is to be found at Madam Hawkins in Queen Anne's Co. She is seeking information on her husband, who from his letters dated 1734, 1736, and 1737, lodged at one John Van

Boskerk's in Philadelphia Co., in the Manor of Moreland (*Scott* 1:269 cites *Pa. Gaz.* 31 July 1740).

GILLART, FELIX, son of Felix Gillart, coach maker and auctioneer of Long Acre, St. Martins in the Field, London [actually Mddx.], went to sea and in 1789 or 1790 he was on a ship in the James River and was then called *Delap.* If he applies to Edmund Pendleton, Jr., of Caroline Co., he will hear something to his advantage (*GAVN:* 135 cites the *Virginia Gazette and General Advertiser* 6 Nov 1793).

GIROD, WILLIAM, the friend of Mr. Dennis O'Neal, and Mrs. Shylock, will hear something very interesting to his happiness, if he applies to the offices of the National Intelligencer, Washington, D.C. (*The National intelligencer and Washington Advertiser* 11 Jan 1809).

GLACY, ANTOINE FRANCOIS de PAUL PARAT, formerly in the French military service, a planter in the Island of Guadeloupe, left that island a few years ago, and is supposed to have taken his refuge in the United States, but has not been heard of since. His wife is anxious to know his actual residence. Any information about his existence, residence, or death, may be forwarded to the French Commercial Commissary in Baltimore (*Federal Gazette and Baltimore Daily Advertiser* 7 Nov 1801).

GLANVIL, WILLIAM, of Tavistock, Devonshire, West of England, lately arrived in America. He is residing at Mrs. Davis', near the head of Hancock's Wharf, Boston, and has been informed that an uncle of his, Jeremy Glanvil, has recently died, bequeathing to him certain property. William wants to know in what part of the United States his uncle died, and to whom the property as been entrusted (*Poulson's American Daily Advertiser* 1 July 1803).

GLASER, CARL, is sought by his cousin Georg Peter Funck, who arrived last autumn from Zweybruecken Region and is serving in Germantown with John Jones, tanner (*Pennsylvanische Geschichts-Schreiber* 1 April 1751).

GLEN, WILLIAM, about 19 years of age, a wheelwright by trade, sailed from Port Rush, Co. Antrim, in the Ship *Rainbow,* Capt. Osburn, and landed at New Castle last October. It is supposed he went towards Lancaster. If he is living, his brother, Robert Glen, in the Forks of the Delaware, asks him to write, or if William is dead, Robert would like to know of that (*Pa. Gaz.* 26 May 1763).

GLOESZ, ERHART, smith, near Lancaster, on the road past Peter Eby's Mill, has information that Henrich Knoblauch has arrived in America with an important letter for him, and he urges Knoblach to forward his letter (*Hocker:* 40 cites the *Pennsylvanische Geschichts-Schreiber* 1 Feb 1754).

GLUCK, JOH. CONRAD, from Darmstadt, is sought by Simon Keppler, who will be returning to Germany in three weeks (*Eyster:* 38 cites the *Pennsylvanische Staatsbote* 4 Aug 1775).

Conrad Gluck arrived in Philadelphia on the *Lydia*. He took the usual qualifications [oath of fidelity] to the Government on 19 Oct 1749 (*PGP* 1:421).

GOEBELL, JOHANN WILHELM, son of Johann Wilhelm Goebell, one of the merchant and magistrates of Windau, left home some time ago, supposedly for Philadelphia. He is entitled to a legacy from his mother, Maria Elisabeth, who has died, and from his late father-in-law, Heinrich Coht, who died in 1783. Goebell is sought by the city of Windau (*Hocker:*174 cites the *Philadelphische Correspondenz* 7 Feb 1786).

GOETTMAN, JOH. LEONHART, from Kirchbrunndach, aus dem Obenwald, notifies his brother-in-law, Johannes Nicolas Arnold, who came to America seven years ago, that he (Goettman) has arrived this summer from Germany, and that he was very sick on the ship *Union,* Capt. Bryson (*Hocker:* 126 cites the *Wochentlicher Pennsylvanischer Staatsbote* 19 Oct 1773).

Joh. Leonhart Gottmann arrived on the *Union* on 27 Sep 1773 (*Eyster:*33).

GOODMAN, JOSEPH, came from Peterborough, England, many years ago to reside in Maryland. He is urged to apply to Evan Thomas of Montgomery Co. or to Elias Ellicott on Baltimore (*Maryland Journal and Baltimore Advertiser* 10 March 1789).

Joseph Goodman was indicted for theft and tried at the Old Bailey on 4 Dec 1751. He stole property from his landlord Thomas Pullen, who kept the York-Minister [Tavern or Inn] at Hyde Park Corner in London. Goodman was found guilty and sentenced to transportation (www.OldBaileyonLine.org) He was sentenced to transportation in Middlesex between Oct 1751 and Jan 1752 (*CBEB*). He was transported from London in the *Thomas,* Capt. James Dobbins, in March 1752, and arrived in Annapolis in April 1752 (*KPMV:*134).

On 8 March 1762 Joseph Goodman received a payment from the estate of Oneal Robinson of AA Co. (MDAD 47:311).

A Joseph Goodman, blacksmith, drowned last week while attempting to ride over the Falls of Patapsco. He left four children, and a wife big with a fifth child (*AMG* 12 March 1767).

In 1790 a Joseph Goodman (not yet proven to be a relation) was head of a family in Frederick Co., MD, with one white male over 16, one white male under 16, and three white females (*1790MD,* p. 70, col. 3).

GOODRICK (or GUTRIDGE), Mr. [-?-], lately a resident of Alexandria, married a Widow Edelen of Fredericksburg. He may hear of something to his advantage by applying to the printer (*GAVN:* 137 cites *The Virginia Gazette and Alexandria Advertiser* 3 Sep 1789).

GOODRIDGE, WILLIAM, of Salisbury, Wilts., left England about 50 years ago to reside in some part of this colony. If he or any descendants are living they will be informed of something to their advantage by applying to John Smith of Hanover Town (*GAVN:* 137 cites the *Virginia Gazette* 2 June 1768).

GOODWIN, EDWARD, came from England to America on 23 July 1767 for five years. He will hear something to his advantage if he contacts James Taylor, coach maker in

Annapolis (Annapolis *Maryland Gazette* 1 Aug 1771).
On 29 June 1776 an Edward Goodwin of Frederick Co., MD, was enrolled by Capt.
Benjamin Spyker in the Maryland Flying Camp (*ARMD* 18:43).

GORDON, JAMES and **THOMAS GORDON**, about 1730, sailed from Belfast, Northern Ireland, in a passenger ship, bound for Philadelphia; the Master's name was M'Laughlin. If any of James' or Thomas' offspring will signify their progenitors by letter to Dr. John Nevill Cowan at New York, directed to the care of John and Oliver Goodwin, druggists, they may hear of something to their advantage (*Claypoole's American Daily Advertiser* 18 June 1796).

GORDON, ROBERT, son of Thomas Gordon, of Carnstroan, Co. Antrim, some time ago, emigrated to this country. If he or his legal representatives will call on Hugh Kennedy, of Hagerstown, he or they will be informed of an estate in Ireland, of £1000 per annum, to which he or his heirs are entitled by the death of a Mr. John Gordon, lately dec. (*Kline's Carlisle Weekly Gazette* 30 Nov 1804).

GORDON, THOMAS, son of James Gordon, was born at Lurgan, Co. Armagh. He sailed from Belfast about three years ago. He is asked to apply to the printer to hear something to his advantage (Scott 3:233 cites *The New York Gazette and Weekly Mercury* 10 Dec 1781).

GORHAM, JOHN, is asked to call at the Powhatan Manufacturing Company's warehouse, No. 197 Market St., he may hear of something to his advantage (*Baltimore Patriot* 9 July 1817).

GOTZ, JOH. JACOB, married Catherine, the sister of the mother of Anna Eva Frauenfelder, from Darmstadt, Litzelbach, near Neukirchen in Lichtenberg, who about three years ago, married Philip Hartman of Oley, near the Church. Anna Eva wants to know the whereabouts of her aunt Catherine (*Eyster:* 18 cites the *Pennsylvanische Berichte* 4 Feb 1758).

GOULD, DAVID, formerly of Sheffield, Old England, but lately a resident near Deer Creek, MD, is asked to apply at the Golden Swan, N. Third St., and he may hear of something to his advantage, or any information respecting him will be thankfully received (*Claypoole's American Daily Advertiser* 15 June 1797).

GRACEBERRY, WILLIAM, a tailor, born near Belfast, in the North of Ireland, and sailed from thence for New York or Philadelphia in the Year 1736. If he is still alive, and will convey a letter directed to William Maine, Surveyor, at the Indian Land, in South Carolina, to the care of Messrs. Smith and Nutt, Merchants, on the Bay, in Charles Town, acquainting him with the place of his abode, and how a letter may be safely conveyed to him, the said Maine can give him such intelligence as will be extremely agreeable, and considerably to his advantage, in relation to his three sisters, Elizabeth, Mary and Margaret, who, with his brother James (since deceased) sailed from Belfast, and arrived in Charles Town in the said Year, 1736 (*Pa. Gaz.* 17 April 1760).

William Graceberry was born c1711 in Co. Armagh, Ireland, and died in Penns Neck, Salem Co., New Jersey. He married Mary [-?-], born c1715 in Penns Neck. According to data posted by Barbara McCormick on Ancestry World Tree, William and Mary were the parents of: MARGARET, b. c1738 in Pittsgrove, Salem Co., New Jersey, m. Cornelius Dubois.; JAMES, b. c1741 in Pittsgrove, m. Beulah [-?-]; MARY, b. c1743 in Pittsgrove, m. Thomas Mayhew; and ANN, b. 28 June 1749 in Pittsgrove.

GRACIE, THOMAS, living at the head of Big Spring, Cumberland County PA, is expecting a brother of his, and he believes he may be the John Gracie, who has a little halt in his walk, cabinet maker by trade, lately from Galway in Scotland, and who has been inquiring for a brother he has in this state (*The Carlisle Gazette and the Western Repository of Knowledge* 11 July 1792).

GRAEMLING, JACOB, came in a ship, arriving in Maryland, perhaps five years ago. His brother Georg Graemlng, from Sennfeld, near Adelsheim, arrived in Philadelphia five years ago. Georg now lives in Skippack, Montgomery Co., at Welcker's Mill, is seeking information about Jacob (*Esyter:* 17 and *Hocker:* 64 cites the *Pennsylvanische Geschichts-Schreiber* 26 Nov 1757).
     Joh. Georg Graemling arrived 23 Sep 1752 on the *St. Andrew* (*Eyster:*17).

GRAESZEL, PHILIP, has been in America seven years. His brother, Jacob Graeszel, of Allemangel, Lynn Twp., Lehigh Co., PA, is seeking Philip (*Hocker:*97 cites the *Pennsylanische Geschichts-Schreiber* 18 Dec 1761).

GRASBURG, JOHN, of Amsterdam, in Holland, left home in 1806, as an apprentice for ten years to Capt. Richard Isaac of New York. His mother, a widow, is seeking information about him (*Poulson's American Daily Advertiser* 7 Dec 1820).

GRAUENINGER, MARTIN, born at Erlingen, near Sinsheun, arrived in this country in 1738 with his brother Johann Gottlieb. They were separated, and Johann Giotlieb, now at Anwell, New Jersey, seeks news of his brother (*Hocker:*3 cites the *Pennsylvanische Geschichts-Schreiber* 16 May 1745).

GRAY, JAMES, is supposed to have left Aberdeen some years ago and gone to Jamaica, where he stayed for some time, and then went to the Granades, where he soon died. If his parents or near relatives are still alive, and will apply to Ninian Johnson, merchant of Aberdeen, they will hear of something to their advantage (Dobson, *Aberdeen Journal* 11 Dec 1769; issue # 1144).
     James Gray, son of James Gray, a day laborer of Aberdeen, was sent to Grenada, and died in 1769 (*DSSA:* 84 cites the Aberdeen Propinquity Books).

GRAY, RICHARD, born at Falmouth in Cornwall, Eng., shoemaker, is asked to apply to the printer, where he may hear something to his advantage (*Scott* 3:237 cites *The New York Gazette and the Weekly Mercury* 5 Aug 1782).

GRAY, ROBERT, a native of Baslybay, Co. Monaghan, Ireland, son of James Gray and Elizabeth Gray, *alias Corry*, emigrated to this country about 1803 or 1804. Any information concerning him should be sent to James Gray at Mr. Scott's Manufactory, 626 Greenwich St., NY (*Baltimore Patriot* 7 July 1815).

GRAY, WILLIAM, who came to MD from Fotheringhay, Eng., some years ago, is sought by his nephew, James Stevens, son of John Stevens, chandler and grocer, who has recently come to MD (Annapolis *Maryland Gazette* 23 Oct 1751).

GREADY, ANN, wife of James Gready, and daughter of James Purtle of New London, Chester Co., and three of her children, were carried off on the 2nd day of July last from York Co., by the Indians. James Purtle, to encourage scouting parties against the Indians, will give 50 lbs., current money to anyone who will bring back his daughter Ann and her three children: Elisha, 10 years of age, Jane, age 6, and Mary, age 3, alive (or ten pounds for each of the children, and twenty pounds for the mother (*Pa. Gaz.* 11 Aug 1757).

GREEN, JOHN, of Lancaster Co., PA, is hereby notified that if he applies to Thomas Williams, hatter, in Second St., Philadelphia, opposite the Quakers' Meeting House, he will hear of something much to his advantage (*Pa. Gaz.* 29 May 1746).

GREEN, RICHARD, left Mansfield, New Jersey, about five years ago, and settled in Maryland. His father, Thomas Green, formerly lived for a time in East Jersey, and now lives in Turkeyfeet Twp., Bedford Co., PA. He is seeking news of his son (*Maryland Journal and Baltimore Advertiser* 10 Nov 1778).

GREENE, NATHANIEL, late of RI, is asked to apply to Messrs. Goddard and Langworthy, printers of Baltimore, where he may hear of something to his advantage (*GAVN:*143 cites *The Virginia Journal and Alexandria Advertiser* 31 March 1785).

GREENWAY, JOHN, of Liverpool, Eng., left that town about 35 years ago to reside in MD; he is urged to contact the printer (*Maryland Journal and Baltimore Advertiser* 10 Jan 1786).

GREENWOOD, JOSEPH, son of Daniel Greenwood, of Enfield, Eng., went to MD in the ship *Expedition*, Capt. English, about three years ago. News of him is sought, and it should be sent to the post office in Philadelphia (*Pa. Gaz.* 27 Jan 1747).
    He may be the Joseph Greenwood who died by May 1764, when his real and personal estate was to be sold (*Pa. Gaz.* 3 May 1764).

GRIERSON, WILLIAM, second son of Mr. Grierson of Ganock, in the Stewartry of Galloway, Scotland, is asked to apply to Mrs. Caimes of Bambarrack in the said Stewartry, he may hear of something greatly to his advantage. The said William Grierson may obtain some further information by applying to Capt. Thomas Losh, of the *Flora*, now in this port, or to Philip Nicklin & Co., Philadelphia (*Pennsylvania Packet and Daily Advertiser*4 Dec 1790),
    William Grierson, born in 1751, a smith, resided in Galloway, and sailed in Oct 1774 - May 1775 from Greenock to Philadelphia in the *Sally*, J. Brice, captain (David Dobson. *The Original Scots Colonists in America, 1612-1783.* Baltimore: Genealogical Publishing Co., 1989, p. 122; *DSSA:* 85).

GRIFFITH, Capt. JOHN, native of Haverford West, Wales, and a citizen of New York for almost 50 years, and for many years a commander in the London, Amsterdam, and Carolina trade, died 5 Nov at his house in Smith St., New York City, aged 74 (*Scott* 3: 242 cites *The New York Gazette and the Weekly Mercury* 10 Nov 1783).

GRIFFITH, OWEN, living with Landon Carter, Richmond Co., "though in a little time free," has an account with his brother at the Duke of Montague's that his father sent him some goods and has since died. Griffith will be going home to a really very good estate (*GAVN:*145 cites Rind's *Virginia Gazette* 6 Sep, 26 Sep 1770).
   In 1790 an Owen Griffith was listed in the census of Baltimore Co., MD, p. 23 (*AIS 1790 U.S. Federal Census Index*).

GRIFFITH, THOMAS, son of Thomas Griffith, of Bristol Twp., Philadelphia Co., PA, is absent, and is desired to come to the said township, where he shall hear of something to his advantage (*Pa. Gaz.* 3 July 1784).
   Thomas Griffith of Bristol Twp., Philadelphia Co., yeoman, died leaving a will dated 12 Oct 1782 and proved 1 March 1786. He named his wife Elizabeth, son Thomas, and the following grandchildren: Hugh Griffith (son of son Benjamin), Benjamin Armitage (son of dau. Rachel), William, Thomas, Joseph, Charles, and Cornelius Kite (sons of dau. Rebecca Kite). Son-in-law Joseph Kite of the Jerseys, and Joseph Spender were named executors. Jonathan Likens, Susannah Likens, and John Child witnessed the will (Philadelphia Co. Wills T:290).

GROGAN, EDWARD, son of Edward Grogan of Dublin, should apply to Gilbert Bigger of Baltimore, MD. Edward, Jr., left Dublin about twelve years ago, and was in Baltimore in 1784 (*Federal Intelligencer and Baltimore Daily Gazette* 22 July 1795).
   N.B.: On 24 Jan 1760 an Edward Grogan of Dublin, Gent., witnessed the will of Robert Boswell of Ballycurry, Co. Wicklow (*Eustace* 2:127).

GROOM, WILLIAM, formerly of Royal Exchange Lane, Boston, and at least 70 years old, or his heirs, are asked to apply by letter to James Travis of Beaufort, South Carolina, as they will hear of something greatly to their advantage (*United States Gazette* 17 Oct 1805).

GROOMBRIDGE, JAMES, native of England, who lived for some time at or near Slade's Tavern on My Lady's Manor, and kept a school, is asked to apply to Wallace and Muir of Annapolis (*Maryland Journal and Baltimore Advertiser* 12 Jan 1787).
   James Groombridge and Sarah Wyle were married on 15 Jan 1765 in St. John's Parish, Baltimore County (*SJSG:*227).
   James Groombridge was listed as a creditor in the inventory of Moses Goodwin of BA Co. on 15 Aug 1767 (MINV 97:256).
   Groombridge, of Baltimore Co., was a non-juror to the Oath of Fidelity in 1778 (*BARP:*112). In 1790 James "Grumsbridge" [*sic*] was head of a family in Baltimore County, with one white male over 16, and one white female under 16 (*1790MD:*343, col. 1). James Groombridge, aged 77, was buried on 12 Jan 1799 in St. James Parish (*BAJA:*52).

GROSS, MARIA CATHERINE WEISSIN, from Langen Candel, bey Lindau, is the wife of Frantz Gross, a weaver, who has a brother-in-law near Lancaster, Stoffel Geiger. Her sister, Maria Elizabeth Weissin, is now the wife of David Rittman; they arrived in New York in 1755 and are in New York with Adam vin dem Berg (*Pennsylvanische Geschichts-Schreiber* 22 May 1761).

GROSZ, LEOPOLD VALENTIN, and his son **JOHAN FRIEDRICH GROSZ,** are sought by Leopold's daughter Eva Rosina Barbara Groszin, who is now with Johann Stauffer, Warwick Twp., Lancaster Co. (*Hocker:* 91 cites the *Pennsylvanische Geschichts-Schreiber* 3 July 1761).

Leopold Valentin Gross arrived in Philadelphia on the *Two Brothers*, Thomas Arnot, commander, from Rotterdam, last from Cowes, and took the Oath to the Government on 15 Sep 1752 (*PGP* 1:478).

Johan Friederich Gross was in Philadelphia Co. in 1752 (*AIS Census Index: Pre-1790* gives no other documentation).

In Sep 1754 Peter Schertz of Bart Twp., Lancaster Co., PA, advertised that his German servant Efrosina (Eva Rosina) Barbara Groszin, age 35, had run away (*Hocker* cites the *Pennsylvanische Geschichts-Schreiber* 1 Sep 1754).

GRUENSZWEISS, GOTTFRIED, a woolcomber, is sought by his brother-in-law, Georg Heinrich Reinoehl, from Wurtemburg, a smith, now living in Conestoga, Lancaster Co., PA, with Christian Weber, near Jacob Bayerle's mill (*Hocker:*25 cites cites the *Pennsylvanische Geschichts-Schreiber* 1 April 1751).

George Heinrich Reinoehl, married at Nedlingen, Wurtemburg, Eva Catharina Gruneszweiss, dau. of a schoolmaster. Reinoehl arrived on the snow *Good Intent* on 9 Nov 1749 (*PGP* 1:426). Hocker (above) incorrectly transcribed his name as Steinohl. Henry "Reinole" was in Lebanon Twp., Lancaster Co., in 1771, and Henry "Reinehl," Sr., was in Labanon Twp. with George, Henry, and Conrad Reinehl (Yoder's *PGI* 102-103).

Henry Reinoehl, son of Henry and Catherine, was born on 18 Dec 1741 in Germany, was baptized, and came to America in his 8th year (1749), and conformed. He married 1st, Juliana Gephart (by whom he had four children), and 2nd, at Quitopohila Lutheran Church, on 23 June 1779, Cath. Matter (by whom he had six children). He died 14 Feb, and was buried 16 Feb 1835, aged 83 years and 2 months. (*Lebanon Churches*).

Henry and Juliana were the parents of ("Records of Quitapohila (Hill) Lutheran Church," *Lebanon Churches*): ANNA MARY, b. 24 Aug 1771, bapt. 22 Sep 1771 Sp.: George Pawter and wife Anna Mary); ANNA CATHARINE, b. 4 Oct, bapt. 17 Oct 1773 (sp.: George Henry Reinoehl and wife Eva Catharine); MARY ELIZABETH, b. 15 March, bapt. 20 March 1778 (sp.: Mary Elizabeth Schomacher, single). Henry and Catherine were the parents of: ANNA CHRISTINA, b. 26 Oct, bapt. 12 Nov 1780 (sp. George Henry Reineohl and wife Anna Christina; and JULIANA, b. 2 Jan 1783, bapt. 12 Jan 1783 (sp.: Jacob Matter and wife).

GUTBROD, MAGDALENA, from Tuebingen, Wurtemberg, came to America in 1754 with her husband and several children. The husband died on the voyage, and others settled in Canajoharie, NY (*Hocker:*191 cites the *Philadelphische Correspondenz* 22 Jan 1793).

HAART, JACOB, unmarried, from Heppenheim, near Alzey, arrived in America about a year ago. Henrich Landes, of Perkasie, Bucks Co., his brother-in-law, seeks him (*Hocker* 16 cites the *Pennsylvanische Geschichts-Schreiber* 1 Dec 1749).

Jacob Hardt arrived on the *Patience and Margaret* on 25 Oct 1748. Heinrich Landes arrived on the *Isaac* on 27 Sep 1749 (*Eyster:*7).

HABERSTOCK, TOBIAS, who went away six years ago, is being sought by Philipp Conrad Christ, a native of Beuerbach, Nasssau-Usingen, son of Joh. Philipp Christ, master linen-weaver. Christ came here last fall, intending to visit his friend Mr. Bott, master smith, from Stockenroth, Idstein.. (*Eyster:* 26 cites the *Pennsylvanische Staatsbote* 14 April 1772).

HADLOW, ROBERT, son of Joseph Hadlow of Co. Kent, Eng., came to this country some time ago. He was last heard of in 1768 at Thomas Hopkins, Esq., in Binglons, near Philadelphia. If he is still alive he should apply to Miers Fisher in Philadelphia, for news of a considerable legacy bequeathed to him by a relative in England (*Pa. Gaz.* 5 Oct 1774).

HAEKERMANN, CARL DIEDRICH GUSTAV, former Secretary of the Council and Court of Justice at Barth, in Swedish Pomerania, sailed from Amsterdam in 1780, for Charleston, with a Mr. Buchholtz. Ludwig Henrich Luering, 93 Race Street, Philadelphia, is inquiring for him (*Hocker:*189 cites the *Philadelphische Correspondenz* 15 Nov 1791).

HAFFNER, [-?-], formerly "Churfaeltzlicher" Renovator in Heidelberg, went to Holland two years ago and then came to Pennsylvania. C. L. Boehme, the Reformed Pastor in Lancaster, is seeking information about him (*Hocker:*138 cites the *Wochentlicher Pennsylvanischer Staatsbote* 24 Jan 1775).

HAG, JOH. GEORG, from Frankenbach, is sought by Christian Buhler, lately returned from Germany (*Eyster:* 35 cites the *Pennsylvanische Staatsbote* 4 Oct 1774).

In 1748 Hans Georg Hag was in Philadelphia Co., PA (*AIS Census Index: Pre-1790* gives no other documentation).

Joh. Georg Hag and his wife Appolonia were sponsors at the baptism of N. Peter Radebach, son of Peter Radebach in Oct 1765 at the Little Tulpehocken Church (Bucks Co.?) (*Egle's Notes and Queries, Annual Volume, 1899:*206).

HAGER, HARMANUS, who came about five years ago from Germany to PA, is notified that three of his children, Jacob, Anna Margarietta, and Valentine, have arrived in New York City in the ship *Sarah Galley*, Capt. Thomas (*Pa. Gaz.* 24 Oct 1754; *Scott* 5:44 cites the *New York Post Boy* 21 Oct 1755).

HALL, CHARITY, dau. of Thomas Hall of Dublin, came to PA some years ago, and lived on Brandywine Creek, Chester Co., will hear something to her advantage by applying to William Reynolds of Charlestown, near Moor Hall, Chester Co. (*Scott* 1:250 cites the *Pa. Gaz.* 29 Jan 1740).

HALL, ELIJAH, ship-carpenter, and his heirs have inherited about 200 a. of land in Anne Arundel Co., on the Patpasco River, now in the possession of Capt. Thomas Mortimer of Baltimore Town, who claims the land [under the will?] of Charles Hall, but whereof only one-half of the land was willed to him. Elijah and Charles Hall are cousins and served their apprenticeship to ship carpenters on Fells Point. The land was willed to them by their grandfather Nathan Pumphrey. Elijah Hall served his time about 20 years ago with a Mr. Wells, ship carpenter, from whence he went about 18 years ago to Chincoteague to repair a vessel burnt down by the British. He is or was a married man and had children. This notice was placed by Elijah's friend James Bonadye (*Federal Intelligencer and Baltimore Daily Gazette* 23 Oct 1795).

Nathan Pumphrey of AA Co. died leaving a will dated 16 Aug 1761 and proved 24 April 1764. to Thomas Bennett, son of Phebe Bennett, he left furniture. He left cattle to Mary Hall, dau. of Dasian [*sic*] Hall. He left the residue of his estate to Sarah Hall. But if they die without issue, then Sarah Hall's dau. Sarah Hall should inherit the residue of his estate. If she dies without heirs, the Charles and Elijah Hall, sons of Casian and Ann Hall should inherit. The first named Sarah Hall was named executor. Philip Hammond, Richard and Nathan Shipley, and Edward Tyler witnessed the will (MWB 32:58).

Thomas Mortimer was in Baltimore Town on 9 Oct 1782 when John Peter Smail, age 18 on 30 March 1782. was bound to him to learn the trade of a mariner (BOCP 1:76).

In 1790 Elijah Hall was head of a family in AA Co., with five white males 16 and over, one white male under 16, and four white females (*1790MD:*13, col. 1).

HALL (or HALLY), JAMES, and JOHN, left Scotland some 50 years ago, and went to New Castle on the Delaware, not far from Philadelphia. Their friends at Carnlea, Co. of Perth, North Britain, would like to know of they are alive or dead, and if dead, if they left behind any children. Anyone with information is asked to contact Peter Graham & Co., of Philadelphia, James Peter, Sheriff's clerk, Perth, North Britain, or James Riddle, esq.. of New Castle, DE ([DE] *American Watchman* 19 Oct 1816).

HALL, PATRICK, is asked to write to his brother, Robert Hall, who came from the Bayres in the Parish of Haddington, in East Leuthian [Lothian], Scotland. Patrick should write to him, directed to Esquire Brinlie, in Roxbury, near Boston (*Pa. Gaz.* 15 Dec 1743).

HALLBERG, MICHAEL, a goldsmith, emigrated from Denmark between 1740 and 1750, and established himself in Philadelphia. He was a merchant in Philadelphia between 1750 and 1770, and had a son who died while acting as a surgeon in the service of the United States during the Revolutionary War. Any descendants of Hallberg, or anyone who can give information about the family, are asked to communicate with F.G. & R.S. Smith, 201 S. Front St., Philadelphia (*Poulson's American Daily Advertiser* 29 Oct 1819).

HALLIDAY, Mrs., formerly of Newry, Ireland, is supposed to have lived for some time in Baltimore. Anyone having information about her is asked to communicate with Granville S. Oldfield, 4 Charles ST., Baltimore (*Baltimore Patriot* 20 Dec 1820).

HALY, MARGERY, wife of the late Capt. Hutchinson of New York City, and her sister, **CATHERINE** (or **ANNE**) **HALY** (who came to America in 1745), are asked to apply to Hugh Gaine, as a sister of theirs wishes to see them (*Scott* 3:214 cites *The New York Gazette and Weekly Mercury* 20 and 27 April 1778).

HAMILTON, Capt. ALEXANDER, of the New York Co, of Artillery, may hear of something to his advantage by applying to the printer of this paper (*The Pennsylvania Evening Post* 25 Jan 1777).

HAMILTON, JAMES, shoemaker, left Glasgow, and is supposed to have arrived on some part of this continent in the year 1769. If he is living he should apply to Robert Hamilton at the Sign of the Boot, in Leesburg, Loudoun Co., VA, where he may hear of something to his advantage (*Pa. Gaz.* 3 March 1773).

James Hamilton, son of Robert Hamilton, shoemaker, resided in Kilmarnock, Ayrshire, and settled in Loudoun Co., VA, by 1786 (*SOCD:* 65).

Robert Hamilton, born 1720, died by 1786, innkeeper and cordwainer, resided at Kilmarnock, and settled in Loudoun Co., VA, by 1740. He married Margaret McKee, and had at least one son; JAMES (*SOCD:* 66).

HAMILTON, JOHN, son of Jeffry Hamilton, **WILLIAM HAMILTON** of White Castle, and **SAMUEL HAMILTON** were all natives of Ireland who came to this country some time ago. They have not been heard of in some time, and are urged to write to their friends in Philadelphia (*Lancaster Journal* 30 Nov 1804).

HAMILTON, THOMAS, came from Nickmany, Co. Tyrone, Ireland, about 30 years ago. He, if he is living, or any of his family, should know that David Cockran, a sister's son of his came to Philadelphia, and cannot get any information about Hamilton. Any person who can inform Cockran about Hamilton is asked to send a letter to Patrick Anderson, Charlestown, Chester Co., PA (*Pa. Gaz.* 8 Dec 1763).

A Thomas Hamilton and Margaret Twining were issued a marriage license by Gov. James Hamilton in Jan 1749 (*PVR* 1:503). Stephen Twining of Wrightstown, Bucks Co., PA, made a will on 8 mo., 8 d., 1771, naming his dau. Margaret, wife of Thomas Hamilton, and her children (*Bucks Co. Will Book 3*).

HANBURY, JOSEPH, about 18 or 20 years ago, embarked from England to Pennsylvania; he was brought up as a clerk to Ironworks, and served as a clerk under Caple Hanbury, Esq., Iron Master, at Ponty Pool, South Wales. After his arrival he settled in Vincent Twp., near French Creek, Chester Co., PA. His brother William Hanbury, now residing at the North East Forge in MD, would be glad of news of him (*Pa. Gaz.* 29 Nov 1764).

HANNAM, MINTY, left England about 1768, and was last heard of at Christopher Cardiff's, Great Choptank River, Bolingbroke, Talbot Co., MD, in 1771. He should apply to Rev. Reader Wareham in Dorchester, Eng. Anyone knowing of his death should apply to Messrs. John and Thomas Gilliate of Richmond, VA (*Maryland Journal and Baltimore Advertiser* 13 March 1789).

Minty Hannam, formerly of St. John, Southwark, Surrey, but lately of Dorchester Co., MD, died by April 1791. Administration was granted to his cousin-german, Hester Read, since his relict, Mary Holland, formerly Hannam, was cited but did not appear (*AWAP*:138).

HANNAM, WILLIAM, from Crondall in Hampshire, may hear of something to his advantage. Anyone with information should contact Townsend Speakman, apothecary, four doors below the Friends Meeting House on the west side of Second Street (*Pennsylvania Packet and General Advertiser* 22 July 1784).

HARDMAN, JOHN, from the North of Ireland, came from Antigua about two years ago. If he will repair to the printer, he will receive a letter and some proposals to his advantage (*Pa. Gaz.* 29 June 1738).

HARNETT, JOHN MAURICE, a native of Ireland, and a tanner by trade, came to this town last November in the Brig *Baltimore*, from Cork. He should apply to the printer (*Maryland Journal and Baltimore Advertiser* 13 Aug 1790).
    In 1790 John Harnett was listed in the Census of Baltimore Town with one white male over 16, three white males under 16, and one white female (*1790MD* 18, col. 3).

HARRIS, HENRY, from Wales, settled in this Province (it is thought near to Philadelphia) who died, and left a son Henry Harris. Whether there are more children is not known, who also died, and left issue. These are to desire any of them to apply to the New Printing Office, where they may hear of something to their advantage (*Pa. Gaz.* 24 Feb 1763).

HARRIS, JOHN, a peddler, last 21 Feb came to the house of Nicholas Grubb in Nockamixon Twp., Bucks Co., and said he lived near the Drawbridge, Philadelphia. He was sick at Grubb's house and finally died on 10 March. Grubb took an inventory of his goods, and now wishes to inform Harris' relations that if they present the proper certificates to Grubb, they may have his goods, upon paying the funeral and other charges (*Pa. Gaz.* 3 April 1782).

HART, HYMAN, tailor, had lived at Dr. Charles Carroll's, Annapolis, but later moved to the Eastern Shore. Richard Burdus has a letter from London for him (Annapolis *Maryland Gazette* 14 May 1752).
    Coldham shows a Hyam Hart [*sic*] who was sentenced to transportation from Somerset in July 1744 (Coldham *British Emigrants in Bondage* 430).

HARTMAN, HENRICH, who arrived from Siegen in Nassau two years ago, is sought by Anthon Stutt near Peter Jung's (*Eyster:*12 cites the *Pennsylvanische Berichte* 1 April 1752). Henrich Hardtman arrived on the *Patience* on 19 Sep 1749 (*Eyster:*12).
    Henrich Hartman, of Philadelphia, unmarried, miller, is in prison for a debt of £17.10.0. He is willing to serve anyone who will pay the debt (Hocker cites the *Pennsylvanische Geschichts-Schreiber* 20 Aug 1757).
    Henrich Hartman of Rockhill Twp., Bucks Co., was mentioned in the *Pennsylvanische Geschichts-Schreiber* of 9 Nov 1759 (*Hocker* 82).

HARTMAN, PHILIP, of Oley, near the Church, states that about three years ago, he took a wife from Darmstadt, Litzelbach, near Neukirchen in Lichtenberg, by the name of Anna Eva Frauenfelder, who wants to know the whereabouts of her mother's sister, Catherine, who was married to Joh. Jacob Gotz. Gotz can send a note to Hartman or to the printer (*Eyster:*18 cites the *Pennsylvanische Berichte* 4 Feb 1758).

Paul and Philip Hartman advertised for news of their brother Gottlieb Friedrich, who was indentured eight years ago at Raritan, NJ. Anyone with information should contact Matthes Reichert, Falckner Swamp, Montgomery Co., PA (*Hocker:* 89 cites the *Pennsylvanische Geschichts-Schreiber* 22 May 1761).

HARTMANN, FRIEDRICH, and his five children, **FRIEDRICH JOHANN PAULUS, GOTLIEB FREDERICK, JOH. PHILIP, WILHELM,** and **ROSINA,** all arrived in America bout seven years ago, and now are sought by their son and brother, Johann Eberhart Hartmann, who is serving with David Auen, Upper Saucon Twp., Northampton (now Lehigh Co.) (*Hocker:*85 cites the *Pennsylvanische Geschichts-Schreiber* 11 Aug 1760).

Eberhart, Friederich, and Wilhelm Hartmann were in Philadelphia Co. in 1753 (*AIS Census Index: Pre-1790* gives no other documentation).

HARTMANN, Sieur GEORGE CHARLES FREDERICK, formerly a subaltern officer in the Brunswick troops, in 1780, resided in Loudoun Co. He settled near Knowland's Ferry, about three miles from the Potomac where he married a farmer's dau. She was a linen weaver and he took up the same profession. He should apply to David Anderson, Jr., Hanover Town, he will receive the proper credentials of his being heir to a very considerable inheritance in Brunswick. He must present himself there by the last of Feb 1788 to claim it (*GAVN*:155 cites the *Virginia Independent Chronicle* 15, 22 Aug 1787, *Virginia Journal and Alexandria Advertiser* 6 Dec 1787).

HARTMANN, GOTTFRIED, was indentured at Raritan, NJ, eight years ago. Now he is sought by his brothers Paul and Philip Hartmann (*Hocker:*89 cites the *Pennsylvanische Geschichts-Schreiber* 27 May 1761).

HARVIE, SARAH, who is said to have lived near Upper Marlborough, and later went to Frederick Co., MD, if living, should apply to Ignatius Digges so she may receive the balance of a legacy left her by William Mordent [*sic*]. If she is dead, her heirs may apply. (Annapolis *Maryland Gazette* 31 Oct 1776).

William Mordant of Prince George's Co. died leaving a will dated 31 March 1741 and proved 20 April 1741. He named his granddau. Elizabeth Burgess and left Sarah Harvie personalty belonging to his deceased wife. He left the residue of his estate to Jonathan and David Lewis and Sarah Harvie. Ignatius Digges was named executor. John Osborne, Robert Riddell, and Peter Parker witnessed the will (MWB 22:351).

William Harvey married Margaret Norman on 2 Feb 1726 in All Hallow's Parish, Anne Arundel Co., MD She evidently died as he married Mary Sherbert in All Hallows on 2 March 1730. Mary was baptized the same day (*AACR:* 41, 45). William and Mary were the parents of four children, whose births were recorded in All Hallows (*AACR:* 170): SARAH, b. 20 July 1737; JOHN, b. 20 June 1741; ELIZABETH, b. 19 March 1750/1; and ANN, b. 2 March 1751/2.

HARWOOD, WILLIAM, arrived from England about 1774 with his son, aged 10 or 11, and is supposed to have settled near Fredericksburg or Alexandria. He will hear something to his advantage if he applies to T. Green, printer, in Fredericksburg (*GAVN:*156 cites the *Virginia Herald and Fredericksburg Advertiser* 24 June 1790, the *Virginia Gaz. and Alexandria Advertiser* 1 July 1790).

HASTEY, JAMES, was born at Matching Green, Essex, son of James Hastey, and enlisted in the 7th Regt. of Guards in 1774. He was at St. Vincent's in 1775, and was ordered thence to Boston. If he will apply to Capt. Normand Tolmey at the shipyards he will hear something to his advantage (*Scott* 3:239 cites *The New York Gazette and Weekly Mercury* 6 Jan 1783).

HASZLER, BASTIAN, is sought by his brother Jacob, who arrived in this country a year and a half ago. Notify Hansz Zimmerman, Cocalico, Lancaster Co. (*Hocker:*27 cites the *Pennsylvanische Geschichts-Schreiber* 1 June 1751).

Hans Jacob Hasler made his mark when he arrived on the *Crown*, Michael James Master, from Rotterdam, last from Cowes, on 30 Aug 1749 (*PGP* 1:391).

HATTON, ROBERT, left Dorchester Co., MD some 12 or 15 months ago. He is invited to come to John Bennett. He has nothing to fear from Bennett or any other creditor in DO Co. (Annapolis *Maryland Gazette* 9 Dec 1762).

HAUGHTON, JOHN, carpenter, and wife **SARAH**, about twenty years ago [c1768], came from Wicklow, Ireland, to Annapolis or Baltimore. If they are alive they should apply to the printer to hear something to their advantage (*Pa. Gaz.* 1 Dec 1788).

HAUPT, JOHANNES, several years ago was the servant of a captain in Philadelphia. His mother in Tuebingen, Wurtemberg, is seeking him (*Hocker:*163 cites the *Philadelphische Correspondenz* 10 April 1782).

HAUPTMAN, HENRY, was born in Elssatz, near Strasburg, and came to Philadelphia in the year 1773. If he will apply to his brother Jacob Hauptman, at Bourie Lane, No. 8, in the city of New York, or to Mr. Joseph Cruikshanks' Printing Office, on the north side of Market street, between Second and Third Streets, Philadelphia, he will hear of something to his advantage. "New York. June 2, 1783" (*Pa Gaz.* 11 June 1783; *Hocker:*165 cites the *Philadelphische Correspondenz* 10 June 1783).

HAUSER, BARBARA, and her children, **JOHANNES, CHRISTOPH, REGINA** and **BARBARA**, are in this country, and are sought by their son and brother Casper Hauser, who is serving in Skippack, Montgomery Co., Pennsylvania, with Georg Weidner (*Hocker:*62 cites the *Pennsylvanische Geschichts-Schreiber* 25 June 1757).

Johann and Christoff Hauser arrived on the *Speedwell*, Capt. James Creagh, from Rotterdam, but last from Cowes, on 25 Sep 1749 (*PGP* 1:410).

HAUSMANN, LUDWIG CARL, born in Hesse-Hanau, son of the late Hesse Cassel First Lieutenant Franz Theodor Hausmann. Ludwig Carl came to America with the Hesse Hanau troops as fireworker, was at the Albemarle Barracks in VA, left there in June

1780, and is believed to have been in Rockingham Co., VA, with the brothers Zeller, and later with Col. Schmidt, but after he left there he has not been heard from (*Hocker* 172 cites the *Philadelphische Correspondenz* 14 Dec 1784).

HAUSSER, CASPAR, now 10 or 11 years old, son of Heinrich, who came from Switzerland to Philadelphia two years ago. Heinrich and his wife were sick on the ship and he died. Their children were indentured, and the mother lost trace of them. She has since located three of the children, and she now is seeking her son Caspar, who is 10 or 11 years old (*Hocker:*4 cites the *Pennsylvanische Geschichts-Schreiber* 16 Nov 1745).

Heinrich Debarts Hausser was in Philadelphia Co., PA, in 1763 (*AIS Census Index: Pre-1790* gives no other documentation).

A Casper Hauser, German, was naturalized in Baltimore Co., Maryland on 12 Sep 1763 (*CMN:*45).

HAWK, HENRY, left Philadelphia, PA with his dau. **MARY** about 17 years ago to purchase land in the backcountry. His eldest daughter Susanna seeks news of her father and sister. Information may be sent to John Rabhun, breeches-maker, in Third St., opposite the Workhouse, in Philadelphia (*Pa. Chronicle* 6 March 1769).

In 1782 a Henry Hawk was in Hampshire Co., VA (*AIS Census Index: Pre-1790* gives no other documentation).

HAWLEY, BENJAMIN, left England, between 20 and 30 years ago, for North America. If he is alive, and will come to the New Printing Office, in Market Street, he will hear of something to his advantage. Or, if the said Benjamin Hawley (who is supposed to have been a schoolmaster) is dead and has left any children, they are desired to apply as above (*Pa. Gaz.* 15 Dec 1757).

HAWTHORN, ALEXANDER, came from Merow, Co. Derry, Ireland. He has goods sent him from his friends. These are now in the hands of William Applebee, near the Stone Bridge in Second St. (*Pa. Gaz.* 24 May 1764). Hawthorn had a letter waiting in the Philadelphia Post Office in July 1768 (*Pa. Gaz.* 16 July 1768).

HAY, EDWARD, of Boston, a hatter and dealer in goods, about 15 years ago married one Mehitabel Webb of Wethersfield, CT. In the same year they moved to Lenox, MA, where they had one child. Thence they moved south, and the best information that their friends have obtained was that they were at or near Philadelphia in 1794. Since then no information has been received concerning them. It is feared that they have fallen victims to the fever, which in a subsequent year raged in that city. Possibly one or the other of them or some child survived. If they be living and will contact or visit their relatives, they may hear of something to their advantage. Anyone with information is asked to contact Rev. Joshua Williams or Harwinton, Litchfield Co., CT, or William Webb, Wethersfield, Hartford Co., CT (*The United States Gazette* 16 Dec 1807).

HAYLEY, THOMAS, Esq., formerly of Southgate, Mddx., and then of Bedford Row, London, came over to Philadelphia on or about 1754, where he resided some time, and then went to Chester Co., where it is supposed he died about 1767, or in Cecil Co., Maryland. Information about his death, and where, should be given to John Hill, surveyor or draftsman in Arch St. (*Pennsylvania Packet and Daily Advertiser* 14 Nov 1789).

HAYMAN, NICHOLAS, and **JOHN HAYMAN,** sons of Nicholas Hayman, dec., are asked to apply to Verplank & Crommelin, merchants in New York City for news of a legacy (*Scott* 5:20 cites *The New York Post Boy* 21 May 1750).

    JOHN, GILES, and **NICHOLAS HAYMAN** (sons of Nicholas Hayman, late of Christiana Bridge, Newcastle Co., dec.), who left the country some years ago, may claim their share in the estate of John Hayman, late of Amsterdam, dec. Their brother Peter Hayman is also expected to share in the inheritance (*Pa. Gaz.* 30 July 1752). The brothers are to appear before the High Sheriff and Aldermen of Amsterdam to prosecute their claim "on pain of eternal silence" (*Pa. Gaz.* 23 Aug 1753).

HAYNES, JOHN, of Warwick, England, born in 1758, was apprenticed in London to a S-occa [*sic*] [stucco?] plasterer. He left his apprenticeship and came to America about 8 years ago. Whoever will give information of the said John Haynes to Joseph Frobisher of Montreal, Canada, will hear of something to his advantage (*Gazette of the United States* 26 Oct 1802).

HEANE, JOSEPH, tailor, son of Thomas Heane, wheelwright, of Loughborough, Co. Leicester, Eng., came to America about 1774, and wrote to his father from MD in 1775. He is urged to contact his father or Taylor and Rogers in New York (*Maryland Journal and Baltimore Advertiser* 13 Feb 1784; *GAVN:*159, cites *The Virginia Gazette or American Advertiser* of 21 Feb 1784).

HEATON, THOMAS, left England on 26 Sep 1797. He was about 5', 6 or 7" tall, and would have been 51 in Oct 1811. The last accounts from him stated he was leaving Philadelphia for New Jersey to superintend the building of a mill for boring cannon. Anyone having information about him is asked to contact John Field, 138 S. Fourth St., or Robert Nash in Alexandria, VA (*Poulson's American Daily Advertiser* 22 March 1822).

HEBBENHEIMER, DAVID, living two miles from Easton, PA, with Stofffel Buettenbinder, is seeking information on his father's brother, who came to America several years earlier (*Hocker:*75 cites the *Pennsylvanische Geschichts-Schreiber* 5 Jan 1759).

    David Hebbenheimer, married Christina Graf on 20 Feb 1763 at The Lutheran Church in New Hanover (Falkner Swamp) Montgomery Co., PA (*PGCR* 2:347).

HEBENER, CASPAR, came to America many years ago with his brothers Georg and Heinrich. Georg now lives in Carolina. Heinrich, born in Hanover, and now working with Johann Andreas Rohr, locksmith, Second St., Philadelphia., is seeking Caspar, who formerly worked in Richard Wister's glass house in Salem, NJ (*Hocker:*113 cites the *Wochentlicher Pennsylvanischer Staatsbote* 7 April 1772).

HECKER, CAROLINE CHARLOTTE, dau. of Johann Jacob Hecker, of Quitaphilla, Lebanon Co., near Herman Ohrendorff, about six years ago indentured her to Johann

Conrad 1st. Now Hecker wants to know her whereabouts (*Hocker:*17 cites the *Pennsylvanische Geschichts-Schreiber* 16 Jan 1750).

HEDGES, THOMAS, late of Williamsburg, carpenter, left there about two years ago, saying he intended to move to SC or GA. He is asked to advise the printer where to write to him so that he may be advised of an estate fallen to him in Oxfordshire. If he does not make his claim soon, his uncle intends to enter upon it as heir, under the pretense that the said Thomas is dead without issue (*GAVN:*159 cites *The Virginia Gazette* 19 May 1738).

In Dec 1769 the Prerogative Court of Canterbury granted administration on the estate of Thomas Hedges of Wilmington, NC, widower, dec. (*CBE4*).

HEFT, JOH. PETER, from Rohrbach, near Heidelberg, a cooper by trade, in 1750 traveled to America, and since then, has not been heard from. Please inform the publisher of this paper whether he is alive or dead, and if the latter, please send a certified Burial Certificate (*Eyster:*35 cites the *Pennsylvanische Staatsbote* 14 Oct 1774).

HEIBERG, HENDRICK FINDE, native of Norway, resided in New York City in the year 1807 and at that time followed the sea. By the death of his uncle, Claude Finde, he, with others, becomes an heir to his uncle's estate. If he is alive, he is asked to contact Samuel S. Newman of New York, of Wm. Pearce and Sons, Gloucester, MA ([DC] *Daily National Intelligencer* 7 Dec 1819).

HELDTIN, MARIA CATHARINA, dau. of Maria Magdalena, two years ago was indentured by her mother to Jacob Eschelman, a smith, living two miles from Lancaster. Now the mother would like to hear from her daughter (*Hocker:*27 cites the *Pennsylvanische Geschichts-Schreiber* 1 April 1751).

HELLIER, JOHN, came from Bristol many years ago and settled on the Freshes of the Rappahannock River. If any of his descendants apply to Roger Dixon of Fredericksburg, they will hear something to their advantage. Dixon has heard of a Hilliard Family that came from Bristol and settled near the late Col. Turner on the Rappahannock (*GAVN:*159 cites the *Virginia Gazette* 20 June 1771).

In late April or early May 1721, Mr. John Hellier, bound from Bristol for Virginia was a shipper aboard the *Little York*, Capt. William Pearks (*CBE2*).

HENDRICKS, JOHN, was in Philadelphia in 1714. If he or his brother, as it appears he had one, will apply to the printers, they may hear of something to their advantage (*Pa. Gaz.* 31 Oct 1765).

HENDRICKS, WILLIAM, son of Paul Hendricks, of Towamensing, Co. Philadelphia, died last Feb. In his will, Paul left a legacy to his eldest son William, who left him about 18 years ago, and has not been heard of since. If said William is still alive, he should apply to John and Paul Hendricks, executors of the said Paul Hendricks, within one year of the latter's death, to receive his legacy; otherwise he will be excluded, agreeable to the will (*Pa. Gaz.* 15 March 1775).

HENISY, Mrs., arrived in the ship *Thomas Gibbons,* from Cork. If she will leave a line at the Post Office, addressed to H.B., she will hear something to her advantage (*Baltimore Patriot* 16 Sep 1819).

HENLEY, [-?-], son of Rev. Phocion Henley of Dorsetshire, Eng., came to America five or seven years ago. He has inherited an estate and should contact Daniel Chamier of Balto. Town (Annapolis *Maryland Gazette* 1 April 1768).

HENRY, JAMES, ELEANOR HENRY, and **JANE HENRY,** children of the nephew of Hugh Henry, Gent. (late of the Jewel Office in the Tower of London, who died on 10 Sep 1769), are to claim their shares of his estate from the High Court of Chancery (*GAVN:*161 cites *The Virginia Gazette* 3 Nov 1774).

HEPENSTIEL, [-?-], a family from Grafschaft Wittgenstein, has been in America more than thirty years. An inquiry is made for them (*Hocker:*192 cites the *Philadelphische Correspondenz* 10 May 1793).

HEPP, JOH. ULRICH, from Gesslingen, on the Staig, in Ulm, is sought by Ernst Ludwig Baisch (*Eyster:*40 cites the *Pennsylvanische Staatsbote* 26 Nov 1776).
    A Johannes Hepp was in Philadelphia Co. in 1771 (*AIS Census Index: Pre-1790* gives no other documentation).

HERBERT, Mr. JOHN, late merchant on the James River died in 1704 or 1705. His coat of arms was cut on his tombstone. He married Mrs. Frances Anderson and left three children: Butler Herbert, Richard Herbert, and Martha Herbert who married James Powell Cock. If any of his descendants apply to the printer, they may hear something to their advantage (*GAVN:*162 cites *The Virginia Gazette* 7 Aug 1752).
    John Herbert's tombstone, bearing arms and crest, reads: "Here Lyeth Interred the body of/ John Herbert, Son of John Herbert/ Apothecary, and Grandson of/ Richard Herbert Citizen & Grocer/ of London who departed this Life/ the 17th day of March 1704/ in the 46th year of his age." The tombstone was removed from Puddledock in Prince George's Co., VA. and placed in Blandford Churchyard (C. G. Chamberlayne, "Old Blandford Tombsotnes, *Virginia Vital Records,* Baltimore: Genealogical Publishing Co.).

HERBSTER, JOH. DAVID, from Graben in Durlach, is sought by Christian Buhler, lately returned from Germany, who has a letter and a present for him (*Eyster* 35 cites the *Pennsylvanische Staatsbote* 4 Oct 1774).
    A David Herbster was in Philadelphia Co. in 1750 (*AIS Census Index: Pre-1790* gives no other documentation).
    A David Herbster of Lebanon [Twp.] and Anna Maria Barbara Hacker were married on 19 Feb 1760 ("Marriage Record of Rev. John Casper Stoever, 1730-1799," *Egle's Notes and Queries Annual Volume 1896,* 99). David and Anna Maria were the parents of ("Records of the Hill Church," *Egle's Notes and Queries Annual Volume 1898,* 240): JOHN, b. 18 Aug, bapt. 23 Aug 1765 (sp.: John Hamster and wife); AGNES MARY, b. April, bapt. 22 April 1768 (sp.: Jacob Haecker and wife Agnes)

HERMANN, PHILIP HENRICH, a tailor, came to America six or seven years ago. His sister, Margaretha Dorothea Hermannin, from Betsdorf, Alsace, arrived in Philadelphia on 30 Sep 1770. She later married Jacob Paulus, a tailor. Now she is seeking her brother, and asks that word be sent to Metzner, the German apothecary, in Philadelphia (*Hocker:* 105 cites the *Philadelphia Staatsbote* 15 Jan 1771).

For more on the Hermann Family, see Burgert's *Alsace:* 246-247.

HERRINGHAM, WILLIAM, MARY, and FRANCIS, children of William Herringham, late of Greenwich, Co. Kent, Eng., left England about 25 years ago to go to some part of the West Indies, and then settled in the northern colonies. They should contact William Russell of Piscataway, Prince George's Co., MD (Annapolis *Maryland Gazette* 9 April 1767).

William Herringham was in Chesterfield Co., VA by 5 March 1753, when he witnessed the will of Stephen Gill of Dale Parish (Weisiger, *Chesterfield Co. Wills, 1749-1774*).

William Herringham married Prudence [-?-]. They were the parents of a son WLLIAM, b. on 15 May 1742 in Bristol Parish, Prince George's Co., VA (C. G. Chamberlayne, *The Vestry Book and Register of Bristol Parish, Virginia, 1720-1789*).

HERRIOTT, WILLIAM, son of Rachel Norberry, late of Middletown, Chester Co., PA., is asked to apply to Abraham Martin of Aston Twp. or to Jacob Howell, of Marcus hook, in the said county, or at the Register Office in the said county, he will hear of something greatly to his advantage. Herriott is supposed to be in some part of the Jerseys or in the New York Government (*Pa. Gaz.* 5 May 1768).

Rachel Norbury, spinster, of Chester Co., died leaving a will dated 15 March and proved 2 June 1766. Her nephew Jacob Norbury and her nieces Mary wife of William Key, and Sarah wife of Thomas Pedrick were to have £5 each. All remainder of estate real or personal was to go to son William Herriot and was to be put into the hands of Jacob Howell and his wife Ann as Trustees. Abraham Martin was named executor. Joshua Cowpland and Elisha Price witnessed the will (*Wills of Chester County, Pennsylvania.* Westminster: Family Line Publications).

HESS, HENRICH, from Hechleim, was in service in New York. Now he is sought by his brother-in-law Nicolaus Salede from Bergzeberne, but now of Tulpehocken Twp., Berks Co. (*Hocker:* 77 cites *Sower's Newspaper* 13 April 1759).

Nicholas Salade and Henrich Hess arrived on 16 Oct 1752 on the snow *Ketty* (*Eyster:* 20).

HESSIN, ANNA, HENRICH HESS, and JOHANNES HESS, and a sister who married Bastian Geringer, are sought by their sister, Anna Margretha Hessin, who is in service of James Wilson of Derry Twp., Lancaster [now Dauphin] Co. (*Hocker:* 75 cites the *Pennsylvanische Geschichts-Schreiber* 5 Jan 1759).

HEST, JOHANN PETER, was born at Rohrbach, near Heidelberg, and came to America in 1750. Michael Diffendoerfer, Lancaster, is seeking information about him (*Hocker:* 136 cites the *Wochentlicher Pennsylvanischer Staatsbote* 16 Oct 1774).

HEYWOOD, JAMES, should apply to J. Buchanan and W. Robb. A native of the Isle of Man, he left Baltimore for the West Indies about two years ago (*Maryland Journal and Baltimore Advertiser* 20 Jan 1792).

HIBBARD, RALPH, the nephew of the late Ralph Tunneliffe of Rotherham, Yorkshire, England, left Rotherham about forty years ago and was supposed to go to America. If he is now living and will apply at the offices of Messrs. Wheatley and Badger, in Rotherham, he will hear of something to his advantage (*The American Beacon and Commercial Diary* 28 Aug 1817).

HIGGINS, JOHN, late teacher of the Mathematicks in Albany Co., is asked to apply to Col. Thomas Proctor of Artillery at Philadelphia or elsewhere, where he may hear of something greatly to his advantage (*Pa. Gaz.* 18 July 1778)

HILLDRUP, SAMUEL, a native of Berkshire, old England came from Exton to this continent about 27 years ago (c1743). If he is alive and will apply in person, or direct a line for Z.Z., and will leave it with the printer, he may hear something to his advantage (*Pa. Gaz.* 22 Jan 1767).

He may be the Samuel Hildrup *alias* Grove, who was reprieved for transportation for 14 years in Devon, in Aug 1740. Transportation Bond to VA was posted (*CBEB*).

A Samuel Hilldrup was living in Annapolis in July 1743 when he advertised for the return of a runaway servant man named Thomas Overington (*Pa. Gaz.* 14 July 1743). On 14 June 1745 Samuel Hildrop [*sic*] received a payment from the estate of John Watkins of Anne Arundel Co., MD (MDAD 21:172).

Samuel Hildrup [*sic*] married Elizabeth Barbee in Spotsylvania County in Feb 1745 ("Spotsylvania Marriage Licenses," *Virginia Marriage Records,* Baltimore: Genealogical Publishing Co., p. 552).

He may be the Samuel Hilldrup who married in Oct 1753, Elizabeth Barbee, b. 1715 in Essex Co., VA. In May 1754 he was appointed guardian to Mary and Sarah Redd, orphans of Thomas Redd, and also guardian to Thomas and William Collins, orphans of Thomas Collins (William Armstrong Crozier. *Spotsylvania County Records*).

HIRTH, CHRISTOPH, needlemaker from Geildorf, Wurtemburg, is sought by Ernest Ludwig Baisch (*Eyster:*27 cites the *Pennsylvanische Staatsbote* 28 July 1772).

HOCKLIN, ELEANOR, age c60, whose maiden name was Eleanor Nicholas, was born in the Parish of Constenton, Cornwall. About eight or ten years ago she went from the Parish of Camborne, and resided in New York City. She should apply to the printer to hear something to her advantage (*Scott* 3:242 cites *The New York Gazette and Weekly Mercury* 6 Oct 1783).

HODGKINSON, JOHN, son of Peter Aris Hodgkinson, a boy of about 13 years old, was taken by a Spanish Privateer in his passage from Dublin to Philadelphia in a Brigt [Brigantine?] commanded by Zacharia Whitepain, and as the father can have no satisfactory account of him, is any person will take care of the boy, if on the Continent, among the English inhabitants, and send word to his father in Burlington [NJ], he shall receive £5 for the boy (*Pa. Gaz.* 14 Dec 1744).

HODNET, JOHN, merchant from London, may arrive in any of these parts of America. He should apply to the printer and be informed where his father-in-law lives (*The Virginia Gazette* 22-29 Oct 1736).
A John Hodnet was in Buckingham Co., VA, in 1779 (*AIS Census Index: Pre-1790* gives no other documentation).

HOFFMAN, ADAM CHRISTIAN, was born in Berlin, and was employed on business in Hamburg, London, and later Kingston, Jamaica until 1760. He left Jamaica without telling anyone where he was going. Now his sister is seeking information on him. Address any information to Johann Carl Hekker, merchant, Londonderry Twp., Dauphin Co (*Hocker:*120 cites the *Wochentlicher Pennsylvanischer Staatsbote* 16 Feb 1773).

HOFFMAN, GOTTLIEB DANIEL, born at Wertin, near Halle, was the son of a clergyman. He went to Hamburg as the servant of a merchant, and then emigrated to America several years ago. The only letter received from him came from Philadelphia and was dated 21 Aug 1786. He said he was in the service of Herbert & Potts, Alexandria, VA (*Hocker:* 203 cites the *Germantauner Zeitung* 27 Oct 1789).
   In 1790 Gottlieb Daniel Hoffman was listed in the census of the Northern Liberties of Philadelphia, p. 204 (*AIS 1790 U.S. Federal Census Index*).

HOFFMANN, JOHANN GEORG, a smith, arrived in this country five years ago from Nassau-Dillburg. His brother, Johann Jacob Hoffmann (now in Allemangel, Linn Twp., Lehigh Co., with Philip Moser), a wheelwright, arrived four years ago, and is seeking Johann Georg (*Hocker:*65 cites the *Pennsylvanische Geschichts-Schreiber* 29 Oct 1757).
   Joh. Georg Hoffman arrived on the *Forest* on 10 Oct 1752. Joh. Jacob Hoffman arrived on the *Edinburgh* on 2 Oct 1753 (*Eyster:*17).
   Johann Georg Hoffman and Henrich Schenk of Conestoga, Lancaster Co. were mentioned in the *Pennsylvanische Geschichts-Schreiber* 1 Feb 1752 (*Hocker:* 30).

HOFFMANN, JOH. MICHAEL, from Heilbrunn, is sought by Christian Buhler, lately returned from Germany (*Eyster:*35 cites the *Pennsylvanische Staatsbote* 4 Oct 1774).

HOFFSESSIN, MARIA, is sought by her mother Margretha Hoffsessin, who recently arrived in this country and is now at Oley with Antoni Jaeger (*Hocker:* 17 cites the *Pennsylvanische Geschichts-Schreiber* 1 Jan 1750).
   Margaretha Hoffsaess, from Grotzinger, Wurtemburg, after private communion, left for Pennsylvania on 15 May 1748, with Johannes Gentner, and Michael, Jacob, and Margaretha Mueller (Yoder's *PGI* 68).

HOGAN, DENNIS, about 11 years ago came to America from Co. Tipperary, Ireland, and is thought to have settled in New England. he is asked to get in touch with his brother Thomas Hogan, who came to America last fall, and is living at John McCurdy's in Albany (*Scott* 3:57 cites *The New York Gazette and Weekly Mercury* 1 Nov 1756).

HOGAN, MARGARET, four years old last spring, is sought by her mother Mary Hogan, who left her daughter with Nicholas Williams, a Frenchman, then living near Liberty Town, while she was taking care of business in Philadelphia. On her return she found that Williams had moved away, taking the child with him to some place that "all [her] vigilance has failed to find out." Williams is a silversmith, but mostly follows peddling. He and his wife, who is an Irish woman, call the child their own (Hagerstown *Washington Spy* 17 Oct 1792).

HOHREIN, TOBIAS, from Frankenbach, is sought by Christian Buhler, who has lately returned from Germany (*Eyster:*35 cites the *Pennsylvanische Staatsbote* 4 Oct 1774; *Hocker:*136).
    As Robie Hohrein, a native of Wurtemburg, he was said to have died at Fredericktown, MD in the year 1773. If his heirs will apply to the Department of State, they will receive some information that probably (Washington, D.C. *Monitor* 25 March 1809).

HOLLAND, AGNES, mother of Capt. William Holland, or her daughter Elizabeth, are asked to inquire of Henry Holland, Esq., of New York City, as they may hear something to their advantage (*New York Post-Boy* 25 June 1761).

HOLLAND, ELIZABETH, dau. of William Holland, formerly of James River, VA, shipwright, and Agnes his wife, is believed to be living in or near New York {City] on or near James River or Yorktown, VA. She may learn something greatly to her advantage by applying to Alexander Golden, postmaster of New York or to John Dixon, postmaster of Williamsburg (*GAVN:* 166 cites *The Virginia Gazette Aug 1770)*.

HOLLINGSWORTH, SAMUEL, enlisted in the United States' Service under Capt. Sands, in Baltimore in 1824 and was discharged in the South on 6 August 1827, being the termination of his period of service. If he is living, he will hear something to his advantage by application to Wm. J. Wright, S. Charles St., Baltimore (*Baltimore Patriot* 8 Aug 1831).

HOLLYDAY, CLEMENT, at present serving in the U.S. Army, should apply to his sister, Anne Cooke, or to the printer of this paper (*Maryland Journal and Baltimore Advertiser* 12 May 1778).
    Clement Hollyday was a 1st Lieut. in the Flying Camp from Washington Co., from July 1776 to 1 Dec 1776. He was a Pay Master for the 5th Regiment on 10 Dec 1776, and resigned on 25 Feb 1779 (Rieman Steuart. *A History of the Maryland Line in the Revolutionary Way 1775-1783.* Pub. by the Society of the Cincinnati of Maryland, 1969, p. 97).

HOLM, DAVID (or DONALD), house carpenter, from the parish of Rooken, Rossshire, Scotland, arrived at New York during the American War. Afterwards he went to Long Island or Philadelphia, or perhaps further southward (accounts differ). His brother John Holm has arrived from Scotland in very low circumstances, and wishes to hear from him (Frederick *Bartgis' Republican Gazette* 25 Jan 1805; The *Hornet* of 29 Jan 1805 gives his name as Donald Holm).

HOLZMANN, JOHANN HARTMANN, was born at Bonamus, near Frankfort on the Main and went to New York in June 1781, with the English 60th Regiment, under

General Amherst. Relatives in Germany are inquiring for him (*Hocker:*176 cites the *Philadelphische Correspondenz* 5 Sep 1786).

HONEY, THOMAS, son of Thomas Honey, late of Redruth, Co. Cornwall, Eng., if alive, is asked to contact John Halse, master of the ship *Royal Exchange* at Halifax, or Lawrence Kavanagh, merchant at Louisburg (*Scott* 3:99 cites *The New York Mercury* 23 Jan 1764).

HOOD, MARY, formerly Mary Beville, dau. of Joseph Beville, dec. formerly of Nottoway Co., VA, married Roland Hood, and removed to one of the western states several years since. If she will apply to H. R. Anderson, of Morganville, Nottoway, Virginia, she will hear of something to her advantage (*Richmond Enquirer* 17 Jan 1832).

HOOKE, Mr. |-?-|, came into this country about four years ago. He is to apply to Thomas Longstroth, tanner, at Chestnut Hill, or to John Longstroth, in the House of Employment, or to William Hollard, Front St., Philadelphia, merchant, to hear something to his advantage (*Pa. Chronicle* 12 Sep 1768).

HORNSBY, SAMUEL, sailed from Dublin about three years ago in a vessel commanded by Capt. Bartholomew Sinnott. He is said to have run away from the vessel. He is now about 15 years old, tall, of a swarthy complexion, marked with the small pox, and has a stoppage in his speech. If he applies to Mr. Willoughby Loftus, near the Merchants' Coffee House, in New York, he will hear something to his advantage (*Pa. Gaz.* 10 Nov 1768).

HOWARD, SUSANNA, was born in VA about 45 miles from Alexandria. The Anne Arundel County Court has issued a notice that any person who will take her to her place of birth should apply to Thomas Jennings or John Brice (Annapolis *Maryland Gazette* 18 Nov 1756).

HOWARD, Sgt. THOMAS, late of the Pennsylvania Line has died. Richard Fullerton of Philadelphia has his certificates, and asks Howard's heirs to call for them within two months of the date, or they will be returned to the office if there is no application made by that time (*Pennsylvania Packet and Daily Advertiser* 2 March 1785).

HOWE, JOHN, a colored man, sailed from Philadelphia last Dec for Charleston, and from thence to Boston. Anyone with information about him is asked to contact his old, helpless, and greatly distressed mother, Sarah Howe, who lived in Havre de Grace (*Poulson's American Daily Advertiser* 20 March 1817).

HOWEL, THOMAS, with his wife and two children, Ann and Patrick, came over in 1728 or 1729 in the ship *John and Elizabeth*, John Yoakley, master, bound from Derry, Ireland, to New Castle. If they apply to the printer, they will hear something to their advantage (*American Weekly Mercury* 25 July 1734).

HOY, RICHARD, carpenter, came from Cork, Ireland, to MD about 18 years ago. His brother John Hoy, now living on the Chickahominy River, seeks information on him

(*GAVN:* 171 cites *The Virginia Gazette* 17 Feb 1738).

On 11 Dec 1762 Richard Hoy was mentioned in the inventory of Edward Rogers of Kent Co., MD (MINV 80:25).

A John Hoy was granted 309 acres escheat land on 11 Aug 1720, lying in the fork between Pagan Creek and Young's Creek, James City County ("[James City County] Patents Issued During the Regal Government," *Virginia Land Records*, Baltimore: Genealogical Publishing Co., p. 259).

HUBER, DANIEL, for several years with Jacob Reiff, in Skippack, Montgomery Co., recently left. His brother Christian, in Conestoga [Twp.], Lancaster County, is seeking him (*Hocker* 18 cites the *Pennsylvanische Geschichts-Schreiber* 16 April 1750).

Daniel Huber, age 22, with Andreas Huber, age 20, and Jurgen Huber, age 24, arrived on the *Friendship*, Alex. Thompson, master, qualifying on 12 Oct 1741 (*PGP* 1:307).

Daniel Huber and Anna Sophia Meyer were married by Rev. Stoever on 17 April 1743 in Warwick Twp. (Wright, "Baptisms and Marriages by Casper Stoever," Wright, *Lancaster Co. Church Records of the 18th Century*).

Daniel Huber and his wife were sponsors of a child at White Oaks Church, Lancaster Co., PA, in 1754 (Wright, *Lancaster County, Pennsylvania Church Records of the 18th Century*. Westminster: Family Line Publications).

HUBER, MARTIN, native of Bazil, in Switzerland, has been absent from his family for about 10 or 12 Years, and thought to be in some part of America If he will apply to William Bayard, and Company, in New York, he may hear of something very considerable to his Advantage. N.B.: He set out from Brazil for America, and entered as a soldier, but was afterwards discharged. Any person who can give intelligence of him, whether dead or alive will be thankfully rewarded (*Pa. Gaz.* 4 March 1762).

HUBERER, GEORG, now in Carolina, and his brothers Caspar and Henrich arrived many years ago. Casper was formerly in Wister's Glasshouse in NJ. Henrich, born in Hanover and now with Andreas Rohr, locksmith, in Philadelphia, is seeking information about Georg (*Eyster:* 25 cites the *Pennsylvanische Staatsbote* 15 Jan 1771).

Henrich Hubener [*sic*] arrived on the *Lydia* on 19 Oct 1749 (*Eyster:* 25).

HUBLER, [-?-], and [-?-], brothers, from Sendfeld, near Aldesheim, Odenwald, are sought by Ernest Ludwig Baisch (*Eyster:* 27 cites the *Pennsylvanische Staatsbote* 28 July 1772).

HUFT, JOHANNES GEORG, has died and left each of his children £10. Balthasar Vettermann, Upper Milford Twp., Lehigh Co., notifies Philip Peter Huft of his father's death (*Hocker:* 170 cites the *Philadelphische Correspondenz* 13 July 1784).

HUGHES, RICE, of Clagin in the Island of Anglesea, took passage to Philadelphia in 1768. If he is still alive, and will apply to the printer he may hear of something greatly to his advantage (*Pa. Gaz.* 6 Aug 1788).

A later notice stated that Rice Hughes, son of John Hughes, late of Clegyr, in the Co. of Anglesey, gent., dec., who was brought up in the business of a carpenter, and went to Liverpool about 19 years ago, and is supposed to have sailed from there to Philadelphia. If he will apply to Messrs. Wright, Garden Court, Temple, London, or Messrs. Warder, Parker and Co., of Philadelphia, he will hear of something much to his advantage (*Pennsylvania Packer and Daily Advertiser* 23 Dec 1788).

HUMBERT, PHILIP, born at Haette, Lower Alsace, near Cronweissenburg, came to America in 1773 and is believed to be in Maryland. His brother, Bernhardt Humbert, at St. Augustine, East Florida, is seeking him (*Hocker* 142 cites the *Wochentlicher Pennsylvanischer Staatsbote* 4 April 1775).

HUMPHREYS, HUMPHREY, late of Horsham Twp., Philadelphia Co., cordwainer, enlisted as a private soldier in H.M. Service in Philadelphia, in March 1756, and has not been heard of since. If he is living he should contact his relations where he may be found. Anyone who can give true intelligence concerning Humphreys should apply to David Cummings in Elbow Lane in Philadelphia, or Humphrey Jones in Gwynedd Twp., North Wales, same county (*Pa. Gaz.* 24 Sep 1767).

Jane Williams, widow, of Montgomery, Philadelphia Co. made a will on 16 Jan 1763 and named her brother Humphrey Humphreys (Philadelphia Co. Will Book O:365).

HUNT, JANE, in 1767 sailed from Cork to MD. If she writes to Captain George Wolsey, in Baltimore, informing him of her place of residence, she will soon hear of something to her advantage (*Pa. Gaz.* 30 May 1771).

HUNT, JOHN, some years ago came from South Carolina, and is now supposed to be in Pennsylvania or New Jersey. He is desired to apply himself to Mr. Robert Ellis, or he printer of this paper, where he may hear of something of advantage to him, and find a letter for him (*American Weekly Mercury* 26 Sep-3 Oct 1734).

HUNT, JOHN, is asked to call at John Haword's in Kent Co., Maryland, where he will receive a packet from England directed to him at George William Forrester's, containing an account of his uncle's death (*Scott* 2:60 cites the *Pa. Gaz.* 21 Sep 1749).

HUNT, JOHN, saddler, left England and in 1748 resided in St. Paul's Parish. He later removed to Wetstone Parish [*sic*] in the same county; then he went to Georgia. He will hear something to his advantage if he applies to John Merryman, Jr. (Annapolis *Maryland Gazette* 21 Feb 1765).

On 10 Nov 1742 Thomas Broad and wife Anne conv. 170 a. *Broad's Improvement* to John Hunt (BALR TB#C:66). On 20 June 1749 John Hunt, with consent of wife Dorcas, conveyed the 170 a. tract to Daniel Barnett and Peter Mire (BALR TR#C:236).

He may be the John Hunt who married Dorcas [-?-], by whom he was the father of (*BAPA* 1:13, 16): EPICTETUS, b. 8 March 1738/9; PRISCILLA, b. 20 Oct 1734; SENECA, b. 31 July 1736; (son) ONESIPHORUS, b . 19 Feb 1740; and CHRISTINA EBERHARDINA, b. 20 Feb 1742.

HUNT, JOHN, a cooper, lived in Philadelphia some 15 years ago, according to letters from London received by Joseph Richardson, goldsmith, who can inform him of something greatly to his advantage (*Pa. Gaz.* 18 Sep 1766).

HUNT, JOHN, a native of Edinburgh, came to the United States in the fall of 1815, and was in business in the nursery and seed line at a place called New-Corpse, near Washington, D.C., as late as Oct 1815. His brother, William Hunt, now at Charleston, S.C., has written several times, but has received no reply. Anyone with information is asked to contact the brother at Charleston, or Mr. John Kennedy, merchant of Washington, D.C. (*The Daily National Intelligencer* 16 Aug 1817).

HUNTER, Capt. JOHN, died in April 1791. All of his sisters or their issue are to apply to William W. Pepys, Synonds Lane, Chancery Lane, London (*GAVN* 174 cites the *Virginia Gazette & Richmond Chronicle* 13 June 1794).

John Hunter, formerly of Little England, VA, but late of Bath, Somerset, Eng., died by April 1791, when administration was granted to Archibald Hamilton and Osgood Hamilton., since Benjamin Coulbourne had renounced (*AWAP*:160).

HUNTER, SAMUEL, son of William Hunter of Strabane, Co. Tyrone, if alive, is asked to call at the London Coffee House, Philadelphia, where he will receive a letter and hear something considerably to his advantage (*Pa. Gaz.* 13 June 1765).

HUNTER, SAMUEL, an elderly man, a traveler selling indigo, fell ill and died at the house of John Yocum in Douglas Twp., near Pott's Grove, Berks Co. Before he died he said his home was near Albany, where he had a wife and children. After his decease an exact account was taken of what he had with him. If his wife, or others concerned will apply to the said Yocum, and can prove the right they have as heir, they may hear of something to their advantage (*The Pennsylvania Packet or the General Advertiser* 2 Feb 1782).

HURST, CHARLES, of Chester Town, Kent County, MD, lived in this place about three years past. If he will come to the Subscriber, he will be informed of something to his advantage, as he has letters from London for that Purpose. /s/ John Hynson (*Pa. Gaz.* 24 Jan 1765).

Charles Hurst and Elizabeth Games were married on 22 Aug 1756 (by publication of banns) in St Luke's Parish, Queen Anne's Co., MD (*ESVR* 3:21).

On 9 June 1756 Charles Hurst witnessed the will of John Porter of KE Co. (MWB 30:124). On 22 Oct 1757 he and Elizabeth Hurst witnessed the will of Nicholas Brodaway of Queen Anne's Co. (MWB 30:374).

Charles Hurst, about 5'9", with coarse brown bushy hair, a well set fellow, born in England, ran away from the Kent Co. Goal, in MD. He is a very good penman, and kept School for several Years, and has been at Sea. He is about 36 years of age. He loves liquor and is pretty talkative (*Pa. Gaz.* 29 Oct 1761).

HUSCHWADER, CHRISTIAN DAVID, was born at Kircheim in the Kingdom of Wurtemburg, and went from that place about 22 years ago when he was about 42 years of age, in the capacity of a Merchant's clerk. His parents never heard anything from him since his departure. His father died about 20 years ago, and his relatives urge him to return home directly to take possession of his father's estate, which has been in the hands of an administrator. Anyone with information should contact C. W. Karthaus, Baltimore (*Baltimore Patriot & Mercantile Advertiser* 6 Nov 1818).

HUSSA, DEWALD, wheelwright, arrived in this country this year. His friend, Jacob Manny, Durham Twp., Bucks Co., living four miles from Durham Furnace, is seeking him (*Hocker:* 16 cites the *Pennsylvanische Geschichts-Schreiber* 1 Dec 1749).

A Dewald Hushaa of Brecknock Twp., Lancaster Co., PA, was naturalized in Pennsylvania some time between 24 Sep and 5 Oct 1767 (Bockstruck: 144).

HUTTON, JOHN, from Kendall, Westmorland, Eng., should apply to Carlyle and Dalton, merchants in VA, to hear something greatly to his advantage (Annapolis *Maryland Gazette* 18 Dec 1760).

HYDEN, JOHN, a baker by trade and a native of Philadelphia, left that place to go to sea. If he will contact his brother George Hyden at Elizabethtown, Lancaster County, he will something to his advantage (*Lancaster Journal* 29 Sep 1821).

IHLE, EVA MARIA, was born in Idlingen, Germany, and who came to PA in 1752, is sought by her cousin George, who came to PA in 1754. He asks that any news of her be given to Christian Ditrich in Front St., Philadelphia (*Pa. Chronicle* 10 Oct 1768).

Johan Georg Ihle arrived on the *Henrietta,* Johhn Ross, Capt., from Rotterdam, last from Cowes, on 22 Oct 1754 (*Rupp* 342). A Hans Georg Ihle was in York Co., PA by Feb 1772 (*Hocker* 112 cites the *Pennsylvanische Staatsbote* 11 Feb 1772).

George Ihle married Maria [-?-]. They were the parents of (Records of Trinity Lutheran Church, Lancaster Co., PA. *PGCR* 1:45, 51, 60): EVA MARIA, b. 11 Dec 1759, bapt. 11 May 1760; CHRISTINA SUSANNA, b. 27 Sep, bapt. 1 Nov 1761; CATHARINA BARBARA, b. 30 June, bapt. 23 Oct 1763; and ANDREAS, b. 12 June, bapt. 21 July 1765.

INNES, ALEXANDER, a hatter by trade, some time ago was on board the Frigate *Constellation* and in 1798 was in Norfolk, VA. He has not been heard of since. Anyone who knows anything of his situation or address is asked to communicate with Robert Innes, Jr., merchant, of Easton, PA (*National Intelligencer and Washington Advertiser* 1 Dec 1801).

IRVINE, GEORGE, was bred a ship carpenter, and is a well-set middle sized man, about 40 years of age. He went from London to the West Indies, and from there to North America in 1756. If he will apply to Dr. John Kearsley, Jr., of Philadelphia, or will let him know where he is living, he will hear something greatly to his advantage (*Pa. Gaz.* 13 April 1769).

ISSLER, HENDRICK, who came as a passenger on the *Nancy,* Capt. Thomas, from Rotterdam to the Patapsco River, should apply to Thomas Jones of Baltimore Co. (Annapolis *Maryland Gazette* 21 Feb 1765).

JACKSON, JOHN, brother of Robert Jackson of the Town of Armagh in Ireland, is asked to call on Rev. Mr. James Davidson near the College in Philadelphia, to be informed of something agreeable to him (*Pa. Gaz.* 20 Dec 1770).

JACKSON, PEGGY, married [-?-] [-?-], and was lately the mother of two or more children, kept a huckster shop, and took in washing. She was a native of Keswick, Cumberland, Eng. If she will apply without delay to Mr. Isaac Edmondson, 36, N. Second St., she will hear of something to her advantage (*Claypoole's American Daily Advertiser* 16 Feb 17960).

JACOB, JOHANN DANIEL, from Auerbach, near Zweibrucken, arrived in this country three years ago. This autumn, his mother, Anna Maria Jacobin, living with Johannes Berger, Reformed schoolmaster, seeks information on her son (*Hocker:* 12 cites the *Pennsylvanische Geschichts-Schreiber* 16 Dec 1748).

Daniel Jacob arrived on the *Neptune* on 25 Oct 1746 (*Eyster:* 6).

JAFFRAY, HENRY, came to this Province some 23 years ago. He was born in St. Riggings, near Sterling, Scotland. His son Henry has come over on purpose to find him. If anyone knows where he may be found, notify John McCall, tailor, at the Sign of the Hands and Shears, below the Drawbridge, or at the New Printing Office (*Pa. Gaz.* 18 Nov 1756).

JAMIESON, JOHN, tinsmith, came from Glasgow over 10 years ago; his friends have not heard from his since 1775 when he asked them to address [letters] to him care of Robert Hamilton, Ferry Creek, Augusta Co., or Mr. Lamb Lyle, merchant. If the said Jamieson is alive and will apply to Robert Thomson, merchant at Port Royal, Rappahannock, he will hear something to his advantage (*GAVN:* 180 cites the *Virginia Gazette and Weekly Advertiser* 30 Oct 1784).

A John Jameson, 23, tin plate worker, from Westminster, sailed from London the week of 3 to 10 Jan 1773, an indentured servant, sailing for Virginia on the *Adventurer* (*Fothergill:* 124).

JAMMESON, WILLIAM, came from the Shire of Renfrew, Scotland, about 14 or 15 years ago, to Philadelphia, and is now supposed to be living in some part of Virginia. If he will apply to the printer, or send a letter informing him of his residence, he will hear of something to his advantage ([PA] *Independent Gazetteer* 26 Jan 1787).

JEEK, JOHN, *alias* **JOHN TEEK,** of South Brent, Somersetshire, left England, and came to this colony where he was reportedly employed as a bailiff or under-Sheriff to a Mr. Jones; he has not been heard from for eight years. Humphrey Hill of King and Queen Co. advertises for news of him (*GAVN:* 180 cites the *Virginia Gazette* and Rind's *Virginia Gazette* 20 Jan 1774).

JETTER, THOMAS, who served his time in the butcher's trade, has followed his brother, John Jetter, who came into this country about 14 years ago. John would be glad if someone could inform the printers about [Thomas'?] whereabouts (*Pa. Gaz.* 30 April 1767).

John Jetter, Jr., was sentenced to transportation in London, and transported on the *Thames* in April 1753 (*CBEB*).

JOBBSON, RICHARD, about 30 years ago, came with his father Joseph Jobbson, from Ireland to PA. If he will return, he may meet with something considerable by applying to his relations in Cork, or to William Fennell at Surebank near Clonmell. Anyone with knowledge of whether he is alive or dead, and whether he had any legal issue should apply to Thomas Lightfoot (*Pa. Gaz.* 14 Nov 1771).

In 1790 a Richard Jobson was listed in the census of Bucks Co., PA, p. 53. A Joseph Jobson was listed in the census of Upper Providence Twp., Delaware Co., PA, p. 104 (*AIS 1790 U.S. Federal Census Index*).

JOHNSON, JOHN ROSS, is supposed to reside in the State of Pennsylvania, and a nephew of the late Major John Johnson of the Army of the United States. If he will apply to Anthony Gale, Major, Marines at the Philadelphia Marine Barracks, he will hear of something to his advantage (*Poulson's American Daily Advertiser* 25 Nov 1814).

JOHNSON, SARAH, came into PA from Ireland about twelve or fourteen years ago and served her time with one Henry Hatherton, formerly living within fourteen miles of Philadelphia. Sarah's mother Rose Crawford has come to Philadelphia, and would like to see her. Crawford, who lives next door to the Sign of Lord Loudoun in Front St., is also seeking news of her son George Hutcherson, a tailor (*Pa. Gaz.* 27 Sep 1759).

JOHNSON, WILLIAM, age c16, English servant, arrived in VA in 1768 on the ship *Justitia* from London. John Johnson wishes information on him (*GAVN:*182 cites *The Virginia Gazette* 16 April 1772).

William Johnson was reprieved and sentenced for transportation for life at Middlesex in Oct 1768; he was transported on the *Justitia* (*CBEB*).

JOHNSTON, COLIN, son of John and Jane Johnston, was born in Philadelphia, and was bound as an apprentice (by his widowed mother) to one Daniel Shirks, shoemaker of Philadelphia in the year 1759 for 14 years. Shirks is said by some to have removed to Whiteclay Creek in New Castle Co. on the Delaware. Others say that he settled between the Head of Elk and the Bohemia River in Cecil Co., MD.

If Colin Johnston is alive and will apply to his father-in-law, George Traster, living 17 miles from Lancaster, on the Philadelphia Road, or to Thomas Witherspoon in St. George's Hundred, Newcastle Co., he may hear of something to his advantage. If he cannot come in person, he may write to either, giving his place of abode, he may hear of something to his advantage. He may also apply to Daniel Cookson in Pequea. His mother and father-in-law have not heard from him in 14 years. /s/ George and Jane Traster (*Pa. Gaz.* 24 March 1773).

JOHNSTON, GEORGE, late of Kerrimore, Scotland, is asked to apply to the printer to hear something to his advantage (*Scott* 3:236 cites *The New York Gazette and Weekly Mercury* 20 May 1782).

JOHNSTON, JAMES, believed to have settled somewhere in America, is sought by his niece, Eliza LaGrize (nee Jones), who escaped over two years ago from the horrid massacre at Cap Francois, and has been wandering for two years, searching for her uncle. She asks that anyone with knowledge to contact her through the Rev. John Murray of

Boston, MA (*GAVN* 198 cites the *Republican Journal and Dumfries Weekly Advertiser* 23 June 1796).

JONES, AMOS, died testate leaving a sister Mary who married Abraham Griffith, and who had children. Her children, if living, are asked to contact Jacob Thomas of Coventry, Chester County, PA, or Abel Thomas of Exeter, in Berks Co., PA, for news of a legacy. If they were removed from the Province, it would be a kindness if their acquaintance would contact the above named persons (*Pa. Gaz.* 25 May 1774).

Hugh Jones of Hatfield, Philadelphia Co., died leaving a will dated 23 April 1758 and proved 24 Aug 1758. He named his wife Catherine, his mother Margaret Griffith, and his children Amos, Mary, Nathan, Jane and Margaret. He named a cousin Ellis Pugh. The trustees were Amos Griffith, Joseph Griffith, and Rowland Evans. The executors were Catherine and Amos Jones. Nicholas Gelis, Abram Rutt, and John Roberts witnessed the will. (Philadelphia Co. Will Book L:145).

JONES, JACOB, who has a brother at Rosseau, Dominica, is asked to apply to W. Goddard, to hear of something to his advantage (*Pennsylvania Chronicle and Universal Advertiser*, 18-25 June 1770).

JONES, JOHN, a stonemason, native of Ross, Herefordshire, was supposed to have lived in Pennsylvania in the last few years. If he is dead, did he leave any children. Information should be sent to the Post Office in Philadelphia (*Pa. Gaz.* 20 June 1751).

JONES, JOHN, a young man of middle size, and thin of flesh, about 25 years of age, left the neighborhood of Londongrove, Chester Co., in the beginning of First month last. He was heard of in two or three places in the direction of Philadelphia; the last account of him was near the 14 mile stone, on the road leading toward Westchester. Before he departed, it was observed that his mind was much depressed. Any information should be sent to: Thomas Savory, Philadelphia; William Robinson, near the Broad Ford, on Schuylkill, Townsend Lamborn, near Westchester, or Amos Harvy, near Chad's Ford, on Brandywine (*Village Record or Chester and Delaware Federalist* 13 May 1818).

JONES, LUCY, left Halifax in Aug 1819 and shortly afterwards arrived in Baltimore. Since then her mother has not heard from her. Anyone who has information is asked to send it to the office of the New York *Evening Post*, thus conferring a great favor on her parents who live in New York (*Baltimore Patriot* 19 Dec 1822).

JONES, PEREGRINE, a smooth faced middle-sized man, about 48 years old, in 1761 was supposed to have resided in a counting house in these parts or to have acted as a clerk at some iron works. If he is living he is asked to contact James Gibson of London of his place of residence and occupation, by a letter directed to John Boreman at the House of Amos Strettel in Philadelphia (*Pa. Gaz.* 24 May 1764).

A Peregrine Jones had his property over the Blue Mountains, about 18 miles from Easton [PA] seized in execution. The property will be sold on 22 June 1774 (*Pa. Gaz.* 1 June 1774).

In 1790 a Peregrine Jones was listed in the census of Luzerne Co., PA, p. 149 (*AIS 1790 U.S. Federal Census Index*).

JONES, WILLIAM, formerly of the City or County of Cork, came into this country about twenty years ago, and his relations have not heard from him for the past eighteen years. If he is still living, he is asked to direct a letter to James Rose opposite the "George," in Arch St., Philadelphia, giving his place of residence (*Pa. Gaz.* 10 Feb 1763).

JOURDAN, HENRY, formerly of Co. Down, Ireland, left Ireland before the American War, and was a resident of Baltimore after the war. In a letter he stated he was married and intended to remain in Baltimore. He had with him a sister Jane Jourdan who had also gotten married (*Federal Intelligencer and Baltimore Daily Gazette* 26 Aug 1795).

Henry Jordan and Elizabeth Murfort were married 26 Oct 1778 in BA Co., MD (Marriage returns of Rev. Thomas Chase). That same year Henry Jordan of Baltimore Co. was a non-juror to the Oath of Allegiance (*BARP:* 147).

In 1783 Henry Jordan was a taxable in Baltimore East Hundred, BA Co. His household consisted of two white males and two white females (Bettie S. Carothers, *1783 Tax List of Baltimore County, MD.* Lutherville: 1978: p. 10). In 1790 Henry "Jordon" [*sic*] was head of a family in Baltimore Town, with one white male over 16, one white male under 16, and five white females (*1790MD,* p. 20, col. 1).

Jane Jordan m. Thomas Williams, in BA Co., MD, on 25 Nov 1781 (Marriage Returns of Rev. William West in Robert Barnes, *Maryland Marriages, 1778-1800.* Baltimore: Genealogical Publishing Co.).

JOUVENAL, MAGDALEN, came last fall with her father from Holland in a ship consigned to James Pemberton. She was sold to one Richard Bowman. Her father is seeking news of her. Any such news of her should be brought to said Pemberton or to Anthony Benezet in Philadelphia (*Scott* 2:227 cites the *Pa. Gaz.* 19 April 1753).

KAIN, WILLIAM, of England's Grove, about 54 miles from Philadelphia, came to Pennsylvania about 46 years ago, and had three sons by the wife he first married, all settled in these parts. His brother [*sic*], John Keenhan (Keenban), of the Township of Ballymony in the Barony of Ballybrit, King's Co., Ireland, has arrived at Philadelphia, but he cannot by any means find out the said William, or any place called England Grove. John Keenban is at the house of Thomas Howard, joiner, Second St., Philadelphia (*Pa. Gaz.* 28 May 1730).

KATLER, PETER, son of Stephanus and Magdalena Katler (who came to Philadelphia nine years ago) went to the Raritan region of New Jersey, and was with some Dutch people there. His father has died, and Peter is sought by his brother Michel, who is with Michael Schenck, one mile from Lancaster (*Hocker:* 73 cites the *Pennsylvanische Geschichts-Schreiber* 28 Oct 1758).

A Michael Katler married Charlotte [-?-], and they were the parents of: ANDREW, b. 9 Oct 1764, bapt. 14 Oct 1764 at Christ Evangelical Lutheran Church, York (Bates and Wright. *York Co. Church Records,* vol. 2).

KAVANAGH, MATTHEW, carpenter, lately of New Port, in Nova Scotia, left there in 1789 and came to some part of the United States. He is supposed to be in Kentucky. His brother Patrick Kavanagh, of Halifax, Nova Scotia, asks him to write to him as it would be much to his advantage (*GAVN:* 189 cites *The Examiner* 26 March 1799).

KEAN, MARY, about 15 years of age, came over from Ireland, with Capt. Clark, in the ship *Providence,* and was sold at New Castle two years [ago] this Fall. Her mother doesn't know where she was sold or to whom, and asks anyone who knows of her to write to the Mother, living in Windsor Twp., Middlesex Co., East Jersey, at Mr. John Lecount's (*Pa. Gaz.* 20 Sep 1764).

KEARNS, JOHN, native of Ireland, near Cumber. Co. Down, died in Oct 1781 in Newtown, long Island, and it is supposed that some of his relations now reside in the State of Pennsylvania. If they will apply to Messrs. Jacob Benning Hove and Co., of Philadelphia, or Mr. Peter Dustan, they will hear of a sum of money found, which is supposed was the property of the deceased (*Poulson's American Daily Advertiser* 5 May 1809).

KEATING, WILLIAM, formerly a resident of London as an attorney, is now supposed to be near Winchester [Virginia]. If he will apply to Samuel Pleasants, printer of Richmond, he will hear something to his advantage (*GAVN:* 190 cites *The Richmond and Manchester Advertiser* 26 Nov 1795; *Bowen's Virginia Centinel and Gazette* 14 Dec 1795).

KEAY, PHILIP, of VA, was sent a letter from a relative in Whitechurch, Shropshire, Eng. (*GAVN:* 190 cites the *Va. Gaz.* 29 Nov 1770).

KEENS, MICHAEL, a Dutch lad was imported into this country a year ago and sold to Christopher Yust. John Keens, Michael's father, wishes to hear from his son (*Scott* 2:234 cites the *Pa. Gaz.* 24 May 1753).

KEEPER, CHRISTIAN, miller, born in Hanau, came to America 18 or 19 years ago. Friederich Mayer, 92 Market St., Charleston, SC is inquiring for him (*Hocker:* 189 cites the *Philadelphische Correspondenz* 29 May 1791).

KELLER, JOHANN GEORG, arrived in America with his mother nineteen years ago, and with his mother served with Jacob Fries, Gohansey, Salem Co., NJ. He is seeking his mother who went to VA some three years ago. Notify Johannes Fries, Race St., Philadelphia (*Hocker:* 151 cites the *Wochentlicher Pennsylvanischer Staatsbote* 21 May 1776).

KELLY, RICHARD, son of John, of Galway, Ireland, came to America in the Year 1750, and has formerly taught school near Mr. Robert McMullin, in Darby Township. If he will repair to the printers hereof next Saturday, or any other Saturday till the first of next April, and, by certain marks, proving himself to be the same, may hear of something greatly to his advantage. N.B.: The Reason why on Saturday, and no other day in the week, is because the person who can give proper Intelligence, as he lives in the country, cannot with convenience attend on other days. If said Kelly is living, he is required to leave a memorandum at the New Printing Office (*Pa. Gaz.* 13 Nov 1760).

Richard Kelly, a native Irish servant man ran away on 19 April 1755. He might change his name as his indenture shows the name Richard Benson. He is about 19 years old, 5'5" high, well set, of a red complexion, much freckled on his face and on his hands. He can speak good English, can read and write well, and understand something of the Latin tongue. He is a sensible crafty fellow, and may forge himself a pass and other writings to help him along (*Pa. Gaz.* 24 April 1755).

KENNEDY, JOHN, who came from London to MD in Oct 1773, was asked to apply to the Baltimore Post Office (*Maryland Gazette or Baltimore General Advertiser* 9 May 1775).

KENNEDY, JOHN, from Connecticut, went to the Eastern Shore of Maryland to sell horses and mules. A person was sent from Dover to find him, and tracked him to Cambridge, and then to Easton. He returned to Choptank Bridge, and then set out for Dover. He was last heard from on 2 February. He is about 24 years of age, slender built, nearly six feet high. Anyone with information is asked to contact Daniel Hindsdale at Hartford, CT (*Gazette of the United States* 18 March 1797).

KENNEDY, NICHOLAS, son of John Kennedy of Co. Entrim [Antrim], Ireland, is urged to contact his brother Neal Kennedy, care of Patrick Green, Lancaster Co., where Neal Kennedy plans to live (*Lancaster Journal* 27 Aug 1803).

KENT, Mr., reportedly lived in Lancaster Co., VA, and enlisted under Capt. Wright Westcot to serve on board the *Norfolk Revenge* galley. His heirs are asked to apply to Joseph Scott, Jr., in Suffolk Co. or to John Scott in Nansemond Co., for a sum of money left at his decease (*GAVN:* 193 cites *The Virginia Gazette* 17 July 1778).

KERCKHART, VELTEN, came into this country seven years ago from Reuberem, on the Brem. He is sought by Arion [?] Kerckhart, over the Susquehanna, near York, who arrived last autumn from Neu Hemsbach, and who calls Velten his "vetter" (cousin or uncle) (*Hocker:* 22 cites the *Pennsylvanische Geschichts-Schreiber* 16 Sep 1750).
  Andon Kirchhart arrived on the *Edinburgh* on 15 Sep 1749 (*Eyster:* 9).

KERN (KIRN), HANS GEORG, wheelwright from Grossen Astbach, Wurtemburg, is sought by Ludwig Batsch (*Eyster:* 23 cites the *Pennsylvanische Staatsbote* 12 June 1770).
  Hans George Kern arrived 17 Oct 1749 on the *Fane* (*Eyster:* 23).

KERTZ, FRIEDRICH, butcher servant in PA, came from Dornstatt, Wurtemberg, some twelve years ago (*Hocker:* 114 cites the *Wochentlicher Pennsylvanischer Staatsbote* 28 July 1772).

KESZLER, JOH. GEORG, ADAM KESZLER, ANNA MARGARETHA KESZLER, and **EVA KESZLER,** four children of Wilhelm Keszler, of Nieder Husselbach, Ober-Amt Herrstein, dec. Friedrich Sebastian Marker, master tailor, Pine and Seventh Sts., Philadelphia, is seeking them (*Hocker:* 178 cites the *Philadelphische Correspondenz* 17 April 1787).

Johann George Kessler was in Philadelphia Co. in 1772 (*AIS Census Index: Pre-1790* gives no other documentation).

KEUCHELER, CHRISTOPH, son of Johannes, of Conestoga Twp., Lancaster Co., PA, near Mansz Graff, was indentured by his father for his passage costs. The son was transferred from one master to another, and the father lost trace of his son, whom he is now seeking. He was last known to be living with Robert Betz (or Bates) (*Hocker:* 7 cites the *Pennsylvanische Geschichts-Schreiber* 16 April 1747).

KEYSER, JOHANN ULRICH, came to America twenty years ago with his wife and child. Now he is sought by his sister's son, Johannes Ostertag, linenweaver from Hohen Meiningen, Wurtemberg, who arrived this autumn in Capt. Smith's ship. His wife died on the voyage, and he is not yet free from the ship (*Hocker:* 119 cites the *Wochentlicher Pennsylvanischer Staatsbote* 8 Dec 1772).

KILRAN [KIDRAN?], LUKE, aged about 48 or 49, a native of Ireland, was last heard from residing among the Creeks in Georgia, about 20 years ago. Any information about him will be thankfully received by the editor of the *Franklin Repository,* Chambersburg (*Carlisle Republican* 29 June 1819).

KING, JOHN, mariner, son of Esther King, late of King and Queen Co., VA, dec., was in Liverpool at the time of his mother's decease. He has inherited a considerable portion of the estate of Mrs. Anne Clowes of Liverpool. He has not been seen in the latter city for some six years (*GAVN:* 196 cites *The Virginia Independent Chronicle and General Advertiser* 26 May 1790).

KINGSLEY, GEORGE, a mariner, short and thick set, and originally from Carolina, is supposed to have died at Fell's Point in 1797. Anyone possessing any of his papers, or having any information about him is asked to apply to Messrs Bedford and Martin, No. 42 Water St. (*Federal Gazette and Baltimore Daily Advertiser* 19 Oct 1801).

KINSELL, FREDERICK, *alias* **FREDERICK BENJAMIN OTTO KUNTZELL,** hairdresser, and teacher of English, was in Philadelphia in 1784, and in Baltimore in 1788. He is summoned to return to Demmin to claim a small patrimony, or else make it over either his sister-in-law Elizabeth Schenekin, now married to a man named Schultz, or to his sister Catherine Juliana Kuntzell, now married to a shoemaker named Kobrow, since bankrupt and living at Dargum in Mecklenburg. The regiment in which Kinsell was enrolled also claims the money. /s/ The Burgomaster and Senate (*Maryland Journal and Baltimore Advertiser* 11 Dec 1792).

　　In 1790 Fred'k Kinsell was head of a family in Baltimore Town, with two white males over 16, one white male under 16, and four white females (*1790MD* 21, col. 1).

　　Frederick Kinsall was leader of a class at the Baltimore City Station, M.E. Church (*BCMR* 1:195).

KIRK, THOMAS, was transported from London c1765; about 1771 he told relatives he was an usher to a Mr. Hart, a schoolmaster in Baltimore, or some other place in MD. He is reported to have left MD and gone to Berkeley Co., VA, near Winchester, and kept a school.

Thomas Kirk was sentenced to transportation and transported in April 1765 on the *Ann,* from London (*CBEB*).

Thomas Kirk came into this country about 18 years ago from England. He is asked to apply to Dr. John Stevenson of Baltimore Town (*Maryland Journal and Baltimore Advertiser* 5 Sep 1783).

He is said to have died in 1783, but a Mr. Kirk was in Winchester in 1787 and in 1788 was in Baltimore. He or his children have a legacy in England (*GAVN:* 197 cites *The Virginia Centinel or Winchester Mercury* 14 May 1788).

KIRKPATRICK, THOMAS, a native of Scotland, and a stout well-made man, used to travel as a peddler in the neighborhood of Chesnut Hill and Whitemarsh, has been for a long time missing. Anyone who may know of his death or departure, or who may know of any property left by him, is asked to contact James & Richard Smith (*Pa. Gaz.* 18 July 1748).

KIRSCHMAN, CATHARINA, and her daughters **MARIA KIRSCHMAN,** and **CATHARINA KIRSCHMAN,** are sought by their son and brother, Johan Martin Kirschman, from the Wurtemburg domain of the Palatinate Duke in Weiler, and now of Maidencreek Twp., Berks Co., who is also seeking information about his two brothers-in-law Christian and Friedrich Schwartz (*Hocker:* 87 cites the *Pennsylvanische Geschichts-Schreiber* 13 Feb 1761).

Hans Martin Kirschman arrived 19 Sep 1752 on *Edinburgh,* James Russell, capt., Amsterdam, last from Cowes (Rupp, *Names of Thirty Thousand Immigrants:* 273).

KIRWAIN, Capt. MATTHIAS, of DO Co., master of the schooner *Sally,* took a cargo of wheat on board on the Rappahannock River addressed to A. Houghan, and has not been heard of since. Anyone with information is asked to contact A. Houghan (*Baltimore Patriot and Mercantile Advertiser* 16 Oct 1818).

KISTLER, HENRICH, who arrived in this country twelve years ago, is sought by his brother Johann, from the "Berner Gebiet, von Boetzen," who arrived this year, and is with Abraham Herr, Conestoga, Lancaster Co. (*Hocker:* 17 cites the *Pennsylvanische Geschichts-Schreiber* 16 Jan 1750).

Heinrich "Kistner," age 40, arrived on the *Charming Nancy* on 9 Nov 1738; Johannes Kessler arrived on the snow *Good Intent* on 9 Nov 1749 (*Eyster:* 7-8).

John Kistler of Berks Co., PA, was naturalized on 10-12 April 1762 (Bockstruck:159).

KLAAR, SIMON, arrived in this country six years ago, and was indentured as a servant. His sister Barbara became free two years ago, and is now seeking her brother (*Hocker:* 8 cites the *Pennsylvanische Geschichts-Schreiber* 16 May 1747).

Simon Clar married Margaretha [-?-]. They were the parents of at least two children, baptized at St. Matthew's Lutheran Church, York Co., PA (*York Co. Church Records*): ELISABETHA, b. 26 Feb 174, bapt. 10 July 1774 (spon.: Frederick Eyler and Catharina

Reinecker): and SUSANNA, b. Feb 1776, bapt. 7 April 1776 (spon.: Jacob Schlegel and Susanna Schlegel).

KLEIMENHAGEN, JOHN HENRY, possibly living in Baltimore, MD, is sought by his brother, William Kleimenhagen, from Waldeck, Upper Waroldern, Germany, who is now living with Abraham Kegy of Lancaster Co., PA (*Maryland Journal and Baltimore Advertiser* 10 April 1789).

KLEIN, CARL, locksmith, from Zweibruecken, came to America a year and a half ago, with his son Georg, 12 years old, who was indentured to John Dunlap, printer, Philadelphia. Dunlap is now seeking information about Klein (*Hocker:* 140 cites the *Wochent-licher Pennsylvanischer Staatsbote* 7 March 1775).

KLEIN (or KLAEN), HANSZ MICHAEL, age 14, and **ANDREAS KLEIN,** age 12, sons of Matheus, who arrived in America last autumn from Rexingen, Nassau, and indentured the two sons. Matheus was sick at the time and received no indenture papers, nor did he know the names of the masters. He died and now the widow is seeking her two sons. Information may be sent to David Schaefer at Philadelphia (*Hocker:* 48 cites the *Pennsylvanische Geschichts-Schreiber* 1 May 1755). (*Eyster* gives the name as Klan)
For more on the Klein or Klaen family, see Burgert's *Alsace* 297.

KLEIN, PHILIP, was born in Adenbach and served his time as a redemptioner fifteen miles from Philadelphia. Jacob Marx is seeking him. Notify Jacob Ableiter, living at the seven miles tone, Germantown (*Hocker:* 165 cites the *Philadelphische Correspondenz* 22 July 1783).

KLEIN, PHILIP HENRICH, was born in Limbach. His wife is a sister of the mother of Johann Martin Puff, son of Joh. Peter Puff, of Nassau-Itstein. Johann Martin Puff was indentured to John Hutchinson, of Bristol, Bucks Co., PA, and now is seeking Klein. (*Hocker:* 127 cites the *Wochentlicher Pennsylvanischer Staatsbote* 10 Nov 1773; *Eyster:* 34 cites the *Pennsylvanische Staatsbote* 30 Nov 1773).
Joh. Martin Puff arrived on the *Charming Molly* on 22 Oct 1773 (*Eyster:* 34).

KLEINBEHL, JOHN, of Dornheim, Hesse-Darmstadt, baker, son of John Daniel Kleinbehl of the same place, dec., came to Philadelphia about 1754. At the age of about 20 he was bound to Obadiah Robin of Cumberland Co., West New Jersey. His relations in Germany would be glad to hear from him. If he is living, and will apply to Peter Miller, Notary Public in Second St., near Race St., Philadelphia, he may hear something to his advantage. Philip Sansfelder, a relation of Kleinbehl (or Leinbehl) is going to Germany, with Capt. Smith (*Pa. Gaz.* 23 Oct 1766)
Johannes Kleinbehl arrived on the *Neptune*, Capt. Ware, from Rotterdam, on 30 Sep 1754 (*PGP* 1:622).

KLEMEKE, CHARLES WILLIAM, formerly of London, left England for the United States in 1796. If he is living he should apply personally or by letter to John Carrere in Baltimore, or to Messrs. Isaac Hazlehurst and son in Philadelphia, where he may hear of something greatly to his advantage (*Federal Gazette and Baltimore Daily Advertiser* 15 May 1798).

KLINGENMEYER, CONRAD, aged about 14, came to this country in Oct 1751 on the ship *Duke of Wirtemberg*, Capt. Montpelier. He was bought by a man who lives 30 miles from Philadelphia on the Germantown Road. Conrad's father, Conrad Klingenmeyer, seeks information on his son, News to be sent to David Hall (*Scott* 2:200 cites the *Pa. Gaz.* 19 Oct 1752).

KLUNTZ, CONRAD, is sought by his sister Anna Dorothea Kluntzin, now with George Mueller, Maxatawny (Berks Co.), and who arrived in America seven years ago (*Hocker:* 82 cites the *Pennsylvanische Geschichts-Schreiber* 9 Nov 1759).

KNIGHT, [-?-], apothecary at Tottenham, near London, came to this country some years ago. If he will apply to the printers, he may hear something to his advantage (*Pa. Gaz.* 25 May 1774).

KNIGHT, CHARLES, on 8th inst., in the prosecution of his profession, walked out from his family in Philadelphia, promising to return the same evening, but he did not return, and it is presumed some accident has befallen him. He was 27 or 28 years old, 5'10 or 11", fair complexion. He had with him several miniature pictures, with apparatus for miniature painting. Any information concerning him, should be communicated to Mr. Isaac Pearson, stationer, 109 Market St., and will be gratefully acknowledged by a distressed wife and family (*Poulson's American Daily Advertiser* 29 Aug 1806).

KNOEHE, JOANETTE CHRISTINE, late **KIMMEL**, a native of Wisbaden near Frankford on the Main, Germany, who is known to have lived for a considerable time, in East Pennsborough Twp., Cumberland Co., PA, is requested to call at John Halse at Bethlehem, Northampton Co., where she will hear something to her advantage (*The Carlisle Gazette and the Western Repository of Knowledge* 28 Aug 1793).

KNOWLES, JOHN, served his apprenticeship with [-?-] West of Reading, Berkshire, and then resided at Folkestone, Kent. He is a watchmaker, and nephew to William Wood of London. He has been married for some years and has resided at Philadelphia. He left Philadelphia in 1792 leaving a wife and three children. If he will apply to Thomas Stewardson of Philadelphia, or Edward Jansen or Anthony Horne of London, he will hear of something to his advantage (*Poulson's American Daily Advertiser* 2 March 1803).

KNOX, VICTOR, some time ago lived in Lancaster, PA, where he was a peddler. Nothing has been heard from him for a year. Anyone with information is asked to contact Anthony Porter (*Pa. Gaz.* 24 Oct 1751).

Another notice, placed the following week stated that Victor Knox had been dead for six years. James Knox, brother and heir-at-law of the said Victor, asks Porter to contact him (*Pa. Gaz.* 31 Oct 1751).

KOEBLIN, MARIA BARBARA, care of Thomas Clime, Quaker, at Pequea, advertises that her daughter, aged 18, left the Little Brandywine last Christmas for Lancaster to enter service, and has not been heard of since (*Hocker:* 101 cites the *Wochentlicher Pennsylvanischer Staatsbote* 22 May 1770).

KOENIG, GEORGE MICHAEL, and CATHERINE KOENIG, born at Hocksted, Germany, relations of George Stower and Joachim Stower living in Paradise Twp, York Co., came into this country about 25 years ago, but were never heard of since. They are asked to send words to their relations, or to John George Kuhn or Bernard Holzinger in York Town (*Pa. Gaz.* 8 Nov 1764).

KOERGER, JOHANN PHILIP, from the Palatinate, Dorf Krolsheim, near Bingen now lives at Neudorlach, near Schoharie, forty miles west of Albany, NY. He wishes to notify his sister, Anna Maria, wife of Anton Miller, and his sister's daughter, the wife of Valentin Gaul (her father being Matthias Best), who have come from Germany to Philadelphia (*Hocker:* 190 cites the *Philadelphische Correspondenz* 14 Aug 1792).

KOELLERIN, MARGRETHA, widow, arrived in America eight years ago from the Zurich region. Her brother Hans Ulrich Wuensch, Conestoga, Manor Twp, Lancaster Co., with John Ross is seeking Her (*Hocker:* 73 cites the *Pennsylvanische Geschichts-Schreiber* 14 Oct 1758; see also *Eyster:* 19).

Hans Ulrich Wunsch and Hans George Keller arrived on the brigantine *Sally,* on 17 Oct 1750 (*Eyster:* 19).

KOHL, CHRISTIAN, baker, about 50 years old, was born at Frankfort on the Main and left there thirty-four years ago. Nicolaus Kohl, Lancaster, is seeking him (*Hocker:* 178 cites the *Philadelphische Correspondenz* 9 Jan 1787).

KOHLER, JACOB, has been in America for twenty years ago, and nine years ago lived on a farm in NY, but is now believed to be in VA, is sought by his brother Nicolaus Kohler, farmer, from Muelhofen, two hours above Landay, son of Andreas Kohler, arrived in America last autumn (*Hocker:* 115 cites the *Wochentlicher Pennsylvanischer Staatsbote* 23 June 1772).

Jacob Kohler arrived on the *Phoenix* on 25 Sep 1751, Capt. Spurrier, from Rotterdam and Portsmouth (*PGP* 1:471). Nicklaus Kohler arrived on the Brigantine *Recovery,* [-?-] Bull, master, from Rotterdam, last from Cowes, on 30 Oct 1771 (*Names of Foreigners* 498).

KONKEL, PETER, arrived in Philadelphia from Holland [as] a servant, between five and six years ago, and is sought by his brother Andrew, living with Samuel Smith in Burlington, West Jersey. All Andrew knows about his brother is that he was sold to one Isaac Garrett, a few miles over Schuylkill. Garrett or his brother should contact Andrew, or leave word at Shoemaker's Store in Philadelphia (*Penna. Gaz.* 31 Jan 1760).

KRAFFTBERGER, ULRICH, arrived in this country two years ago. His sister, Anna Barbara Krafftbergerin, with Conrad Schwartz, Lancaster, is seeking him (*Hocker:* 45 cites the *Pennsylvanische Geschichts-Schreiber* 16 Dec 1754).

KRAG, GEORGE, son of John and Beatrice Krag, of Whitehall Twp., Northampton Co., PA, who came to this province and brought several children with them, was bound to some person in the Jerseys, down the Delaware River, and has not been heard from since. If he is "yet in being" [is still alive], he is asked to inquire for his said parents at Mr. Sower's, Printer, in Germantown, or to contact George Good, living at Cedar Creek, Northampton Co. (*Pa. Gaz.* 5 March 1761).

KRAUEL, JOHANN CONRAD, a miller, who came to America from London four years ago, is sought by his brother, Johann Andreas Krauel, at the Golden Swan Inn, Third St., Philadelphia, and who was born in Grossen Bernden, Brandenburg (*Hocker:* 128 cites the *Wochentlicher Pennsylvanischer Staatsbote* 14 Dec 1773).

KRAUL, ANDREAS, who arrived in America last autumn, is sought by his brother Conrad Kraul, miller, near Lebanon (*Hocker:* 133 cites the *Wochentlicher Pennsylvanischer Staatsbote* 7 June 1774).

KRAUSZ, ELIZABETH, who came to America about 26 years ago from Konsheim, in the Palatinate, is sought by her brother Simon, living six miles above Harris' Ferry, at the English meeting house, Cumberland Co., who came to America about the same time (*Hocker:* 151 cites the *Wochentlicher Pennsylvanischer Staatsbote* 7 June 1776).

For more on the Kraus family, see Annette K. Burgert's *Brethren from Gimbsheim in the Palatinate to Ephrata and Bermudian in Pennsylvania.* Myerstown: AKB Publications.

KREBS, PETER, his wife **MAGDALENA KREBS**, and their family arrived at Philadelphia five years ago last autumn. Their daughter, Anna Maria, was indentured at Lancaster, to English people, who removed to Charlestown, MD, and then to Williamsburg, VA. Maria was freed and is now in Baltimore, with Samuel Hook, and she is seeking her mother (*Hocker:* 70 cites the *Pennsylvanische Geschichts-Schreiber* 10 June 1758).

In 1790 Petter [*sic*] Krebs was head of a family in Codorus Twp., York Co, PA (*AIS 1790 Census Index*).

For more on the Krebs Family, see Burgert's *Alsace* 314-315.

KRISCHERIN, SOPHIA, MARIAMEL KRISCHERIN, and **MARIA KRISCHER LIEBERIN**, from Alzey, are sought by their brother, Jacob Krischer of Lancaster, Pennsylvania (*Hocker:* 99 cites the *Pennsylvanische Geschichts-Schreiber* 9 April 1762).

KRUG, THEODORE, arrived at this port in Sep [1817? 1827?] from Brunswick, Germany. If he will come to the City of New York and call upon F. S. & P. Schlesinger, No. 112 Pearl St., or John Hildreth, No. 22 Nassau St., he will hear something much to his advantage. The last information from Mr. Krug is that he left the employ of Mr. John

Kulp in Andalusia, PA in June 1828. There is a letter her from Germany with important information in it (*Baltimore Patriot* 3 Nov 1829).

KUDER, JOH. PETER, and JOH. BERNHARD KUDER, from Frankenbach, are sought by Christian Buhler (*Eyster:* 35 cites the *Pennsylvanische Staatsbote* 4 Oct 1774).

KUEMMERLY, HANS, born in Schleydorf, Wurtemberg, who came to America fifteen years ago, is sought by his brother Michel Kuemmerly of Tyrone Twp., York Co., Pennsylvania. Their father died on the voyage, and their mother died soon after arriving at Philadelphia. Address in care of William Walker, storekeeper in Tyrone Twp (*Hocker:* 101 cites the *Wochentlicher Pennsylvanischer Staatsbote* 19 Dec 1769; *Eyster:* 23 gives this name as Michael Kummer).

KUHN, ANNA MARIA, is sought by her parents, Johannes and Barbara Kuhn, who are living in New York, opposite the High School, and who have not seen their daughter for thirteen years (*Hocker:* 85 cites the *Pennsylvanische Geschichts-Schreiber* 11 Aug 1760).
    Johannes Kuhn, farmer, and Anna Barbara, dau. of Hans Jacob Adam, the village watchman, went to Pennsylvania in 1753 with her old father and three children (Marriage Register of Schlaitdorf, Wurtemberg). Johannes Kuhn and Hans Jacob Adam arrived 17 Sep 1753 on the ship *Richard and Mary.*
    Johannes and Anna Barbara were the parents of: ANNA BARBARA [*sic*], b. 10 Oct 1742; JOHANN JACOB, b. 22 Oct 1744; EUPHROSINA, b. 16 Oct 1746; and ANNA CATHARINA, b. 28 Sep 1749 (Yoder's *PGI* 81).

KUHN, FRANZ PAUL, tanner, who came to America in 1764, is being sought by his brother Ludwig Conrad Kuhn, born at Aldensimmern, innkeeper at Mannheim, in the Palatinate at the Sign of the Elephant in the house that was formerly a pipe factory, and who arrived at Philadelphia on 3 Oct in the ship *Mary,* Capt. Fitzpatrick. In Feb 1791 Ludwig Conrad Kuhn announced he was going to Germany in March (*Hocker:* 186, 187 cites the *Philadelphische Correspondenz* 15 Oct 1790, 4 Feb 1791).

KUHN, MARTIN, son of George Martin Kuhn, is sought by his uncle Johann Georg Kuhn, who is living near the Gwynedd meeting House, Montgomery Twp., Montgomery Co., (*Hocker:* 78 cites the *Pennsylvanische Geschichts-Schreiber* 5 June 1759).
    Hans Georg Kuhn, and Margaretha Kuhn, in 1752 left Webenheim, Oberamt Zweibrucken for America. Johann George Kuhn arrived 14 Sep 1753 on the ship *Edinburgh* ("List of Emigrants from Zweibrucken, 1750-1771," in Yoder's *PGI* 324).
    Newman, in *Maryland Revolutionary Records,* p. 117, states that the marriage of a John George Kuhn to Catherine Smith about 1800 probably in MD, was established by a Revolutionary Pension application.

KUHRT, MARGARET, dau. of John Ernest Kuhrt (now at Quitipshiullin Creek, Lancaster Co., near Jacob German's plantation), on 22 Sep 1753 was bound before the Mayor of the City of Philadelphia to one Robert Ludlam, but his place of abode is not mentioned in the Indenture. John Ernest Kuhrt, is anxious to locate his daughter (*Pa. Gaz.* 8 Oct 1761).

J. Ernst Kurt arrived on the ship *Queen of Denmark*, Capt. George Parish, from Hamburg, last from Cowes, and qualified on 11 Sep 1753 (*Names of Foreigners* 382).

KURTZIN, ELISABETHA BARBARA, born in Ober Amt Kayserslautern, Dorf Katzenbach, came to Philadelphia eight years ago, served in Lancaster, and married Johannes Ziegler. Heinrich Kurz [*sic*] is seeking information about her. Notify Friedrich Dietz, tailor, in Philadelphia (*Hocker:* 149 cites the *Wochentlicher Pennsylvanischer Staatsbote* 16 Feb 1776).

LABRETECHE, PIERRE-MARIE-ANNE-FRANCOIS, born at La Fire in the *ci-devant* Picardy on 14 Aug 1761, embarked with a passport to the United States on 10 Feb 1790, on the ship *le Patriote*, Capt. Legros, as a passenger. He is requested to submit to his family, the Certificate of his uninterrupted residence among a free people, the ally of the French Republic, in the form prescribed by a decree of the National Convention. This will preserve his name from appearing in the list of the Emigrants, save his fortune and that of his father and sisters, who wish as much from attachment as for their personal tranquility, to receive as soon as possible the above certificates, and his power of attorney for the partition of the estate of his mother, deceased, in the first days of October 1793 ([PA] *Aurora General Advertiser* 12 Nov 1794).

LACY, SAMUEL, born in Northants., Eng., who came to America about 20 years ago with Charles French, who lives at Ancocus Creek in Burlington Co., West Jersey, will hear some thing to his advantage if he will come to Henry Flower, postmaster in Philadelphia (*AWM* 18 April 1722).

LAECKIN, ELIZABETH, dau. of Paul Laeck, who left the family twenty years ago, and for a time was at Pottsgrove, is sought by her sister Polly Laeckin, at the Inn of Andreas Drumber, Lower Milford Twp., Bucks Co. (*Hocker:* 189 cites the *Philadelph-ische Correspondenz* 23 March 1792).

LAFFERTY, EDWARD, was a soldier in the 4th PA. Regiment. Edward Butler of Carlisle is holding a certificate for 42.4.5 specie in Lafferty's name, and urges him or his heirs to apply to him. Butler will be at Carlisle for two weeks (*The Carlisle Gazette* 1 March 1786).

LAMB, JAMES, cooper from Scotland, said to live in West Caln Twp., Chester Co., may hear of something to his advantage by applying to Stuart & Barr, Philadelphia *The Pennsylvania Packet and Daily Advertiser* 4 Sep 1788).

LAMBERT, J.B., departed Baltimore last January, leaving a wife and two children behind him. The wife has since died, and the children are very much in want of him. Last Feb he was in Augusta and Savannah, GA, and Charleston, SC. Any information concerning him should be sent to the office of the *American* (*Baltimore Patriot & Mercantile Advertiser* 12 Jan 1819).

John B. Lambert married Pheby Eleanor Higdon on 22 Dec 1793 in King George's Parish, PG Co. (KGPG:387). John and Pheby were the parents of (KGPG:400): ANN, b.

15 Dec 1797, prob. the Ann Lambert of PG Co., who was m. 14 Dec 1820 by Rev. Anger to John B. Spalding, also of PG Co. (Washington *National Intelligencer* 20 Dec 1820).

LAMONNERIE, AUGUSTE, came some time ago from St. Vincente and resided in Baltimore or Baltimore Co. If he applies to Nathaniel Lewis and Son in Philadelphia, or to William Robb, 77 South St., he will hear of something to his advantage (*Federal Gazette and Baltimore Daily Advertiser* 6 April 1796).

LAMOTTE, LOUIS VALENTIN, and **JACQUES MERCIER LAMOTTE,** planters of St. Domingo, are anxiously sought by their relations and friends. Information may be sent to the French Commercial Commissary in Baltimore (*Federal Gazette and Baltimore Daily Advertiser* 7 Nov 1801).

LAMPHIER, THOMAS, arrived from Ireland at Port Tobacco on Potomac River MD, where he set up a brewery about 1740. If he or any of his heirs are alive, and will inquire of Mr. A. B. at the house of Mr. Morgan Edwards by the Baptist meetinghouse in Second St., Philadelphia, they hear of something to their advantage (*Pa. Gaz.* 4 Oct 1764).

For more information on Thomas Lamphier's Irish relatives and descendants in MD, see Robert Barnes, *British Roots of Maryland Families II.* Baltimore: Genealogical Publishing Co., 2002.

LAMY, MARTIN, came to Philadelphia from Holland with his father and mother in the year 1741 in a vessel belonging to Stedman and Robertson, and was bound to a carpenter in Oley Twp., Berks. If he is living, he is asked to inform his brother at the Mill called New Brandywine in Northampton Twp., Burlington C., West Jersey. /s/ John Lame [*sic*] (*Dunlap's Pennsylvania Packet, or the General Advertiser* 17 July 1775).

LANDRY, ANTHONY, and his wife, of the Inhabitant's River, Nova Scotia, were sent to the some of the King's colonies, and his children are in Philadelphia. Any news of Landry and his wife should be sent to the following commissioners: William Griffits, Jacob Duchee, and Thomas Say (*Pa. Gaz.* 25 March 1756).

One Antoine Landry, Acadian, took the Oath the King at the Mines, Pisquit, Nova Scotia, on 31 Oct 1727. Another Antoine Landry, also an Acadian, took the Oath of Allegiance in 1730 (*Bockstruck:* 171).

LANG, JOHANNES, a smith, from Oeszweiler Thal, Zweibrueckischen, came to America 26 or 27 years ago. Now Friedrich Hoffman, from the same place, is seeking him (*Hocker:* 125 cites the *Wochentlicher Pennsylvanischer Staatsbote* 31 Aug 1773).

Johannes Lang arrived on the *Leslie* on 7 Oct 1749 (*Eyster:* 32). In 1754 Johannes Lang was in Philadelphia Co., PA. (*AIS Census Index: Pre-1790* gives no other documentation).

LARWOOD, JOHN, lived in Queen Anne's Co., MD, about 30 years ago. He died recently in Amsterdam. He left his estate to his son John, whom he left in this Province. If John is dead, any lawful heirs should inherit. John or his children should apply to John Gassaway near South River, Anne Arundel Co. (Annapolis *Maryland Gazette* 29 July 1746).

LATSHAW, JOHN, late an inhabitant of Baltimore Town, Maryland, left this place on a business trip last August intending to be gone only a month. His wife Magdalena is seeking knowledge of his whereabouts (*Maryland Journal and Baltimore Advertiser* 24 Jan 1786).

LAVERTY, JOHN, died at the house of Moses Van Camp last 13 July. He has a brother (Christian names not known) living in PA, supposedly in Lancaster or York Counties. If the brother will apply to Moses Van Camp at Walpach, or to Peter Trexler in Northampton Co., PA, he may hear of something greatly to his advantage (*Pa. Gaz.* 5 Sep 1781).

On 18 1773 John Laverty of Ireland was indentured as a servant to serve William Kennedy of Philadelphia for one year and six months. Kennedy was to provide meat, drink, washing, lodging, one coat, three shirts, and two pair of trousers during Laverty's term of service (PGS. "Indentures:" 242).

LAWLER, MARY, *als.* **PHELAR,** dau. of Richard Lawler of Stradbally, Ireland, arrived in Baltimore in 1774 or 1775. She is urged to contact the printer (*Maryland Gazette or Baltimore General Advertiser* 24 Nov 1789).

Mary Lawler of Ireland, age 20, came to Maryland as an indentured servant on the *Baltimore*, Mr. John Henrick, sailing 28 March-5 April 1774 (*CBE4:*59; *Fothergill:*62).

LAWTON, WILLIAM, born in some part of New England, and brother of Joseph Lawton, late of Stokes Co., NC, should apply to John McKim of Baltimore, or to Seth Griffin of Stokes Co., NC (*Maryland Journal and Baltimore Advertiser* 13 Aug 1794).

In 1782 a William Lawton was found in Portsmouth, Newport Co., RI (*AIS Census Index: Pre-1790* gives no other documentation).

In 1790 a William Lawton was listed as a head of a family in Chatham Co., NC. Another William was listed as head of a family in Newport co., RI (*AIS 1790 Census Index*).

LAYTON, ISAAC, of Philip Lane near London Wall, London, jeweler, went to North America in 1766 and resided in Philadelphia under the assumed name of Charles Freeman. In July 1774 he was living in Alexandria in Potomac in VA. Nicholas Toke, late of Lenton, Co. Kent, has died and left the said Layton £500 and a share of the clear residue of his estate. Layton is asked to contact John OFD [*sic:* Ord?] of Lincoln's Inn, London (*GAVN:* 201 cites the *Va. Gaz. and General Advertiser* 5 Nov 1785 and the *Va. Gaz. and Weekly Advertiser* 20 Aug 1785).

LEA, GEORGE, of Newry, Co. Down, Ireland, as had a legacy left him in that country. If he or any of his relations will call upon the printer of this paper, they will hear of something to their advantage (*The Pennsylvania Packet and Daily Advertiser* 5 Sep 1788).

A later advertisement asked George Lee, formerly of Newry, Co. Down, Ireland, to apply to James Calbraith, Chesnut St , Philadelphia, where he will hear of something very much to his advantage. If he is dead and left a wife or children, either of them, by applying, shall be entitled to the same advantage (*Federal Gazette and Philadelphia Evening Post* 9 Dec 1790).

LEADAM, WILLIAM, came to America some years ago from the Town of Beverly in Eng. and lived somewhere near Ocracoke, NC. He is asked to apply to the postmaster of Williamsburg, VA (*GAVN:* 201 cites the *Va. Gaz.* 4 Aug 1774).

In 1755 a William Leadam was in Granville Co., NC (*AIS Census Index: Pre-1790* gives no other documentation).

LEADER, MAJOR, some time ago left a son or daughter at or near Philadelphia. If that son or daughter will apply to Ensign Duncan, Paymaster to General Abercrombie's Regiment, or to Mr. John Malcolm in Water St., he or she may hear of something much to his or her advantage (*Pa. Gaz.* 16 Dec 1756).

LEARMOUTH, JOHN, son of Alexander Learmouth of Edinburgh, who some years ago was a pilot from Philadelphia, and resided in Lewis Town, is asked to contact Dr. William Moore of No. 5, Wall St., New York City, to hear something to his advantage (*Scott* 3:228 cites *The New York Gazette and Weekly Mercury* 8 Jan 1781).

On 11 Sep 1784, John Learmonth [*sic*], mariner in Philadelphia, appointed William Mitchell in Dundee, Angus, his attorney to collect money from Arthur Miller, Ann Learmonth, and John Learmonth, all of Edinburgh. William West, Thomas Dick, and John Shields witnessed (*DSSF* :68 cites RD4.236.762).

LEDUC, ALEXANDER SAINVILLE, about 16½ or 17 years old, of blue eyes, brown hair, fair complexion, and speaks French, Spanish and English, son of M. Le Duc, Surgeon and Physician at New Orleans, left the Natchez in October 1788 and went to Louisville, KY, in company with several Americans. If he will apply personally, or by letter, to Barbie [*i.e.*, Barbe] de Marbois, Esq., Consul General of France, or Mr. John Leamy, merchant, both of Philadelphia, he will hear of something to his advantage (*The Pennsylvania Packet and Daily Advertiser* 29 May 1790).

LEE, WILLIAM, son of William Lee, had been bound to a weaver at Carrickfergus, Co. Antrim, Ireland. He left his apprenticeship, and sailed from Newry in 1763 as a servant, for America, and has not been heard from since. If he applies to William Love, a friend of his, lately arrived in Philadelphia, he will hear of something to his advantage, left to him by his uncle, also named William Lee, late of Tandergee, dec. (*Pa. Gaz.* 22 Aug 1765).

William Lee, servant man, served for four years with one Christopher Wilson, in New Castle County, and now has run away from his current master, David Scholefield, living in Christiana Hundred, New Castle Co. Lee is about 21 years old, 5'3" high, fair complexion, with light straight hair cut pretty close to the top of his head. He has a slight stammering in his speech. He may change his name to Brian Daily (*Pa. Gaz.* 7 Jan 1768).

LEECH, THOMAS, formerly of the Twp. of Worsley near Manchester, Eng., is asked to apply to Mr. F. Nichols, No. 70 Chesnut St., Philadelphia, as he will hear something to his advantage (*Gazette of the United States* 25 May 1803).

LEFEUER, DAVID, of Cumberland Co., and his children, **DAVID, JR., JAMES,** and **CATHERINE**, the wife of Robert Thompson, are entitled to sums of money under the will of David Lefueuer of London, dec., whose executor cannot locate the heirs (*GAVN* 204 cites the *Va. Gaz.* 21 June 1770).

LEGLER, JACOB, is sought by his sister-in-law, Maria Judith, who was born at Pfaffenhofen, Wurtemberg (*Hocker:* 4 cites the *Pennsylvanische Geschichts-Schreiber* 16 Sep 1745).

LEHMAN, CHIRSTIAN TRAUGOTT, of Zittau in the Province of Upper Lusatia, Germany, aged 13 years, left his native place in 1813 with Jacob Schmal of Dresden, Saxony, for Neuvied on the Rhine. They are presumed to have come to the United states of America, put the parents of Christian have never heard any thing from him since. Anyone with knowledge of him is asked to contact the editor of the *American Daily Advertiser* (*Poulson's American Daily Advertiser* 28 Jan 1819).

LEIBROCK, JOHANN DEWALT, was born in Vogelbach, Zweibrucken, and came to America eleven years ago. His cousin Anna Elizabeth Eigen is seeking him (*Hocker:* 162 cites the *Philadelphische Correspondenz* 29 Aug 1781).

For more on the Leibrock family, see Burgert's *Western Palatinate:* 220-221.

LENTZ, FRIEDRICH, a butcher, from Dornstatt, Wurtemberg, came to America twelve years ago. Ernest Ludwig Baisch is seeking information about him (*Hocker:* 117 cites the *Wochentlicher Pennsylvanischer Staatsbote* 29 Sep 1772).

A Frederick Sigismund Lentz was naturalized in New York City on 18 Oct 1763 (*Bockstruck:* 180).

In 1790 a Frederick Lentz, grocer, was listed as living on North Front St., between Market and Race Street, west, with one male over 16, one male under 16, and three females (*1790PA:* 219).

LENTZ, JOHANN, arrived in America five years ago, and is seeking his three daughters and one son. Notify Johannes Pfister, Northampton Twp., Bucks Co. (*Hocker:* 80 cites the *Pennsylvanische Geschichts-Schreiber* 17 Aug 1759).

LEONARD, THEODORE, left a Printing Office in Boston, last summer, where he as an apprentice, unknown to his parents or his master, and has not been heard of since. He is 5' 7-8" tall, with dark hair, eyes and complexion (Frederick *Rights of Man* 5 Oct 1796).

LESTER, GEORGE, a bricklayer, left SC about a year ago. If he is in this Province he may hear something to his advantage if he will leave a letter, addressed to L. L., with the printers of this paper (*Pa. Gaz.* 28 June 1770).

LEVY, ASHER, son of Isaac Levy of the City of Philadelphia, dec., is asked to apply to the printer, and he will hear of something to his advantage (*The Pennsylvania Packet and General Advertiser* 13 Dec 1783).

LEWIS, CHRISTIAN BENJAMIN, a native of Rotterdam, of small stature, a watchmaker and jeweler, speaks the German language fluently. He came to Baltimore about three years ago, and has not been heard of for a considerable length of time. Anyone with information is asked to contact C. Q. Phillips as it will contribute much to Lewis' advantage if he could be heard from (*Baltimore Patriot* 18 Jan 1821).

LICHTENSTEIN, JOHANNES, a native of Durn, near Sinsheim, was married in Laudenbach on the Mountain Pass, came to this country about 18 years ago. If he is living, will he be so good as to inform Jacob Hitzheimer on 7th St., Philadelphia, and he will hear from his daughter in Germany. If he is not living, will someone please notify Hitzheimer (*Eyster:* 34 cites the *Pennsylvanische Staatsbote* 30 Nov 1773).

(*Hocker:* 128 transcribes this name as Johannes Liebenstein).

LIGHTFOOT, FRANCIS, a native of New Kent Co., and formerly a resident of VA, if living, or has any legal heir or descendant living in the United States or elsewhere, by applying, either in person, or by special agent, and giving sufficient proof of their being such a legal descendant, to William or Nicholas Lightfoot of James City Co., or to James Poindexter, of Powhatan, will hear of something highly important and much to their advantage (*The Enquirer* 19 Nov 1805).

LIGHTFOOT, JAMES, left his wife about two years ago in Bristol, England, and sent for her [to come] over here. She arrived here on 19 Nov in the *Prince George,* and since that time has heard he was at work at John Inch's, in Annapolis. She has written several letters, but is uncertain whether her husband has received them as she has never had an answer. If any person can give information about him, he is asked to direct a line to Esther Lightfoot at Mr. John McMichael's, Philadelphia (*Pa. Gaz.* 29 May 1760).

LINDQUIST, CASPAR, a cabinet maker, embarked at Tonningen in September 1807, in the ship *Three Sisters,* bound for Philadelphia, but his distressed mother and relations have never received any account of him since that time. Anyone with information is asked to address themselves to the editor of the *American Daily Advertiser* (*Poulson's American Daily Advertiser* 8 March 1817).

LINDSAY, Capt., born in Edinburgh, came to New York City about 1758. If he applies to the printer, he may hear something to his advantage (*Scott* 3:256 cites *The New York Gazette and the Weekly Mercury* 18 March 1782).

LINFORD, JAMES, son of Rebecca Linford, late of the City of Bristol, dec., left England about 1755, was a sailor, and, according to his brother William, married Christian Van Riper, dau. of a farmer at Aquanunck, NJ. He lived in NJ, and as a boatman, carried timber to his sloop to New York City. He is asked to apply to the printer to hear something to his advantage (*Scott* 3:223 cites *The New York Gazette and the Weekly Mercury* 1 May 1780).

LINSEY, WILLIAM, was a native of James City Co., which he left some time ago. Edmund Linsey, administrator of the estate of Elizabeth Linsey, William's mother, advises that William of his heirs may receive their legacies (*GAVN:* 209 cites *The Virginia Independent Chronicle and General Advertiser* 6 Jan 1790).

LINWELL, JAMES, in 1795 lived near the Gap Tavern, Salisbury Twp., PA. From thence, he is supposed to have moved to NY. Anyone who can send information about the said Linwell, by sending a line to Dan Eaton, Missquitoee [*sic*] Creek Post Office, Trumbull Co., OH, will convey a favor on the widow McCurdy, formerly of Salisbury

Twp., who at this time is in a pitiful situation ([DE] *American Watchman* 5 Aug 1818; *Baltimore Patriot* 22 July 1815).

LIPERT, SARAH, married 1st, Adam Garret, and 2nd Sebastian Steinmeyer, and left home about 15 years ago. Her brother, Adam Lipert, living in New Virginia between Martinsburg, the Warm Springs, and Potomack River, wishes to inform her of the death of her father and a legacy of 200 pounds (*York Recorder* 18 June 1800).

LIPOP, JOSEPH, a native of Rome, was at Alexandria in the year 1811 in the service of Mr. Serrurier, the minister-plenipotentiary of France. He was there employed also by Mr. Taylor, a coach-maker. He then went to Washington City. Ornamenting coaches was his usually business. If Mr. Lipop is living, he may hear of something to his advantage by applying at the office of the *Alexandria Gazette*. /s/ Joseph Bonfanti, 305 Broadway, New York (*Alexandria Gazette & Daily Advertiser* 23 Sep 1819).

LIPPENCOTT, JUDIAH, of the late 3rd Regt. of Foot, will hear of something to his advantage by calling on Richard Fullerton, Philadelphia, who also asks the heirs of Thomas Howard, and James M'anally, late of the Pennsylvania Line, both dec., to call on Fullerton for the certificates belonging to the soldiers (*The Pennsylvania Packet and Daily Advertiser* 2 March 1785).

LITHGOW, HECTOR, about 1764 was a private in H.B.M. 77th Regt., then quartered at Halifax, [Nova Scotia]. He left for Great Britain, and then went to the East Indies where he d. in 1784. He left a considerable property to his sons John and Hugh Lithgow, and their mother, Frances Sweeting. Hugh Lithgow is supposed to be in some part of the Eastern Shore of Maryland, where he married some years ago (*MJBA* 1 Aug 1788). The sons or their mother may hear about his estate if the apply to Thomas Pope, Esq., at Philadelphia, or to Archibald Gay or Letitia Court (*GAVN*: 209 cites the *Virginia Herald and Fredericksburg Advertiser* 3 July 1788, and the *Norfolk and Portsmouth Journal* 23 July 1788). His sons John and Hugh were born in Halifax Nova Scotia, and lately resided there. Their mother was Frances Sweeting (*Carlisle Gazette* 3 Sep 1788).

Hannah Lithgow was listed as a creditor in the account filed 24 Oct 1772 of Isaac Molis of Worcester Co. (MDAD 69:330). She may be the Hannah Lithgow, whose house on Mulberry (commonly called Arch) St., was one of several houses owned by the Pennsylvania Land Company in London, and was to be sold in May 1765 (*Pa. Gaz.* 2 May 1765). She died by Sep 1781 in Philadelphia, when Amos Loney, of Baltimore Co., MD, advertised he would settle her estate (*Pa. Gaz.* 19 Sep 1781).

LITT, PETER, was found dead upon the Great Road, Springfield Twp., Bucks Co. An inquest was held upon him according to the law. He had with him some shoe buckles, needles, and pins. His relations, if he has any, may have the goods again, paying the charges and applying to Samuel McCammon (*Pa. Gaz.* 3 May 1780).

LITTLE, CHARLES, sailed from the Port of Baltimore last summer, intending to come to Philadelphia. Since then his friends have not heard from him. Anyone with information is asked to contact his wife at 163 Chestnut St., Philadelphia (*Baltimore Patriot* 17 Aug 1819).

LITTLE, MICHAEL, and his wife and daughter recently arrived from Belfast, Ireland, with Mr. Ore, merchant, and are thought to have left Philadelphia last 16 Nov. They are asked to inform Andrew Cosgrave, now living in Baltimore Town, care of Christopher Curtis, cooper (*Pa. Gaz.* 14 Feb 1765).

In June 1766 Little informed Andrew Cosgrave who "advertised his wife in the papers last summer, that she and her father (Michael Little), are living in Baltimore county, within fifteen miles of the town, in the Forks of the Gunpowder, on part of Mr. Nicholas Darnall's land (*Pa. Gaz.* 10 June 1766).

LOCK, [-?-], *alias* **SLUT**, a shoemaker in, or near, Philadelphia, is advised that if he applies to William Murray, at his House, on the East Side of Second Street, between Spruce and Union Streets, opposite to Mr. Charles Stedman's, he will hear of something to his advantage (*Pa. Gaz.* 26 Dec 1765).

LOCKARD, PATRICK, son of Aaron Lockard, late of Abington Twp., Philadelphia Co., dec., enlisted about three years ago in HM Service. If he will come to John Shoemaker, miller, in Cheltenham Twp., Philadelphia Co., he will hear something considerably to his advantage. If he is dead, Shoemaker will reward anyone who can tell him, of the circumstances of Lockard's death and whether he left either a widow or children. John Shoemaker and Elizabeth Lockard were administrators of Aaron Lockard's estate (*Pa. Gaz.* 31 May 1770).

LOEDY, DANIEL, age 24, and **HANSZ LOEDY,** age 13, his brother, arrived in this country, and were indentured by their mother, Magdalena Haussmanin, who received no papers, and now she is seeking information about them. She is with Hansz Adam Schneider, near Schnecker's Mill, Conestoga, Lancaster Co. (*Hocker:* 29 cites the *Pennsylvanische Geschichts-Schreiber* 1 Oct 1751).

LOHMAN, JOHN DANIEL, a German by birth, left Barnum's Hotel on 2 Sep last, and has not been heard from since. For several years past he has been the Billiard keeper at the Hotel. He is about 45 years of age, and is supposed to have become deranged, and may have destroyed himself. Any information will be thankfully received by D. Koster, 20 S. Calvert St., or at the Bar of the City Hotel (*Baltimore Patriot* 17 April 1834).

LONG, JOHN, lately in the Maryland Flying Camp, in Capt. Buffy's Co., and now supposed to be in Philadelphia, will call upon Mr. Hugh McAllister, living in the upper end of Second Street, near the Barracks, he may hear something to his advantage (*Pennsylvania Evening Post* 4 Feb 1777).

In 1790 a John Long was listed as head of a family in Baltimore Co., MD (*AIS 1790 Census Index*).

LONSDALE, WILLIAM M., if in Baltimore, should call on Henry Long, where he may hear something to his advantage (*Baltimore Patriot* 11 Feb 1825).

LOPDELL, HENRY, kept a school for some years on York River. He has not been heard of for some time. If he applies to Col. George Braxton on York River, he will receive information on something much to his advantage (*GAVN:* 211 cites the *Va. Gaz.* 8 Jan 1739).

LORCH, JACOB, from Druchtelfingen in Wurtemburg, is sought by Ludwig Batsch (*Eyster:* 23 cites the *Pennsylvanische Staatsbote* 12 June 1770).

Jacob Lorch arrived on the *Forest* on 10 Oct 1752 (*Eyster:* 23).

LORT, JOHANNES, born at Grunberg, Darmstadt, came to America twenty-one years ago. Now his father is seeking him. At one time the Newlander Becker offered twenty shillings to anyone who could find him. Now Johannes Sauter, who will be returning to Germany in about ten days, is seeking him (*Hocker:* 144 and *Eyster:* 38 cite the *Wochentlicher Pennsylvanischer Staatsbote* 30 June 1775).

In 1790 a John Lort, carpenter, was listed in Philadelphia, living on Spruce St., between Fifth and Sixth Sts. In his household were two white males over 16, and one white female (*1790PA:* 244).

LOTHIAN, ELIZABETH, dau. of Baillie John Lothian of Bruntisland, North Britain, has been in this country about nine years. If she will inform the post office, she will receive a letter from a relative, but she must inform the printer of her grandmother's name on her mother's side, "for what reason he disna ken" (*GAVN:* 312 cites the *Va. Gaz.* 31 March 1774).

LOVE, ROBERT, from Swadlinbar, Co. Caven, Ireland, is informed that his sister, Martha Love (now M'Mullin) now resides in Lancaster Co., PA, and wants to hear from him (*Lancaster Journal* 24 Aug 1804).

LOWE, JAMES, later calling himself James Brown, was apprenticed to one O'Dear, Carver and Gilder, in Warder St., London. He left his master, went to Dublin, and bound himself to Capt. Robert Miller, of the ship *Connelly,* and sailed for Philadelphia from Dublin on 30 March 1770, arriving in June or July following. If he applies to Bernard and Jugiez, Carvers, at the corner of Chesnut and Thirds Sts., he will hear of something greatly to his advantage (*Pa. Gaz.* 29 Aug 1771).

LOWE, ROBERT, son of Robert Lowe, was born in Philadelphia, in the year 1732, and served his apprenticeship to a shoemaker in this city. If he is living (or his widow or children, if he be dead) and will apply to Dr. William Chancellor, in Market St., they may hear of something considerably to their advantage (*Pa. Gaz.* 9 Sep 1762).

LOWE, THOMAS, son of Edward and Mary Lowe of Marylebone, London, came to MD about 35 years ago with his uncles John and Robert Chesley. He is urged to contact Zachariah Forrest (Annapolis *Maryland Gazette* 9 March 1786).

LUCAS, WILLIAM, son of Thomas and Passibella Lucas, was born in Accomack Co., VA. He is requested to apply to William Beavens of that county, to be informed of something to his advantage (*GAVN:* 213 cites the *Va. Gaz.* 25 April 1755).

LUDERT, LUDWIG, from Memel. Prussia. left London for America fourteen years ago. Information about him is sought (*Hocker:* 179 cites the *Philadelphische Correspondenz* 1 May 1787).

LUDWIG, GEORG, of Herborn. in Ocanien Nassau-Dillenburg. died some time ago, leaving his daughter, the widow of Johann Jost Metzeler 2000 gulden (*Hocker:* 165 cites the *Philadelphische Correspondenz* 24 Dec 1782).
  In 1790 a George Ludwig was listed as head of a family in Berks Co., PA (*AIS 1790 Census Index*).

LUECKHARDT, BERNHARD, has been in America for 19 or 20 years. His sister, Johanna Maria Lueckhardtin, who came on the ship *Union*, is seeking him and asks him to fetch her the soonest possible from the ship *Union*, Capt. Bryson (*Hocker:* 127 and *Eyster:* 36 both cite the *Wochentlicher Pennsylvanischer Staatsbote* 23 Nov 1773).

LUKE, JAMES, born in Northampton Co., VA, is requested to return home, some affairs being settled to his advantage. He was in the Province of PA some 18 months or two years ago. Isaac Luke living in Portsmouth. Norfolk Co., VA, is seeking James (*Pa. Gaz.* 26 June 1766).

LYLE, FARRELL, came from Ireland about five years ago and landed at Hobb's Hole. If he will apply to James Mulllaghan, Kingston Parish, Gloucester Co., he may hear something to his advantage (*GAVN:* 213 cites Purdy. Clarkson and Davis' *Va. Gaz.* 11 Oct 1776).

LYON, THOMAS, of Lancaster Co., PA, is asked to apply to the printers of this paper where he will be informed of something considerably to his advantage (*Pa. Gaz.* 27 April 1791).
  Thomas Lyon of Lancaster Co. took the Oath of Fidelity to the United States of America on or before 2 June 1778 before Stewart Herbert (Lancaster Co. Deeds L:379).
  In 1790 a Thomas Lyon lived in Leacock Twp., Lancaster Co., with one white male over 16, one white male under 16, and five white females (*1790PA:* 138).

LYSAGHT, NICHOLAS, son of John Lysaght of Hertfordshire, left his father in 1739. If he applies to Benjamin Franklin, he will hear something to his advantage (*Scott* 2:302 cites the *Pa. Gaz.* 29 Aug 1754).

M'ANALLY, JAMES, late of the Pennsylvania Line has died. Richard Fullerton of Philadelphia has his certificate, and asks his heirs to call for them within two months, or they will be returned to the office (*Pennsylvania Packet and Daily Advertiser* 2 March 1785).

M'CANDLISH, GEORGE, a farmer in Craig near Whitehorn in the county of Wigtown, N. Britain, and Agnes Smith. his wife, about the year 1774 left Scotland and went to America. They are understood to have lived somewhere in Pennsylvania. They died about 1790, leaving children. If any of these children or their descendants are alive, they should "lose no time" in applying to the gentlemen named below, where they will hear of something to their advantage. /s/ Mr. John Bainbridge, 45 Bread St., London, Mr. James Smith, Wigtown, Scotland, or Messrs. Joshua and Thomas Gilpin, Philadelphia (*Poulson's American Daily Advertiser* 11 Nov 1817).

M'CARTHY, JOHN, a ship carpenter, who served his apprenticeship with John Maloney at Brickfields, Cork, about four years arrived in the State of Virginia from the city of Cork, and since then his relations in Cork have never heard from him. If he lives in Virginia, or any person can inform the subscriber where he may be found, it will be greatly appreciated. /s/ Henry Harris. (*American Beacon and Norfolk & Portsmouth Daily Advertiser* 5 May 1819).

M'CARTY (McCARTY), MICHAEL, about 20 years of age, was in Quebec and was intended to have gone to Baltimore, but nothing has been heard of him since. His brother, Mr. Callahan McCarty, a native of Ireland, arrived in the town of Alexandria, VA in the brig *Eliza*, John Clifford, master, from Quebec, via St. Andrews, leaving his brother Michael in Quebec. He is now anxious to hear concerning his brother (*Alexandria Gazette & Daily Advertiser* 13 March 1820).

M'CLACKEN, |-?-|, is a son of Patrick McClacken, a peddler who traded on the Eastern Shore of Maryland and VA, who died last Dec. The son may hear something to his advantage by applying to William Duffey of Drawbridge, VA (Kline's *Carlisle Weekly Gazette* 13 June 1798).

M'CLASKEY, ALEXANDER, from Ireland, brother of Robert M'Claskey who died in Salem, West Jersey, is asked to apply to Clement Acton, exec. of the said Robert, he will receive the whole of Robert's estate (*Herald of Liberty* 18 Jan 1802).

M'CLEAN, JOHN, who left Dublin some years ago, and resided with his wife Susannah at the house of Capt. Hyson, will hear something to his advantage if he will go to Chatham, Morris Co., NJ (*Scott* 3:201 cites *The New York Gazette and the Weekly Mercury* 12 Feb 1776).

M'CLUNG, WILLIAM, was in this city about two months ago. If he will apply to Benjamin Armitage near Spruce St., in Second St., he will hear of something to his advantage (*Pennsylvania Packet and General Advertiser* 11 May 1772).

M'COMMON, THOMAS, came from Ireland in the ship *Rose* in 1766, and served time with John Montgomery. If he is living, and will apply to his Bartholomew Mather in Cheltenham Twp., Philadelphia Co., he may hear of his brother and something to his advantage. Direct letters giving information to Bartholomew Mather, to be left at the London Coffee House, Philadelphia, to oblige John McCommon (*Pa. Gaz.* 10 Oct 1771).

M'CONNELL, WILLIAM, foot chapman or peddler, late of Donegal Twp., Lancaster Co., PA, died at the house of James Scott in Montgomery Twp., Franklin Co., on the 20th inst. These are to notify his heirs, and those with accounts of money of the deceased deposited with them are to give their names to John Scott, Esq., in Chambersburg or to James Scott, the subscriber (*Kline's Carlisle Weekly Gazette* 6 April 1796).

M'CRACKEN, WILLIAM (who came into this province from London some time last summer), by applying to Lewis Gordon, in Norris Alley, Philadelphia, may hear of something to his advantage (*Pa. Gaz.* 24 Dec 1751).

M'DANIEL, ANNE, was born c1717 in Dublin. She came to MD c1741/2 and once lived with a minister in Annapolis, but may have later moved to the Eastern Shore. She is urged to contact her friends through Jonas Green (Annapolis *Maryland Gazette* 6 Sep 1753).

M'DANIEL, JAMES, who came to America from Ireland, about last June 12 month, age about 20, is asked to communicate with Edes and Gill at Boston (*Scott* 3:136 cites *The New York Gazette and Weekly Mercury* 30 Jan 1769).
      In 1790 a James McDaniel was head of a family in New York co. (*AIS 1790 Census Index*).

M'DONEL, ALEXANDER, Sgt.-Major of the Second South Carolina Regiment, or **Mr. M'DONEL**, clerk at Ms. Leappiner's brewery, lately from New York, may hear of something to their advantage by applying to Mrs. Shaing, opposite Mr. Hare's brewery, Water St. Jacob Kalipoffer will greatly appreciate any information that can be given (*Pennsylvania Packet or the General Advertiser* 14 Nov 1780).

M'DONNALD, THOMAS, is supposed to have left Virginia in 1776. If he is still living, and will apply to the printers, he may hear of something very much to his advantage (*The Pennsylvania Packet and Daily Advertiser* 23 March 1789).

M'DOUGALL, JOHN, a native of Scotland, arrived in this country some time ago. He will hear something to his advantage by applying to F. S., at the head of Bond St., Fells Point (*Baltimore Patriot and Mercantile Advertiser* 6 April 1818).

M'FALL, ABBEY, and **POLLY M'FALL**, are daughters of Neil M'Fall, late sergeant in the British 26th Regiment of Foot, who died in the city of New York after the conclusion of the late war. If they are living, or either of them, and will apply at the office of this newspaper, they will hear of something to their advantage (*Claypoole's American Daily Advertiser* 22 Feb 1797).

M'FARLANE, WALTER, son of Andrew M'Farlane, of Glenfroun in North Britain, will hear something to his advantage if he contacts Joseph Scott in Philadelphia, Walter and Thomas Buchanan of New York City, or William Duegued in Boston (*Scott* 3:176 cites *The New York Gazette and Weekly Mercury* 16 Aug 1773).
      In 1790 a Walter McFarland [*sic*] was listed in Hopkinton, Middlesex Co., MA (*AIS 1790 U.S. Federal Census Index*, cites p. 277).

M'GILL, DAVID, physician or surgeon, Gent., son of Arthur M'Gill of Kemback, Co. Fyfe, Scotland, came into MD some 50 years ago and married a woman named Bond or Bonn and now has two sons. He should contact the printer (Annapolis *Maryland Gazette* 20 June 1765).

David M'Gill married Grace Boon on 6 March 1708/9 at Christ Church Parish, Calvert Co. (*CRSM*:83). She was a dau. of Grace Brooke who died leaving a will proved 30 Oct 1725. She named her son John Boon, her dau. Grace Magill and Grace's children Arthur and Mary Magill, and other relatives (MWB 18:424).

D. Mackgill witnessed the will of James Mackall of Calvert Co. on 26 Dec 1716 (MWB 14:232). David and Grace Makgill witnessed the will of John Hall of St. Mary's Co. on 29 Nov 1727 (MWB 19:302).

David McGill of St. Mary's Co., MD, died by 18 April 1744 when his personal estate was appraised at £24.9.8 by Samuel Abell and John Raley. Mary Wilkeson and Mararel Abell signed as next of kin. Grace McGill filed the inventory on 3 July 1744 (MINV 29:248).

M'GONNEGAL, FRANCIS, lately arrived from Londonderry on the ship *Hannah,* Capt. Mitchell, is urged to contact his brother Morris McGonnegal, shoemaker, living near Bald Friar Ferry, Susquehanna (*Maryland Journal and Baltimore Advertiser* 24 Aug 1774).

M'KEAN, ELIZABETH, wife of William McKean, merchant of Philadelphia, is asked to apply to John Fenno, editor of this newspaper, 119 Chesnut St., Philadelphia, as she will hear of something to his advantage (*Gazette of the United States* 29 July 1797).

M'KENNY, FRANCIS, brother of Anne M'Kenny (now de la Hoyde), late of SC, if living should apply to George Sikes of Charleston, SC, to hear something to his advantage (*GAVN:* 220 cites the *Va. Gaz.* 30 Oct 1778).

M'KILRONAN, MATTHEW, was born in the Parish of Templefort, Co. Cavan, and a weaver, has been in this country for three years. If he applies to John Clifton, weaver in Third St., Philadelphia, he will hear something to his advantage from his sister in Ireland (*Scott* 1:161 cites the *Pa. Gaz.* 14 July 1737).

M'LEANE, HUGH, late of Sherry in the Parish of Dunaughy, Co. Antrim, arrived in Baltimore in June 1774. He wants to contact his son Hugh who left the same place about 18 months earlier (*Maryland Journal and Baltimore Advertiser* 18 June 1774).

M'MURRY, JOSEPH, formerly of Derryaghy, Ireland, is asked to apply to Edward Jones of Walnut St., where he will hear of something to his advantage (*Pennsylvania Evening Herald and the American Monitor* 6 July 1785).

M'NACHTEN, NEIL, born in North Britain, shoemaker, came to Boston where he lived for nine years; his brother Alexander of the Island of Isla has come to America and is seeking him (*Scott* 3:11 cites *Bradford's New York Gazette 4 Dec 1738*).

M'NESH, JOHN, if living, is sought by William, Jesse, and George Hall who wish to have some information from him concerning the estate of George Hall, dec.; the estate is in Newbury Twp., York Co., on Fishing Creek (*The Carlisle Gazette* 17 Jan 1787).

MAAR, JOHANN, from Mt. Taschendorf in Frankischen Kreis of Germany (Franconia), belonging to Reichsfreyherr von. Kuentsberg, Amt. Obersteinbach, left for America in 1766, with Johann Leonard Schloepp (See elsewhere) (*Hocker:* 188 cites the *Philadelphische Correspondenz* 9 Sep 1791).

MacDID, CORNELIUS, born in the Parish of Lake. Co. Donegall, came to PA about four years ago in the ship *Happy Return* from Londonderry. His brother James asks that Cornelius come to Capt. Thomas Gray's on Ridley creek, near Newcastle (*Pa. Gaz.* 20 July 1745).

MACHAN, ARCHIBALD, from Londonderry, lately sailed out of New York. If he is alive he is desired to apply to Margaret Berwick at the Sign of the Three Mariners, Front St., where he will hear something considerably to his advantage (*Pa. Gaz.* 6 April 1738).

A query concerning Archibald Machan who immigrated to America c1736 was published in the "Interest List" of the *Ulster Genealogical & Historical Guild* 9 (1986), p. 27.

An Archibald Machan married by 17 Sep 1776, Margaret, dau. of John Dunwoody of West Nantmeal Twp., Chester Co., PA (*Chester Wills*).

MACKAY, WILLIAM, was born in Cox-Town, parish of Golsby, Shire of Sutherland, Scotland, and has been in MD some 12 or 13 years. His brother Robert Mackay has lately come into the country with Sir John St. Clair, Quarter-Master of H. M. forces in North America, and wants to get in touch with him. (Annapolis *Maryland Gazette* 27 Feb 1755).

William Mackay settled Sugar Loaf Mountain, Montgomery Co., MD, by 1790 (*SOCD:* 98).

MAGEE, JOHN, died, leaving a brother who came to PA some seven years ago and lived near Middletown and Neshaminy. The brother is urged to contact Sarah Weatherly, living in Greenwich Twp., Gloucester Co., and Province of West NJ, to receive a small legacy of cash and wearing apparel, left by his brother (*Pa. Gaz.* 28 July 1773).

MAHLER (MOHLER), FRIEDRICH, born in Sulzbah, Alsace, arrived in America two years ago last autumn. His brother Conrad, a carpenter, near Lancaster, is seeking Friedrich. Conrad, who is now free, is employed with George Eberle, in Lancaster (*Hocker:* 107 cites the *Pennsylvanische Staatsbote* 11 June 1771).

Conrad Mahler, came in the *Hamilton,* Charles Smith, on 6 Oct 1767. Friedrich Mahler came on the *Betsy,* Capt. Samuel Hawk, master, 26 Oct 1768 (*Names of Foreigners* 480, 487).

For more on the Mahler Family, see Burgert's *Alsace* 352.

MAIBEN (or MAVEN), JAMES, from Ireland, settled in this country about 1770. His friends in Co. Sligo are anxious to know if he is still alive. Please inform James Dunlop of Port Royal, VA (*GAVN:* 224 cites the *Virginia Herald and Fredericksburg Advertiser* 24 July 1788).

MAIN, FRANCIS, a well set lad of 14 years, with dark hair, and a scar over one eyebrow, came to MD as a servant about 1727 or 1728 on the ship *Grove*, Capt. Babb. He is urged to apply to the printer (Annapolis *Maryland Gazette* 27 April 1748).

MAINS, THOMAS, born in the Parish of Cumberland, Co. Down, Ireland, brother of Matthew Mains, will hear something to his advantage by applying to H. Gaine (*Scott* 3:204 cites *The New York Gazette and Weekly Mercury* 1 July 1776).

MAJOR, EDMOND, planter in VA or MD, died about 40 years ago. If he or his descendants apply to Cary Michell in Hampton, they may hear something to their advantage (*GAVN*:224 cites the *Va. Gaz.* 27 Oct 1788).

MAN, JOHN, in 1757 lived at Marsh Creek, Cumberland Co. His wife and two boys were taken prisoners by the Indians, who killed the mother and one son. They brought the other to Montreal, and sold him to a French officer. When the town was taken [by the English], the boy came, almost naked, to Finlay and Campbell, merchants of Montreal, who clothed him and took care of him. They would like him to be claimed by his relatives (*Pa. Gaz.* 2 April 1761).

John Man, of Marsh Creek, and other children, are now at the State House in Philadelphia. During the war they had been taken captive by the Indians from several parts of the Province, and have been lately released by General Amherst. They are to be returned to their parents or other relations, who are desired to come forthwith and receive them (*Pa. Gaz.* 2 July 1761).

MANSFIELD, RACHEL, formerly lived in Dover, but in the last four or five years settled in or about Philadelphia. Anyone with information is asked to contact her son Thomas Mansfield, Enquire at 133 S. Sixth St. (*Poulson's American Daily Advertiser* 19 June 1811).

MANUEN, LAWRENCE, shoemaker, left the town of Gallway, Province of Connough, Ireland, about 17 years ago. If he is living he should apply to the printers, to be directed to his brother Daniel, who lives in Philadelphia. Direct to Daniel Manuen to care of Philip Neill, near the Salutation in Water St. (*Pa. Gaz.* 14 May 1767).

MANWEIT, JOHANN PHILIPP, a baker in Philadelphia, several years ago, now is sought by Philip Rothenhauser (*Hocker:* 171 cites the *Philadelphische Correspondenz* 19 Oct 1784).

MARGGRANDEN, ADAM, cooper from Eggenstein, Germany, lived with Reuben Haines of Philadelphia, for several years and left him in 1777. He was a substitute in the militia in the campaign against the Indians at Shamokin, and on returning, two years ago, it was reported that he had drowned in a millpond near Northumberland. Now Haines wants proof of his death (*Hocker:* 301 cites the *Germantauner Zeitung* 14 Nov 1786).

He is probably the George Adam Marggrander [*sic*] who came on the *Charming Molly*, Robert Gill, master, from London, on 29 Sep 1774 (*PGP* 1:759).

MARINER, Dr. [-?-], came to VA from Bristol about 1758 with his son **JAMES MARINER**. They may hear something to their advantage if they apply to post office in Williamsburg (*GAVN:* 226 cites the *Va. Gaz.* 11 Dec 1772).

MARKLIN (MAERKLEY), HANS, was born in Dueren. He brought his wife Barbara (born Tschoppin) and their seven children to America from Switzerland. Johann E. Schweighaus, Second Street, Philadelphia, is seeking them (*Hocker:* 613 cites the *Philadelphische Correspondenz* 10 April 1782).

Hans Marklin [*sic*] was baptized 2 March 1742 in Thurnen, Amt. Homburg. He married Barbara Tschopp from Bretzwill. In 1771 he was a silk-reeler and a day labourer. He paid £20.0.0 for his manumission and £28.0.48 for his 10% tax. He had a hard time supporting his family, and was induced to emigrate by news of a relative who had emigrated and been successful in PA (*Faust* 2:180).

Hans and Barbara were the parents of the following children, probably baptized at Thurnen (*Faust* 2:180): ANNA, bapt. 6 Jan 1756; HANS JACOB, bapt. 8 Jan 1758; HEINRICH, bapt. 8 April 1762; ANNA MARGRETH, bapt. 8 Jan 1764; BARBARA, bapt. 3 Nov 1765; ESTER, bapt. 20 Dec 1767; and JOHANNES, bapt. 10 Oct 1769.

MARSHALL, JOHN, son of Alexander Marshall of Over Stoway, near Taunton, Co Somerset, has been absent a considerable time at sea or beyond the seas. A reward is offered for information concerning him (*American Weekly Mercury* 2 Jan 1728).

MARSHALL, WILLIAM, son of Henry Marshall of Manor Cunningham, Co. Donegal, is asked to apply to Capt. George Marshall in New York City, or to Thompson and Alexander (*Scott* 3:137 cites *The New York Gazette and Weekly Mercury* 6 Feb 1769).

MARTIN, ALEXANDER, merchant in Salisbury, NC, is hereby informed that his father, Hugh Martin, of Hunterdon Co., NJ, died last 9 March, and named him and his brother James as executors. Alexander Martin is desired to come home, if not inconvenient to his business, to settle his father's affairs; however, his mother requests that if his coming is attended by any disadvantage, he is not to come (*Pa. Gaz.* 10 Dec 1761).

In 1790 an Alexander Martin was head of a family in Richmond co., NC (*AIS 1790 Census Index*).

MARTIN, ALEXANDER, has been at Havana since Sep 1826, to administer (by order of the Spanish Government, in the presence of physicians appointed for that purpose), the Anti-pestilential liquors, discovered by Dr. J. J. Giraud of this city, for the cure and prevention of the yellow fever. The three experiments were to have been completed this year, and they were successfully used during three epidemics. No information has been received from Mr. Martin (*Baltimore Patriot* 19 Oct 1822).

MARTIN, JOSEPH, left Bally Martin, Co. Down, near Killiney, Ireland, on 10 July 1750, and took his passage from Lairn, for New York. He kept school for some time in the Jerseys. If he is alive, and will come to the New Printing Office in Market St., Philadelphia, he will hear something to his advantage (*Pa. Gaz.* 17 Jan 1760).

MARTIN, JOST, from Traben, near Trarbach, is sought by Ernest Ludwig Baisch (*Eyster:* 27 cites the *Pennsylvanische Staatsbote* 28 July 1772).

Jost Martin married Elizabeth Miller on 20 May 1776 at the First Reformed Church in Lancaster, PA (*Lancaster Churches* vol. 2).

MARTIN, RICHARD, a short, thick, well set boy, is sought by James Tait of PG Co., who states that Martin has either eloped or [was?] misled of his wife ([DC] *Columbian Chronicle* 30 June 1795)

MATTHEWS, WILLIAM, was left a legacy by his father's will. If he will apply to the executor, he may receive it (*GAVN:* 229 cites the *Va. Gaz. and Weekly Advertiser* 8 Nov 1783).

MAYER, ANTON, arrived four years ago. His brother Hans Heinrich Mayer, from Pinkel, Switzerland, and now living in Greenwich Twp., Maxatawney, Berks Co., PA, came here 14 years ago, and is seeking his brother Anton (*Eyster:* 18 cites the *Pennsylvanische Berichte* 4 Feb 1758).

Henrich Meyer arrived on the *Phoenix* on 30 Sep 1743 (*Eyster:* 18).

MAYER, HANS CONRAD, came here 27 years ago. His sister Anna Mayer, born at Winckel in Zurich District, is seeking him. She is living at Middletown, NJ. He may write to Jacob Rittenhouse in Germantown, or to Abraham Mayer at New Gossenhoppen (*Eyster:* 21 cites the *Pennsylvanische Berichte* 27 March 1761).

Conrad Mayer arrived on 29 May 1735 on the *Mercury* (*Eyster:* 21).

MAYER, JOHN MICHEL, formerly a citizen of Gratzingen, is now living in PA. A letter is waiting for him at the Printer's; the cost is one shilling (*Eyster:* 6 cites the *Pennsylvanische Berichte* 1 Dec 1748).

Michael Meyer of Grotzingen [*sic*], Wurtemburg, married Anna Maria [-?-]. Michael and his wife and one child took Communion privately, and left with other emigrants who had taken communion on 9 May 1747 and left that day. In 1749 Mayer was noted as being in PA (Yoder's *PGI:* 91).

Michael Meyer arrived on the *Lydia* on 24 Sep 1747). Another Michael Meyer and Philip Jacob Meyer arrived on the *Restoration* on 9 Oct 1747 (*PGP* 1:364).

Michael and Anna Maria Meyer were the parents of at least two children (Yoder's *PGI:* 91): JOHANN GEORG, b. 21 July 1740, and MICHAEL, b. 7 March 1743.

MAYNE, SAMUEL, native of Co. Down, Ire., emigrated to the United States, and worked in different parts of PA as a cabinet maker, occasionally as a carpenter. His friends have received no word of him since 1809, when he was in New York. His brother Hugh Mayne, now in Baltimore, is seeking information about him (*Baltimore Patriot* 7 Feb 1821).

McDEAD, JOHN, JAMES McDEAD, GEORGE McDEAD, and **PATRICK McDEAD,** if living, are asked to apply to Thomas Tagart, Esq., of Cecil Co., MD, to hear of something to their advantage (*Pa. Gaz.* 5 Oct 1769).

McDONALD, KITTY, and her two children, came from Ireland with Thomas Burl in the ship *Norfolk,* Capt. Wilson. One of her children was taken away by Thomas Burl's father to Patterson Town, and is now in Philadelphia. Anyone with information is asked to contact Kitty McDonald at 167 S. Second St., Philadelphia. (Wash., D.C. *Centinel of Liberty* 5 Feb 1799).

McGINLY, NEAL, had sent letters to his brother Hugh McNeal, of the Parish of Lefford, Co. Donegal, Ireland, who has recently arrived in this country. Hugh cannot locate his brother, and asks Neal to contact him at Mr. James Montgomery, near the Brick Meeting House, East Nottingham, Chester Co. (*Pa. Gaz.* 8 Feb 1770).

McILHENEY, JOHN, of West Fallowfield Twp., Chester Co., PA, age 19, of fair complexion and about 5'6" tall, left his father's house about nine weeks ago, intending to get employment as a waggoner in the continental service. Since that time his parents have heard nothing from him, and they are very uneasy. If he is living, he is asked to write to them /s/ William McIlheney (*Pa. Gaz.* 13 Jan 1779).

William McIlheney of West Fallowfield Twp., Chester Co., died leaving a will dated 28 March 1779 and proved 18 March 1800. He left al his personal estate to his daughters Margaret, Jane, and Elizabeth. All his land was to be sold, and son John was to have £20.0.0, and the same amount was left to his grandson Jacob. Grandson Ezekiel was to have £10.0.0. His son-in-law James Gillam was to have 10 shillings. The remainder was to be divided equally among his seven children: John, Margaret, George, Mary, Jane, Rebecca, and Elizabeth. Son George and daughter Elizabeth were named executors. James Noble, James Sterrett and John Croson witnessed the will (*Chester Wills*).

McKAIN, GEORGE, a lusty well set man, supposed to be about 40 years of age, came many years since from Ireland into this country. He was in Philadelphia about two years ago. If he be yet living, and will apply to the printers hereto, he may hear of something greatly to his advantage; and if deceased, a particular account thereof, from any of his friends or acquaintance, when and where he died, and what children he has left, shall be thankfully rewarded (*Pa. Gaz.* 12 Aug 1762).

McLEALAND, SAMUEL, from the Parish of Fahan, near Londonderry, should apply to George Conneley, soap boiler, in Union St., between Second and Third Sts., to receive some goods sent from Ireland by John Devlaghan (*Pa. Gaz.* 17 Nov 1768).

McPHERSON, JOHN, Jr., being *non compos mentis,* hath lately left the house of his father, John McPherson, Sr., in Sadsbury Twp., Chester Co. All persons are asked to secure the son and send word to his father by letter, directed to the Rev. Adam Boyd or Mr. Andrew Stirling (*Pa. Gaz.* 6 Jan 1757).

About three years ago, John McPherson, age 27, somewhat disordered in his senses (occasioned by a fall from his horse), left his father's house. He is a pretty good English scholar and some time after his departure, taught an English school in the Forks of the Delaware, but soon departed from thence. He leaves a father, mother, and a young wife (*Pa. Gaz.* 7 Feb 1760).

McQUEAD, PATRICK, son of John McQuead living in the Parish of Derrylichin, Co. Antrim, came to America some twelve years ago from England. If he will send a letter to the care of Nathaniel Grubb pf Chester County, the favor will be thankfully acknowledged by Arthur McQuead (*Pa. Gaz.* 2 Oct 1755).

MEAR, JOHN, formerly of Bridgewater, Co. Somerset, is asked to apply by letter or otherwise to Peter Blight of Philadelphia, as he will hear of something to his advantage (*The Pennsylvania Packet and Daily Advertiser* 28 Dec 1785).

MELI, JOHANN, born at Baar, Alsace, is informed that his sister Catharina Meli has died unmarried last Feb in Brussells (*Hocker:* 166 cites the *Philadelphische Correspondenz* 30 Sep 1783).

MENGES, JOHANN GEORG, born at Hebstel, Granschaft, Furstenau, tailor, arrived in America eight years ago. His brother Johann Conrad Menges, of Upper Milford Twp., Northampton (now Lehigh) Co., with his brother-in-law Mazius, one and a half miles from Abraham Meyer of New Gossenhoppen, is seeking his Johann Georg (*Hocker:* 67 cites the *Pennsylvbanische Geschichts-Schreiber* 24 Dec 1757).

"Conrath" [*sic*] Menges arrived on the *Albany,* Robert Brown, Master, from Rotterdam last from Cowers, on 2 Sep 1749 (*PGP* 1:395). Another "Conrath" Meyers arrived on the *Mary and Sarah* on 23 Oct 1754 (*Eyster:* 17).

John Conrad Menges, a widower, married Anna Catherine, dau. of Peter Bechtel and his wife, on 10 Jan 1764. They were the parents of (Records of Christ Church, Bieber Creek, the Mertz Church, *Berks Churches* 4): JOHAN CONRAD, b. 27 Feb 1765; ANNA MARGRETHA, b. 27 Feb 1767; PETER, b. 29 July 1771; CATHARINA ELIZABETHA, b. 26 Dec 1773; JOHANN JACOB, b. 12 Aug 1776; JACOB, b. 17 Sep 1777; and ANA MARIA, b. 25 Dec 1783.

MENSCH, JOHANN NICKEL, arrived in this country four years ago from Deimberg, "aus dem Crumbacher Amt." He is 28 years old and is probably indentured. His brother, Adam Mensch, of Cohansey, Cumberland Co., NJ, is seeking him (*Hocker:* 63 cites the *Pennsylvanische Geschichts-Schreiber* 25 June 1757).

Adam Mensch arrived on the *Brothers,* Capt. Muir, from Rotterdam, on 24 Aug 1750 (*PGP* 1:437).

For more on the Mensch family, see Burgert's *Western Palatinate* 237-238, and Frank W. Mensch, *The Mensch Genealogy,* Philadelphia, 1921.

MERCER, RICHARD, a plasterer by trade, left West-Whiteland, Chester Co., PA, on or about 12 Aug 1819. His relatives and friends have not heard from him since. Anyone with information is asked to contact his mother, Patty Mercer, residing in West-Whiteland Twp., Chester Co., PA (*Republican Star and General Advertiser* Nov 1829).

MERCKEL, CHRISTIAN FREDERICK, son of the deceased Collector of Customs at Gatersburg, in the Principality of Halverstadt, paid a visit to his mother in 1789, and was seen to be returning on horseback to Halverstadt where he was apprenticed to a merchant named Schmidt. He never returned to his mother or his employer and has not been heard of since. His mother has died, and he has become heir to a considerable fortune, which, since 1798, has been under the management of guardians appointed by the Royal Prussian Court of Administration. Anyone with information is asked to communicate with I. E. A. Steinmetz, Consul of His Prussian majesty at Charleston, SC, or the Court of Administration at Gatersleben /s/ Roloff, High Bailiff of the Principality of Halverstadt (*U.S. Gazette* 21 Nov 1804).

MERIRIEUX, Citizen, was born at Carcassonne, Dept. of Aude, and for a few years lived at Fort, *ci-devant* Dauphin, on the Island of St. Domingo. Anyone who can supply information about him is asked to send to the Minister or Consuls of the French Republic in the United States ([PA] *Aurora General Advertiser* 21 Nov 1794).

MERKER, PAULUS, miller, was born at Langen Sulzbach and came to America about thirty years ago. Now he is sought by his nephew, Philip Jacob Lischer, son of Merker's sister, living with Conrad Hess on Race St., Philadelphia (*Hocker:* 162 cites the *Philadelphische Correspondenz* June 1781).

For more on the Merker family, see Burgert's *Alsace* 343, 361-362.

MERKESON, JOHN, HARMAN SHOEMAKER, or MATHIAS SHOEMAKER. Or any of their heirs, should apply to Walter Johnson of Skippack Twp., Philadelphia Co., PA, as they will hear of something to their advantage (*The Pennsylvania Packet or the General Advertiser* 10 Aug 1782).

METZ, JOHANNES, and **VALENTINE METZ,** five years ago they and their brother Peter, were indentured. Peter is now free and is trying to find them (*Hocker:* 6 cites the *Pennsylvanische Geschichts-Schreiber* 15 Aug 1746).

Peter Metz, age 18, came on the *Molly,* John Cranch, master, on 26 Oct 1741 (*PGP* 1:314).

METZGER, JOHANNES, linenweaver from Valengin, Wurtemburg, is sought by Ernest Ludwig Baisch (*Eyster:* 27 cites the *Pennsylvanische-Staatsbote* 28 July 1772).

Hocker: 117 cites the same notice adding that he is believed to be in the Shenandoah Valley of Virginia, with the Dunkers.

MEYBERG, DANIEL, a smith, arrived in this country eighteen years ago. His brother, Friedrich Meyberg, arrived here this autumn, having passed through the East Indies and Holland, and is seeking Daniel. Friedrich is at Deep Run, Perkasie, Bucks Co., with Abraham Schwartz (*Hocker:* 45 cites the *Pennsylvanische Geschichts-Schreiber* 16 Dec 1745).

MEYER, CHRISTIAN, from Dandeshoff in Meissenheim, was born in 1733 and arrived in 1743. His mother, who lives among the Welsh in Montgomery Co., PA, is seeking him (*Eyster:* 5 cites the *Pennsylvanische Berichte* 16 Sep 1746).

Christian Meyer of Philadelphia Co., PA, was naturalized in PA on 11 to 1 April 1743 (*Bockstruck:* 200).

Hocker: 6 cites the *Pennsylvanische Geschichts-Schreiber* 16 Sep 1746 adding that five years ago at Christmastime, a widow complained to a man in the street in Philadelphia that she had many small children, and could not pay for their passage on the ship. The man took Christian Mayer, then aged 8 to his home, some thirty miles away, to consult his wife on the matter if retaining the boy. The mother did not get the man's name, and now she wishes to hear from him.

MICHEL, CARL, and his brother **CASPER MICHEL** came to Pennsylvania from Germany three years ago. Their sister, Maria Dorothea Michel, married Bernhard Reinschmidt and had come to American about ten years ago. Reinschmidt is now in the service of Jacob Frisch as furnace master at Mount Hope, Morris Co., NJ, and is seeking his wife's two brothers (*Hocker:* 142 cites the *Wochentlicher Pennsylvanische Staatsbote* 4 April 1775).

MILLAR, JAMES, of dark complexion, aged about 20, 5'6 or 5'7 in height, and a carpenter or joiner by trade, was born at Stratham in Surrey. On 2 May 1764 he indented himself to Mr. Sydenham, merchant in London, and sailed immediately in the brig *Brothers,* James Morris, master, bound to Patapsco in Maryland, and was con-signed to Mr. Fishwick there. Anyone who can give information about Millar, alive or dead, is asked to send a few lines to Charles Allen, to be left at Mr. Joseph Yeates, at the Three Tuns in Chesnut St., Philadelphia. "Philadelphia, 6 June 1765" (Annapolis *Maryland Gazette* 13 June 1765).

MILLEN, HUGH, son of Quinten Millen of New York is asked to apply to Josa. Follins, Jr., John Little, or Henry King, who are executors of his late brother Alexander Millen, or to Col. Robert Gable of the City of Richmond, as he will hear of something to his advantage. "Edenton N.C., 3 July " (*The Enquirer* 11 July 1807).

MILLER, Mr. [-?-], was a Justice of the Peace in Philadelphia during the late war. He had two daus., one of whom married a M. Pater, of Guadeloupe. Anyone with information is requested to communicate with the French Boarding House, 105 N. Front St. (*Aurora General Advertiser* 20 Nov 1795).

MILLER, CATHERINE, dau. of Adam Miller of Bucks Co., PA, went away with Jacob Conrad into MD or VA about 14 or 15 years ago. She is asked to apply to John Weaver or Conrad Sherman (*Maryland Gazette or Baltimore General Advertiser* 26 Feb 1788).

MILLER, JOHN, son of Francis and Susan Miller of London, left Great Britain on the *Litchfield* for MD or VA in 1752. He or his heirs may hear something to their advantage of they reply to Aeneas M'Lean of New York (*GAVN:* 235 cites Rind's *Va. Gaz.*9 Feb 1769).

John Miller, felon, from Surrey was transported from London to MD on the *Litchfield,* Capt. Leonard Gerrard, in May 1752 (*KPMV:* 136).

MILLER, JOHN, of Philadelphia, PA, went to Baltimore Co., MD about 1791, as a miller. He is urged to contact William Johnson of Philadelphia (Baltimore *Daily Intelligencer* 14 Feb 1794).

MILLER, JOHN GEORGE, a native of St. Gall in Suisse [Switzerland], should apply to Jacob Ehrenzeller at the Sign of the Bay Horse in Third Street, near the Academy, to hear something to his advantage (*Pa. Gaz.* 25 Oct 1775).

MILLER, MARIA CATHERINE, came to Philadelphia. From Germany about six years ago, and was sold into the country, so her brother Christian Miller has not been able to get any intelligence of her. She is asked to inform him of where she is living. Christian is living with John Hare, Lampeter Twp., Lancaster Co. (*Pa. Gaz.* 9 Oct 1755).

Christian Miller arrived on the *Phoenix*, John Mason, master, late from Rotterdam, last from Cowes, on 15 Sep 1749 (*PGP* 1:406).

MILLER, RUDOLPH, and **BARBARA MILLER,** came from Switzerland to this Province with their father, Jacob Miller, and their sister Regina. Rudolph and Barbara were bound out as apprentices. Regina has married Daniel Kahn, living at Conestoga Ferry, near Lancaster, and would like to hear from her brother and sister (*Pa. Gaz.* 30 Oct 1760).

Daniel Kahn, born in Canton Zurich, and living in Lancaster, advertised that he had returned from a journey abroad and that information was sought on the Vies family who came to America about 35 years ago (*Hocker:* 105 cites the *Wochentlicher Pennsylvanische Staatsbote* 15 Jan 1771).

MILLES, PHILIP, came from London, about ten or eleven years ago to VA in the ship *Painter*, Capt. Miller, and there agreed with Henry Man of VA to work at the cabinet-making trade. On 4 Aug 1775 he worked with Thomas Bryant, cabinet-maker, in Philadelphia. He enlisted soon after in the Continental Army, and was taken to Fort Washington. He "listed" in the British army in the new levies, and was again taken with Earl Cornwallis at Yorktown. Two years ago he was a prisoner at Rockingham Court House, and at Mr. Rutherford's tavern there. If he is still alive and will apply to William Graham in Philadelphia, he will hear of something greatly to his advantage (*Pa. Gaz.* 6 July 1785).

MILLIGAN, JOHN, late of Charleston, merchant, has died. His nearest heirs will hear of something advantageous by applying as soon as possible, to Robert Walker of Charleston (*Daily National Intelligencer* 2 Nov 1820).

MILWARD, JOHN, an Englishman, 35 years old, 5'6" tall, square set, brown hair, rather curly, fair complexion and light eyes, left England in the beginning of 1783 in the brig *Iris*, Capt. Caldcleugh, for New York, from which ship he ran from on her arrival at that place. He was on board His Britannic Majesty's ship *Roebuck*, Capt. Hammond, on the New York station, during the latter end of the American war. If he will apply to Mr. Peter W. Galloudet, Second St., Philadelphia, or Mr. George Douglas, Queen St. New York, where he will hear of something considerably to his advantage. If living he is supposed to be on board some of the coasting vessels (*The Pennsylvania Packet and Daily Advertiser* 8 June 1789).

MINGLE, WILLIAM, now about 22 years old, sailed from Philadelphia on 1 March 1813 in the privateer *Shadaw*, commanded by Capt. Haight. He was taken prisoner by the

British the following April and sent to Stapleton Prison, somewhere in the interior of England. Since then his mother, Elizabeth Mingle, has not heard from him and does not know whether he is alive or dead. [No address is given for the mother] (*Baltimore Patriot* 8 Aug 1815).

MINHARD, JOHN JACOB, a German, died on board the schooner *Bee*, George Stewart, master, belonging to Curacao, on his voyage to Baltimore. If his proper heir applies to the printer, he may hear of something to his advantage (*Pennsylvania Packet or the General Advertiser* 30 Oct 1779).

MINSON, HENRY, for many years was captain of several vessels on the James River. His wife, Elizabeth Minson, of Charles City Co., is seeking him. He left her with his five children, without any reason. A few days ago she learned that he was brought to Williamsburg as a Tory, and never since heard of him, but she believes he may be in Hampton or Norfolk (*GAVN:* 235 cites Purdy, Clarkson and Davis' *Va. Gaz.* 21 June 1776).

MITCHELL, WILLIAM, formerly lived in the Parish of Desart Creaght, Co. Tyrone, and came to these parts in 1769. He enlisted in the Regiment of Royal Americans in 1770. His brother David Mitchell arrived in Philadelphia last 19 July and left their father, mother, and brethren all in good health on last 10 May when he left them. David earnestly requests that William write to him as soon as possible, care of Mr. William Carson, tavern keeper, in the Third St., at the Sign of the Harp and Crown (*Pa. Gaz.* 30 Sep 1772).

MOLEGAN, JOHN, ROBERT, and **MOSES**, sons of John Molegan, came from Co. Armagh, Ireland, have a legacy left them by one Thomas McKeterick. If they apply to Hugh McCollom, executor, living at Freehold, Monmouth Co., NJ, they may be further informed (*Pa. Gaz.* 10 Feb 1757).

In 1790 a John Molegan was in North Huntingdon Twp., Westmoreland Co., PA, on p. 264 (*AIS 1790 U.S. Federal Census Index*).

MOLENHAUPT, JOHANN PHILIP, from Alsdorf in Anspach, is now in New York, and he notifies his cousin, Heinrich Guntermann, that he came to America, in response to a letter from Guntermann promising to free him upon his arrival. As he heard nothing from Guntermann, he was compelled to go into service, he has three years left to serve, and he owes 8 guineas (*Hocker:* 177 cites the *Philadelphische Correspondenz* 5 Dec 1786).

MONDELL, WILLIAM, aged 55, 5'6" or 7" tall, of ruddy complexion and stout build, has been missing from Fells Point for a week. It is supposed that he left in a deranged state, and come to Philadelphia. Anyone with information is asked to contact Samuel Chubb, at 151 N. Third St., his disconsolate wife, or John Sykes and Son, Baltimore (*Poulson's American Daily Advertiser* 10 Oct 1819).

MONDUCET, Mr. GUILLER de, a French gentleman from Nogent Le Rotrou, is now supposed to be in the continent of North America. By the death of his parents, he has become the heir to a very large fortune in France. Anyone having news of him is asked to contact Messrs. Lacaze and Mallet, merchants, in Philadelphia (*Pa. Gaz.* 12 Feb 1783).

MONRO, HECTOR SHIRLEY, son of Hector Monro, Esq., of Co. Down, Ireland, will learn something to his advantage if he applies to Rev. Philip Hughes (Chaplain to the Regt. of Maj. Gen. Abercrombie), or to Messrs. Cunningham and Nesbit, or to Hugh Wallace of NYC, merchant (*Scott* 3:47 cites *The New York Mercury* 6 Sep 1756; *Pa. Gaz.* 19 Aug 1756).

MONROE, JOHN, about nineteen years ago lived with John Way in Newcastle Co., DE. He was eight years old when his mother, Rebecca Monroe, left him and moved to Fayette Co., PA. About six years ago she received a letter from John Way saying he son had left him, and since then she has heard nothing of her son. Anyone with information is asked to contact his mother, Rebecca Monroe, of Fayette Co, PA (*Poulson's American Daily Advertiser* 9 July 1808).

MOORE, DAVID, and his wife **JANET MOORE**, who came this fall in the ship *Holderness*, Capt. Simpson, from Leith, Ireland, are sought by Margaret Lenox, sister of Janet Moore. Margaret lives at John Mick's in Nottingham, PA (*Scott* 2:210 cites the *Pa. Gaz.* 14 Dec 1752).

MOORE, JACOB, left Holland about six years ago and came to America. His sister Barbara has been in America for about three years and would like information about her brother (*Scott* 3:39 cites *The New York Mercury* 18 Aug 1755).

MOORE, JAMES, son of Acheson Moore of Aughnacloy, Ireland, should apply to the printers (*Maryland Journal and Baltimore Advertiser* 7 Sep 1790).

MORAS, CITIZEN [-?-], of Bordeaux, France, resident in Port Royal, Martinique, arrived in the continent after the said island fell into the power of the English. His brother-in-law wishes to know his residence and asks him to write to him in care of Citizen Myers of Norfolk, who will forward letters to the French ship *L'Eclatant*, on board which Citizen Page, Officer of Health, and son-in-law of the widow Moras resides (*GAVN:* 240 cites the *American Gazette and Norfolk and Portsmouth Public Advertiser* 21 April 1795).

MOREMAN, THOMAS, son of Peter Moreman, near Exeter, in Old England, if alive, may hear of something to his advantage by applying to Joshua Howell (*Pa. Gaz.* 28 June 1758).

MORESS, TORANS, who came over with Hugh Alexander (*q.v.*), is lame. If he will apply to Mr. Carson, may hear of something to his advantage (*Pa. Gaz.*, 24 July 1760).

MORGAN, JAMES, left Delaware last 12 June, and has not been heard of since. He was a clerk at the Union Factory, and more recently kept a store in New Castle Co., near St. George's. It is understood that he has been employed in a factory near New York. His distressed wife, Elizabeth Morgan, is now in New York, and is seeking information about him. Letters containing information may be addressed to he office of the *Baltimore Patriot* or to Rev. Lewis Richards (*Baltimore Patriot* 14 Dec 1824).

MORGAN, JOHN, son of John Morgan of Milnehouses, Co. Durham, left England some 24 years ago. The son is urged to contact his father as all his brothers have died without issue, and he is now the heir (*Pa. Gaz.* 5 March 1730).

MORRIS, DANIEL, of Skippack, about two years ago went to the Lower Counties, and has not been heard of since. John Morris of Skippack, Philadelphia Co., offers a reward for news of his brother (*Pa. Gaz.* 16 Aug 1733).

MORRIS, OWEN, of the Parish of Kemmis in Montgomeryshire, Wales, left there 40 years ago, and was not heard of until 1736, when he wrote his brother Richard Morris, asking that a relative might come to him to be heir to his estate. He gave his address as The White Hart in Boston. Ann Roberts, dau. of a nephew Owen Roberts, Jr., came to America, but cannot find Owen Morris the Elder, now nearly 80 years old. Ann Roberts, now at Edward Nicholls, in Philadelphia, will pay a reward for news of Owen Morris the Elder (*Pa. Gaz.* 8 March 1739).

MORRIS, THEOPHILUS, a native of South Wales, from Trelech, in Carmarthenshire, by trade a shoemaker, between 60 and 70 years of age, lived some time in Chester County. If he is alive, and will come to the New Printing Office, in Market Street, Philadelphia, he will hear of something to his Advantage (*Pa. Gaz.* 6 Nov 1760).

MORRIS, Rev. WILLIAM, late of Montgomeryshire, North Wales, is urged to contact Rev. William Barroll of Cecil Co. (Annapolis *Maryland Gazette* 24 May 1764).
Later he was described as being of Garthsire, Co. Montgomery. He left his country and stayed with Rev. Jones in Cecil Co. He will hear something to his advantage if he applies to John Merryman, Jr., of Baltimore Town (Annapolis *Maryland Gazette* 21 Feb 1765).

MORRIS, WILLIAM, from Finrona, Co. Tyrone, Ireland, some time ago resided in Northumberland Co., PA, near Sunbury. If he is living he is urged to contact his sister Anne McKinney and family, lately come into this country, by writing to Alexander McIntire, Lancaster, PA (*Lancaster Journal* 12 Feb 1802).

MORRISON, DANIEL, a peddler, formerly lived in Chambersburg, PA. He left home about eight months ago, intending to go to the western part of Pennsylvania or Virginia. Since then he has not been heard of. He is about 5' tall, sandy complexioned, and thick set. Anyone with information is asked to contact his disconsolate family. /s/ Nancy Morrison, Chambersburg (*Democratic Republican* 24 Feb 1817).

MORTON, ALEXANDER, left Scotland about two years ago for MD. He is urged to contact William Webster near Piscataway (Annapolis *Maryland Gazette* 27 Sep 1770).
An Alexander Morton died in Dorchester Co., MD by Nov 1771. His personal estate was appraised by Julius August Jackson and Clement Bayly at £423.18.0. John Fisher, admin., filed the inventory on 15 Nov 1771. A second inventory totaling £203.5.3

was filed by John Fisher on 10 March 1773 (MINV 107:268, 111:346). No administration account was filed in the Prerogative Court of Maryland.

MORTON, THOMAS, bookbinder, a native of Petersburg, VA, is believed to have lately resided in Philadelphia. If he applies to F. G. at 212 Market St., Baltimore, he may hear of something to his advantage (*The Tickler* 2 May 1810).

MOSELEY, MATTHEW, son of Anthony Moseley, came over from England in 1734. If he or his children are alive they may hear something to their advantage if they apply to Bassett and Alexander Moseley, Norfolk (*GAVN*: 242 cites Rind's *Va. Gaz.* 12 May 1768).

A Matthew Moseley was in Dobbs Co., NC in 1780 (*AIS Census Index: Pre-1790* gives no other documentation). Matthew Mosley [*sic*] was head of a family in Dobbs Co., NC in 1790 (*AIS 1790 Census Index*).

MOSER, WALBURGA, and her sister **MARGRETHA MOSER**, went to SC about 21 years ago, married and are now believed to be Ebenezer, GA. Their brother, Jacob Moser, in the service of Adam Erben, brandyburner of Philadelphia, was born at Langenau, near Ulm. He is seeking information about his two sisters (*Hocker*: 124 cites the *Wochentlicher Pennsylvania Staatsbote* 13 July 1773).

Jacob Moser arrived on the ship *Hope* on 3 Dec 1772 (*Eyster*: 32).

In 1790 a Jacob Moser was in Bucks Co., PA (*AIS 1790 U.S. Federal Census Index*).

MOSERN, GEORGE. JOHN, and **BARBARA**, children of Eve Hatfield, who died by April 1764, are sought by their relations who do not know whether they are living or where they reside. If they are living they are to apply to Paul Mosern in Falconer's Swamp, in New Hanover Twp., for their share of their mother's estate (*Pa. Gaz.* 19 April 1764).

MOWORN, HENRY, and **ADAM MOWORN**, came from Germany with their parents about 24 years ago. The vessel was cast away on the capes, but the passengers got to Lewes Town, where the boys were given away by their father. He and his wife then proceeded to Philadelphia, where both parents soon died, leaving a daughter, Mary, who is still living at Philadelphia, and is anxious to know if her brothers are still living (*Pa. Gaz.* 5 Nov 1765).

MUELLER, HENRICH, from Zurich Gebiet, Switzerland, arrived in America, about eight years ago with his daughters Elizabeth, and **REGELY MUELLER**, and they were separated. Elizabeth is with Peter Zimmerman at Swamp, and will be free in the autumn of next year. She is seeking news of her father and sister (*Hocker*: 33 cites the *Pennsylvanische Geschichts-Schreiber* 16 April 1752).

MUELLER, JOH. GEORG, born in St. Gallen, Switzerland, is asked to send word of his whereabouts to Jacob Ehrenzeller at the Brown Horse Inn, Fourth St., near the Academy, Philadelphia (*Hocker*: 119, 144 cites the *Wochentlicher Pennsylvania Staatsbote* 4 July 1775).

MUELLER, JOHANNES, from Knillingen, the son of a gold refiner, arrived in America sixteen years ago. This autumn his brother Andreas arrived, and is with Paul Koester, Skippack, Montgomery Co., PA, and is seeking Johannes (*Hocker:* 32 cites the *Pennsylvanische Geschichts-Schreiber* 1 March 1752).

MUELLERIN, ROSINA, arrived in this country five years ago from Undinge. Her brother Jacob, from Undienge, in Aurach, Wutrtemburg, at present living over the River in Maidenhaet, with Johannes Enerson, is seeking her (*Hocker:* 44 cites the *Pennsylvanische Geschichts-Schreiber* 16 Nov 1754).

MULLEN, ANN, now about 21, daughter of Mary Moore, was taken prisoner by the Shawanese Indians from the Cow Pasture, Augusta Co., VA, about six years ago. She and one Laney Pussey made their escape from the Lower Shawanese Towns, and were later taken by the Onandagoes, with whom they remained for eleven months. They made their way to Raritan, in the Jerseys where some relatives of Laney Pussey live. Her mother is now at Fort Pitt, having lately been released by the Shawanese, waiting for her children to be brought to her. Ann Mullen was often called Ann Moore, her mother having married while the girl was young (*Pa. Gaz.* 17 March 1763).

MULLEN, JAMES, is sought by his brother Henry Mullen, who has not heard from him for some time. If Mullen will come immediately to Baltimore, and apply at the house of Felix Hughes, Market St., he will hear of something decidedly to his advantage (*Baltimore Patriot* 9 Aug 1831).

MUNN, WILLIAM, DANIEL MUNN, and JOHN MUNN, now or late of Philadelphia, are sons of the late Daniel Munn of Bartholomew Close, London, dyer and scourer who died in June 1756 and left each of his sons a small legacy at age 21. Those who are of age should apply to Alexander Mann, carpenter, at the Golden Key, facing Picadilly, London, or to Jacob Fletcher, button seller, in Cloth Fair, executors of the said Daniel Munn, Sr. (*Pa. Gaz.* 31 Jan 1758).

William Munn had a letter waiting for him at Philadelphia Post Office (*Pa. Gaz.* 3 Aug 1758).

MURALT, GASPARD de. native of Switzerland, is said to be settled near this city. If he will apply to Joshua Fisher and Sons he will hear something to his advantage (*Pa. Gaz.* 7 May 1772).

MURPHY, PETER, a youth about eleven years old, was sometime ago, bound to Giles Sheperd, cordwainer of Philadelphia. Sheperd has absconded, taking the youth with him, contrary to engagement. Daniel Swan offers a reward for news of Peter Murphy (*Pa. Gaz.* 12 Feb 1767).

The 1790 Censuses show a Peter Murphy in Baltimore Co., MD, p. 18, and another one in Washington Co., PA, p. 251 (*AIS 1790 U.S. Federal Census Index*).

MURPHY, TERRENCE, was lately discharged from employment at the U.S. Capitol. His wife, who has been rescued from the wreck of the *Constellation,* and is now in this city and in utmost distress, is seeking information about him ([DC] *Daily National Intelligencer* 7 Feb 1820).

MUTZ, CORNELIUS, from Buttenhausen, near Graveneck, Wurtemburg, is sought by Ernest Ludwig Baisch (*Eyster:* 27 cites the *Pennsylvanische Staatsbote* 26 Nov 1776).

NASH, MATTHEW, served part of his time with Joshua Gaither, and the remainder of his time with Neal Clark on Elk Ridge, MD. He should apply to William Woodward at Head of Severn, to hear of something to his advantage, from his friends in England (Annapolis *Maryland Gazette* 23 Aug 1764).

On 25 Sep 1755 Matthew Nash was indicted for stealing two cheeses, value 5 s., the goods of John Blest. At the trial on 22 Oct 1755 Blest testified that he lived in Great Marlborough-street, Carnaby-market; he was a cheese monger. The prisoner came into my shop on the 29th of September, and Blest saw him take one cheese, and walk out. Nash testified in his own defense that he had been coming from his mother's to go to his lodgings in Swallow St., when Blest lost two cheeses; he came and took hold of me, and said, I had taken two cheeses, but I had no cheeses upon me. Nash was found guilty and sentenced to transportation (www.oldbaileyonline.org).

Matthew Nash was transported from Middlesex Gaol to MD in the *Greyhound,* Capt. Alexander Stewart. The ship sailed in Jan 1756 and arrived in MD in April 1756 (*KPMV:* 53).

NEALE, Mrs. ANNE, or **ANNE LADBROOKE,** from Daventry in Northamptonshire, left London on 2 Feb 1713, and was known to have lived with a lady on the Bristol or Rappahannock Rivers in Virginia about three years ago. She is urged to contact her brother John Neale, who has sent her a letter (Annapolis *Maryland Gazette* 9 June 1730).

NEGLEY, CATHERINE, dau. of Philip Negley, of Stoney Ridge, Middleton Twp., Cumberland Co., left her father's plantation on Sunday morning last, without permission, perhaps because she was afraid of receiving some chastisement from her parents, who are quite concerned about her safety, and hope she will return home (*The Carlisle Gazette* 25 July 1787).

NEIL, MATTHEW, came over in the Ship *Glasgow,* from Glasgow, last fall, and proposed going to Cumberland Co., as well to purchase land as to sell a few dry goods, will direct a line to William Semple, merchant, in Philadelphia (who has not heard from him since he left that place) he may hear of something in which he is materially concerned (*Pa. Gaz.* 15 Dec 1773).

In 1790 a Matthew Neal was head of a family in Cumberland Co., PA (*AIS 1790 Census Index*).

NELSON, JOHN, of Franklin Co., NC, formerly of Kingsess, PA, died intestate last November in NC. Any of his relations, now living are asked to apply to James Dyer at Mr. Robert Furniss' in Newcastle on Delaware, or to Col. Simon Jefferey's in NC, where they will may hear of something greatly to their advantage (*The Pennsylvania Packet or the General Advertiser* 8 Sep 1781).

NESBIT, BETSEY, is supposed to live in Antrim Twp, Franklin Co, PA, about six miles from Chambersburg, and sometime with the Rev. Mr. Lin. Her sister, Anna Nesbit, of Morris Town, NJ, has been in this country for 10 years, and has endeavored in vain to discover where Betsey is living. Anyone with information is asked to contact Anna (*Poulson's American Daily Advertiser* 2 April 1812).

NESTER, FRIEDRICH, is living in the vicinity of the Blue Mountains. Peter Schmidt, born in Carlsruh im Durlachischen, arrived in Philadelphia recently with Capt. Smith, and is now in the employ of Andrew McGlone, merchant, at the lower bridge (drawbridge), Philadelphia. Peter is a son of Sigmund Schmidt, who is still in Germany, and is inquiring for Nester (*Hocker:* 119 cites the *Wochentlicher Pennsylvanischer Staatsbote* 17 Nov 1772).

NEWLANDS, JAMES, aged about 35, came five or six years ago as an indentured servant from Glasgow to one of the plantations in America. He has succeeded to a considerable fortune. Alexander Newlands, skinner, of Edinburgh, is seeking information about him (*Scott* 3:19 cites *Bradford's New York Gazette* 24 Oct 1737).

James Newlands, age c35, went from Glasgow five or six years ago as an indentured servant to one of HM plantations. He has lately succeeded to a considerable estate. Alexander Newlands, skinner, in Edinburgh, seeks information on him (*GAVN* 249 cites the *Va. Gaz.* 21 April 1738).

NICHOLAS, RICHARD, from Cornwall, Eng., formerly lived in PA, but then went to some part of MD, is hereby informed that his brother's son, John Nicholas, is now in Philadelphia, and would be glad to hear from him. John Nicholas can be reached at Arnold Bailey's, at the upper end of Front St., Philadelphia (*Pa. Gaz.* 30 Aug 1759).

About 1757 Richard Nicholas was listed as a creditor of the estate of John McDermot of Cecil Co., MD (MDAD 41:152).

NICHOLS, WILLIAM, came into MD as a transport for seven years, and was sold to William Keeley (or Kelly) living on the Garrison Ridge in BA Co. he should contact Charles Homewood for news of a legacy in England (Annapolis *Maryland Gazette* 23 April 1752).

On 27 June 1748 William Nicholls [*sic*] was indicted for stealing nine pounds weight of brass, the property of Richard Smith, He was tried at the Old Bailey in London on 6 July 1748. The Prisoner had been apprenticed to Mr. Smith, who said he was a very good workman, and a very ingenious boy. Nicholls begged of Mr. Smith to take him again, but he would not agree to it. Nicholls was found guilty and sentenced to transportation (www.oldbaileyonline.org).

He may have been the William Nicholls transported from London to Virginia by the *Mary,* Capt. John Ramsay, in July 1748 (*KPMV:* 117).

NICODEMUS, JOHANN ADAM born at Medenbach, Nassau Dilleburg, and now living near Lancaster, is asked to apply to Johann Caspar Lapp, pastor at Anwell, NJ, with regard to his son, who has been freed from a harsh master, Georg Trimmer, of Anwell (*Hocker:* 55 cites the *Pennsylvanische Geschichts-Schreiber* 16 May 1756).

Johann Adam Nicodemus arrived on the *Edinburgh,* Capt. John Lyon, from Rotterdam, qualifying on 2 Oct 1753 (*PGP* 1:578).

NIXON, ROBERT, house carpenter, formerly of Ireland, served his apprenticeship to Thomas Simpson of Drogheda, in said Kingdom. If he will inform the printers where he can be found he may hear of something to his advantage (*The Independent Gazetteer* 8 Oct 1783).

NIXON, WILLIAM, left Ireland some years ago, and removed with this family into this Province, and is said to have since lived in Maxfield Twp., Bucks Co. If he applies to the Post Office in Philadelphia, he may hear of something to his advantage (*Pa. Gaz.* 9 April 1752).

NIXON, WILLIAM, lived in Ireland and was bred up in the County of Fermanagh, and tenant to Esquire Brooks. If he is in America, and will come before the Governor of this Province, and shall prove himself to be of Cline, a Town Land belonging to Mr. Patrick Lendrum, he shall be paid 50 pounds Pennsylvania currency by Thomas Mullan at the sign of the Anchor and Hope in Philadelphia (*Pa. Gaz.* 25 Dec 1760).

NOBLE, RICHARD, formerly a surveyor in PA, has an heir at law who is asked to apply to Thomas Harrison so he may hear something to his advantage (*Pa. Gaz.* 24 Nov 1773).

NOERLINGERIN, ELISABETH, born in Wurtemberg, am dem Kloster Boebemhauser Amt, came to America twenty-two years ago, and now Johannes Elinger, Reestown, Bedford County, is seeking her (*Hocker:* 147 cites the *Wochentlicher Pennsylvanischer Staatsbote* 20 Oct 1775).

NOLAN, NICHOLAS, left Gallway last May or June and came to PA or MD in a vessel from Londonderry. If he applies to the printers, he will hear something to his advantage (*Pa. Gaz.* 6 Nov 1770).

NORRIS, A. B., resided in Baltimore in the summer of 1822. If he or his friends will advise "X. Y." at the office of the *Baltimore Patriot* he will hear of something to his advantage (*Baltimore Patriot* 23 Jan 1826).

NORTON, PEIRCE GEORGE COPE, now aged about 22, arrived in Philadelphia about seven years ago in a vessel commanded by Capt. Duncan, he is asked to apply to Hugh Gaine to learn something to his advantage (*Scott* 3:220 cites *The New York Gazette and Weekly Mercury* 27 Sep 1779).

NORTON, RUTH, who came about 27 years ago from Ireland as a gentlewoman's servant, and is supposed to have married Thomas Brown, mariner, will learn something to her advantage by going to George Brown, clerk to John Moore of Philadelphia, Esq. (*American Weekly Mercury* 23 July 1724).

NOWLAND, HANNAH MATILDA, now in her 22nd year, dau. of James and Sarah Ann Nowland, is believed to reside in Goshen, Loudon Co., VA, where she was raised. Her brother, William P. Nowland, living in Baltimore, MD, has neither seen nor heard anything about her for ten years. Up to now his circumstances have not allowed him to make a search for her, but he would like to have news of her (*Baltimore Patriot* 24 Jan 1816).

James Nowland and wife Honor were the parents of the following children, baptized in St. Peter's Catholic Church, Baltimore (*Piet:* 92, 93); WILLIAM, b. 21 March 1794, bapt. 4 Aug 1796; and MATILDA, b. 7 Dec 1796, bapt. 1 Aug 1797.

NUFFER, CHRISTIAN, and his sisters **CHRISTINA, CATHARINA**, and **VERONICA NUFFERIN**, are sought by their mother Christina Nufferin, from Rothenburg on the Necker, who came to America about thirty-four years ago and lived at Allentown. (*Hocker:* 165 cites the *Philadelphische Correspondenz* 3 June 1783).

Christoph Nuffer of Neuffen, Wurtemburg, married Christina [-?-]. He arrived on the *Phoenix* on 25 Sep 1751 (*PGP* 1:471). Christoph and Christiana were the parents of (Yoder's *PGI* 97): ELEANORA CATHARINA, b. 12 Oct 1750; CHRISTIAN; CHRISTIANA, and VERONICA.

NUNIS, SOLOMON. See **LOCKY CURLE.** (1833)

NUSLY, ULRICH, is asked to come to Jacob Peter at the Blue Mountains, or to Joseph Pfeiffer, to learn of the legacy left him by his uncle Ulrich Nusly, native of Switzerland, lately of Flower Town, Philadelphia Co., who has died (*Pa. Gaz.* 21 Dec 1774).

OBERLE, MICHAEL, is sought by Valentin Marter from Gungenheim, who will be free in the spring. Marter is at Martin Fritz's in Manetani, at the White Horse, below the Swede (*Eyster:* 13 cites the *Pennsylvanische Berichte* 16 Jan 1754).

O'BRIEN, JOHN, born in the county of Latrem [Antrim?], Ireland, came to Philadelphia in 1772, and worked as a laborer. He is about 64 years of age. If he is in any part of the United States, or if any person knows of him, he or they are asked to address a line to David and William, at 40 Market St. or to Alexander Wallace, 30 S. 2nd St., Philadelphia (*Poulson's American Daily Advertiser* 17 March 1810).

OERTER, GEORG, came to America seven years ago. His brother Michel, from Ober Otterbach, in Gutenberger Amt, is seeking information about him and can be contacted at Dietrich Welcker's ironworks (*Hocker:* 72 cites the *Pennsylvanische Geschichts-Schreiber* 10 Sep 1758). [**N.B.:** *Eyster:* 19 reads this name as Orter]

George Daniel Orter arrived on the ship *Brotherhood* on 3 Nov 1750 (*Eyster:* 19).

Michel Oerther [*sic*] arrived on the *Barclay*, Capt. John Brown, from Rotterdam, but last from Cowes, and took the usual oaths and declarations to the government, on 14 Sep 1754 (*PGP* 1:600). As Michael Erter [*sic*] he was in Frederick Co., MD by 8 Oct 1765 when Thomas Logsdon, with the consent of his wife Mary sold Erter 10 a. of *Good Fellowship.* On 8 Oct 1765 William Wilkson sold Erter 10 a. of *Addition to Full Bottle* (FRLR K:48-50, 50-51). As Michael Arter [*sic*] he was in Frederick Co., MD by 21 April 1767 when he purchased 60 a. of *Fellowship* from Jacob Gable (FRLR K: 1190-1191).

In 1790 a Michael Arter was listed in the Frederick Co. Census with two white males over 16, two white males under 16, and three white females. Nearby was Daniel Arter with one white male over 16, five white males under 16, and five white females (*1790MD* p. 60, col. 1).

OGILVIE, JAMES, came from Keith, in the North of Scotland. If he is in this town, he will confer a favor by calling at the post office for some letters sent him a friend in New York, or upon Capt. Samuel W. Turner of the schooner *Leonidas,* now lying at Smith's wharf; he will hear of something to his advantage (*Baltimore Patriot and Mercantile Advertiser* 15 Feb 1819).

OGLE, HENRY, late of Newry, Ireland, is supposed to be found Shippensburg, Cumberland Co., Penna., c/o Henry Patterson. Ogle is hereby informed that there are letters for him in the hands of Thomas Ledlie Birch of Washington [Co.?], Penna., including one from his relative Hans Ogle (*Herald of Liberty* 22 Aug 1801).

OGLE, SAMUEL, Esq., former Governor of Maryland, resided at Annapolis. His children or next of kin may hear something to their advantage by applying to Mr. Robert Donovan, Attorney at law, Peter St., Dublin, Ireland (*Universal Gazette* 1 Aug 1799).

Samuel Ogle, Governor Maryland, died 3 May 1752 and was buried at Annapolis. He had a half-sister, Meliora Ogle, who died 1774 in Dublin, Ireland (*BDML* 2:618).

OGLE, WILLIAM, native of Ireland, is supposed to have landed at New York some time last summer. This is to inform him that his parents now reside in the Village of Columbia, ten miles from Lancaster, and they are anxious to hear from him (*Lancaster Journal-Extra* 15 Feb 1804).

OLIVER, JOSEPH and **JOHN OLIVER,** sons of Joseph and Mary (Knap) Oliver of the Island of Guernsey, will hear something to their advantage by applying to William Foster, surgeon, in Guernsey (*GAVN:* 254 cites the *Va. Gaz. and General Advertiser* 7 Dec 1791).

O'MERA, MICHAEL, has been 40 years in this country, living in some part of VA, and if living , is a widower, and has only one daughter. A relative who has recently arrived from Ireland is seeking him, and asks that any information be directed to S.F., care of Robert Grant, 48 Lombard St. (*Poulson's American Daily Advertiser* 29 April 1819).

ORME, Rev. JOHN, died. His children or their heirs should apply to Thorowgood Smith of Baltimore (*Maryland Gazette or Baltimore General Advertiser* 4 Feb 1785).

John Orme married Ruth, daughter of Archibald Edmondston, who, on 25 March 1730, conveyed to his beloved son-in-law, Rev. John Orme, 248 a. of *Leith,* to contribute to the comfort of him and his wife Ruth Orme (PGLR M:564).

Rev. John Orme, for many years the Pastor of a dissenting congregation at Upper Marlborough, died 28 April 1758 in PG Co., age 67 years (*Maryland Gazette* 11 May 1758). Rev. Orme died leaving a will dated 28 Oct 1757 and proved 24 Aug 1758. He named his wife Ruth (who was to be extx.), and children John, James, Archibald, Jane, Elizabeth, Septima, Octava, and Ebenezer Edmonston. He also named a granddau. Nancy. Robert Bradley, Ruth Allen, and Jno. Belt., Jr., witnessed the will (MWB 30:562).

John and Ruth (Edmondston) were the parents of: JOHN, JAMES, ARCHIBALD, JANE, ELIZABETH, SEPTIMA, OCTAVA, and EBENEZER EDMONSTON.

ORR, DANIEL, blacksmith, who formerly lived in Chester Co., PA, is desired to apply to James Caldwell, administrator of Patrick Orr, dec., where he will hear something to his advantage. Patrick Orr, was a storekeeper late of Leacock Twp., Lancaster Co., and Caldwell asks all persons indebted to the estate to settle their accounts (*Pa. Gaz.* 24 April 1775).

ORR, JOHN, formerly of Hurtletoot, Co. Antrim, Ireland, came to Baltimore in the summer of 1829 in the Brig *William.* Capt. Larmour, from Belfast. He had a considerable sum of money in his possession. Information will be thankfully received by Wm. & Thos. Adair. Editors of county papers will confer a favor on Mrs. Orr by giving the above insertion (*Baltimore Patriot* 21 Jan 1834).

ORR, THOMAS, peruke maker, may have lived at Pequea. He is asked to call on William Carson, peruke maker, in Front St., Philadelphia, before 1 Oct next, where he may learn of something that will contribute greatly to his advantage (*Pa. Gaz.* 20 Aug 1761).

The 1790 Census of Pennsylvania lists two Thomas Orrs: one in West Marlborough Twp., Chester Co., PA, p. 74, and the other in Washington Twp. of Westmoreland Co., p. 268 (*AIS 1790 U.S. Federal Census Index*).

ORSER, JOHANNIS, was born in New York, and died recently at or near Egg Harbor, NJ. His children or heirs, is any are alive, are asked to apply to Daniel Dunscombe of the City of New York, who will inform them of something to their advantage. The heirs are asked to be speedy in their application (*The Pennsylvania Journal,* 14 Dec 1758).

OSBORNE, THOMAS, was born in Sheffield, Yorks., and was aged about 38. He arrived at Charleston, SC from Eng., some three or four months ago, and left Charleston for this Province [VA] some 10 weeks ago. If he applies to the printer he will hear something greatly to his advantage (*GAVN:* 255 cites the *Va. Gaz.* 11 June 1767).

In 1787 a Thomas Osborne was living in Charleston, SC (*AIS Census Index: Pre-1790* gives no other documentation).

OSTADE, HOON VAN, served in the United States Army under the name Charles Williams, from Aug 1806 to Aug 1812. His family is anxious to ascertain whether he is living or dead. Anyone with information is asked to communicate with the editor of this paper (*The Daily National Intelligencer* 14 Jan 1818).

OTTERBACH, WILHELM, born in Amt Burbach, Nassau-Dillenburg, who arrived in New York in 1785 on the ship *Watson.* His brother Jost Otterbach of <Middle Paxton Twp., Dauphin Co, PA, nine miles from Harrisburg, is seeking him (*Hocker:* 192 cites the *Philadelphische Correspondenz* 23 April 1793).

Johan Jost Otterbach arrived on the *Minerva,* Capt. Thomas Arnott, from Rotterdam, last from Cowes, and took the Oath on 17 Sep 1771 (*Names of Foreigners:* 496).

Johann Wilhelm Otterbach and Anna Elisabeth Bucherin arrived in Sep 1785 on the ship *Watson* from Amsterdam, and were consigned to Sears and Smith, NY (*Hocker:* 185 cites the *Philadelphische Correspondenz* 26 May 1789).

OVER, THOMAS, of the City of Gloucester, who in 1715, came from Bristol to New York in the ship of Capt. Totterdel. He is said to have married, and to be living in Pennsylvania or the Jerseys, is to come to Obadiah Hunt in New York City, who will inform him of an estate he has inherited; his sister, who came to America with him, has also been left a legacy (*American Weekly Mercury* 9 May 1722).

OWEN, JOHN, came from England in the ship *Diana,* William Montgomery, captain. He is urged to contact his brother, Hugh Owen, shoemaker, No. 8, Grace Church St., London (Annapolis *Maryland Gazette* 20 Jan 1774).

PAINTER, PETER, age c18, was born in Germany and came to America about four years ago, and was bought by Peter Knot. His friends are seeking him Information may be given to Cornelius Tanner in Lancaster Co., PA; a letter for Tanner may also be left with Mrs. Mary Lawler, tavern keeper at Newton (*Scott* 2:17 cites the *Pa. Gaz.* 27 May 1748).

PALMER, CHARLES, Quaker, age between 20 and 30, son of William Palmer of Litchfield, Eng., is sought as heir to an estate (*Scott* 3:6 cites *Bradford's New York Gazette* 10 June 1734).

PARKER, NICHOLAS, is supposed to have come to America seeking his brother Thomas Parker, who gives notice that he lives in Waterford Twp., Gloucester Co. [NJ], ten miles from Philadelphia (*Pa. Gaz.* 30 Sep 1742).

In 1774, Thomas Parker was living in Gloucester Twp., Gloucester Co., NJ (*AIS Census Index: Pre-1790* gives no other documentation).

PARKER, RICHARD, joiner and house carpenter, who had come lately from England, will hear something to his advantage by inquiring at the post office (*GAVN:* 258 cites the *Va. Gaz.* 26 May 1768).

PAU, HANS MICHAEL, a Dutch boy, about 14 years of age, last year was sold to a person in the country for seven years, and his mother, Christina Pau, does not know the person's name or where he lives. Anyone knowing of the boy is asked to send notice of him to the Post Office in Philadelphia (*Pa. Gaz.* 25 Dec 1750).

PAUL, THOMAS, a mason from Maryland, sought work in Philadelphia. His wife Maria, has heard nothing from his for three months. She is seeking information about him, or she will be forced to indenture their children (*Hocker:* 70 cites the *Pennsylvansiche Geschichts-Schreiber* 13 May 1758).

A Thomas Paul was a Sergeant in the Commissary Department between 27 April 1777 and 1 Aug 1779, and was discharged on 27 April 1780 (Henry C. Peden, Jr.,

Revolutionary Patriots of Kent and Queen Anne's Counties, Westminster: Family Line Publications, p. 198).

PAUST, CHRISTOFFEL, of Hanover Twp., has a letter from Ober Sultzen, Hanover, waiting for him at the Printer's. It contains nothing (*Eyster:*7 cites *the Pennsylvanische Berichte* 1 Nov 1749).
Christoph Paus arrived on the *St. Andrew* on 12 Sep 1734 (*Eyster:* 7).

PAYAN, Mr., born at Le Ciota in Provence, and is about 36 years old. He has lived for several years in Baltimore, but left in 1792 for Cape Francois, which he left with three young children, and came to Philadelphia. He stayed there a short time and then moved to the country. A person lately arrived from France, wishes to be informed of his residence and has things of the greatest consequence to communicate to him. Anyone having information about him should direct it to Mr. Fabre at Schweighaiser and Co., New York (*Federal Gazette & Baltimore Daily Advertiser* 5 Jan 1797).

PAYER, FREDERICK, of Low Bergen, and some other children, are now at the State House in Philadelphia. During the war they had been taken captive by the Indians from several parts of the Province, and have been lately released by General Amherst. They are to be returned to their parents or other relations, who are desired to come forthwith and receive them (*Pa. Gaz.* 2 July 1761).

PECKIN, WILLIAM, born at Eccleshall, Staffs., was a soldier in the 17th Regt. of Foot at Fort Stanwix in Oct 1763. He is asked to apply to Noel and Hazard, booksellers in New York City (*The New York Gazette and Weekly Mercury* 2 Dec 1771).

PENN, WILLIAM, a practitioner of physic in the British settlement in the Bay of Honduras, has died. If any of his relations are living they are requested to apply to Alexander Macauley at York or to the printers, where they may hear something to their advantage (*GAVN:* 262 cites *American Gazette and Norfolk and Portsmouth Public Advertiser* 21 May 1794).

PENNOYER, DENNETT, as Daniel Penneroy, [*sic*], left Philadelphia about 12 years ago, probably to settle in MD or VA. If he will apply to Edward Evans of Philadelphia, he will hear something to his advantage (*GAVN:* 262 cites *The American Weekly Mercury* 17 May 1739. The *Pa. Gaz.* of 12 July 1739 gives his name as "Bennett Penneroy").
He was bapt. 1690 at Clifford, son of Thomas Penoiyre, who died c1727 Hereford, and Elizabeth, dau. of John Dannett of Bosbury.
On 20 Dec 1726, as Danet Penoyre, he witnessed the will of John Burbage, Sr., weaver, of Somerset Co., MD. (MWB 19:115).
Dennett died in PA c1728, having been a claimant to an estate in Mddx, England. A deposition by John Lee, tailor, of Philadelphia, and wife Sarah, states that in 1727 Pennoyry had kept a school in Somerset County, MD, and had come from the vicinity of Hertfordshire. He told them he had been an officer in the Army and went to Antigua before going to Philadelphia and then to MD, where he died in 1728 (Coldham, "Genealogical Gleanings in England," *NGSQ* 59 (3) 176-177).

PERRY, JOHN, of Choptank River, about 20 years ago moved to New Topsail, NC and died owning a small estate of land. His only son is also dead. Any of the same name living at Choptank [who] may be of the same family, should inquire of William Hedges, living in Cecil County, for details of the estate (Annapolis *Maryland Gazette* 30 Jan 1751).

In 1742 a John Perry was in Bertie Co., NC (*AIS Census Index: Pre-1790* gives no other documentation).

PETRI, [-?-], has been in America for 40 years, and is said to be a justice in a region called "zum Korb." His nephew Anton Petri, from Breitschit, Nassau-Dillenburg, arrived in America last autumn, and he is seeking his "vetter" (cousin or uncle) (*Hocker:* 48 cites the *Pennsylvanische Geschichts-Schreiber* 1 April 1755).

Anton Petri arrived on the *Edinburgh* on 30 Sep 1754 (*Eyster:* 15).

PETRY, GERMAIN JOHN, late of Pisguit River, Nova Scotia, is now in Philadelphia. His seven children had been sent to some of the king's colonies, and Petry wants any news of them (*Pa. Gaz.* 25 March 1756).

PFARIN, ANNA MARIA, was indentured several years ago to an Englishman by her stepfather George Koeling. She is free this year, and may find her mother and stepfather in the Oley Hills, near Conrad Preisz, Bucks Co. (*Hocker:* 58 cites the *Pennsylvanische Geschichts-Schreiber* 13 Nov 1756).

PFAU, HANSZ MICHEL, was indentured last year to an Englishman, and now his mother, Christina Pfauin, widow, from Sultz, Wurtemberg, wants to know where her son lives. (*Hocker:* 21 cites the *Pennsylvanische Geschichts-Schreiber* 1 Sep 1750).

In 1790 a John Pfau was listed as head of a family in the Northern Liberties of Philadelphia, PA (*AIS 1790 Census Index).*

PFEIFFERIN, FRONY, is sought by her sister, Anna Maria Linck, who is with Joseph Flegel, Chestnut Hill, Philadelphia County (*Hocker:* 77 cites the *Pennsylvanische Geschichts-Schreiber* 11 May 1759).

PHELPS, RICHARD, came over from London about 1764 with Leonard Brooke. He lived as a schoolmaster with Dr. Leonard Hollyday at Patuxent. He is urged to contact Will Deakins, Jr. (Annapolis *Maryland Gazette* 14 Dec 1775).

There were several Richard Phelps in Anne Arundel Co., MD, in the 18th century.

One Richard Phelps was in Anne Arundel Co., MD in 1778 when he took the Oath of Fidelity (*AIS Census Index: Pre-1790* gives no other documentation).

One Richard Phelps of Anne Arundel Co. died by Oct 1795 when William Phelps advertised he would settle the estate (Annapolis *Maryland Gazette* 29 Oct 1795).

PHIBBS, JOHN, formerly of Washington, PA, if living, will hear of something highly advantageous by communicating his place of residence to Samuel E. McCabe, near Pittsburgh, PA ([DC] *Daily National Intelligencer* 23 Oct 1820).

PHILLIPS, CATHERINE, John Frizzell, and William Frizzell (*qq.v.*), all resided in Baltimore in 1808. If any of them are now living, they are request-ed to call at the Office of Wm. & Thos. Adair, 175 Baltimore St. (*Baltimore Patriot* 25 Aug 1834).

PHILLIPS, DANIEL, from Kingsbridge, [Co. Devon] Eng., supposed to reside in NJ. He is to apply to Jonathan Thomas, postmaster in Burlington, where he will hear something to his advantage (*Scott* 2:92 cites the *Pa. Gaz.* 26 July 1750).

PHILLIPS, PATRICK, an Irishman, resided at Hungerford Market London, and came to this country about 25 years ago. He is said to have resided in this district. If he is living, he is asked to communicate with Thomas C. Wright ([DC] *Daily National Intelligencer* 27 Dec 1820).

PHILLIPS, ZACHARY, is asked to come to John Wheldon, cordwainer in Philadelphia, where he may hear of something to his advantage. Wheldon will defray his traveling charges, and satisfy him for his loss of time (Philadelphia *American Weekly Mercury* 7 – 16 March 1731/2).

PICKFORD, THOMAS, of Congleton, Cheshire, is said to have worked for some years in Philadelphia as a bricklayer or labourer. If living, he may hear of a considerable estate left him (*Scott* 2:134 cites the *Pa. Gaz.* 20 June 1751).

PINDLE, THOMAS, a native of Maryland, left Annapolis about two years ago, possibly entered on board either the *Columbia,* or the *Alfred,* vessels of war, at Philadelphia. He is asked to apply to his brother-in-law, Samuel Watson, living near Annapolis (Annapolis *Maryland Gazette* 5 June 1777).

Martha Pindle of Annapolis died leaving will dated 10 April 1777 and proved 5 June 1777. She named her sisters Mary Ford and Ruthy Fowler. She left her money, goods, and chattels to her brother Samuel Watson. Her Negro girl Jane was left to the care and direction of Mr. Joshua [Fearon?] until her husband, Thomas Pindle should call for her and demand her. Catherine Bowney and Benjamin Harwood witnessed the will (AAWB EV#1:7).

In 1790 a Thomas Pindell [*sic*] was listed as head of a family in Baltimore Co., MD (*AIS 1790 Census Index*).

PIPER, Capt., left the country about six years ago. His heirs, supposed to be living in one of the lower counties on the Eastern Shore, should contact Capt. Coolidge at Selby's Landing on the Patuxent (Annapolis *Maryland Gazette* 28 July 1763).

PLACE, [-?-], anyone of that name who had an uncle Aaron Place in England is to apply to Jonathan Thomas, postmaster in Burlington (*Scott* 2:92 cites the *Pa. Gaz.* 26 July 1750).

PLEDGER, JOSEPH, ship joiner, left the town of Salem, West Jersey, some time in June or July 1765 and has not been heard of since. If he is still living, he may hear of something to his advantage by applying to Robert Johnson, living in the said town (*Pa. Gaz.* 22 Jan 1767).

The 1790 Census of North Carolina shows a Joseph Pledger living in Robeson Co., p.50 (*AIS 1790 U.S. Federal Census Index*).

POLLOCK, ROBERT, is supposed to have come to America in 1726 from the Parish of Mernes in Renfrewshire, North Britain,. He will learn of an inheritance, if he will come to Patrick Willson who lives at Batchelor's Hall in the Northern Liberties of Phila., or to Andrew Bradford (*American Weekly Mercury* 7 Dec 1732).

POMMER, JOHANN ULRICH, who arrived in America on 14 Aug on the ship *Sally*, Capt. Stephen Jones, has disappeared from the Widow Kreiderin's Golden Swan Inn, Third St., Philadelphia. Pommer is about 30 years old, and for a time worked in a sugar house in London (*Hocker:* 135 cites the *Wochentlicher Pennsylvanischer Staatsbote* 13 Sep 1774).

PORTER, Mrs., widow of Thomas Porter, an Englishman who died in 1793 of the yellow fever, was left her with two small children. She was living in 1795 and worked at the Taylor work. Anyone with information about her or her children is asked to contact William Young, at the corner of Shippen and Fifth Sts., they may hear something to her or their advantage (*Poulson's American Daily Advertiser* 26 Jan 1808).

PORTER, THOMAS, was born in the West Indies; knowledge of his whereabouts is desired (*Scott* 3:13 cites *Bradford's New York Gazette* 24 Sep 1744).

POSEY, Capt. JOHN, who married Miss Elizabeth Adair in 1769, should contact Jonathan Waddle of Charlestown, SC (*Annapolis Maryland Gazette* 12 May 1774).
    Christian Adair of KE Co. died by 23 May 1769 when her estate was administered by John Moore, who cited an inventory of £253.10.7 and payments of £38.9.0. A second account, filed 1 Aug 1769 mentioned payments to her dau. Elizabeth, wife of Capt. John Posey (MDAD 61:257, 62:185).

POTTS, JOHN, lately lived at Salem, New Jersey. If he will apply to the printer, he may hear of something to his advantage (*The Pennsylvania Evening Post* 19 April 1777).

POVALL, PETER, (commonly called **POVEY**) of Oswestry, Shropshire, sailed from Liverpool on the *Hope* in March 1759. He left the ship in Philadelphia that same year. Information on his whereabouts is desired (*GAVN:* 269 cites *The Virginia Gazette* 18 Jan 1770).

POWELL, JOHN, a sawyer, is asked to contact the printer (Annapolis *Maryland Gazette* 28 Nov 1750).

PRESTON, THOMAS, formerly held land on Winters' Run, Broad Neck, Gunpowder Neck, and several parts of Harford Co. The heirs of his children Thomas Preston and Mary Skates, are urged to contact the printer (*Maryland Journal and Baltimore Advertiser* 2 Dec 1791).
    A Thomas Preston was listed in 1790 as head of a family in Harford Co., MD (*AIS 1790 Census Index).*

PRICE, JOHN, born in Kidderminster, Worcestershire, Old England, shipped himself from Liverpool to America about 14 years ago, and served his time in Queen Anne's Co., MD, in Greenwood Neck, with George Teat and John Chambers. He is heir to a good estate, and his friends have a great desire to see him. If he will apply to Joseph Yeates at the Three Tuns in Chestnut St., Philadelphia, he will be more particularly informed about his affairs, and if any money is wanted to clear him of debts, it shall be advanced by Joseph Yeates. (*Pa. Gaz.* 7 Aug 1766).

Earlier, his brother had earnestly entreated him to return home (*GAVN*: 271: cites the *Va. Gaz.* 25 Oct 1765).

PRIGG, WILLIAM, JOSEPH PRIGG, and **MARY PRIGG**, in 1750 or 1751 lived at the Coventry Iron Works, belonging to Mrs. Ann Nutt of PA. Their brother John, of Sampitt, SC, left PA in the year 1750 or 1751. William, Joseph, or Mary their sister, or their legal descendants are asked to apply to Thomas Fenning, of Sampitt, near Georgetown, SC, where they will hear of something greatly to their advantage (*Pa. Gaz.* 27 June 1792).

PRIGG, JOHN FREDERICK (AUGUSTUS), came into this country some time ago from Copenhagen [Denmark], where his father still lives. He is urged to contact Michael Earle in Cecil Co., MD (Annapolis *Maryland Gazette* 10 Feb 1757).

As John F. A. Priggs he was a Quartermaster in the 11th Battalion on 13 Jan 1776. As John Priggs he served on the Board of Patuxent Associators who signed a resolution pertaining to the defense of the defense of the Potomac and Patuxent Rivers on 21 April 1781. The estate of John F. A. Priggs was opened on 14 June 1796 (*RPPG:* 248).

John Frederick Augustus Priggs settled in PG Co., MD, where he married and was the father of (MOPG:225): FREDERICK AUGUSTUS, b. 27 Oct 1749, bapt. 10 March 1749/50; and (poss.) HEDWICK, who m. Clement Hollyday by PGML dated 18 Dec 1784.

PROBART, WILLIAM, lived in St. Mary's Co., MD, in 1739. He was urged to contact Dr. David Ross at Bladensburg for news of a legacy in England (Annapolis *Maryland Gazette* 19 Dec 1750; *Scott* 2:125 cites the *Pa. Gaz.* 25 April 1751).

In June 1751 William Lane of WO Co., MD petitioned the Court of Chancery that William Probart of WO Co., mariner, had married the petitioner's dau. who is still living, and who had borne him five children. For some time Probart had been deprived of his reason and was unable to manage his affairs. Lane stated that Probart thought he was the Queen of England (MCHR 8:652).

In July 1751 William Probart advertised about the false rumor that Thomas Lambden of Worcester Co., merchant, had illegally obtained bills from Probart (Annapolis *Maryland Gazette* 3 July 1751).

On 21 March 1770 William Probart of Worcester Co., MD, signed the inventory of John Johnson as one of the creditors (MINV 107:60).

PROCTOR, WILLIAM, about 1749 went away from Prince George's Co., MD, leaving his wife behind him. He went with Charity [Tydings: *q.v.*] Sellman, once the widow of Solomon Sparrow of Anne Arundel County, and took with them their daughter Sophia

Sparrow, aged about 10, into the Colony of VA (Annapolis *Maryland Gazette* 5 Oct 1752).

William Proctor married Jane Partridge on 12 April 1726 in Queen Anne's Parish, Prince George's Co., MD (PGQA: Marriage Reg.: 4).

William Proctor was in Prince George's Co. on 15 Feb 1727 when he was listed as a creditor of the estate of George Shirley (MDAD 8:508). On 30 Nov 1744 he was a debtor to the estate of Richard Marsham Waring of PG Co. (MDAD 21:65).

PROTHERO, MARY, came to VA from Bristol some six or seven years ago, with Sarah Syfers, when both were about age 20. They lived with one Coleman, a biscuit baker on York River. If she applies to Capt. John Cawsey of the ship *Brothers* she will hear something to her advantage (*GAVN*: 273 cites the *Va. Gaz.* 18 Feb 1768).

Mary Prothero's husband, Robert Taylor of Bedford Co., advertised that she had run off with a silversmith named Cuttings, and that they will go to England, to get some money which she has inherited by the death of Samuel Prothero of Bristol (*GAVN*: 273 cites the *Va. Gaz.* 6 July 1769).

PUSSEY, LANEY, had been captured by the Indians. About four years ago she made her escape with one Ann Mullen (See elsewhere in this work). They were captured by the Onandagoes, who held them about eleven months, and then the girls made their way to Raritan in the Jerseys, where some of her relations lived (*Pa. Gaz.* 17 March 1763).

QUARRIER, ALEXANDER, about 30 years ago left Scotland for this country and for many years resided in the City of Richmond. Advertisements appeared in several American newspapers, and the editor of the *Intelligencer* is asked to transmit any such copies to the Hon. James Caldwell of the House of Representatives (*The Daily National Intelligencer* 22 Nov 1814).

RAMSAY, Miss MARIA, late from Montreal, if she is still in this city, is asked to call upon Mr. James Gorman, at 10 South Water St., where she will hear of something greatly to her advantage (*Poulson's American Daily Advertiser* 4 Aug 1820).

RAMSEY, JAMES, came from Co. Antrim, Ireland, to Little Britain, Lancaster Co., PA, and then removed to the Jerseys. He will hear something to his advantage by getting in touch with William Gillilands, merchant, of New York City (*Pa. Gaz.* 17 Jan 1766).

RAMSEY (or RAMSAY), JOHN, and JAMES RAMSEY, formerly of Lancaster Co., VA, sons of John and Jane Ramsey, dec., are advised that they may hear something to their advantage if the return to Lancaster Co. before 10 May 1769. /s/ Dale Carter and Samuel Yap (*GAVN*: 276 cites Rind's *Va. Gaz.* 28 April 1768).

RANDALL, RICHARD, and JOSEPH RANDALL, sons of Christopher and Hannah Randall of the Parish of St. Magdalen, Bermondsey, Surrey, Eng., are advised to apply to Capt. George Dobbie of Hobb's Hole, they may hear of a considerable legacy left to them. Joseph Randall is believed to be in MD (*GAVN*: 277 cites the *Va. Gaz.* 26 May 1768).

A Joseph Randall died in Queen Anne's Co., MD, some time before 1 June 1751 when his personal property was appraised (MINV 47:66).

RAPER, THOMAS, was born at Epsom, England. A carpenter, or joiner, he came from England to Maryland some eight or ten years ago. A relation of his has lately died in England and left a considerable estate, which falls to him. He was last heard of about Amboy or Burlington [NJ] some eight or ten months ago. There is a letter for him at the Post Office in Philadelphia (*Pa. Gaz.* 8 Nov 1739).

RECHER, ELIZABETH, and her sister **MARGARETHA RECHER**, were indentured 11 years ago with their brothers Friedrich and Johannes, who was born at Brattle, two miles above Basel. Johannes is now in Amwell, NJ, with Peter Rockenfelder [Rockenfeller?], and wishes to hear from his sisters (*Hocker:* 14 cites the *Pennsylvanische Geschichts-Schreiber* 1 Aug 1749).

Johann Recher (making his mark "H") and Fritz Recher arrived on the snow *Enterprise*, Lyonell Wood, commander from London, and qualified on 6 Dec 1738 (*PGP* 1:249, 250).

A Hans Recher married Kindeld Lichtlen some time before June 1743. They were the parents of: JOHANNES, bapt. 19 June 1743 at Muddy Creek Reformed Church (sp.: Abraham Witman and Magdalena Steyl (*Lancaster Churches*).

REDDIKER, CATHERINE, about nine years ago was aged 3, and was brought to America from Amsterdam by Capt. Bailey, with her father, who was ill at the time. News of her is sought by Hendrick Heter, baker, of New York City (*New York Post-Boy* 24 Oct 1748).

REDDINGTON, MICHAEL, late of Ballivane, near Cork, left Ireland two or three years ago. He has inherited a large property from his father, Thomas Reddington, Esq. (*Scott* 3:230 cites *The New York Gazette and Weekly Mercury* 9 July 1781).

REDING, THOMAS, peruke maker, bound himself, about seven years ago to Thomas Buttington of Bradford Twp., Lancaster Co., PA. He will hear something to his advantage if he will go to the Post Office in Philadelphia (*American Weekly Mercury* 23 May 1734).

REDWOOD, WILLIAM, and wife Sarah (late Sarah Pope) left England on 1768 and went to reside in "Rhode Island in the Province of New Hampshire [*sic*]," North America. They, if living, or any of their children or next of kin, should apply to His Excellency John Collins, the Governor of Rhode Island, as they will hear of something greatly to their advantage (*Newport Herald* 26 Nov 1789).

In 1790 a Sally Redwood was head of a family in Newport Co., RI (*AIS 1790 Census Index*).

REES, WILLIAM, son of Evan Rees, was born in Casbuchan, near Cardiff, in Glamorganshire, South Wales, and came from Bristol to Philadelphia about five years ago. If he is still alive, and will call at the New Printing Office in Market St., Philadelphia, he will hear of something to his advantage (*Pa. Gaz.* 29 May 1760).

REICHERT, GOTTFRIED, left Staeten unterm Heuchelberg seven years ago. Information is wanted about him (*Hocker:* 16 cites the *Pennsylvanische Geschichts-Schreiber* 16 Oct 1749).

Reichert, from Staeten unterm Heuchelberg, has heard that his father, Martin Reicherthas arrived in America, and wishes to hear from him (*Hocker:* 34 cites the *Pennsylvanische Geschichts-Schreiber* 16 June 1752).

Gottfried may be the John Gottfried Rieger [*sic*] who arrived 21 Sep 1742 on the ship *Francis and Elizabeth* (*Eyster:* 7).

REICHERT, CHRISTINA, is supposed to be in service in Conestoga, Lancaster Co., and is sought by her father, Simon Reichert, who arrived in America last autumn and is with Valentine Jung, Upper Saucon, Lehigh Co. (*Hocker:* 38 cites the *Pennsylvanische Geschichts-Schreiber* 16 May 1753).

REIGHTER, JOHN, son of Peter Reighter, who has recently died, is sought by Thomas Smith and Thomas Duncan who have recovered a sum of money for Reighter's heirs. They have frequently written to John Reighter, one of the sons of said Peter, addressed to his direction to the care of John Holmes, Jr., merchant, in Baltimore, MD. They now believe that John Reighter has removed from Baltimore, and they give notice they will pay the money to the [other] children or guardians (*The Carlisle Gazette and the Western Repository of Knowledge* 1 Feb 1792).

REINER, MICHAEL, from Schwewigern, near Heilbrunn, is sought by Ernest Ludwig Baisch (Newlander) (*Eyster:* 40 cites the *Pennsylvanische Staatsbote* 26 Nov 1776).

Michael Reiner and Catharina Rush were married by license on 15 Feb 1774 at St. James Episcopal Church, in Lancaster Co., PA (*Lancaster Churches,* vol. 3).

Michael Reiner of Lancaster Twp., Lancaster Co., advertised he would sell or lease five acres of land, three miles from the borough, on which stands a large stone dwelling house and a mill house (*Pa. Gaz.* 15 Jan 1794).

REINHARD, JOHANN THEODOR, is sought by his mother, Anna Margretha Regina Reinhardin, widow, who was born in Hempele, and living in Wetzler, Germany. Her only son, Johan Theodor Reinhard. He studied for five years in the Gymnasium in Weilburg, taking French, English, Italian, Greek, Hebrew, and the Oriental languages. In his 16th year, he went to the University of Leipzig to study law, and after remaining there for two and a years, he left for Goettingen, where he intended to spend a year at the University. He traveled by way of Hamburg, and Bremen. At Bremen, a ship was about to sail for America. He had heard and read much about America while in Leipzig, and on April 28 he wrote to his mother that he intended sailing for America the following day, but he did not give the name of the ship or captain. His father, who died in 1783, was assessor of the local court of justice. Johan Theodor was born in 1770 in Neustrelitz, Mecklenburg (*Hocker:* 186 cites the *Philadelphische Correspondenz* 13 Oct 1789).

REINLANDER, PHILIP JACOB, tanner, who formerly lived at Derckem, on the Hart, is sought by Leonhardt Gesell of Tulpehocken, Berks Co., PA, near Conrad Weiser's (*Hocker:* 23 cites the *Pennsylvanische Geschichts-Schreiber* 16 Nov 1750).

Philip Jacob Rheinlender [*sic*], with five in his family arrived in the *William and Sarah* on 21 Sep 1727. Joh. Leonhard Gesell, age 31, arrived on the *Lydia* on 10 Sep 1743 (*Eyster:* 9).

REITZ, GEORG HEINRICH, who was indentured in West Caln Twp., Chester Co., PA, in Cuilbertson's mill, is sought by his brother, Johann Philip Reitz. Johann Philip intends to return to his home in Rossdorf, and leaves instructions where his letters may be left (*Hocker:* 113 cites the *Wochentlicher Pennsylvanische Staatsbote* 14 April 1772).

Gorg Heinrich and Johann Philip Reitz arrived on the *Sally,* John Ostman, commander, from Rotterdam, last from Cowes, and too the oaths on 23 Oct 1767 (*PGP* 1:714).

REMINGTON, RALPH, if still living should contact John Jones in Hampton for news of a considerable estate in England (Annapolis *Maryland Gazette* 10 Oct 1759).

Remington was again advised that he might hear of something to his advantage by applying to John Flanagan in Second St., Philadelphia. If anyone could confirm Renington's death, so that his heirs can have the same advantage, Flanagan would be grateful (*Pa. Gaz.* 8 April 1762).

REMUS, BASTIAN, if living, is informed by his wife Anna Maria Remus, that she is settled with her mother on a good farm in Little Conewago Twp., York Co., PA, and has taken the same for nine or ten years. If her husband will come to her, she will endeavor to contribute all in her power for their future benefit. However, it has been reported that her husband has been taken, with others from Conecocheague, some time before General Braddock's defeat, to help in clearing the road up Potomac River to Will's Creek or Fort Cumberland, when it was reported that he went by the name John Everhart. Anna Maria Remus will pay twenty shillings to anyone who can tell her if the said Remus, or Everhart, ot alive or dead (*Pa. Gaz.* 1 June 1758).

Bastian Remus, a Dutch servant man, ran away from Joseph Williams in Lower Merion Twp, Philadelphia Co. He is of short stature, black swarthy complexion, black curled hair, and over 40 years of age. He professes to be a miller, and a good Dutch scholar, and understands something of the Latin tongue (*Pa. Gaz.* 7 June 1753).

RENDERTS, Mr., first name not known, left Holland about 1787 for the West Indies, and then left for the United States of America. If he will direct a line to Mrs. Anna Moore of Washington, D.C., he will received information about his daughter, who with her mother (now long deceased), resided at Dockurn, West Friesland, when her father left for the West Indies (*The National Intelligencer and Washington Advertiser* 13 Aug 1806).

RENER, CHRISTOFFEL, who had been in America for six years, is sought by his brother, Abraham Rener, in New York, by the fresh water, who would like to inform him that his father, mother, brother and sister are all well (*Hocker:* 82 cites the *Pennsyl-vanische Geschichts-Schreiber* 9 Nov 1759).

RENSHAW, JOHN, by trade a tailor, was the son of Thomas and Hannah Renshaw who were formerly of Harford Co., MD, but later moved to Baltimore Co., MD, when John took his departure. His parents were informed that he lived at one time in the neighborhood of Harrisburg. Any information concerning Mr. John Renshaw, his residence, or whether he is alive or dead, will thankfully received by his aged mother, Mrs. Hannah Renshaw, now living in Georgetown, Potomac (*Oracle of Dauphn and Harrisburgh Advertiser* 18 Oct 1802).

RENT, ALEXANDER JOHANNES, wrote to Germany, telling his "Baasze" (aunt or cousin) Anna Maria Rentin, to join him in Pennsylvania. She crossed the ocean two years ago with her husband, Philip Odenwalder, a smith, and now she seeks the aforesaid Rent (*Hocker:* 4 cites the *Pennsylvanische Geschichts-Schreiber* 16 Dec 1745).

RENTZ, JOHANNES, baker and innkeeper, of Ebenezer, SC or GA, is informed that his brother, Johann Georg Frent, from Weihl, in Schoenembuch, arrived in Pennsylvania, and is seeking information about him (*Pennsylvanische Geschichts-Schreiber* 22 May 1761).

REPPIN, ANNA MARIA, arrived last autumn and is now in Germantown seeking news of her brother, Johann Casper Repp, "aus der Wetterau von Dauerheim," who arrived in this country six years ago, and then notified his sister, Anna Maria Reppin, also to come (*Pennsylvanische Geschichts-Schreiber* 26 June 1743).

RETTERIN, CATHARINA, care of George Eyerich, near Yellow Springs, Pikeland Twp., Chester Co., came to America sixteen years ago with her father Melchior Retter, now dec., her mother Eva, her eldest sister Anna Maria, her second sister, Margaretha, and her third sister Magdalena. These three sisters were indentured in Philadelphia, and Catherine was indentured to Lorenz Hippel in the country ("*in dem Busch*"). She is seeking news of her family (*Wochentlicher Pennsylvanische Staatsbote* 9 Oct 1770).

REYNOLDS, STEPHEN, died on his way to the western country in August 1803. He is supposed to have been a native of New Hampshire or one of the eastern states. If his heirs will apply to John Rine, administrator, living in Cumberland, Allegany Co., MD, they will hear of something to their advantage (*National Intelligencer and Washington Advertiser* 2 May 1805).

REYNOLLS, Mr., an Irish gentleman, formerly of the 4th or King's Own Regiment in the British Army, left the service and came to the United States about eight or ten years ago. If he will apply to Messrs Keatinge, Simons, and Son, factors, Charleston, SC, he will learn some domestic occurrences of high importance to him (*Republican, or Anti-Democrat,* 18 April 1803).

RICERT, JOHN MARCUS, is one of two children of George Adam, and his wife Crates, who came in here from Germany, in the Year 1754, and landed at Philadelphia, and both died soon after. They left two children, Magdalen, and John Marcus Ricert; the said John was sold into the country, and left his said sister on board the ship, and has never heard of her since. He is very desirous of hearing from her, she being the only relation he has in this country. If she is alive, and hears of this advertisement, or if any person will be kind enough to inform her of it, they may acquaint her, that she will hear of her brother, by applying to Richard Mason, joiner, in Second Street, Philadelphia, or to Isaac Chapman, in Wright's Town, Bucks County. /s/ John Marcus Ricert. (*Pa. Gaz.* 26 June 1766).

RICHARDET, DANIEL, purchased large property in this country in 1781 and 1782. Anyone with information is asked to contact Messrs. Nottnagel, Montmollin and Co. (*Federal Gazette and Philadelphia Evening Post* 4 Oct 1790).

RICHARDSON, WILLIAM, son of John, came to MD and was a servant in 1754 to Samuel Tipton on Patapsco River. If he contacts the printer, he will hear something to his advantage (Annapolis *Maryland Gazette* 8 Jan 1767).

RICHMOND, GEORGE, a carpenter and millwright, left the Island of Jamaica in 1786 and went to VA or MD. If alive, he should apply to Mr. Charles Campbell, 3 S. Fourth

St., Philadelphia, where he will hear of something to his advantage (*The Philadelphia Gazette & Universal Daily Advertiser* 5 Aug 1796).

A later notice sought George Richmond, a carpenter, native of Scotland, who left Jamaica about 13 years ago for the continent of America, and has not been heard of since, notwithstanding diligent enquiry, and publication in the Winchester *Sentinel* in May 1802. If he is alive and will apply to George Lind, of Strasburg, Shenandoah Co., VA, he will hear of something to his benefit (*The National Intelligencer and Washington Advertiser* 7 Sep 1804).

RIDDING, WILLIAM, was born in Pequemon's [Perquiman's] Co., NC. If he will come to the printer of the *Post-Boy,* he will learn something to his advantage (*New York Post-Boy* 19 March 1759).

RIDDLE, FRANCES, came about 26 years ago as a servant and supposedly married one Richard Wagstaffe (*q.v.*), a Leicestershire man, will hear something to her advantage if she is alive and will call at the New Printing Office (*Scott* 2:195 cites the *Pa. Gaz.* 21 Sep 1752).

RIDDLE, JOHN, Jr., arrived at James Stoddart's Inn in Allegany Co., MD, on the 4th inst., in the accommodation stage from Frederick, where he had paid his passage to Wheeling. The passengers told the innkeeper he as unwell, and required refreshment but cautioned him not to give him anything to drink. Riddle became unmanageable, and had to be tied. The next morning he had disappeared. He was about 30 years old, and about 5'8" tall. Anyone with information is asked to contact James Stoddard (*Baltimore Patriot* 29 Aug 1834).

RIEHLE, GEORG FRIEDRICH, has been in America for twenty years. His brother, **JOHANN MICHAEL RIEHLE,** a flour miller, has been in America for four years. Johann Friedrich Kuecherer, of Raccoon Creek, Gloucester Co., twenty miles from Philadelphia, is seeking news of them (*Wochentlicher Pennsylvanische Staatsbote* 22 March 1776).

RINCKER, JACOB, a Swiss, arrived in this country four years ago and still has a year to serve. His mother, who is free, and who lived near Germantown, is seeking information about him and wants him to come to see her and his brothers, Casper and Henrich, living with Thomas Lorentz, about four miles from Merton Meeting House, across the Schulkill in Montgomery Co., PA (*Hocker:* 8 cites the *Pennsylvanische Geschichts-Schreiber* 16 July 1747).

In 1750 Jacob Rincker was in Philadelphia Co., PA (*AIS Census Index: Pre-1790* gives no other documentation).

RITCHIE, ROBERT, late of Philadelphia, has died. If his heirs will apply to James Hughes of Cecil Co., MD, they may hear of something, perhaps to their advantage (*The Pennsylvania Herald and General Advertiser* 14 July 1787).

RITCHIE, WILLIAM, a native of Leith, emigrated to the United States about 40 years ago, and was understood to have settled on Fell's Point, Baltimore, where he engaged in the business of ship carpenter: the advertiser does not know whether it was a master, or a journeyman. If he is alive, or if he is dead, anyone with information, is asked to contact James Ronaldson, Cedar by 9th Street, Philadelphia (*Baltimore Patriot* 4 May 1831).

In 1796 William Ritchie, mariner, lived at 1 Fleet St., Fell's Point. In 1799 he was a rigger, at 24 Lancaster St. He does not appear in the City Directory for 1807 (*Baltimore City Directories* for the years indicated).

In 1799 William Ritchie of Baltimore, MD, was listed as a brother of James Ritchie, weaver in Perth (*DSSB* 2:172 cites Services of Heirs, and the *Scottish Genealogist; DSSD:* 120).

RITZMANN, HERMANN, a smith, is past 80 years of age. He was born at Am Seister Deich, four miles from Hamburg, established a factory in Moscow under Czar Peter I and later came to American, having been in New York 50 years ago. His four sisters and brother, whom he left in Germany, are all dead. His nephew Ulrich Otto, chemist, who arrived in New York last October is seeking him. Send information to Dr. Adam Simon Kuhn, Lancaster, or Mr. Wiltenberger, Market St., Philadelphia (*Pennsylvanische Staatsbote* 7 Sep 1773).

ROACH, JOHN, came from Belfast, a redemptioner, on board the ship *Prince George*, Captain Beatty, and arrived here the 11th of June, 1767, will apply to the printers hereof, he will be informed of something to his advantage (*Pa. Gaz.* 1 Sep 1768).

ROACH, PHILIP, aged about 15, son of a widowed mother, left Baltimore on 8 July 1822 with James Bremner (*q.v.*), and has not been heard of since. Any information concerning him should be sent to Samuel Russell, near Pratt St. Bridge (*Baltimore Patriot* 6 Sep 1822).

ROACH, TIMOTHY, mariner, native of Bristol, England, or his legal representative, is asked to apply to the office of the New York *Evening Post,* either by letter or personally, as they will hear of something greatly to their advantage (*Washington Federalist* 6 Jan 1804).

ROBERTS, JOHN, a clock and watchmaker from Bury St. Edmunds, Eng., about the year 1795, removed with his family to Philadelphia. If he or any of his descendants are living, they may hear of something to their advantage by applying to 117 Race St. (*Poulson's American Daily Advertiser* 13 Jan 1818).

ROBERTS, LYDIA, dau. of John Roberts, late of Bucks Co., PA, is supposed to have gone with David Anderson to Carlisle, PA, when she was a child, from Kent Co., DE. She may have married and had children. If she or any of them will apply to Mary Roberts of Middletown, Bucks co., PA, and prove that they are the dau. or grandchildren the said John Roberts, they will hear of something to their advantage (*Poulson's American Daily Advertiser* 23 Jan 1812).

ROBERTSON, JAMES, Jr., wagonmaker, a native of Currie, shire of Edinburgh, who lived for some time at Fells Point, where he had a wife and four children, three of whom are named James, Ann, and Elizabeth, should apply to Alexander Finlater or the printer, so he will have an opportunity to see his father who has just arrived here (*Maryland Journal and Baltimore Advertiser* 18 Aug 1786).

ROBESON, ALEXANDER, came to PA some 30 years ago, and is now supposed to be in Gloucester Co., NJ. Before he left Ireland the said Alexander lived with his uncle, a linen weaver, near Lisburn. His brother James Robeson is lately arrived in this Province from Lisburn, and is living with Samuel Martin at Paxton, Lancaster Co., PA, and wants to see his brother Alexander. (*Pa. Gaz.* 28 April 1768).

ROBINSON, AGNES, served part of her time with Big John Glen on Yellow Breeches. She is asked to send an account of her residence to John M'Dannel on Conndoguinett Creek, near Carlisle. This will oblige her disconsolate mother, Agnes Robinson, who also wishes to know if William Robinson who lived with Elizabeth Wiley, or her son Samuel in Paxton, near Harrisburg, be living ([PA] *Kline's Weekly Carlisle Gazette* 11 April 1798).

ROBINSON, RICHARD, hatter, of Philadelphia, left that place about the middle of last August, and went to Norfolk and Petersburg in Virginia, and is supposed to have died on his passage, by water, home from Norfolk sometime the September following. Anyone knowing anything about the time and place of his death or anything relative thereto, is asked to transmit it to William Shannon, 183 Market St., Philadelphia (*Philadelphia Gazette and Universal Daily Advertiser* 8 July 1795).

ROBINSON, SAMUEL, of the parish of Bangar, near Belfast, in the north of Ireland, blacksmith, about 15 or 16 years ago came over and settled some where in this Province; and as there are some persons lately come from England, who want to see or hear of him, this is therefore to request any person that knows where his place of residence is, that they will give intelligence thereof to Mr. Alexander Lunan, merchant, in Philadelphia, or to the Printer hereof, and the favour shall be gratefully acknowledged, by John Robinson (*Pa. Gaz.* 21 July 1753)..

ROBINSON, THOMAS, is supposed to be an Englishman, and to have lived with one Samuel Jackson, in this city. If he will apply to Joshua Fisher, and Sons, he may hear of something to his advantage; or if the said Robinson, be deceased, and has left any creditors, they may hear of something to their advantage, by applying as above (*Pa. Gaz.* 15 Sep 1768).

ROCK, JOHANNES, from Rohrum, near Frankort-on-Main, will learn something to his advantage if he sends his address to Simon Keppler from Aidlingen in Boblinger, Wurtemburg (*Eyster:* 38 cites *Pennsylvanische Staatsbote* 4 Aug 1775).

RODGERS, HEZEKIAH, late of Marshfield, Gloucester Co., Eng., blacksmith, son of Ezekiel Rodgers, blacksmith, of Glos., Eng., came to PA, some time ago, and resided in Maxfield Twp., Bucks Co., PA. He is requested to communicate with the printer (*Pa. Chronicle* 23 March 1767).

John Dyer of Plumstead, Bucks Co., noted in his diary for the 2 d., 7 m., 1780, that "Hezekiah Rodgers, an old man, died this morning" (*Bucks Churches* 4:64).

RODOVALHO, FRANCISCO DE PAULA, native of the Island of Terceira, if, in this country, is asked to communicate with March & Benson, 47 South St., New York, as he may hear of something to his advantage (*Poulson's American Daily Advertiser* 15 Aug 1805).

ROGERS, RICHARD, son of Richard Rogers, Clerk of H.M. Victualing Office on Tower Hill, London, came to America, about 15 years ago, and is supposed to have lived in Rhode Island or on long Island. He is requested to send information about his place of abode to George Ross, peruke maker, in Philadelphia (*American Weekly Mercury* 8 May 1735).

ROGERS, RICHARD, came to America from England about 1750, and as late as 1750 was keeping school in Lunenberg Co., VA, when he was last heard from. Persons in London are seeking information about him (*GAVN*: 291 cites the *Va. Gaz.* 20 May 1773).
    In 1783 a Richard Rogers was listed on the tax list of Holland District of Nansemond Co., VA (*AIS Census Index: Pre-1790* gives no other documentation).

ROMIG, GEORG MICHEL, GEORG ROMIG, and **CHRISTIAN ROMIG,** have been in America for many years. They are sought by their brother Johannes Romig, who comes from Newstadt, an der Groszen Linden, and is with Valentin Kuehle, Rockhill Twp., Bucks Co., PA, Notify Adam Wittman, Reading (*Pennsylvanische Geschichts-Schreiber* 12 Oct 1759).

RORICH, NINGES, his wife **ANENGLE RORICH,** their children **FRIEDRICH,** and **JULIANA RORICHIN,** are sought by their daughter and sister, Sophia Dorothea Elisabetha Rorichin,, of New York, who is with Mr. Gebel (*Pennsylvanische Geschichts-Schreiber* 15 Feb 1760).

ROSS, JAMES, a single man of Co. Derry, Ireland, came to PA about four years ago, and served his time with Mr. Speers, near St. George, in MD [poss. St. George's Parish, then in Baltimore, now Harford, Co., MD]. William Pattan, his brother, has come into this country and would like to hear where he is, to hear something to his advantage (*Pa. Gaz.* 6 Feb 1766).

ROSS, RICHARD. came from Koningsburgh in 1763, being then in the 25th year of his age, and is said since then to have resided in this City. If he will apply to the Subscriber, he may hear of something greatly to his Advantage /s/ William Drewry (*Pa. Gaz.* 23 April 1752).

ROUGHSEDGE, WILLIAM, late of Prescott, Lancs., came as an import in the *Swaile* in 1763 and was bound to Mr. Burch of Wicomico, Charles Co., MD. He will hear of something to his advantage by applying to Jacob Allan of Williamsburg (*GAVN*: 293 cites the *Va. Gaz.* 15 April 1772).
    William Roughsedge, felon was sentenced to transportation at Lent, 1763, from Lancashire (*CBEB*).
    Roughsedge took the Oath of Fidelity in 1778 in Montgomery Co., MD, before the Hon. Richard Thompson. In July 1780 he was a private in the 8th Co., Lower Battalion of Militia (*RPMO* 290).

ROURK, LAWRENCE, about eleven years ago came to America from Co. Tipperary, Ireland, and is thought to have settled in New England. He is asked to contact his brother John Rourk, who came to America last fall, and is living at John McCurdy's in Albany (*Scott* 3:57 cites the *New York Gazette and Weekly Mercury* 1 Nov 1756; *Scott* 5:57 cites *The New York Post Boy* 1 Nov 1756).

RUD, WILLIAM, son of John and Avis Rud, late of Henrico Co, VA, but more recently of Chesterfield Co., VA, left VA 16 years ago, saying he planned to go to Annapolis. He is urged to contact his brother Thomas Rud in Chesterfield Co, VA (Annapolis *Maryland Gazette* 27 Dec 1749).

RUDD, ELIZABETH, some years ago from the county of Warwick, Eng., and is supposed to be living in some part of America. She is asked to contact her father, Samuel Rudd of Charles City Co., VA (*GAVN:* 294 cites the *Va. Gaz.* 26 Sep 1745).

RUMBOLD, THOMAS, late of Long-Alley, near Moorfields, Mddx., Eng., and his bro. **WILLIAM RUMBOLD** of the same place (sons of Thomas Rumbold of the same place, stocking trimmer, dec., who was a son of William Rumbold, formerely of King's Clere, Co. Southampton, yeoman, dec.), are supposed to have come to North America about 16 or 17 years ago. If still living, they, or their heirs are to apply to Capt. Thomas Miller in New York City, or to Messrs., Bristow and Winterbottom in London, or to James Gwyn in London (*Scott* 3:126 cites *The New York Mercury* 5 Oct 1767).

The heirs of Thomas and William Rumbold, namely William Rumbold, Mary wife of Alexander Laing (both of MD), Mary wife of Garret Blackford of NJ, [-?-] Rumbold of Cashel, Ireland, Rodolphus Rumbold of Tipperary in Ireland, William Rumbold of Jamaica, and William Rumbold of the Bay of Honduras, are asked to enter proof of their claims as heirs before John Eames, one of the Masters of the High Court of Chancery of England (*Scott* 3:162 cites *The New York Gazette and Weekly Mercury* 4 May 1772).

Pursuant to a Decree of the High Court of Chancery in England, William Rumbold, Mary wife of Alexander Laing, both of the Province of MD, Mary the wife of Garrett Blackford of NJ, [-?-] Rumbold of Cashell in Ireland, Rodolphus Rumbold of Tipperary in Ireland, William Rumbold of Jamaica, and William Rumbold of the Bay of Honduras, and all other persons claiming to be heirs of Thomas Rumbold, late of Long Alley, near Moorfields, Co. Middlesex, or of William Rumbold, of the same place, his brother, who were sons of Thomas Rumbold of the same place, stocking trimmer, dec., who was the son of William Rumbold, late of King's Clere, in the County of Southampton, yeoman, dec., are to come and enter into proof of their respective claims of being the heirs at law of the said Thomas and William Rumbold, before John Eames, Esq., one of the Masters of the said court, at his Chambers in Symondinn, Chancery inn, London (*Pa. Gaz.* 4 May 1774).

RUTHERFORD, GEORGE, should apply either personally or by letter to William Tannehill, Jr., of Bladensburg, he will hear something to his advantage relative to his estates in Roxburghshire, Scotland (Washington, D. C. *Federal Republican* 28 Jan 1814).

RUTHERFORD, JOHN, native of Scotland, and formerly a lieutenant in the British Navy came to this country some years ago. He is supposed to have married in this country. If he is still alive, he may hear of something to his advantage by applying to the editor of this paper (*Poulson's American Daily Advertiser* 21 Aug 1816).

RUTTER, CHRISTIAN, last spring in Germany borrowed some money from Hansz Georg Schneider, from Gilstein, in Hernnberger Amt. They came to PA on different ships, and Schneider, now living on the Ridge (Ridge Avenue, Philadelphia), is seeking Ruffer (*Hocker:* 30 cites the *Pennsylvanische Geschichts-Schreiber* 1 Jan 1752).

Hans Georg Schneider arrived on the *Anderson*, Hugh Campbell master, from Rotterdam, last from Cowes, and qualified on 25 Aug 1751 (*Names of Foreigners:* 328).

ST. CLAIR, THOMAS, native of Scotland, related to the family of Roslin, embarked at Nantz [Nantes] in France, about two years ago in a brig bound for Baltimore. He should apply to Col. McGregor in New York or Luke Wheeler in Baltimore. He is about 25 years of age, fair complexion, and six feet high (*Maryland Gazette and Baltimore Advertiser* 21 June 1785).

He may be the Thomas St. Clair who married Mary [-?-]. They were the parents of (*BAJA*: 37, 47): MARY ANN, b. 5 April 1801; ELIZABETH RUTH, b. 2 July 1813.

ST. JOHN, JAMES, son of Capt. Richard St. John of Ballysheen, Co. Clare, Ireland, about 21 years ago left Ireland for America. Samuel and John Morton, merchants in Philadelphia, seek knowledge of him. Capt. Charles Edmundstone of the 18th or Royal Irish Regiment. of Foot, quartered in Philadelphia, and Col. Gisborne of the 16th Regiment of Foot in New York. and Capt. Robert Delaway of the 10th Regiment of Foot quartered in Quebec also seek knowledge of him (*Pa. Chron.* 8 Feb 1768).

SAVEY, ABRAHAM, and his wife were demised 50 a. of land by James Ransome, of Gloucester Co., VA, on 23 Nov 1670 for 99 years. G. Wythe now possesses the land and is advertising for the person entitled to the reversion (*GAVN:* 279 cites the *Va. Gaz.* 8 March 1770).

SCHAAF, HENRICH, living with Christophel Heumacher, on the Little Lehigh, "in der Schmaltzgasz," had his brother Friedrich come to America this year. Now he finds that in the Philadelphia Mayor's Book. Friedrich Schaff was indentured to Johannes Bauman, whose place of residence is not given. Henrich is seeking information about Bauman (*Hocker:* 27 cites the *Pennsylvanische Geschichts-Schreiber* 16 Dec 1752).

Henrich Schaaf came on the *Phoenix*, John Mason, master, from Rotterdam, and qualified on 15 Sep 1749 (*Names of Foreigners* 289).

For more on the Schaaf Family, see Burgert's 's *Northern Alsace* 421-422.

SCHAAF, JOHANN PETER, of Lebanon, is notified of the arrival of his cousin Johann August Leonhardt, from Hitzenhahn, bey der Gentzbacher Muehl, near Dillenburg, and that Leonhardt is very sick, at Abel James' place, Frankford, five miles from Philadelphia (*Hocker:* 126 cites the *Wochentlicher Pennsylvanischer Staatsbote* 19 Oct 1773).

Joh. Jost Leonhardt arrived on the *Union* on 27 Sep 1773. Joh. Peter Schaaf arrived on the *Neptune* on 28 Sep 1751 (*Eyster:* 33).

SCHAAK, JACOB, weaver, from Lorraine, arrived last fall. If he is alive and in good health, he should come to Jacob Keiter in Skippack, who needs to speak with him (*Eyster:* 6 cites the *Pennsylvanische Berichte* 16 March 1748).

Jacob Schorck and Johannes Schauch arrived on 9 Oct 1747 on the ship *Restauration* (*Eyster:* 6).

SCHAEFER, ADAM, is sought by his brother-in-law, Peter Edelman, [living?] on the Altilana, near Christian Kuhn, formerly of Fuerstenguischen, near Eberbach, or Heidelberg (*Hocker:* 52 cites the *Pennsylvanische Geschichts-Schreiber* 16 Oct 1755).

Peter Edelman and Joh. Adam Schafer arrived on the brig *Mary & Sarah* on 26 Oct 1754 (*Eyster:* 15).

Peter Edleman, of the City of Philadelphia, tavern keeper, died leaving a will dated 28 Jan 1762 and proved 20 April 1762. He named his children George and Elizabeth, and named his wife Christian as extx. The witnesses were Mathias Startz and Andrew Liburt. (*Phila. Wills.* Vol. 3, cites Philadelphia Co. Will Book M:276).
Peter and Christian were the parents of: GEORGE; and ELIZABETH.

SCHARTLE, MELCHIOR, born in Lobrunn, Zabergen, Wurtemburg, came to America about thirty years ago, and settled in the Blue Mountains. His youngest daughter Maria Barbara, is the mother of Juliana Kummerlin, who arrived in America and is now with Jacob Bartsch, formerly landlord of the White Lamb Inn, Market St., Philadelphia. She is seeking her grandfather (*Hocker:* 122 cites the *Wochentlicher Pennsylvanischer Staatsbote* 25 May 1773).

SCHAUB, MARTIN, from Zanzsingen, or Basel, arrived in this country with his brother Johann. Both were indentured and became separated. Johann, now with Moses Peters in Montgomery Twp., is seeking Martin (*Hocker:* 47 cites the *Pennsylvanische Geschichts-Schreiber* 1 March 1755).
Hans Schaub and Martin Schaub arrived on 15 Aug 1750 on the ship *Royal Union* (*Eyster:* 14).

SCHAUTZ, EVE, arrived at Philadelphia from Germany some time in October 1753 and was bound to one Randle Hutchinson of Bucks Co. Her brother, Johannes Schautz, of Conecocheague, Cumberland Co., about thirty miles above Carlisle, and ten miles from Jacob Schnebele, will appreciate it if anyone can inform him about her (*Pa. Gaz.* 21 Feb 1765).

SCHEINTS, GEORGE, came to Philadelphia from Frankfort, Germany, some 14 years ago. If he is still alive, and will apply to Richard Moore in Alloway Creek, Salem Co., he may hear of his brother Henry Scheints, who will be glad of the opportunity to see him (*Pa. Gaz.* 22 March 1769).

SCHELLBASZ, LUDWIG, from Rohre, Darmstadt Region, miller, living nine miles from Frederick, MD, seeks information about one of his sisters, who came to America. He left three sisters in Germany, and does not know which one came to America. Notify Conrad Grosch, at Frederick [MD?] (*Hocker:* 76 cites the *Pennsylvanische Geschichts-Schreiber* 2 March 1759).

SCHEMPP, MATHES, from Belinger Amt, Wurtemberg, came to America about forty-five years ago. Martin Miller, Kensington, Philadelphia Co., PA, is inquiring for him (*Hocker:* 191 cites the *Philadelphische Correspondenz* 18 Sep 1792).

SCHENCKEL, JACOB, born at Faroldorf, Zurich, a butcher, came to Philadelphia twenty years ago, and later returned to Europe for his family. Through a misunderstanding, his children had sailed for Nova Scotia before he arrived. Jacob then returned to Philadelphia, and his relatives have heard nothing from him. His daughter Elizabeth married Johann Rudolph Schmidt, butcher, in Quebec, and she is now seeking information about her father (*Hocker:* 143 cites the *Wochentlicher Pennsylvanischer Staatsbote* 18 April 1775).

SCHICK, MARGARETHA, arrived in this country, two years ago last autumn. Her brother, Michael Schick, near Hansz Fretz, Bedmister Twp., Bucks Co., is seeking her (*Hocker:* 60 cites the *Pennsylvanische Geschichts-Schreiber* 5 March 1757).

SCHIRR, GERARD HENRY, a native of Hamburg, left London in 1758, and arrived in Annapolis, where he lodged with William Clajon, schoolmaster, and then with John Thompson. He was last heard from in 1759 (Annapolis *Maryland Gazette* 19 Jan 1775).

SCHLAYER, HENRICH, arrived in America nine years ago. His brother George, of New Gossenhoppen, at Johann Mack's mill, is seeking him (*Hocker:* 92 cites the *Pennsylvanische Geschichts-Schreiber* 31 July 1761).

SCHLEMB, PETER, lived somewhere in NJ is. Peter has been in this country for 13 years. His brother Frederick Schlemb, born in Longen Condto [prob. Langenkandel, Rhenish Bavaria], came to this country last fall, and is seeking Peter. If Peter is alive he may inquire of Deterick Taub, shoemaker in Second Street, Philadelphia (*Pa. Gaz* 14 Jan 1768).

    Johan Peter Schlemb arrived on the *Peggy,* Capt. James Abercrombie, from Rotterdam, and qualified on 16 Oct 1754 (*PGP* 1:638). Joh. Friederich Schlemb arrived on the *Sally,* John Osman, master, and took the Oath of Allegiance on 5 Oct 1767 (*Names of Foreigners* 480).

    In early pioneer days, two German brothers by the name of Schlemb came to this county. Frederick Schlemb settled in Smyth Co., VA. As the name was gradually adjusted to the English language, the heavy B sound was changed to the voiceless lip sound of p, and the name became Schlemp. The "ch" was later dropped, and the name became plain Slemp, the name of a large and prominent family in Virginia. Frederick Slemp's son John removed to Turkey Cove and took up land in 1789. His wife was Alpha Smyth Slemp. They had a son named Sebastian S. Slemp. We have no record of other children. (J. M. Moseley. Gateway To The West, Manuscript on file in the Archives of The Historical Society of Southwest Virginia. A Small Overall History of Lee County, VA).

SCHLOEPP, JOHANN LEONHARD from Mt. Taschendorf in Frankischen Kreis of Garmany (Franconia), belonging to Reichsfreyherr von Kuentsberg, Amt Obersteinbach, left for America, in 1766, with Johann Maar (see above)., Schloepp wrote to his parents on 16 June 1784 from the potash factory in New York, where he was employed as a cooper (*Hocker:* 188 cites the *Philadelphische Correspondenz* 9 Sep 1791).

SCHLOWEISZ, JOHANN GOTTLIEB, is sought by his sister, Catherine Ehlerin, from Kleebrun, Wurtemburg, who lately lived in Luneberg, near Halifax, and has now come to Philadelphia. She is now in her second marriage, to Mr. Hirschmann, of Luneberg, Philadelphia, and staying with Johann Georg Schneider, apothecary in Race St. (*Hocker:* 65 cites the *Pennsylvanische Geschichts-Schreiber* 29 Oct 1757).

SCHMELL (or SCHNELL), JOHN ADAM, from Cassel, has been in America for fourteen years. He is sought by his sister Anna Elizabeth Loch, widow of Lorentz Loch, from Braunholder, Zweibrucken, arrived in this country last autumn, and lives at North Wales (Gwynned Twp., Montgomery Co.), with Nicolaus Schmell [Schnell?]. She is seeking her brother Johann Adam Schmell [Schnell?] (*Hocker:* 20 cites the *Pennsylvanische Geschichts-Schreiber* 16 June 1750).
   For more on the Loch Family, see Burgert's *Western Palatinate:* 223.

SCHMIDT, JOHANN ADAM, a clothmaker, arrived seven years ago. His brother Jacob Schmidt, care of Antony Jaeger, Oley (Berks Co.), near the New Furnace, arrived in America six years ago, from Langenbramig, and is seeking his brother (*Hocker:* 91 cites the *Pennsylvanische Geschichts-Schreiber* 3 July 1761).
   Jacob Schmidt arrived 30 Oct 1754 on the ship *Mary and Sarah.* Joh. Adam Smitb arrived on 30 Sep 1753 on the ship *Windsor* (*Eyster:* 21).

SCHMIDT, JOST, has been in America for thirty years. He was born at Amt Wetter, Nieder Espy, Hesse. His brother's son, Johannes Schmidt, Springfield Twp., Philadelphia (now Montgomery) Co., PA, is seeking him (*Hocker:* 170 cites the *Philadelphische Correspondenz* 29 June 1784).

SCHMITT, ANN FRY WELLER, married Johann Christ Schmitt. Her brother, Peter Weller, of Amity Twp., on Manatawny Creek, Berks Co., PA, with Philip Boyer, came to America nine years ago, with his two sisters, one of who married Johann Christ Schmitt. Her name is Ann Fry. The other sister is Eva Maria Wellerin. He is seeking information about them (*Hocker:* 18 cites the *Pennsylvanische Geschichts-Schreiber* 16 March 1750).

SCHMITT, JOH. WILHELM, from Nussbaum, back of Creutzenbach, is asked to inform the printer so that he may learn of something to his advantage (*Eyster:* 12 cites the *Pennsylvanische Berichte* 1 Feb 1752).
   Joh. Wilhelm Schmitt arrived on the *Two Brothers* on 14 Sep 1749 (*Eyster:* 12).

SCHMOLTZE, PETER, was born in Zweibrucken, and has been in America for two or three years. His father, Daniel, is seeking him. Notify Adam Grim in NY (*Hocker:* 121 cites the *Wochentlicher Pennsylvanischer Staatsbote* 7 April 1773).
   Daniel Schmoltze arrived on 9 Nov 1767 on the ship *Minerva* (*Esyter:* 30).

SCHNAESZ, HENRICH, is sought by his brother Nicolaus, of Tuplehocken, Berks Co., living with Jacob Lederman (*Hocker:* 11 cites the *Pennsylvanische Geschichts-Schreiber* 1 Nov 1748).

SCHNEIDER, MARIA and **PHILIPPA SCHNEIDER,** have recently arrived from Hire, Germany. Their sister Ann Elizabeth, came to America from Hire in 1752. She has advertised for her two sisters (*Maryland Journal and Baltimore Advertiser* 21 Aug 1776).

SCHNEIDER, DANIEL, came from Nassau-Siegischen two years ago. Two of his brothers Caspar and Hansz Heinrich, arrived last autumn, and are living at Anwell, NJ, near Peter Jung, together with their brother-in-law Anton Stutte. Stutte also news for Henrich Hartman, who arrived in America two years ago, also from Nassau-Siegischen (*Hocker:* 32 cites the *Pennsylvanische Geschichts-Schreiber* 1 April 1752).

Daniel Schneider arrived on the ship *Nancy,* on 31 Aug 1750 (*Eyster:* 12).

SCHNEIDER, ELIZABETH, and her daughters **CATHERINE** and **ANNA MARIA** came to Philadelphia about four years ago. Elizabeth's son, Henrich, from the Dillenburg Region, arrived in New York five years ago, and is now with Sebastian Graf, one mile from Lancaster. He is seeking his mother and sisters (*Hocker:*76 cites the *Pennsylvanische Geschichts-Schreiber* 2 March 1759).

SCHNEIDER, HANSZ HEINRICH, age 23, and **PHILIP SCHNEIDER,** 25 years old, are sought by their father, Imanuel Schneider, living at Christophel Obel, Macungie, Lehigh Co. (*Hocker:* 13 cites the *Pennsylvanische Geschichts-Schreiber* 1 June 1749).

SCHNEIDER, JOHANN GEORG, and his brother **GEORG PETER SCHNEIDER,** are sought by their father, Johannes, living back of the Blue Mountains, Chestnut Hill Twp., Northampton (now Monroe) Co. He came to America in 1764, with his two sons, whose whereabouts he is seeking. The sons were indentured with Joseph Morrison, Cumberland Twp., Marsh Creek Settlement, York (now Adams) Co. The older son, Johann Georg, was free on 14 Aug 1773, and the younger, Georg Peter, was free on 14 Aug 1776 (*Hocker:* 151 cites the *Wochentlicher Pennsylvanischer Staatsbote* 7 June 1776).

Johannes Schneider arrived on the ship *Chance* on 8 Aug 1764 (*Eyster:* 40).

SCHNELL, JACOB, came into this country in 1751 and Ursula Schnell, his mother, has not heard from him for some time. Anyone knowing of his whereabouts is asked to contact his mother, living at Skippack, or Lewis Frederick, watchman in Wood St., Philadelphia (*Pa. Gaz.* 18 Sep 1755).

He may be the Jacob Schnell who came on the *Ann,* John Spurrier, master, from Rotterdam, and qualified on 28 Sep 1749 (*Names of Foreigners:* 299).

SCHROETER, CHRISTINA and ELISABETH SCHROETER, were indentured last autumn by their father Martin, Schroeter, who is with Johannes Schneider of Lancaster Co., PA, and wants to know what became of them (*Hocker:*19 cites the *Pennsylvanische Geschichts-Schreiber* 1 June 1750).

For more on the Schroeter Family, see Burgert's *Alsace:* 455.

SCHUECHEN, SEBASTIAN, born in Niedermerschbach, near Hochenburg, with Jacob Duenschman, left Amsterdam on 29 May last for Philadelphia. Jacob Fischer, Reformed schoolmaster in the stone church, Bern Twp., Berks Co., PA, is seeking them (*Hocker:* 172 cites the *Philadelphische Correspondenz* 22 Feb 1785).

SCHUHMAN, JOHANN PETER, arrived in this country seven years ago with his sister, Maria Catherine, who is now inquiring for him (*Hocker:* 9 cites the *Pennsylvanische Geschichts-Schreiber* 16 Dec 1747).

Johan Peter Shoeman, age 30, arrived on the *Friendship*, William Vittery, commander, from Rotterdam, and qualified 23 Sep 1740 (*Names of Foreigners* 197).

SCHWARTZ, ADAM, late of Northampton Co., PA, from whence he is said to have moved to NJ, if still living, is asked to call upon George Hertzel within one year of 28 Jan 1785, for a legacy left him by his brother Michael Schwartz, dec. Otherwise, Hertzel, who is the executor, will pay the money to the other heirs "Franconia Twp., Montgomery Co." (*Pa. Gaz.* 2 Feb 1785).

SCHWARTZ, BERNHARD, is sought by his brother Philip Leonhard Schwartz, from Duehrn, one-quarter hour from Brackenheim (*Hocker:* 116 cites the *Wochentlicher Pennsylvanischer Staatsbote* 28 July 1772).

Philip Leonhard Schwartz, arrived on the *Peggy*, from Rotterdam, last from Plymouth, James Abercrombie, commander, and qualified on 24 Sep 1758 (*Names of Foreigners* 398).

SCHWARTZ, FRIEDRICH, and CHRISTIAN SCHWARTZ, are sought by their brother-in-law Johan Martin Kirschman, from the Wurtemburg domain of the Palatinate Duke in Weiler, and now of Maidencreek Twp., Berks Co. (*Hocker:* 87 cites the *Pennsylvanische Geschichts-Schreiber* 13 Feb 1761).

SCHWARTZ, WILHELM, blacksmith, 50 years old, and his wife arrived last autumn on the ship *Britannia,* Capt. Peter. They left Henrich Haen's inn, Third Street, Philadelphia three months ago (*Hocker:* 129 cites the *Wochentlicher Pennsylvanischer Staatsbote* 15 March 1774).

SCHWEICKERT, EVA MARGARETHA and **ELIZABETH SCHWEICKERT,** came from Alsace seven years ago, and were servants, six miles from Lancaster, in Warwick Twp. Their brother, Johann Martin Schweickert, serving with Henrich Eckel, Bucks Co., PA, thirty miles from Philadelphia, is seeking them (*Hocker:* 138 cites the Philadelphia *Staatsbote* 31 Jan 1775).

Johannes Martin Schweickert came on the *Union,* Andrew Bryson, master, from Rotterdam, last from Cowes, on 30 Sep 1774 (*PGP* 1:759).

For more on the Schweickert Family, see Burgert's *Alsace 458.*

SCOGGIN, JOHN, left this place about five years ago, If living, he is desired to return, and he will hear of something to his interest. The several printers of newspapers in the United States, to whose notice these may come, are requested to give them a place in their papers for a short time. "Salem, New-Jersey, 4 Jan 1800" (*Pa. Gaz.* 9 April 1800).

SCOTT, NATHANIEL, late of Edenderry, Ireland, but now of New York, informs his brother Henry Scott, shoemaker, for some time a resident of Philadelphia, or parts adjacent that their father, Jonathan, has died leaving a legacy for Henry (*Scott* 2:66 cites the *Pa. Gaz.* 9 Nov 1749).

Nathaniel Scott, now of Charlestown, SC, advertises that he still has not heard from the said Henry, who is entitled to 20 guineas per annum, provided Henry comes within three months of this advertisement. Henry's last known place of residence may have been in Burlington, in West Jersey (*Pa. Gaz.* 14 June 1758).

SEELIG, JOHN LUDWIG, native of Kirchberg in the Circle of Franconia (Germany) left that place in 1776 and went to North America, and has not been heard of since. His brother Frederick Seelig, living at Pirmasens, near Deux Ponts (Zweybruken), Germany, and his other relations are anxious to hear from him. Anyone with information is asked to contact the editor of this paper (*Poulson's American Daily Advertiser* 6 Jan 1817).

SEGAR, CHARLES, son of the late Henry Segar of the kingdom of Bavaria, is asked to inform the Department of State of his residence, and he will be informed of something to his advantage. In a letter dated 18 Oct 1803 the said Charles Segar announced his intention of embarking at Tonningen to proceed to his uncle, David Segar, merchant, of Philadelphia, to learn about commerce (*The National Intelligencer and Washington Advertiser* 11 July 1811).

SEGRAIS, LEDET de, left Paris last April. If he is present in this country, he will hear something to his advantage by calling on C. & M. Humphreys of Baltimore (*Baltimore Patriot* 21 Sep 1816).

SEIBERT, JOHANNES, was born unter Altertheim bey Werthheim am Mayn, and arrived in America in 1750. His brother Bastian Seibert is at the old sugar house in Philadelphia, and is seeking him (*Hocker:* 85 cites the *Pennsylvanische Geschichts-Schreiber* 11 Aug 1760).

In 1790 a Sebastian Seybert was listed as head of a family in the Northern liberties of Philadelphia, PA (*AIS 1790 Census Index*).

SEITZ, FREDERICK WILLIAM, of Manheim, Germany, age 17, left London on a transport sailing for America in Aug 1777. His aged father and unhappy family are trying to get in touch with him. Any information should be sent to the publisher of the Philadelphia Gazette or to Mr. Unich Hencke, Secretary to the Amsterdam and American Post Offices in Hamburg (*GAVN:* 304 cites the *Virginia Herald and Fredericksburg and Falmouth Advertiser* 11 July 1797).

SEITZ, HANSZ MICHEL, arrived in this country six years ago last autumn. His son of the same name was indentured. The son is asked to notify his parents of his whereabouts. They are with Mordecai Thomson, Ridley Twp., Chester Co. (now Delaware Co.) (*Hocker:* 56 cites the *Pennsylvanische Geschichts-Schreiber* 1 June 1756).

Hans Michel Seitz took the Oath of Allegiance when he arrived on the *Lydia,* Capt. John Randolph, from Rotterdam, on 13 Oct 1749 (*Names of Foreigners:* 302).

He may be the Michael Seitz who was described as aged near 40 years, pretending to be a miller; who ran away from the John Baus, tavern keeper on Chestnut Hill (*Pa. Gaz.* 17 March 1768).

SELLE, CHARLES, on 28 May 1802 left Hamburg for Philadelphia, on the *Pennsylvania,* Capt. Peter Yorke. If he is still alive he is asked to contact F. A. Schneider, 164

N. Third St., where a communication of a very interesting nature will be made to him (*Poulson's American Daily Advertiser* 3 April 1817).

SELTZER, BALTHASAR, was born at Rotheim, Hesse-Hanau, and was last heard from in Philadelphia in 1753. His only daughter, Anna Margaretha Seltzer, is inquiring for him. She was left at home in 1752 when her father and his wife left Germany for America (*Hocker:* 187 cites the *Philadelphische Correspondenz* 26 Nov 1790).

Baltzer Seltzer came on the *Friendship*, from Amsterdam, last from Gosport, on 21 Oct 1754 (*PGP* 1:643).

SENNET, JOHN *alias* JAMES, son of John, and Sarah Abbott, formerly residents of New York, removed to Madeira, where John parted with Sarah. If he will apply to the printer, he will hear something to his advantage (*GAIN:* 304 cites *The Virginia Gazette and General Advertiser* 7 Nov 1792).

John Sennet, son of Sarah Sennet (*alias* Abbott), who lived near New York and who removed thence to Lisbon and afterwards to Madeira, where he left her with the intention of returning to America and settling near James River, and has not been heard of since. If he will apply to Mr. Samuel Green, post master in Annapolis, he will hear of something to his advantage (*Dunlap's American Daily Advertiser* 27 Feb 1793).

SERAZINO, REMIGIUS, born in or near Strasburg, was last heard of in 1761, when he wrote a letter from New York, while he was living with Mrs. Daniel Wittib, leather worker. His brothers and sisters want to hear from him (*Hocker:* 173 cites the *Philadelphische Correspondenz* 14 June 1785).

SEYLER (SAEYLER), FELIX, came from Rucheim about two years ago, and wrote a letter from his ship to his brother Joh. Peter Seyler, not far from Falckner Swamp, near to Heinrich Deringer's, who has been in this land for over 24 years. The letter went to the wrong place, and Peter has only just now received it. He was would like to know where his brother is. Felix came here from Rucheim, and when he sees this he will come to Peter (*Eyster:* 10 cites the *Pennsylvanische Berichte* 1 Sep 1751).

Peter Seyler, with family, arrived (possibly on his second voyage) on the ship *Johnson,* galley, on 18 Sep 1732 (*Eyster:* 10).

Felix Sailor [*sic*] came on the *Phoenix* in 1749, but did not sign (*PGP* 1:407). Felix Seyler, son of the late Benedict Seyler from Ittling(en) in Herrschaft Gemming(en), married on 3 June 1732, Anna Margaretha Bast, dau. of the late Daniel Bast of Ellerstadt, Grafschafft Hartenburg. The marriage record has an added note: "moved to Pennsylvania in 1748" (Burgert's *Palatine Origins:* 338-339).

SEYLERIN, ANNA BARBARA, living at 81 Appletree Alley, Philadelphia, received word from her husband two years ago, whole she was in Germany, directing her to come to America. She has not heard from her husband since. He lived in Baltimore for six years (*Hocker:* 198 cites the *Philadelphische Correpondenze* 18 Sep 1798).

SHAILDS, PETER, resided some time ago in the western part of Maryland, at or near Hagerstown, will hear of something to his advantage by applying to 92 Chesnut St., Philadelphia (*Claypoole's American Daily Advertiser* 3 April 1799).

SHAWCROSS, JOHN, was in or about Philadelphia on 14 Oct 1766. He is asked to call upon John Britton in the Northern Liberties, near Pool Bridge, and prove he is the person inquired for he may hear of something to his advantage (*Pa. Gaz.* 31 Jan 1771).
    John "Shallcross" is listed in the 1790 Census of Lower Dublin Twp., Philadelphia Co., PA (*AIS 1790 U.S. Federal Census Index*).

SHEAFER, GEORGE, resided in Lancaster, PA, about seven years ago, and followed the baking business, will hear of something to his advantage by applying to the Editor of the *Franklin Repository*, Chambersburg. The last time he was heard of he resided somewhere within 40 miles of Pittsburgh (*The True American* 26 Jan 1814).

SHEALS, PETER, came from the North of Ireland, and is supposed to be somewhere about Reading or in the western parts of the state, is requested to apply immediately at No. 2 North Front St., where he will find several letters and agreeable news from his parents and friends (*Claypoole's American Daily Advertiser* 20 Nov 1798).

SHEAN, ARTHUR, left Baltimore County some time ago. He should apply to Basil Magruder of Montgomery County (*Maryland Journal and Baltimore Advertiser* 9 July 1782).
    Arthur Shean (or Shane) was born c1756 in America. He enlisted on 5 July 1776 as a private in Col. Ewing's Battalion. He was 5'5½" high, and had long light colored hair (*BARP:* 239)

SHEEN, JOHN, late of Castemangner, Co. Cork, landed in Baltimore in 1772. He lived with Capt. Woolford of Blackwater, MD. His brother Timothy Sheen now lives in Raccoon Settlement, near Fort Pitt, in Washington Co., PA (*Maryland Journal and Baltimore Advertiser* 3 June 1783).
    A Timothy Shean of London, age 31, bricklayer, sailed for MD 25 Feb-7 March 1774 as an indentured servant on the *Geddis*, Mr. John Harrison (Coldham, *Emigrants from England to the American Colonies, 1773-1776:* 51; *Fothergill:* 37).

SHERGOLD, WILLIAM BERROW, came some years ago from England, and is supposed to live now in Pasquotank, Perguimans, or Currituck Cos., NC. He is asked to apply to the printer, to hear something to his advantage (*GAVN:* 307 cites the *Va. Gaz.* 12 Sep 1745).

SHOEMAKER, HARMAN, or **MATHIAS SHOEMAKER**, or any of their heirs, should apply to Walter Johnson of Skippack Twp., Philadelphia Co., PA, as they will hear of something to their advantage (*The Pennsylvania Packet or the General Advertiser* 10 Aug 1782).
    They left Holland about 60 or 70 years ago. If their heirs will apply to the printers they may be informed of something to their advantage (*Pa. Gaz.* 17 Nov 1784).
    In 1790 a "Harmon" Shoemaker was listed in the Greenville District of SC, p. 70. Matthias Shoemaker was listed in Montgomery Co., PA (*AIS 1790 U.S. Federal Census Index*).

SHOTWELL, JOHN, Jr., aged about 26, small sized, middling thick set, fresh complexion, with an impediment in his speech, lately went from the Scotch Plains, in East Jersey. If he will return to his friends there, he will hear of something greatly to his advantage. Anyone who can give information about him, to David Bacon in Philadelphia, or to John Smith Shotwell at Scotch Plains, will be handsomely rewarded (*Pa. Gaz.* 15 June 1785).

SIDDON, JOHN, was born in England, and came from thence several years ago, and is supposed to be a shoemaker, somewhere in PA. If he will apply to James Bringhurst, he may hear of something to his advantage (*Pennsylvania Packet General Advertiser* 1 June 1784).

SIEBENBERGIN, ELIZABETH SOPHIA, was born in Hattingen, in dem Clerischen, near Wesel. She was expected to come to America, with a High German family to visit her brother, but she did not come, and her brothers in America and Holland are seeking her. Johannes Benninghof, Philadelphia, care of Valentin Schales or Johannes Beiszler, merchants, has information of an inheritance for her (*Hocker:* 80 cites the *Pennsylvanische Geschichts-Schreiber* 28 Sep 1759).

SILVIAS, NICHOLAS, of Plow Park, and other children, are now at the State House in Philadelphia. During the war they had been taken captive by the Indians from several parts of the Province, and have been lately released by General Amherst. They are to be returned to their parents or other relations, who are desired to come forthwith and receive them (*Pa. Gaz.* 2 July 1761).

SIMPSON, JOHN, formerly a dyer, near Preston, Lancs., came over in the snow *Planter*, Capt. Bowen, to VA about 17 months ago. He intended to go to Philadelphia. If he will apply to his friends at Preston, or to the printers, he will hear something to his advantage (*Pa. Gaz.* 22 Feb 1775).

SIMPSON, PATRICK, a traveling merchant, passenger to this part in the *Friendship*, June 1786, should apply to William Young, bookseller, corner of Second and Chestnut Sts., Philadelphia, where he will hear of something to his advantage (*The Pennsylvania Packet and Daily Advertiser* 5 Aug 1785).

SIMPSON, THOMAS, from VA, enlisted in the service of the United States at New Orleans, from on board a privateer, about 1812 or 1813, since which time he has not been certainly heard from by his friends in Virginia. Anyone (perhaps some of the officers of the U.S. Army) with information as to whether he is alive or dead is asked to contact the editors of the Richmond *Enquirer* or the Washington, D.C. *National Intelligencer* 19 Jan 1820).

SKELTON, JOHN, from Beckermouth, near Whitehaven, tailor, left England about 14 years ago. His brother, on board the *Waters*, lying in the James River, requests information about him (*GAVN:* 311 cites the *Va. Gaz.* 27 Oct 1768).

A John Skelton appears in a 1783 tax list of Shenandoah Co., VA (*AIS Census Index: Pre-1790* gives no other documentation).

SLEAMING, MATHIAS, a lad, served part of his apprenticeship to the breeches-making business with Henry Snobble, in Germantown. In the year 1780 he assigned over his indenture to [-?-] Cooper, in Philadelphia; in the year 1782 said Seamen [*sic*] left Philadelphia, and no account has been given of him since that time. Any person who can give information of him, whether living or dead, will please to leave a few lines at Hall and Sellers' Printing Office. (Signed) Matthias Sleaman, Sr., Germantown Township, June 25, 1794 (*Pa. Gaz.* 2 July 1794).

SMITH, BETTY, age c17, dau. of Peter Smith, in 1772 came from Tenderagee, Co. Armagh, Ireland, to Baltimore. Anyone having news of her is asked by Charles Ellitt, to contact Andrew McCallum in Salem Co., opposite Newcastle (*Pa. Chronicle* 17 Jan 1774).

SMITH, ELIZABETH, is sought by William Boor and Jacob Witmer, the executors of her grandfather Peter Smith ([PA] *Kline's Carlisle Weekly Gazette* 21 June 1797).

SMITH, JAMES, farmer and gardener, came from Philadelphia last winter, and is said to have a wife and no children, and is employed some where between Baltimore and Annapolis. If he will apply to Daniel Larrabee, at the corner of Bank and Calvert Streets, he may hear of something to his advantage (*Baltimore Patriot* 29 Oct 1819).

SMITH, JEREMIAH, formerly a corn-chandler in England in 1739, wrote to his friends from the late Governor's in Annapolis. If he applies to the printer, he will hear something greatly to his advantage (Annapolis *Maryland Gazette* 8 Aug 1754).

SMITH, JOSEPH, formerly of Kensington in the Northern Liberties of Philadelphia, and late of Chesterfield, Burlington Co., NJ, has died. His relatives, who are entitled by law to a share of his estate, are asked to call on Ruth Smith, his widow and admx., at her house in Mount Holly (*Pa. Gaz.* 27 Jan 1772, 4 Oct 1775).

SMITH, ROBERT, late of Ouncle, in the County of Northampton, in Old England, should apply to John Elliott, in Chestnut Street, Philadelphia, he will hear of something to his advantage by the death of a relation. If the said Robert Smith is dead, any person who can give a satisfactory account concerning him, by applying as aforesaid, shall be handsomely rewarded for their trouble (*Pa. Gaz.* 15 Sep 1757).

SMITH, SAMUEL, from Ireland, about 27 years old, has been missing for near six weeks, and his friends are afraid he has drowned or met with some other accident. Anyone with news of him is asked to inform the printer or Michael Wallace at Elk River. Smith is of middle stature, sandy complexion and pockfretten. When last seen at Philadelphia, he had on a blue great coat, black stuff jacket, and leather breeches, and rode on a bay mare (*Pa. Gaz.* 24 Nov 1743).

SMITH, WILLIAM, was born at Stroud, Co. Gloucester, and came to America about four years ago. He is asked to apply to Daniel Shatford in New York City (*Scott* 5:3 cites the *New York Post Boy* 6 Aug 1744).

SMITH, WILLIAM, from Trillick, Co. Tyrone, Ireland, some time ago lived with a Daniel Dunlap in Carlisle, PA. If he is still living, he is urged to contact his brother-in-law, James Alexander and family, who have lately come into this country. He should write to write to the said Alexander, c/o of Joseph Walker, Sadbury Twp., Lancaster, PA (*Lancaster Journal* 30 Oct 1802).

SMITHIN, ELIZABETH, whose maiden name was Watkins should apply to the printer, if she is living, for a message to her advantage (Annapolis *Maryland Gazette* 25 March 1746).

An Elizabeth Watkins, was sentenced to transportation, and was transported in June 1728, from London, in the *Elizabeth*. She was given a Landing Certificate at Potomack in Aug 1729 (*CBEB*).

SMOCK, JOHN, moved to NC about three years ago, leaving his children in the care of the subscriber, James Wilson of WO Co. (Annapolis *Maryland Gazette* 3 Jan 1788).

SPAHR, [-?-], a wheelwright, and **MARIA CATHARINE** [his wife?], at Conestoga, Lancaster Co., PA, are sought by Maria Catharina's sister Rosina Dorothea Rostin (or Rostli), born Kauffmaennin, from Waldenburg aus dem Hohenlohischen, who arrived at Patapsco on 12 Nov 1753 on the ship of Capt. Rattray, and was sold at vendue. Information about them may be sent to John Jansen, merchant, Annapolis, MD (*Pennsylvanische Geschichts-Schreiber* 16 Feb 1754).

SPARLING, ELIZABETH, was born at Coat, near Lancaster, Eng., and came to New York City about 30 years ago, if she applies to William [Algeo?] of New York City, merchant, she will hear something to her advantage (*Scott* 5:32 cites the *New York Post Boy* 27 July 1752).

SPECHT, CHRISTINA, was born at Gumbertshorn, in the Elector Palatine's Dominions, and came with her brother and sister to this country 14 Years ago, and was a bound servant for 9 Years in New Jersey. She is sought by her sister's husband, Conrad Frech. Whoever knows any thing about her, is desired to give Intelligence to the aforesaid Frech; or if this should come to her knowledge, she is invited to come to her said brother-in-law and sister, or to let them know where she lives (*Pa. Gaz.* 28 Oct 1762).

SPENCE, CATHERINE, the "Old Post Woman," lived for many years in this colony. Her children are asked to apply to John Martin of King William Co., VA, to be informed of something to their advantage (*GAVN:* 318 cites *The Virginia Gazette* 4 Sep 1746).

SPENCER, RICHARD, kept a store or a tavern in Pittsburgh about ten or twelve years ago. Afterwards he was an officer in the American Army. If he is alive and will apply to David Anderson, Jr., of Hanover Co., he will hear of something to his advantage (*GAVN:* 318 cites *The Virginia Gazette and the Independent Chronicle* 28 Oct 1786).

SPERI, THOMAS, arrived in this country twelve years ago His brother, Nicklaus Speri, arrived this year, and is in Long Swamp, near Maxatawny, Berks Co., with Nicolaus

Schwartz, and he is seeking Thomas (*Hocker:* 22 cites the *Pennsylvanische Geschichts-Schreiber* 16 Oct 1750).
    For more on the Speri family, see Burgert's *Western Palatinate* 306-308.

SPINDLER, PHILIP DAVID, a sieve-maker from Halle, arrived in this country in 1752. His brother, Lorentz Spindler, a tailor, Lancaster Co., living near Hans Ulrich Huber and Jacob Huber, is seeking him (*Hocker:* 45 cites the *Pennsylvanische Geschichts-Schreiber* 16 Dec 1754).
    Johann Philip David Spindler arrived on the *Phoenix*, Capt. Jno. Spurrier, from Rotterdam, but last from Portsmouth, 2 Nov 1752 (*PGP* 1:502).
    Philip David Spindler was sold in Nov 1752 to John Neave for three and one-half years, but his brother, John Lorens Spindler cannot get any news of Neave or his brother, he asks either of them to inform him by letter to John Lorens Spindler, living near Jacob Hubar, in Lancaster Co. (*Pa. Gaz.* 9 Oct 1755).

SPOR, CONRAD, has been in America for twenty years. His sister Anna Catharina Wilhelm, born Sporin, in Neukirchen, near Ziegenhayn, Hesse, and lately arrived in Philadelphia, is inquiring for him. She is at Georg Water's House, Third St., Near Market (*Hocker:* 197 cites the *Philadelphische Correspondenz* 15 July 1796).

SPRAGG, ISAAC, who came from Litchfield, Eng., is asked to apply to the printer, where he may hear of something to his advantage (*Pennsylvania Packet and the General Advertiser* 14 June 1773).

SPRIGG, THOMAS OTHO, of Frederick Co., MD, should apply to the post-master at Fort Wayne Indiana to hear something to his advantage (*Carrolltonian* 23 May 1835).

SPRING, VENDIAL, and **JACOB SPRING,** brothers, formerly of Lancaster Co., PA, have been absent these many years. They should appear at Cocalico Twp., Lancaster Co, to receive their equal shares of a legacy left them by their brother Powell Spring of said twp. and county, otherwise their shares will be paid to their sisters, according to law (*Pa. Gaz.* 23 Nov 1774).
    Hocker: 137, citing the *Wochentlicher Pennsylvanische Staatsbote* of 29 Nov 1774 names the brothers as Wendel, Jacob, and Paul Spring.

STALTZ, ABRAHAM and MATHIAS, are sought by their brother Wendle Staltz, who has not heard from them for seven years past, and is seeking information about them. He can be reached through the Post Office in Market St., or at Casper Ulrick's, whereby he may be enabled to go and see, or write to them (*Pa. Gaz.* 13 Dec 1748).

STAN, NELIUS, age about 10 or 11, a former captive, was delivered by the Shawnaese Indians, to the subscriber, J. F., Davenport, in Cherry St., near the Academy. Stan says his relatives were of the Sect called Meninists [Mennonites] or Dunkers (*Pa. Gaz.* 17 March 1763).

STARK, JOHN and his brother Charles, natives of Messerbacher Hoss, near Rogenhausen, in the Elector Palatine's dominions, came into this country six years ago, both at one season, but in different vessels. Since then, Charles Stark has heard nothing from his brother, and takes this method of informing his brother that he at present lives with Ander Anderson at Encobus, in the Palatine County in NJ, where his brother John may come to see him (*Pa. Gaz.* 10 Jan 1771).

Johann and Carl Starck arrived on the *Prince of Wales*, James Edgar, master, from Rotterdam, last from Cowes, and took the Oath on 5 Nov 1764 (*PGP* 1:701). Hannes Starck arrived on 20 Oct 1764 on the *Richmond* (*Eyster:* 24).

STAUFFER, HENRICH, son of the late Daniel Stauffer of Mount Joy Twp., Lancaster Co., PA, is sought by his brother-in-law, Johannes Schmidt of Donegal Twp., Lancaster Co., PA (*Hocker:* 170 cites the *Philadelphische Correspondenz* 25 May 1784).

STAUS, FRANCIS JOSEPH, DANIEL STAUS, SARAH STAUS, and **SUSANNA STAUS,** are children of the late Belthaser Staus, late of the Northern Liberties of Philadelphia, yeoman, who left a will ordering his estate to be sold, and the money equally divided among his eight children, four of whom are living near Philadelphia, and the four who are missing, named in the heading, and whose shares will be put out [invested] for seven years. Staus named Zacharias Endres his executor.

The executor is informed that Francis Joseph is a skinner, and at one time was paymaster to the British troops in East Florida. Daniel was a captain of a vessel, and inhabitant of the Island of Providence. Sarah married one Andrew Lytel and is living somewhere in North Carolina. Susanna married Andrew Kehr of the 21st Regt. of Scotch Fusiliers. Kehr is said to be a prisoner of General Burgoyne's army, now in VA (*Pa. Gaz.* 18 Sep 1782).

STEEL, JOHN, came from Ireland in 1775. He is asked to apply to William Garigues, admin. of James Steel of Philadelphia, house carpenter, as he may hear of something to his advantage (*Pa. Gaz.* 2 Feb 1785).

STEELE, Mr., recently exhibited the Panorama of the Battle of Waterloo at the Bavilion Gardens. Anyone with information on his current residence, is asked to contact the office of the Baltimore *Patriot* or the Philadelphia *Centinel* (*Baltimore Patriot & Mercantile Advertiser* 12 May 1819).

STEENMEYER, HENDRICK SAMUEL, left Amsterdam in 1803, in the ship *Cora,* Capt. Hutchings, for Baltimore. His friends wish to obtain information concerning him, and ask anyone who can furnish the same to communicate it to Wm. Wilson and Sons, of Baltimore (*Baltimore Patriot* 7 Oct 1823).

STEIN, JACOB, left his dwelling on 24 July 1772. His wife Catherine advertises for news of him (*Maryland Gazette or Baltimore General Advertiser* 16 May 1775).

STEPHENSON, HENRY, late of Trafford Hill, near Yarm, North Riding of York, embarked at London in July 1770 for New York City, but is supposed to have settled in VA or MD in Sep. He is asked to apply to the printer of this paper (*Scott* 3:153 cites *The New York Gazette and Weekly Mercury* 8 April 1771).

STEVENS, HUGH, came from Ireland to Philadelphia some eight years ago in the ship *Andrew,* Capt. Caldwell, and served his time with Samuel White (son of Thomas White) in Little Britain Twp., Lancaster Co. If he will apply to the printer of the *Chronicle* he will hear something to his advantage (*Pa. Chronicle* 22 Aug 1772).

STEVENS, THOMAS, living at the Widow Spencer's on Patapsco, should contact the printer for news of a legacy left him by an uncle (Annapolis *Maryland Gazette* 28 May 1752).

STEVENSON, ROBERT, son of John Stevenson, in the Townland of Cotton, Parish of Bangor, and County of Down, in Ireland, if living, should apply to David Hall, Printer in Philadelphia, or to James McCartney, in New York. He will hear of something greatly to his Advantage. (*Pa. Gaz.* 10 Aug 1762).

Robert Stevenson, son of John and Mary Stevenson, was born in the town land of Cottown, Parish of Bangor, Co. Down, Ireland, and went to America some years ago. He is asked to apply to Messrs. Greg, Cunningham, and Co., merchants, New York City, or Thomas Ewing, merchant of Baltimore (*Scott* 3:190 cites *The New York Gazette and Weekly Mercury* 17 Oct 1774).

STEWARD, PATRICK, Scotchman, Practitioner of Physick and Surgery, late of Somerset [Co.], MD, who left there four sons and three daughters, on last 27 March, died intestate at the subscriber's house in Cape May, NJ, leaving in my hands some few assets to be administered. Those having legal right to the administration thereon, are desired to take the same upon them in three or four months after date, and discharge my bill of funeral expenses, etc., or I shall be obliged to administer, to reimburse myself according to law. /s/ William Smith (*Pa. Gaz.* 1 June 1758).

The inventory of Dr. Patrick Steward of Cape May, NJ, was taken on 28-29 April 1758 by Jeremiah Hand and Jeremiah Smith, and showed a value of £47.1.10, including apparel, medicines, and surgical instruments. William Smith posted bond as administrator on 2 Oct 1758. He filed an account on 13 Nov 1760 (*ARNJ* 32:308 cites Liber 9, p. 313).

STEWART, WILLIAM, tailor, son of Joseph and Martha Stewart, of Ballyeaston Parish, Co. Antrim, Ireland, came into this country about four years ago. His brother Robert Stewart now has also come into this country, and would like to hear from him. Robert is living at the House of Jacob Rush, near the Crooked Billet, on the Philadelphia Road (*Pa. Gaz.* 27 April 1774).

STIERLE, GEORG ALBRECHT, a tanner's apprentice, born at Sinzheim in the Palatinate, left Nancy, France, last Easter Monday, for America. Adam Seitz, Market St., between Third St. and Fourth St., Philadelphia, is seeking him (*Hocker:* 168 cites the *Philadelphische Correspondenz* 25 Nov 1783).

STORCK, JACOB, arrived last summer from Alsace, from Ritters-Hifen in the Hattner-Amt. His mother, Anna Maria Storckin, and her son Dewald, and daughter Anna Maria arrived this autumn, and they are free of passage costs. They are with Johannes Kuhn, near the Reformed Church, and are seeking Jacob (*Hocker:* 31 cites the *Pennsylvanische Geschichts-Schreiber* 1 Feb 1752).

Jacob Stark [*sic*] arrived on the *Brotherhood*, John Thompson, captain, from Rotterdam, and qualified on 3 Nov 1750. Dewald Storch [*sic*] arrived on the *Janet*, Capt. William Cunningham, from Rotterdam, and qualified on 7 Oct 1751 (*Names of Foreigners* 325, 347).

For more on the Storck Family, see Burgert's *Northern Alsace* 492-493.

STREHM, ADAM, and his brother Henrich Strehm (who is now on Cocalico Creek Lancaster Co., one mile from Ephrata, near Abraham Schonauer), came to America five years and six months ago. Henrich is now seeking Adam (*Hocker:* 85 cites the *Pennsylvanische Ge-schichts-Schreiber* 6 June 1760).

Adam and Joh. Henrich Strehm arrived on the *Edinburgh*, James Russel, master, from Rotterdam, and qualified on 30 Sep 1754 (*Names of Foreigners:* 434, 435).

STRETER, MARIA CATHARINE, alias Baker, came over from Germany with her father, Hans Baker, in 1744, and was bound to one Mary Tomlinson (when she was about nine years old, and since then has not been heard from. Her brother Henry Streter, living in Greenwich Twp., Sussex Co., NJ, asks her to come or send to him (*Pa. Gaz.*, 1760, in *ARNJ* 20:513).

STRICKLAND, JOHN, left England in 1775 and arrived in Baltimore. He should apply to Capt. William Dennis of the ship *Hanbury*, or to John Clapham of Annapolis (Annapolis *Maryland Gazette* 5 July 1787).

John Strickland, age 22, of London, gardener, sailed from England to MD, as an indented servant, for four years, 30 Jan-6 Feb 1775, on the *Nancy*, Mr. Gabriel Sund (*CBE4:* 251; *Fothergill:* 132).

He is almost certainly the John Strickland, of the parish of Camberwell, Surrey, who left England in 1775 under indenture from Messrs. Lux and Bowly to serve as gardener. He was asked to contact the printer (*Maryland Journal and Baltimore Advertiser* 23 July 1790).

John Strickland and Alice Perry of Harford Co., MD, were married in St. John's Parish on 30 June 1793 (*SJSG:* 283).

"Formerly of Camberwell, Surrey, but late of Baltimore, MD," he died by Jan 1797, when administration was granted to his brother Charles Strickland, since the relict Ann, now wife of Thomas Shepherd, renounced (*AWAP:* 303).

STROBER, MARTIN, aged 28, disappeared in Aug 1758, and his brother Valentin, of Lancaster Co., is seeking him (*Hocker:* 80 cites the *Pennsylvanische Geschichts-Schreiber* 28 Sep 1759).

STRUDT, CONRAD, arrived in Pennsylvania four years ago from Rothebach, two hours from Hanau, with his wife Maria, and as they could not pay for their passage, they wanted to enter service together. After waiting six weeks without being able to make such arrangements, they sold their clothes to allay their hunger, and finally were indentured separately. The wife has served four years in Williamstown [Wilmington?] in Christiana

Hundred, with Joseph Muddert. She will be free in October and is seeking her husband (*Hocker:* 68 cites the *Pennsylvanische Geschichts-Schreiber* 21 Jan 1758). Conrad Strudt arrived on 3 Oct 1753 on the ship *Louisa* (*Eyster:* 18).

STUBERIN, ELIZABETH, is sought by her daughters Anna and Maria Stuberin, who came to America seven years ago, and were with Emanuel Zimmerman, Jr., Earl Twp., Lancaster Co., PA, are now seeking their mother, Elizabeth Stuberin (*Hocker:* 158 cites the *Wochentlicher Pennsylvanischer Staatsbote* 3 March 1779).

STUMPIN, JULIANA CATHARINA, served her time with George Boehn, married, and then left. She is sought by her brother Herman Stump, who is living with Lenert Christel, Indianfield, at the source of Skippack Creek, Franconia Twp., Montgomery Co., (*Hocker:* 10 cites the *Pennsylvanische Geschichts-Schreiber* 16 May 1748).

STUPSKY, GEORG, born near Danzig, West Prussia, came to America about 1783, and now is sought (*Hocker:* 182 cites the *Philadelphische Correspondenz* 22 July 1788).

STURGEON, JOHN, lived with the subscriber, William Semple, a few years before the late war. His brother **THOMAS STURGEON** sailed out of Marblehead, New England. If either are alive, they may hear of something to their advantage by applying or writing to Dr. John Witherspoon in New Jersey, to Thomas Marshall, merchant in Paisley, north Britain, or to William Semple (*The Pennsylvania Packet and Daily Advertiser* 15 July 1785).

SULLIVAN, CORNELIUS, left Dublin about five years ago and landed in Baltimore. If he is living he should contact his son Philip, now living in York Co., PA (*Maryland Gazette or Baltimore General Advertiser* 17 Nov 1789). He left Dublin about six years ago in company with a Mr. Martin, a surgeon, and landed in Baltimore. Sullivan's son Philip would be glad to hear from him. Letters should be directed to Robert McIlheney at Peter Little's Town, York Co. (*Pennsylvania Herald and York General Advertiser* 7 April 1790).

SULLIVAN, DANIEL, left Christiana Bridge about a year ago. He is asked to apply to the executors of his brother Jeremiah Sullivan, dec., where he will hear of something to his advantage. The executors are Philemon McLaughlin and Con Hollahan (*Pa. Gaz.* 22 April 1767).

SULLIVAN, MORTEY, sailed from Cork in the year 1762 or 1763 and kept school at Cape Fear in NC. He was born in the Barony of Everough, Co. Kerry, Ireland, son of Philip Sullivan, Keanough. Mortey should contact his brother Jeremiah Sullivan, by directing a letter to Mr. Casey's at Front St., Philadelphia, to hear of something greatly to his advantage (*Dunlap's Pennsylvania Packet, or the General Advertiser* 31 July 1775).

SULTAN, WILHELMINA, daughter of Johann Conrad Sultan, was indented for 5½ years to Mr. Alexander M'Dowell of Franklin Co., PA. Anyone who can give information about her will confer a favor on both her paternal and nine fraternal relatives. As Johann C. Sultan is in very unfavorable circumstances, he wishes to know whether his brother **HERMAN SULTAN** is alive or dead. Herman resides in Lexington County, SC. If he should be alive, his brother wishes him to send him one or two hogs, a keg of sourcrout, sausages, knack-worst, liver-worst, etc., for the worst that he can spare will be preferable to what his brother now lives on. Johann C. Sultan has written near 50 letters to his brother and daughter, and has never obtained an answer from either. If his should reach the eye of his brother-in-law, Mr. Denius, residing at St. Croix, he will confer a particular favor of J. C. S. if he should see fit to send him the mahogany he requested long since. J.C.S. thinks this is a reasonable requisition as Mr. Denius is wealthy and mahogany is low in that place. Any information concerning his daughter, brother, or brother-in-law is asked to forward the information to Mr. George Falstaff Brown, tobacconist and inn-keeper, 73 Market St. or to Johann Conrad Sultan, 11th St., between Race and Vine Sts. P.S. The public are informed that his name is not Johann Conrad Sugar, but Johann Conrad Sultan, as his name is more imperial than sweet (*Spirit of the Press* 1 Feb 1807).

SUMMERS, TIMOTHY, or **LAWRENCE SUMMERS**, his brother, who came to PA some years ago from Tillick, Co. Tyrone, Ireland, if alive, are asked to apply to Thomas Lucas at Pequay in Lancaster Co., where they will hear something to their advantage (*Pa. Gaz.* 4 Sep 1755).

SUPPLE, CATHERINE, dau. of Garrit Supple of Limerick, Ireland, seeks information about her brother who arrived in America some years before (*Scott* 3:56 cites *The New York Mercury* 9 Jan 1758).

SYMS, HENRY, is requested to give such information as he may be possessed of respecting a brig called *Success*, of which Richard Sanders was said to be captain, and which is said to have sailed from Boston, for Hamburgh, laden with a variety of articles, consigned to Mr. Conrad Voght, and insurance was directed to be made. The vessel is said to have foundered at sea, but the proof of the loss of the said vessel as not sufficient to recover from the insurers at Hamburgh. If the said Henry Syms will call on Mr. Matthew Muller in Boston, Messrs. John Murray and son or Mr. J. H. Steenbach in New York, he may in turn hear of something which may be of advantage to him: "New York, 22 March" (*Claypoole's American Daily Advertiser* 29 March 1796).

TALL, JOHN, late of Philadelphia, dec., was born in MD, near Wye River. If any of his friends apply to the Joseph Graisbury, they will hear of something to their advantage (*Pa. Gaz.* 3 June 1762).

TALLY, MICHAEL, son of Peter Tally of the Parish of Donaghmore, Co. Tyrone, Ireland, came into this country about 28 years ago as an indentured servant to one William Holmes. If he is living, he is desired to come or send word to Mr. James Alexander at the Black Horse, in Black Horse Alley, near Market St., Philadelphia, where he may hear of a brother of [his?] who is come over in quest of him. /s/ John Tally (*Pa. Gaz.* 2 July 1772).

TARLUCK (or TARBUCK), MARY, came some years ago from Liverpool to the Maryland side of the Potomac. She is urged to contact Christopher Lowndes of Bladensburg, PG Co. (Annapolis *Maryland Gazette* 31 Dec 1745).

TATHAM, JOHN, cabinetmaker, served part of his time in London and part in Carolina. He has a wife and four children. He sent a letter to his brother Thomas Tatham in Pontefract, Yorks, from VA. He is asked to send another letter to his brother at No. 20, Queen St., Bloomsbury, London, to learn something to his advantage (*GAVN*: 230 cites the *Norfolk and Portsmouth Journal* 21 Nov 1787).

TAYLOR, JAMES, came into this country last year. His brother, Samuel Taylor, of Tuscarora Valley, Lack Twp., Cumberland Co., PA, who came from Clochrow, Ireland, is seeking information about James Taylor. (*Pa. Gaz.* 24 May 1775).

TAYLOR, MARLOW, came from Ireland in July 1769 as an indented servant to Thomas McClaine. His time was bought by Mr. Stewart in Lancaster Co. If he will apply to James Gallagher in Second Street, near Market St., Philadelphia, he will be informed of a large legacy left him (*Pa. Packet* 15 Oct 1778).

TAYLOR, MARY, late of Chiseldon, Wilts, came to New York some years since. If she is still living, she should apply to Eleazer M'Comb at the house of John Morton, merchant, New York City (*Scott* 3:131 cites *The New York Gazette and Weekly Mercury* 21 March 1768).

TAYLOR, WALTER, son of the late Walter Taylor, Master Intendant of Woolwich Yard in England, came here about five or six years ago as Master or Mate of the *Charming Nancy* belonging to this place. If he will apply to Capt. John Robertson on Society hill he may hear something to his advantage (*Pa. Gaz.* 19 Oct 1769).

TERRY, WILLIAM, of Penryn, Cornwall, merchant, died about 50 years ago, leaving two sons, Richard and William. One of these sons lived at or near Bristol, and had two sons called Arthur (or Richard), and William Terry. One of these sons, a barber and peruke maker, was at Penryn some 18 or 20 years ago, and told an aunt, Joyce Terry of Penryn, since dead, that he was going to live in America. If he can give proofs he will inherit a house in Penryn (*Scott* 3:179 cites *The New York Gazette and Weekly Mercury* 6 Dec 1773).
    In 1783 a Richard Terry was in W. Riddick's Co., in a 1783 tax list of Nansemond Co., VA (*AIS Census Index: Pre-1790* gives no other documentation).

TERRY, WILLIAM, left Caroline Co., VA about 1764 and may have been in the 96 District of SC in 1786. He is a legatee of Stephen Terry, late of Hanover Co., dec. *GAVN*: 334 cites *The Virginia Independent Chronicle* 29 July 1789).

THEOBALD, CATHARINA, arrived in 1752. She was married on the voyage. **CASPAR THEOBALD** arrived fifteen years ago. Their brother, Johannes, born in Habspeyer, Oberamt Lantern, Chur Pfaltz, arrived in America in 1752. He lives in

Lancaster County, three miles from Ephrata, and is seeking information about his relatives (*Hocker:* 73 cites the *Pennsylvanische Geschichts-Schreiber* 30 Sep 1758).

THIELMANN, JOHN CHRISTIAN, believed to be in Philadelphia, is sought. His father died in Dresden in 1781. (*Hocker:* 164 cites the *Philadelphische Correspondenz* 3 Sep 1782).

THOMAS, MARY, whose maiden name was Clark, and sister to James Clark, late of SC, should apply to Rudeman Robeson, where she may hear of something to her advantage (*Pa. Gaz.* 12 June 1755).

THOMAS, RICHARD, a native of England, left that place in 1783 for Jamaica, where he resided for some time and then left to go to some part of North America; application was to be made to some merchant in Philadelphia, who, it was said would inform Thomas of something to his advantage. An advertisement is said to have appeared in one of the newspapers of this city within three years last past, requesting information about the said Thomas. Any person who may know anything of the inserter of such advertisement, will, by lodging such information at the *Mail* printing office, will greatly oblige said Thomas, who is now living, and my be heard of at the said office (*The Mail, or Claypoole's American Daily Advertiser* 22 Dec 1792).

THOMPSON, JAMES, merchant, formerly of Philadelphia, recently lost his wife. His brother Robert, in England, is seeking news of him (*Scott* 5:49 cites *The New York Post Boy* 20 Oct 1755).

THOMPSON, JOHN, came from England about six years ago. If he will apply to Mr. Jn. Vanderin in Market St., opposite the coffee house, or to the printers, he will hear of something to his advantage (*The Pennsylvania Packet and Daily Advertiser* 4 Nov 1785).

THOMSON, SARAH, dau. of Dr. Thomson of Lurgan, Co. Armagh, Ireland, is 57 years old, and was seen in Philadelphia about 18 months ago. If she will apply to the printers, she will hear something to her advantage (*Pa. Gaz.* 29 June 1769).

THORNE, SAMUEL, late of Crofton, near Wakefield in Yorkshire, Eng., sailed from Liverpool on 9 Aug last, and landed in Philadelphia on 17 Sep. It is supposed he left Philadelphia for Pittsburgh about 25 Sep. His wife and three children have arrived in the *Helvetius,* and earnestly wish to learn where he now is. His family is at present residing at 114 Water St. between Arch and Race Sts. Any information regarding Thorne will be thankfully received by the family, or by Nicholas Cunningham & Co., merchant, Pittsburgh (*American Telegraphe* 17 Jan 1816).

THRASEY, MICHAEL, died last July in Pikeland Twp., Chester Co., PA. At the time he had with him a variety of shop goods. His widow, children, or other relations are asked to come to Valentine Orner, or Samuel Bogner, Overseers of the Poor, to pay off the funeral expenses and to receive the goods (*Pa. Gaz.* 1 Sep 1773).

TIBAUDAU, FRANCIS, late an inhabitant of [Pisguit River?], Nova Scotia, and now in Philadelphia, is seeking information about his wife and seven children, who were sent to some of the king's colonies (*Pa. Gaz.* 25 March 1776).

TIEFFER, [-?-], a stocking weaver, is a native of Duzes, Languedoc. Pierre Seguin, a grenadier in Burgoyne's Infantry that arrived from France on 11 Sep, is seeking information on him (*GAVN* 339 cites *The Virginia Chronicle and Norfolk and Portsmouth General Advertiser* 22 Sep 1792).

TIERNEY, WILLIAM, son of Michael Tierney, and formerly of Limerick, Ireland, left that city about 1777 and embarked at Cork for North America. In 1786 he was supposed to be at Philadelphia, or New York (*Maryland Journal and Baltimore Advertiser* 15 Jan 1790). Anyone who can give information about him is asked to contact Mr. George Roche, merchant in Bristol (*Pa. Gaz.* 13 Jan 1790).

TIPPER, JAMES, butcher, came into this place about 13 or 14 years ago, and served his time with Daniel Wells. After he left Annapolis, he lived some time near Upper Marlboro, and them moved to VA and is supposed to be living near Alexandria. If he is living, he should apply to the printing office to hear something worth Inquiring about (Annapolis *Maryland Gazette* 21 Jan 1762).

In Nov 1754 Sarah Gresham gave notice that James Tepper [*sic*] butcher, had become a bond servant of hers for seven years, and she has paid his debts (*AMG* 28 Nov 1754). By July 1755 James Tepper and others were all in Anne Arundel Co. jail for debt (Annapolis *Maryland Gazette* 17 July 1755).

TIPPER (*alias* SINNOTT), Mrs. MARY, arrived in New York from Ireland some 14 years ago. She is asked to apply in person, or by letter, to Thomas Cullen, in Market St., Philadelphia, to hear of her daughter, who arrived from Ireland, a few weeks ago (*Pa. Chronicle* 12 Oct 1767).

TODD, JAMES, and **WILLIAM TODD**, late of Minemore. Co. Derry, Ireland, are informed that their mother and father have lately arrived in New York City (*Scott* 3:197 cites *The New York Gazette and the Weekly Mercury* 3 July 1775).

TOMLINSON, SAMUEL, dec., went from Lancashire to reside in America, and left five children, who are asked to contact James, Clibborn, & English of Philadelphia, for news of legacies left them by their father's niece, Patience Harrison, widow of Lancashire, who died 14 d., 4 mo., 1798, having made her will on 7 Jan 1797. John Cumming of Hilderstone, commonly called Mossole, in Lancashire, yeoman, and Joh. Albright of Lancaster in Lancashire, are her execs. (*Philadelphia Gazette* 5 Nov 1798).

TOMSON, JAMES, from the Parish of Conner, Co. of Antrim, is to apply to Robert Smyth, hatter in Market St., Philadelphia, or John Smyth from Ireland, to learn something of his advantage (*Pa. Gaz.* 7 June 1770).

TOOPLE, ISAAC, taken near Presque Isle, and other children, are now at the State House in Philadelphia. During the war they had been taken captive by the Indians from several parts of the Province, and have been lately released by General Amherst. They are to be returned to their parents or other relations, who are desired to come forthwith and receive them (*Pa. Gaz.* 2 July 1761).

TRACEY, JAMES, was captured by the Shawnee Indians in 1763 on Stinking Creek, New River. He escaped in the spring of 1773 and went to his former home, where he learned that his father and family had removed "to what they called Virginia." Tracey is now in Fredericksburg seeking information on his family (*GAVN:* 341 cites Rind's *Virginia Gazette* 16 Dec 1773).

TREVORS, THOMAS, hat maker from London, came to MD some years ago. He is urged to contact James Dick (Annapolis *Maryland Gazette* 7 Aug 1766).
   A Thomas Trevor of Mddx. was reprieved for MD in Aug 1713 (Coldham, *British Emigrants in Bondage:* 910)

TRICKETT, JASPER, file smith, left Sheffield, Eng., unknown to his parents and went to VA where they have heard he is overseer to some gentleman. If he writes to his relations he will hear something to his advantage by applying to John Washington of Williamsburg (*GAVN:* 342 cites Rind's *Va. Gaz.* 30 May 1766).

TROUGHER, JOSEPH, blacksmith, who came to North America about eight years ago, is asked to come or send word to Josiah Rolph, merchant at Boston (*American Weekly Mercury* 21 Sep 1721).

TROUTMAN, LYNARD, is sought by his son, (John) Michael Troutman, who was sold about seven years ago to John Groenendike near Kingston, NJ (*ARNJ* 20:315 cites the *Pennsylvania Journal* 11 Jan 1759; *Pa. Gaz. 17 April 1760* gives his name as John Mitchell Troutman).

TROWEL, WILLIAM, native of Derbyshire, and lately a resident of MD is urged to contact the printer, or Edward Ingleton of Lower Ferry, Trenton, PA (*Maryland Journal and Baltimore Advertiser* 5 Aug 1788). In April 1780 he lived in some part of MD, but then lived with a Dr. Bate of Georgetown (*Maryland Journal and Baltimore Advertiser* 27 March 1787, 3 July 1787).
   In 1778 William Trowell was living in Prince George's Co., MD, when he took the Oath of Fidelity before the Hon. Thomas Williams (Peden, *Rev. Patriots of Prince George's Co., Maryland,* p. 300).

TRUAN, FRANCIS, native of France, came to America and served in the Army under the Count d'Estaing in Georgia or some of the Southern States. He is to apply to M. de Gamble of New Orleans to be informed of a sum of money he may command. When last heard of he was a merchant in Richmond, VA (*GAVN:* 343 cites the *Virginia Herald and Fredericksburg Advertiser* 8 July 1790).

TUCKER, SAMUEL, son of Richard and Elizabeth Tucker of Exeter, Old England, has been in the United States army for about the last 12 years. He was late a resident of Washington City, following the trade of house carpenter. He has a brother living in

Philadelphia. If he will call at this office, he may hear of something to his advantage (*Daily National Intelligencer* 12 Oct 1820).

TURNER, EDWARD, who lived some time ago in Talbot County, and then removed to Prince George's Co., should contact the printer to hear some good news (Annapolis *Maryland Gazette* 17 April 1751).

TURNER, WASHINGTON, nephew of Joseph Turner, a young lad who formerly lived in Alexandria, is asked to call on Joseph Riddle he will learn something that is of consequence to a particular friend of his (*GAVN:* 345 cites *The Columbian Mirror and Alexandria Gazette* 16 June 1798).

TYDINGS, CHARITY, married 1st, Solomon Sparrow, by whom she had a daughter Sophia, and 2nd, [-?-] Sellman. About 1749 she went away with William Proctor {*q.v.*] of Prince George's Co., MD, who left his wife behind him. They went into the colony of VA (Annapolis *Maryland Gazette* 5 Oct 1752).

TYLER, WILLIAM, born at Long-Ashen, near Bristol in Somersetshire, came to America, and is supposed to have been a servant of George Bowles of Philadelphia. If he will go to the printer, he will be sent home if he so desires (*American Weekly Mercury* 3 Dec 1730).

UEBELIN, FRIEDRICH, silversmith, born in Basel, Switzerland, has disappeared and is being sought by Ludwig Kuhn, Arch and Third Sts., Philadelphia (*Hocker:*125 cites the *Wochentlicher Pennsylvanischer Staatsbote* 31 Aug 1773).

UHL, ELIZABETH RICKER: her heirs are asked to apply to Thomas Hawkins, of FR Co., so they may hear of something to their advantage (*The Hornet or Republican Advocate* 29 Aug 1810).
      Frederick Uhl married Elizabeth Ricker in 1785 or 1786. After having some children by him, she died. If any of those children are living, and will apply to Thomas Hawkins, they will hear something to their advantage (*The Hornet or Republican Advocate* 29 May 1811).

VALEQUERILLE, M., a French gentleman, served some time in the armies of France, both by land and sea, and was later a prisoner in England, where he learned the English language. He is supposed to have entered the service of the United States of America. If he will call on the subscriber, he will hear something greatly to his advantage. "Princeton, 17 Sep 1783," Samuel Sterett, Private Secretary to the President of the Congress (*The Pennsylvania Packet or the General Advertiser* 27 Sep 1783).

VAN ALSTYNE, SAMUEL, a blacksmith by trade, and late a private in the 23rd Regt. of U.S. Infantry, is asked to communicate with David Bate, auctioneer, on Pennsylvania Avenue (*The Daily National Intelligencer* 3 May 1819).

VANCE, GEORGE, formerly residing at Big Chiques, Lancaster, and a native of Co. Donegal, Ireland, is requested to contact his nephew George Wilson, lately arrived in this country by directing his letters to Patrick Green, Lancaster, PA (*Lancaster Journal* 27 June 1806).

VAN DERWYCK, BARNET, was living in NY or NJ when an advertisement asked anyone who could give an account of him to inform the printer of this paper, when he will learn something to his advantage (*New York Evening Post* 7 May 1750).

van GEMUND, FRIEDERICH HERMAN, born in Hanau, enlisted in the Jaegercrops in Heilbrun at the beginning of February 1776, and later was transferred to the Thirty-third English Regiment. Since Sep 1777 he has been in Albany. Information about him is sought (*Hocker:* 171 cites the *Philadelphische Correspondenz* 26 Oct 1784).

VEIL, JOHANN LORENZ, baker, may have come to America 34 years ago, and now he is being sought (*Hocker:* 202 cites the *Germantauner Zeitung* 12 Dec 1786).

VENTON, SOLOMON, of Talbot or Dorchester Counties, is sought by Anne Venton of Port Tobacco, who wishes to know if he is alive or dead. She offers a reward of 20 shillings to anyone who can inform her or Mr. James Nimmo of Annapolis (Annapolis *Maryland Gazette* 4 March 1746).

On 8 June 1742 Ann Vinton, admx., filed the inventory of William Ansil of Charles Co. (MINV 29:176).

On 22 Aug 1745 Solomon Vinton was listed as a creditor of Peter Mitchell of Charles Co. (MDAD 22:37).

A Solomon Vinton [*sic*] appears in the 1776 census of Bay Hundred, Talbot Co., MD. His household consisted of 1 white male over 50, 2 white males between 16 and 50, 2 white females between 16 and 50, 1 white male under 16, and 1 white female under 16 (Brumbaugh, *Maryland Records,* 2:217).

VESEY, CHARLES, came into MD about 1752 as an indented servant in the quality of a gardener. If he is still living, he should contact Robert Couden, merchant, of Annapolis (Annapolis *Maryland Gazette* 8 July 1773).

VIESZ, NICOLAUS, whose family came to America 35 years ago, is sought by Daniel Tschantz, of Niederwichtract, Zurich Gebiet, because he is due a legacy from Elizabeth Tschantz and from Magdalena Jung (*Hocker:* 105 and *Eyster:* 24 cite the *Wochentlicher Pennsylvanischer Staatsbote* 15 Jan 1771).

VINCENT, JAMES, resided at Detroit in 1803 and later removed to New York City or its vicinity. If he or his heirs, duly proved to be such, will apply to Jos. Watson at Washington City, he or they may receive a considerable sum of money ([D.C.] *Daily National Intelligencer* 21 Nov 1818).

VINCENT, WILLIAM, only surviving son of Abraham Vincent of Dublin, woolen draper, left England as a Steward on a man of war, and is now supposed to reside in VA. News of him is sought (*Scott* 3:86 cites *The New York Mercury* 21 June 1762).

VOIGT, VALENTIN, born in Sultzfeld, one hour from Saxe-Meingen, is believed to be living ten miles from Philadelphia. Relatives in Sultzfeld wish to contact him concerning the death of his stepbrother, Johann Mattheus Voigt. Contact Friedrich Otto, Bethlehem (*Hocker:* 59 cites the *Pennsylvanische Geschichts-Schreiber* 8 Jan 1757).

Johan Valentin Voigt and Johann Mathes Voigt came on the ship *Harle* of London, Ralph Harle, master, from Rotterdam, and took the Oath of Allegiance on 1 Sep 1736 (*Names of Foreigners* 121; *PGP* 1:158).

Valentine Voigt of Philadelphia Co. was naturalized in PA on 10 Sep 1761 (Bockstruck: 312).

J. Valentin Voigt and his wife Catharine were sponsors at a baptism at St. Paul's Church, Amityville, Berks Co., in 1767 (*Berks Churches* vol. 1).

VOKER, CATHERINE, formerly Catherine Keese, should apply to the printer, as she may hear of something to her advantage (*Pennsylvania Packet or the General Advertiser* 24 Feb 1781).

VOLTZ, HANS MARTIN, from Bockingen, is the subject of an official inquiry from Pfortzheim in Baden-Durlach (*Hocker:* 137 cites the *Wochentlicher Pennsylvanischer Staatsbote* 1 Nov 1774).

VON DORSTEN, HERMAN WILBRAND, arrived at Baltimore in 1795, from Bramsche in the Bishopric of Heldesheim, Germany, and from Baltimore, departed to Green Castle, PA. A letter to his address in our possession, authorizes us to believe that he stayed with a Mr. Michael Hively, there. His grandfather, Henrick Wilbrand Portener has bequeathed him a legacy. If Van Dorsten should still reside in this country, he may apply to F. and H. Konig for further particulars (*Federal Gazette & Baltimore Daily Advertiser* 8 Dec 1797).

WADSWORTH, Mr., left his family in London about three years ago. If he is living, and in Philadelphia, he is requested to call on Dr. Rogers, 40 n. Fourth St., and he will hear of something to his advantage. If he is dead, proper information of the same is particularly desired (*The Philadelphia Gazette & Universal Daily Advertiser* 21 July 1795).

WAGEMANN, JOH. GEORG, and JOH. MARTIN WAGEMANN, are sought by Christian Buhler (*Eyster:* 35 cites the *Pennsylvanische Staatsbote* 4 Oct 1774).

Hocker: 136 cites the *Wochentlicher Pennsylvanische Staatsbote* 4 Oct 1774 and states they were from the Heilbrun Region.

WAGNER, GEORGE, from Ruthesheim, Wurtemburg, is sought by Ernest Ludwig Baisch (*Eyster:* 26-27 cites the *Pennsylvanische Staatsbote* 28 July 1772).

He is said to be in Amwell, NJ (*Hocker:* 116 cites the *Wochentlicher Pennsylvanische Staatsbote* 28 July 1772).

WAGNER, JOHANN HENRICH, born in Hesse Cassel, left there thirty years ago, and wrote to his relatives in 1787 from Northampton Co., PA. Now he is being sought (*Hocker:* 193 cites the *Philadelphische Correspondenz* 31 July 1795).

WAGNER, PHILIPP ERNEST, nail smith from Meckmuhle, Wurtemburg, arrived last year. He is sought by Anna Maria Wolfelsperger, born Heimberger (*Eyster:* 12 cites the *Pennsylvanische Berichte* 1 May 1752).

Philipp Ernest Wagner arrived on the *Phoenix* on 28 Sep 1751 (*Eyster:* 13). In 1790 a Philip Wagner was listed as head of a family in Bern Twp., Berks Co. (*AIS 1790 Census Index*).

WAGSTAFFE, RICHARD, peruke and lady's tate maker and hair-cutter, from London, advertised he had settled in Annapolis, where he would also teach reading, writing and accounts, and would take in youth to board and educate at £23 a year. Shortly thereafter he advertised he intended to leave Maryland and asked all those indebted to him to settle their accounts (Annapolis *Maryland Gazette* 3 Jan 1750, 13 June 1750).

By 2 Aug 1750 he had set up his peruke making business in Third St., Philadelphia (*Pa. Gaz.* 2 Aug 1750).

Richard Wagstaffe, a Leicestershire man, married Frances Riddle, who had come to PA about 26 years earlier as a servant. She was advised to contact the New Printing Office to hear something to her advantage (*Pa. Gaz.* 11 Sep 1752).

In July 1754 Wagstaffe was in Philadelphia as a peruke maker, in Chestnut St (Annapolis *Maryland Gazette* 18 July 1754).

Another Richard Wagstaff, relation to the above not proved, married Sarah, dau. of John and Ann Yarnall of Willis Town, Chester Co., PA. She was born 24 d., 2 m., 1724. She died 31 d., 7 m., 1763, and was buried in Friends Burying Ground, at Patapsco. She had produced a certificate from Philadelphia Meeting on 22 d., 6 m., 1763 (Records of Gunpowder Monthly Meeting, Baltimore County, MD, in *QRNM* 1, 42).

WAITE or WAITES, JOHN, from Blyton near Gainsborough, Lincs., and said to be living in MD with one Aquila Carr, is urged to contact the printer (Annapolis *Maryland Gazette* 9 May 1750).

He may be the John Waite, convict from London, who was transported to MD by the *Patapsco Merchant,* Capt. Darby Lux, and registered in Annapolis in October 1732 (*KPMV:* 52).

WALKER, ANDREW, sailed from Londonderry to America on 12 July 1736. His friends in Donnerail have not heard from him since. If Walker will apply to Thomas Jones in Lancaster Co., PA, he may hear something to his advantage (*Scott* 2:64 cites the *Pa. Gaz.* 26 Oct 1749).

WALKER, GUY, formerly of Woodbury, CT, and more recently of FL, died in Baltimore some time last fall, and left a widow named Mary Walker. Her place of residence is unknown, but she is believed to be in destitute circumstances. Anyone acquainted with her present place of residence, will confer a particular favor on her friends, by leaving information at the office of this paper (*Baltimore Patriot* 12 Jan 1830).

WALKER, JEAN, dau. of William Walker of Old Aberdeen, Scotland, came to VA about 50 years ago. John Davidson, cooper at Falmouth, and James Davidson, cooper at

Nansemond Co., VA, came to VA three years ago to find her, but have been unsuccessful (*GAVN:* 352 cites the *Va. Gaz.* 5 May 1718).

WALKER, ROBERT, about 30 years ago came from England with his family and settled on Patuxent or Potomac. He served his time with Henry Mason, a linen weaver in a small town in Durham, and married Sarah Mason. Walker should contact Jonas Green about a relative of his, a freeman, who has recently come into the country (Annapolis *Maryland Gazette:*16 Jan 1755).

WALKER, ROBERT, native of Scotland, resided in T[oe]ks in the Parish of Dunotter until he left for VA some 44 or 45 years ago; at one time his friends heard he was living on the Rappahannock River; he should apply to the printer to hear something greatly to his advantage (*GAVN:* 352 cites Pinkney's *Va. Gaz.* 13 July 1775).

Robert Walker, of Kingston, Scotland, emigrated to VA by 1775. He married Elizabeth Starke c1745, and was the father of: Robert, Richard, David, Bolling, Freeman, Starke, Louisa, Martha, Mary, and Clara (*History of Bristol County, Virginia.* Richmond, 1879).

WALL, HENRY, was born in Warwickshire, Eng., and went from Londonderry to Antigua about four years ago with a Capt. Blacklock. He lately sailed out of Rhode Island. His wife Margaret has come to Philadelphia, and is seeking news of her husband (*Scott* 1:638 cites the *Pa. Gaz.* 2 July 1747).

WALL, JOSEPH. JACOB WALL, and their kinsman **JOHN WALL**, are supposed to have been born in Worcester and to have lately arrived in America. They will hear something their to advantage if they apply to Ebenezer Large in Burlington (*Scott* 2:40 cites the *Pa. Gaz.* 31 Jan 1749).

WALL, MICHAEL, apothecary, native of Ireland, left there about five years ago. If he applies to Stephen Moylan, he will hear something to his advantage (*Pa. Chronicle* 22 June 1772).

WALL, RICHARD, a smith or candlestick-maker from Birmingham, Warwickshire, has been absent five years from his wife Ann. He last wrote to her four years ago when he was a servant to Thomas Gillinger, of Eversham Twp., New Surrey, PA. His wife Ann, who lives at Macclesfield in Cheshire, Eng., has news for him, since a relative recently died and left him a considerable legacy; he left a child in England (*American Weekly Mercury* 23 July 1724).

WALLER, Mrs. ISABELLA, of Plymouth, Eng., is well known to a Mr. Grayson, a native of MD, who is asked to acquaint the printer of her circumstances or situation (*GAVN:* 142 cites Rind's *Virginia Gazette* 7 July 1774).

WALLER, JOHN, ship carpenter, had worked at William Howell's shipyard on Northeast River in Cecil Co., MD. He lately removed to Sussex Co., DE, in the government of Newcastle, Kent, and Sussex on Delaware. If he applies to Benjamin

Rumsey at Joppa, Baltimore County, MD, he will hear something to his advantage (*Pa. Chronicle* 3 June 1771).

On 13 July 1752 John Waller of Great Totham, Essex, aged 16, was bound to serve John Blackwood for seven years in Maryland. (*LEMK:* 234).

WALLEY, HENRY, came as a passenger from London about 14 or 15 years ago on a ship commanded by Capt. John Colvill. He should apply to Richard Piercy of St. Mary's Co., who has an important message for him (Annapolis *Maryland Gazette* 8 April 1746).

On 14 Feb 1750 Henry Walley witnessed the will of John Willson of Charles Co., MD (MWB 28:76).

WALTER, EDWARD, came into this Province from England several years ago, and lived with William Mordant [Mauduit?] near Upper Marlborough, Prince George's Co., MD. He should contact the printer to hear something to his advantage (Annapolis *Maryland Gazette* 30 Oct 1755).

WALTER, PETER, about 60 years old, about 5'11" tall, and of dark complexion, on 7 June last left the Borough of Harrisburg to go to his residence and family near Greensburg, Westmoreland Co., since which time he has not been heard of. As he discovered symptoms of mental derangement about the time he left Harrisburg, his family has become alarmed about his fate. Anyone who can give information is asked to contact Mrs. Mary Walter, near Greensburg, or George Geiger in Harrisburg (*Chronicle of Harrisburg* 4 Oct 1813).

WALTER, WILLIAM, shoemaker, came to Philadelphia about three years ago, and taught school in various parts of the country. He is notified to return to Philadelphia, or to send there and redeem his wife and children, who are greatly distressed for both passage money and other necessaries. She came in the brig *Globe*, Capt. Garrigues, is to be met with at Mr. John Metts, shoemaker, in Water St. (*Pa. Gaz.* 17 Oct 1771).

WALTHER, HANS, of Valendas, and his wife **CATHERINE**, of the family of da Rungs, together with their four Children, **HANS BLASI, HANS, MICHAEL,** and **CATHERINE**, who in the year 1735 went over to the English North American Colonies, as also to their descendants, are hereby notified, by the command and order of the wise Magistrates at Ilantz, and in the Grub, situate in the Upper League of the ancient Rhaetia (or the Country of the Grisons) that, on pain of forfeiting all the estates and effects, together with the right, privileges and prerogatives, belonging to them here, they, or any of them, within the term of six months after the third and last formal publication of this advertisement, do send in their names, and, by authentic documents, do prove and shew forth, that they are the above named persons, or their descendants, to the purpose that, for their own interest, their estates and effects may farther be taken care of; in failure whereof, and after the expiration of this fixed peremptory term, they shall no more be heard, nor their appeals admitted. "Given at Ilantz, Dec. 30, 1759 /s/ George Peter Cabrin." To the Provincial Secretary. N.B. If any one or more of the above mentioned Grisons, or their Descendants, should be found out, they are desired to send the requisite Documents for their legitimation to Mr. Peter Miller, at the Hand and Pen, in Second St., Philadelphia, who will take Care to send them to London, from whence they will be forwarded to Ilantz above said (*Pa. Gaz.* 2 Oct 1760).

WALTMAN, LUDWIG, came to America a year ago. His brother, Johann Nicolaus Waltman, with Daniel Clark in Bucks Co., PA, three miles from Trenton Ferry, is seeking him. Their cousin Johannes Waltman, has also arrived in America (*Hocker:* 114 cites the *Wochentlicher Pennsylvanischer Staatsbote* 21 April 1772).

In 1771 Johannes Waltman was in Philadelphia Co., PA (*AIS Census Index: Pre-1790* gives no other documentation).

In 1790 a Ludwick Waltman was listed as head of a family in York Twp, York Co., PA. (*AIS 1790 Census Index*).

WALTON, JOSEPH, in Nov 1742 was living with, or was well known to, William Denton, living on the south side, near Toppain, Baltimore Co., MD. Walton has not been heard from for near twenty years, and is asked to contact J. Green, the printer (Annapolis *Maryland Gazette* 21 June 1764).

Joseph Walton married Sarah Matheny on 23 March 1746 in St. John's Parish, Baltimore Co. He or another Joseph married Mary Gibbins in St. John's Parish on 31 Dec 1753 (*SJSG*).

WALWORK, JAMES, came into this country some years ago from England is said to have lived at Bladensburg. He should contact the printer to hear something to his advantage (Annapolis *Maryland Gazette* 25 Sep 1755).

WAMBACH, HANSZ GEORG and **PETER WAMBACH,** are being sought by their stepfather, Martin Schroeter, who indentured them last autumn (*Hocker:* 19 cites the *Pennsylvanische Gerschichts-Schreiber* 1 June 1750).

Martin "Wannebach," in service with Michael Drachel, on the Great Lehigh, is seeking information about his parents (*Hocker:* 40 cites the *Pennsylvanische Geschichts-Schreiber* 1 Feb 1754).

For more on the Wambach family, see Burgert's *Alsace* 519-520.

WARBURTON, WILLIAM, son of Robert Warburton, was aged seven or eight years when his father, late of Middletown, in the County of Chester, and Province of Pennsylvania, came from Ireland in the Year 1729. These are therefore to request the said William Warburton (if he has come to any of the neighboring Provinces) to repair to Thomas Pilkinton, in Middletown, aforesaid, where he may be informed of something to his Advantage (*Pa. Gaz.* 5 Nov 1761).

WARE, THOMAS, tailor, native of White Haven, Eng., came to this country in 1818, and was in Augusta, GA, last 19 Dec. Since then he has not been heard from. His wife and two children are now in Baltimore, and need his presence (*Baltimore Patriot & Mercantile Advertiser* 20 May 1819).

A Thomas Ware married Nancy Rummey on 19 Feb 1815 by Rev. Edward Choate (Robert Barnes. *Maryland Marriages 1801-1820.* Baltimore: Genealogical Publishing Co., p. 191). [Although the notice says Ware arrived in 1818, the date of the marriage fits with him having two children-RWB]

WASTLE, TIMOTHY, barber, of Barnard Castle, Co. Durham in Old England, should come to the Post Office where he will hear of something to his advantage (*Pa. Gaz.* 24 Sep 1747).

WATSON, GEORGE, weaver, son of George Watson, blacksmith, in Town head of Bervie, Shire of Kincardine, North Britain, came to Maryland over 30 years ago, when he was aged 22. If he is still living, he is urged to contact the printer, or Robert Barnes in Norfolk (Annapolis *Maryland Gazette* 4 May 1775).

He may the George Watson, laborer, who resided in Banffshire and was a Jacobite, who was taken prisoner at Carlisle and Chester, transported 22 April 1747 from Liverpool to VA on the *Johnson,* William Pemberton, master, and who arrived 5 Aug 1747 at Port Oxford, MD (*SOCD:* 161; David Dobson. *Scots Banished to America, 1650-1775.* Baltimore: Genealogical Publishing Co., p. 223).

WATTS, JOHN was born in Old England, and was in the army at Quebec. Since then he was teaching school at Goshen in Chester Co., PA in 1764. If he is still living, he should apply to Ellis Davies of Goshen, so that he may hear from his mother and learn of something to his advantage (*Pa. Gaz.* 18 Sep 1766).

WATTS, JOHN, came from North Petherton, Somersetshire, about 15 months ago. Ann Liverbe, lately arrived from England, where she lived with Mr. Judney in North Petherton, wants to hear from Watts (*Pa. Chronicle* 26 Dec 1768).

WAUGH, HENRY, came to America in 1736 and is supposed to be in VA or NC. He will hear something to his advantage if he applies to Alexander Moore, peruke-maker in Philadelphia (*Scott* 2:37 cites the *Pa. Gaz.* 13 Dec 1748).

WEBER, AMELIA HOFFMAN, wife of George Weber, was due a legacy of 25 pounds and a trifle more. George Weber has moved to the South Branch, Morefield, VA. If alive, he, or any of his heirs, is requested to call upon Adam Hoffman of Codorus Twp., York

Co., as Hoffman will not pay any interest on the said money (*The Hornet, or Republican Advocate* 27 June 1810).

WEBER, MICHAEL, came to America 13 or 14 years ago from Wetmuehe, near Heilbrun. His relative, Matthis Keehler (*Eyster:* 40 transcribes this name as Joh. Mathes Kohler), tanner, Philadelphia, care of John Haworth, tanner, Fourth St., who has been in Philadelphia for one year, is seeking information about Weber (*Hocker:* 154 cites the *Wochentlicher Pennsylvanischer Staatsbote* 26 Nov 1776).

A Michael Weber of Lancaster Co., PA, was naturalized on 24 Sep 1762 (Bockstruck: 317).

WEBSTER, THOMAS,, servant to Col. Price, died in Jamaica in June 1749., He left a legacy to be claimed from David Verner, Professor of Philosophy at Marischal College (Dobson: *Aberdeen Journal,* Issue # 108).

WEEKS, RICHARD, a miller, aged about 32, about 5'6" tall, left Baltimore last April for England, by way of New York, but has not been heard of since. His brother, Samuel Weeks, 58 Calvert Sr., Baltimore, is seeking any information about him. New York papers are asked to copy this (*Baltimore Patriot* 28 Nov 1834).

WEICHERD, FRIEDRICH, the elder brother, and **HANS BARTEL WEICHERD,** the younger brother, are sought by their sister, Maria Lenora, who is now married to Andrew Heillens, of Shireman's Valley, Cumberland Co. The three were born in Mechelsen, Hanover, and came to America eight years ago, at which time the sister was twelve years old, and all three were indentured to pay for their passage (*Hocker:* 119 cites the *Wochentlicher Pennsylvanischer Staatsbote* 17 Nov 1772).

Joh. Friderich Weger arrived on the ship *Chance* on 8 Aug 1764 (*Eyster:* 29).

WEIDAU, FRIEDRICH, was born in Durlach, and came to America many years ago. He is sought by his brother, Gottlieb Wedau, of Maxatany, Berks Co. (*Hocker:* 158 cites the *Wochentlicher Pennsylvanischer Staatsbote* 24 Feb 1779).

WEILER, FRIEDRICH, was born at Sprengingen, two hours from Kreuzeach, and was a redemptioner in the service of Matthias Schlauch, Lancaster, five years ago. His cousin Andreas Weiler, Douglass Twp., Philadelphia Co. (now Montgomery) is seeking him (*Hocker:* 166 cites the *Philadelphische Correspondenz* 29 July 1783).

Friedrich Weiler was in Lancaster Co., PA, by Sep 1782, when he and his wife, Catharine were the parents of: John, b. 17 Sep 1782, bapt. 1 June 1783 at The First Reformed Church in Lancaster (F. Edward Wright. *Church Records of Lancaster County, Pennsylvania of the 18th Century.* Westminster: Family Line Publications, Vol. 2).

Frederick and Catherine were the parents of the following children, bapt. at the First Reformed Church, Philadelphia Co. (F. Edward Wright. *Early Records of the First Reformed Church of Philadelphia.* Westminster: Family Line Publications, Vol. 2): Jacob, b. 22 March, bapt. 6 Aug 1787 (sp.: Jacob Baumgart and Anna Catherine), bur. 7 Aug 1787, age 1 yr. 4 mos.; Catharine, b. 8 Sep 1787 [*sic*], bapt. 9 Oct 1787 (sp.: Jacob Baumgarten and Catherine), bur. 11 May 1795, age 6 yrs, 8 mos., 3 days; Frederick, bur. 17 Sep 1791, age 2 mos., 5 days.

WEILER, PHILIP, a mason, whose left hand is missing three fingers, arrived in this country in 1753 and was sold to a German in NJ. His parents, living near Ephrata inquire for him (*Hocker:* 47 cites the *Pennsylvanische Geschichts-Schreiber* 1 March 1755).

WEIMER, JACOB, born at Hoffen, near Alsace, near Weissenburg, came to America nine years ago. His brother Andreas, of Albany Co., is seeking him. Notify Peter Paris, Philadelphia, at the corner house at Moravian Alley on Second Street (*Hocker:* 95 cites the *Pennsylvanische Geschichts-Schreiber* 23 Oct 1761).

For more in the Weimer Family, see Burgert's *Alsace* 528-529.

WEIS, ANNA, servant girl, was sold to Richard Parks form four years some time in September. Her father, Johannis Weis, at Lancaster, will give a reasonable reward o anyone who can inform her father where she or Parks lived (*Pa. Gaz.* 11 Oct 1750).

WEISSIN, MARIA CATHERINE, from Langen Candel bey Pindau. She married Frantz Grosz, a weaver, who has a brother-in-law near Lancaster, one Stoffel Geiger. Maria Catherine's sister Maria Elizabeth, married David Rittman. They arrived at New York in 1755 and are there with Adam von der Berg, and are seeking Maria Catherine (*Hocker:* 89 cites the *Pennsylvanische Geschichts-Schreiber* 2 May 1761).

WEITZEL, DIETRICH, and his brother Henrich Weitzel, of Hatfield Twp., Philadelphia Co., now Montgomery Co., living on Jan Henrich's place, arrived in this country three years ago with his brother Dietrich. They were separated, and now Henrich is seeking Dietrich (*Hocker:* 44 cites the *Pennsylvanische Geschichts-Schreiber* 16 Nov 1754).

He may be the Henry Weitzel who died in Lebanon Twp., Lancaster County, PA, leaving a will dated 9 Feb and proved 1 May 1776. He named his children: Martin, John, Elias, Margaret wife of William Kreeg and Magdalena. Casper Snevely and John Ressly witnessed the will. (*Lancaster Wills*).

Dietrick Weitzel died in Lebanon Twp., Lancaster Co., PA, leaving a will dated 9 March and proved 29 March 1765. He named his wife Anna Margaret Weitzel as executrix, and mentioned were four children - names not given (*Lancaster Wills*).

WELCH, JAMES, a surgeon, came into this Province some years ago, and later resided at a place called the Trap, in Maryland. If he will apply to Henry Hill Graham, in Chester, he will hear of something greatly to his advantage (*Pa. Gaz.* 8 March 1764).

William Dunlap, executor, administered the estate of James Welch of Worcester Co., MD, on 4 March 1761. He cited an inventory of £39.17.9, and cited payments of £51.14.9. Distribution was to the accountant (MDAD 46:255). On 17 Dec 1761 William Dunlap, executor, advertised he would settle the estate (*Pa. Gaz.* 17 Dec 1761).

WELLERIN, EVA MARIA, came to America nine years ago with her brother Peter and her sister, Ann Fry, who has married Johann Christ Schmitt. Peter, now of Amity Twp., on Manatawny Creek, Berks Co., with Philip Boyer, is seeking information about his sisters (*Hocker:* 18 cites the *Pennsylvanische Geschichts-Schreiber* 16 March 1750).

WELSH, JOHN, native of England, a house carpenter, left Baltimore in May 1819, and arrived in Bordeaux on the last day June in an American ship, as a carpenter. He traveled from thence overland to London with the captain, and was understood to have returned again to the U.S. He may hear something to his advantage by applying to Hosea Johns, Federal Hill, Baltimore, or to Samuel Chubb, merchant, Philadelphia, or to Stephen Dando, No. 9 Maiden Lane, New York (*Lancaster Journal* 20 April 1821).

WERNER, CASPER, was born at Altengronau, and was a cooper who came to America about two years ago. His brother-in-law Johann Adam Ruppert of Boston is inquiring for him (*Hocker:* 195 cites the *Philadelphische Correspondenz* 6 Feb 1795).

Casper Werner, his wife Margaretha, and his sons Conrad and John, were passengers on the *Columbia,* Capt. William Maley, arriving 8 Sep 1792 (*PGP* 2:52).

WESSELS, JOSEPH, formerly of London, came as a passenger on the ship *Factor* to Philadelphia in 1794. If he will apply to 197 Market St., he will hear of something to his advantage. (*The Philadelphia Gazette & Universal Daily Advertiser* 15 May 1797).

WHELAN, THOMAS, a native of Dongarvan, Co. Waterford, left Ireland, about 14 years ago, and was last heard of as a farmer in Baltimore Co., MD. He is urged to contact his bro. William Whelan (*Maryland Journal and Baltimore Advertiser* 5 June 1795).

WHILEAR[?], JOHN, was a brazier and bell founder of Fairfield, CT. If his child or children are living, they may hear of something to their advantage by applying to Mr. Francis Morgan or Mrs. Sarah Watts of Shepton Mallet, Somerset, Great Britain, or to Ross and Vaughan in Philadelphia (*The Pennsylvania Patriot and Daily Advertiser* 18 May 1787).

WHITAKER, ISRAEL, distiller, if in Baltimore, will something to his advantage by applying to the office of the *Patriot* (*Baltimore Patriot* 27 Nov 1822).

WHITE, ANDREW, is supposed to be in this or some neighboring Provinces. If he inquires of William Allen, Esq., or the printer of this paper, he will hear of something to his advantage (*Pa. Gaz.* 4 Dec 1735).

WHITE, HENRY, wool comber, came from Bristol with Capt. Nathan Cowman about four years ago. He will her something to his advantage if he applies to the printer (*Scott* 1:221 cites the *Pa. Gaz.* 1739).

WHITE, JOHN, came from London, in 1745 with Capt. William Dick, and served his time with Thomas Hall at Port Tobacco. He is urged to contact Jasper Mauduit at Port Tobacco (Annapolis *Maryland Gazette* 6 Sep 1759).

John White of London was sentenced in Jan 1745 and transported in May 1745 on the *Justitia,* Capt. John Johnston (Coldham. *British Emigrants in Bondage:* 964; *KPMV*).

WHITE, JOSHUA, age 19, son of Daniel White of Townsend, MA. left his father's house about two years ago and is supposed to be in some of the southern States, if living. Anyone who can give information about him should contact the Post Master of

Baltimore, or his father, as above (*Baltimore Patriot and Mercantile Daily Advertiser* 2 May 1818).

WHITEHEAD, ELIZABETH, dau. of John Whitehead, formerly of the Parish of St. Sidwell, in Exeter, came to Philadelphia, about 4½ years ago, and was sold to John Tolbert, who then sold her to Ephraim Moore, living eight miles above Lancaster on the Carlisle road. The said Elizabeth's uncle is dead, and has left her a share of her estate. She is asked to come immediately to Philadelphia, and John Reynell will pay her passage and expenses. (*Pa. Gaz.* 31 Jan 1771).

WHITEMAN, ANNE, of a Leicestershire family, but born at Ham, near Stratford, lived in London, near Newgate St. She left England about 1750, and came to MD (Annapolis *Maryland Gazette* 29 Aug 1765).

Ann Whiteman of Middlesex, convict, was transported from London to MD on the *Greyhound,* Capt. Alexander Stewart in Jan 1756, and arrived in April 1756 (*KPMV*: 152).

WHITMAR, JACOB, his brother Jacob [*sic*], and sisters Elizabeth and Margaret, came from Switzerland, nine years ago and were separated. Jacob wishes them to know that he lives at Harman Fisher's, in Upper Hanover Twp., Philadelphia Co. (*Scott* 2:214 cites the *Pa. Gaz.* 16 Jan 1753).

WHITTINGHAM, HEBER: In July and August 1762 the [Annapolis] *Maryland Gazette* ran notices asking for information about Heber Whittingham, a native of Cheshire, England, who had come to Maryland may years previously. Whittingham or his children were urged to contact Thomas Ringgold or the printer for news of a legacy in England.

For the English ancestry of Heber Whittingham, see Robert Barnes, *British Roots of Maryland Families.* Baltimore: Baltimore: Genealogical Publishing Co., 1999, 467-469.

Heber married 1st, Catherine Billington, and 2nd, Mary [-?-].

Whittingham was in Somerset Co. by 10 May 1733 when he was mentioned in the inventory of William Furnis of Somerset Co. (MINV 17:192).

Heber Whittingham made his will on 18 Oct 1749, describing himself as a merchant of Mooresborough, Parish of Middlewick, Eng., and now of Somerset Co., MD. He referred to property left him by Gilbert Symkin, formerly of Cornwall. He named his wife Mary, and children: eld. son Samuel; Heber, Jr.; John; Rebecca; Mary; and Ann (MWB 27:150).

As "Mr. Heber Whittingham," his personal property was appraised on 12 March 1749 at £460.3.2, by Henry Ballard and William McClemmy. McClemmy died and Ballard and John Waters appraised the estate again. Smith Horsey and Samuel Whittingham signed as next of kin. Mary Whittingham filed the inventory (MINV 46:53).

Heber and Catherine (Billington) Whittingham were the parents of: Samuel (eldest son); Heber, Jr.; John; Rebecca; Mary; and Ann.

John Whittingham was a private in the 5th Battalion of Queen Anne's Co. Militia (*ARMD* 18).

WHYTE, ALEXANDER, son of Richard Whyte, merchant of Dublin (who is now dec.) is believed to be in VA since he wrote to a friend in Bristol, and letter was dated "Virginia." His father is deceased, and the executors Mary White and Thomas Dawson advertised that they had empowered Thomas Smith to collect debts and try to locate the said Alexander. Alexander is asked to [post bond] of £700 to the execs. for the use of the estate and his sister Euphemia (*GAVN:* 365-366 cites the *Va. Gaz.* 2 Sep 1757, 30 Nov 1759).

WIDEMEIR, BALTZER, of Nordheim, near Helbrunn, is sought by Simon Keppler, who has a letter for him concerning an inheritance of 600 guilders (*Eyster:* 38 cites the *Pennsylvanische Staatsbote* 4 Aug 1775).

WIEST, PHILIP, arrived some weeks ago in Philadelphia, with Capt. Smith. He was born in Geislingen, near Halle. His brother, Andreas Wiest, living at Great Swatara, Paxton Twp., Lancaster Co., wishes to find Philip. If Philip sees this will he is asked to let his brother know. He can send word to Georg Frey in Middletown, or to Andreas Wiest, above (*Eyster:* 28 cites the *Pennsylvanische Staatsbote* 17 Nov 1772).

Joh. Andreas Wiest arrived on the *Minerva* on 10 Oct 1768 (*Eyster:* 28).

Philip Wiest, from Rotterdam, was indentured in Nov 1772 to Samuel [-?-] and his assigns of Fannet Twp., Cumberland Co., PA, to serve for ten years (PGS. *Indentures* pp. 156-157).

WILCOX, ANTHONY, resided in Westmoreland County, VA, and about 14 months ago left his wife Phoebe, during a severe spell of illness, and with two infant children to support, she is seeking information on his present abode. He was seen in Norfolk about six weeks since, and is believed to have gone to Richmond in a vessel. Wilcox took with him his eldest child, a boy about seven years old, named Henry (*Baltimore Patriot* 26 Oct 1819).

WILEY, PETER, left Balymenough, Co. Antrim, and has been in this country two years. His wife and John McIlroy and his wife have arrived and brought the power of attorney he (Wiley) asked for. They are now living in West Nottingham, Chester County, PA, within two miles of Rev. John Beald's meeting house (*Pa. Gaz.* 26 Sep 1765).

WILEY, ROBERT, from near Loughbricklands, Co. Down, Ireland, some time ago lived in Lancaster Co., PA, and the moved to VA. If he is still living, his aged mother, and brothers and sisters who have lately come into the country, request him to write them. He should direct his letters to Elizabeth Wiley, c/o James Scarling, merchant of Baltimore (*Lancaster Journal* 14 Nov 1801; see also *Gazette of the United states* 20 Jan 1802).

WILLAT, WILLIAM, who left Manchester, in England, at the age of 24, and must now be 83 years of age. If he is living and will apply at the office of [The *Patriot*], he may hear of something to his advantage (*Baltimore Patriot* 25 Oct 1817).

WILLBOUR, PELEG, a wheelwright, was born in New England, and died lately at Amboy. This is to inform his heirs or relations that if they apply to Thomas Fox, Post Master in Amboy, and can prove their right, they may receive the effects he left, which are something considerable (*ARNJ* 19:99 cites the *N.Y. Gazette Revived in Weekly Post Boy* 23 Sep 1751).

On 12 Sep 1751 Thomas Fox, Gent., posted administration bond on the estate of Peleg Wilbor of Perth Amboy, Middlesex Co., NJ, who died intestate. Andrew Johnston, Esq., also of Perth Amboy was his fellow bondsman (*ARNJ* 32:358 cites Liber E, p. 547).

WILLCOX, SAMUEL, was a son of Rev. Mr. Willcox of London. News of him is sought by Capt. William Bryant in New York City (*Scott* 5:42 cites *The New York Post Boy* 27 May 1754).

WILLIAMS, MARY, taken on the Delaware, and other children, are now at the State House in Philadelphia. During the war they had been taken captive by the Indians from several parts of the Province, and have been lately released by General Amherst. They are to be returned to their parents or other relations, who are desired to come forthwith and receive them (*Pa. Gaz.* 2 July 1761).

WILLIAMS, SARAH, lived in York Co., PA, some 15 or 20 years ago. If her children will apply to Thomas Wen of York Town, or to William Webb, near Lancaster, they may hear of something to their advantage (*Pennsylvania Herald & York General Advertiser* 4 March 1789).

WILLIAMS, THOMAS, Sergeant in the Delaware Regiment, was take prisoner at the Battle of Brandywine, and cannot be heard of in Philadelphia. His wife Hannah Williams would be glad to hear from him. She may be heard at Mr. Edward Dickins, painter and glazier in Strawberry Alley, Philadelphia (*Pa. Gaz.* 18 Aug 1778).

WILLIAMS, THOMAS, is deceased. He had had his tongue cut out by the Indians in 1774. If his wife is still living, and will apply to John Shields at the corner of Second and Chestnut Sts., She may hear of something to hers advantage (*Pennsylvania Evening Post* 6 Nov 1779).

WILLIAMS, TIMOTHY, a Welshman, and carpenter by trade, did work at Flower Town last Spring,. Later he was supposed to have gone to Christine Bridge. If he immediately repairs to Mr. Jonathan Adams, at Schuylkill Falls, or to the King David, near the Drawbridge, he will hear of something very much to his Advantage, and his expenses borne (*Pa. Gaz.* 15 July 1762).

WILLIS, JOHN, lead smelter, England about three years ago. If he will apply to John Walter, linen stamper, in Fourth St. Road, he will of something greatly to his advantage (*The Pennsylvania Evening Post* 9 July 1776).

WILLMANS, A. H., from Bielefeld, Grafschaft, Sparenburg, Prussia, is sought by P. E. Delius, who is with Peter Whitesides & Co. (*Hocker:* 166 cites the *Philadelphische Correspondenz* 9 Sep 1782).

WILSON, [-?-], came about 1751, and was living near Lancaster, PA. He is sought by his sister Catherine, Elisabeth Blackett, widow, nee Wilson, who came into this country in a Palatine ship, with Capt. Curtin in 1752. (Annapolis *Maryland Gazette* 26 Feb 1767).

WILSON, CHARLES, late of the Township of Arnold, Co. Nottingham, Great Britain, breeches maker, should apply to William Parr, High Sheriff of the City and County of Philadelphia, to hear something to his advantage. He came into some part of America some 13 years ago, and it was believed to Maryland or Virginia (*Pa. Gaz.* 18 May 1766).

WILSON, GODFREY, left Yorkshire some 40 years ago, and resided some time at the Yallows, Island of Jamaica, and was a carpenter, painter and glazier. If he is still living, he should apply to John Wilson, agent to Mr. Robinson in London (*Scott* 3:131 cites *The New York Gazette and Weekly Mercury* 9 May 1768).

WILSON, JANE, was brought up in Belfast, and took shipping at Londonderry, for America last year. She came over in the *Culloden*, under the care of one Edmondston. Her uncle, William Wilson, in Baltimore County, MD, near Mr. Bay's Meeting House, would be glad to see her (*Pa. Gaz.* 10 Nov 1763).

[Mr. Bay's Meeting House would be Churchville Presbyterian Church in Baltimore, now Harford, Co., MD].

WILSON, SAMUEL, and **ROBERT WILSON**, came from Ireland a few years ago and were said to have resided in Pennsylvania. They are asked to apply to the printers to hear something to their advantage (*Pa. Gaz.* 16 Sep 1762).

WILSON, THOMAS, millwright, and a native of Co. Donegal, Ireland, is requested to contact his brother George Wilson, lately arrived in this country, by directing his letters to Patrick Green, Lancaster, PA (*Lancaster Journal* 27 June 1806).

WINSH (WINTSCH), ANNA MARGARET, was born at Horben in the Swiss Canton of Zurich, and came to this country twelve years ago, with her brother Ulrich, living in Manor Twp., Lancaster County, PA, and who now desires to know her whereabouts (*Pa. Gaz.* 25 Nov 1762).

Anna Margaret married John Usbeck or Reinbeck, and lives some-where in NJ. She is asked to call on Christian Boughman, living in Manor Twp., Lancaster Co., and receive a sum of money left her by her brother, Ulrich Winsh, dec. (*Pa. Gaz.* 4 Oct 1770).

Hans Ulrich Winsh arrived on 17 Oct 1750 on the brigantine *Sally*, Capt. William Hassleton, from the City of London (*PGP* 1:447).

WITHERSPOON, JAMES, came from Glasgow, and resided with John Parnham, then a merchant in Charles Co., MD but has been away from there for the last ten years. He should apply to Jonas Green, printer, to hear something to his advantage (Annapolis *Maryland Gazette* 25 Jan 1749).

WOLFSON, EVES, a Dutch servant woman, age c15, served her time with Bernard Taylor of Bucks Co., PA, some 4 or 5 years ago. William Forster, copper smith, in Second St., Philadelphia, will pay a reward to anyone who enables him to speak to her (*Pa. Chronicle* 12 July 1773).

WOOD, JOHN, son of James Wood, cordwainer, late of Brandywine Hundred, in Newcastle Co., upon Delaware, who has died. James Huston of Derry Twp., Cumberland Co., has in his hands a small legacy belonging to the said John, who is asked to claim his legacy within the term limited by law, or the legacy will be deemed forfeit, and paid to the other heirs of the said James Wood (*Pa. Gaz.* 4 Aug 1773).

WOOD, JOSIAH, left Philadelphia some years ago, and has not been heard of since. If he will return in eight months from the date hereof, he may hear something to his advantage by applying to Thomas Say, of Philadelphia. The said Josiah was a grandson to Mary Pown or Pound, dec. If he cannot come to Philadelphia, he is asked to write to Say, so that a letter may be received within the time (*Pa. Gaz.* 26 March 1767; *Pennsylvania Chronicle and Universal Advertiser* 9-16 March 1767).).

WOOTTON, GEORGE, and **HERBERT WOOTTON,** sons of Samuel Wootton of Bishop's Castle, Shropshire, Eng., and late of Greenock, Scotland, if living, are asked to apply to the printers, so they may hear of a legacy left them. They have lately sailed out of different ports, but from Norfolk and Baltimore in particular (*GAVN:* 377 cites the *American Gazette and Norfolk and Portsmouth Public Advertiser* 21 May 1794).

WORTHINGTON, HENRY, who left Ireland about two years ago, should contact the printer for a present from his mother (*Maryland Journal and Baltimore Advertiser* 4 Sep 1773).

On 16 Oct 1775 Henry Worthington was a private in the Baltimore Artillery Company. In 1778 he took the Oath of Allegiance before the Hon. George Lindenberger (*BARP:* 298).

In 1790 Henry Worthington of Baltimore Town was head of a family, with one white male over 16, one white male under 16, and two white females (*1790MD* 20, col. 1).

WOTHERSPOON, JAMES, came to America some years ago from Colehill Parish, of Old Munkland near Glasgow. His father has since died and left him a legacy (*GAVN:*377 cites *The Virginia Gazette* 22 Sep 1738).

In 1782 a James Wotherspoon appears in a tax list of Orange Co., VA (*AIS Census Index: Pre-1790* gives no other documentation).

WRIGHT, HANNAH, dau. of Thomas Wright, of Middletown, Bucks Co., near Bristol, is sought by her father. She went away last May 24, unknown to any of here friends. She is a little slender body, and hard of hearing she is hard of hearing, and took with her a calico gown, a striped linen short gown, two pair of shoes, one green calimancoe, and the other calfskin. Her other clothes are not known She is asked to let her relations know where she is (*Pa. Gaz.* 14 June 1764).

WRIGHT, RICHARD, of Ireland, lately kept a school at Perth Amboy. His brother Joseph has arrived in these parts and cannot find where he has removed (*Scott* 1:48 cites the *Pa. Gaz.* 7 Oct 1731).

WUST, ELISABETH, from Lomersheim, Wurtemburg, is sought by Ernest Ludwig Baisch (*Eyster:* 27 cites the *Pennsylvanische Staatsbote* 28 July 1772).

YATES, Mr., lately from Liverpool is asked to leave his address with the printer of this paper, as he will hear of something essentially to his advantage (*Philadelphia Gazette* 23 Nov 1798).

YATES, WILLIAM, and THOMAS YATES, of Lancashire are presumed to be in America. Anyone knowing their address should leave it at the office so they may obtain information that may be of service to them (*Baltimore Patriot* 20 March 1821).

YEAL, WILLIAM, a single man, age c40, left Eng., about eight years ago; if he applies to Joseph Pleasants near Richmond, Henrico Co., he will hear something to his advantage (*GAVN:* 379 cites the *Va. Gaz. or the American Advertiser* 4 May 1782).

In 1799 a William Yeal was listed as one white male over 16 in Hanover Co., VA (1799 Tax List).

YOUNG, DAVID, son of Edward Young of Auhagalian, near Omack, Co. Tyrone, Ireland, came to Philadelphia in the Brig *Dolphin,* Capt. Brown, about the latter end of August or beginning of September. If he will apply to Joseph Jacobs, in Market Street, Philadelphia, he may hear something to his advantage (*Pa. Gaz.* 17 Oct 1765).

YOUNG, JAMES, native of Scotland, a joiner, came to America many years ago and last resided in Alexandria. Bolling Stark of Petersburg will inform him of something greatly to his advantage (*GAVN:* 380 cites Rind's *Virginia Gazette* 9 June 1774).

James Davenport of Westmoreland Co. advises that Young died, unmarried, at the house of Edward Sanford, Westmoreland Co. in Feb 1765 (*GAVN:* 380 cites Rind's *Virginia Gazette* 30 June 1774).

ZEMSCH, JOHANN LEONHARD, son of Wilhelm Friedrich Zemsch, former citizen and master needle maker of Rotenburg, ob der Tauber, Franckischen Kreis (Franconia), left home in 1752 for the third time as a journeyman in the needlecraft, going with his cousin Jung, a needle maker from the Marggraflichen Boodischen Residenz Stadt Durlach, and the Jung family. They went to New England on the Stedman ship and landed with Benjamin Shoemaker, merchant, in Philadelphia. Zemsch was indentured for his passage costs to an Irish miller, and his relatives have not heard from him. Information may be sent to the Rev. Mr. Muhlenberg (*Hocker:* 102 cites the *Wochentlicher Pennsylvanische Staatsbote* 7 Aug 1770).

Johann Leonhardt Zemsch (or Zembsch) arrived in Philadelphia on 17 Sep 1753 on the *Richard and Mary,* Capt. John Moore, commander, from Rotterdam, last from Cowes (*PGP* 1:533, 534).

ZENTZERIN, ODILLIA, is sought by her sister Barbara Zentzerin. They and their brother born in Sultz, Lower Alsace, arrived in this country last autumn. Anyone with information should notify Georg Mueller, Tulpehocken, Berks Co. (*Hocker:* 19 cites the *Pennsylvanische Geschichts-Schreiber* 1 June 1750).

ZIEGLER, FRIEDRICH, a native of Stutttgart, Wurtemburg, is sought by a blood relation who wants to know where he is. The relative can be found by addressing a letter to Herr Peter Paris, in the corner house on 2nd St., Philadelphia (*Eyster:* 41 cites the *Pennsylvanische Staatsbote* 10 March 1779).

Friederich Ziegler was in Philadelphia Co., PA in 1743 (*AIS Census Index: Pre-1790* gives no other documentation).

ZIEGLER, MARTIN, from Malsem, Wurtemburg, is sought by Ernest Ludwig Baisch (*Eyster:* 27 cites the *Pennsylvanische Staatsbote* 28 July 1772).

Martin Zeigler [*sic*] was indentured to Joshua Lippincott of Woolwick Twp., Gloucester Co., [NJ?], on 16 Sep 1773, to serve for seven years (*PGS Indentures,* pp. 300-301).

Another Martin Ziegler was in Philadelphia Co., PA in 1751. A Hans Martin Ziegler was in Philadelphia Co., PA in 1766 (*AIS Census Index: Pre-1790* gives no other documentation).

ZIHAN, MARTIN, weaver and saddler, aged about 50 years, left Henrich Schlonecker of Douglass Twp., Montgomery Co., on 24 Feb 1790, and Schlonecker is now inquiring for him (*Hocker:* 188 cites the *Philadelphische Correspondenz* 9 Sep 1791).

ZINCKE, MORITZ, from Lauterberg, Hanover, came to America three years ago. His brother-in-law, Bodo Otto, in Germantown, wants to know where he is (*Hocker:* 56 cites the *Pennsylvanische Geschichts-Schreiber* 1 June 1756).

APPENDIX

The text of this book was taken from advertisements in eighteenth and nineteenth century newspapers. The items in this Appendix are taken from the letters of Dr. Charles Carroll, of Annapolis, MD, published in the *Maryland Historical Magazine*. In a few cases, additional facts about the person sought have been discovered, and are included here.

BENSON, ANN, was the daughter of Richard and Ann Benson of Bristol, Eng., who died some time before April 1729 when Dr. Charles Carroll, of Annapolis, wrote to William Hunt, merchant in London, asking him to find out what part of their estate Richard and Ann Benson left to their daughter Ann. Frances Wall of Bristol was one of the administrators of her mother. Ann Benson, the daughter, may have also had some interest by the death of a grandmother. In April 1730 Carroll again wrote to Hunt and stated that Ann Benson, the daughter, had married a Mr. George Thorpe (*DCC* 18:330, 340).

GARY (GERRIE), STEPHEN, of West Loo, Cornwall, mariner, in 33 Eliz. I, was sold a messuage or tenement in the Borough of Pontpigridge by George Burrows of Plant in Cornwall. Shortly after the purchase, Gerrie came into Virginia, where he married and left one daughter, who left a son. On 21 Oct 1751 Dr. Charles Carroll of Annapolis wrote to Messrs Sedgley and Cheston, merchants in Bristol, to find out by what right Charles Baudon, shipwright in West Loo, is the possessor to inquire into the state of the property (*DCC* 24:262).

Stephen Gary, Gent., immigrated in 1650 and transported Clare his wife in 1653. In 1650 he had a commission to survey 1500 acres on the Eastern Shore of MD (MPL Q:204, 7:581).

Stephen Gary of Dorchester County died leaving a will dated 27 Oct 1675 and proved 6 April 1686. He left personalty to his son Stephen. To his wife Clare he left the tract *Spoacott* for life as well as land in the town of *West Rue* alias *Purpeham* in Cornwall, England. His second daughter Susannah and youngest daughter Clare were to have the said plantation after the death of his wife. His eldest daughter Magdalen and his other daughters were to have 400 acres on the Ridge in Dorchester County and 300 acres at the head of Watts Creek. His grandson Stephen Warner at age 21 was to have 100 acres called *Cornwall* on Fishing Creek, and his grandchild Mary was to have 50 acres *Refuse Neck*. Jno. Stevens of Dorchester Co., and Wm. Sharpe and Wm. Stevens of Talbot Co. were overseers. William Thomas, Lewis [Evans?], and Samuel Coats witnessed the will (MWB 4:202).

HARLOW, JAMES, has been in MD for some thirty years. He claims a right to house in North Yarmouth called the Chequer Inn, which had belonged to his father, who died leaving no other children but the said Harlow. On 6 Nov 1731, Dr. Charles Carroll of Annapolis wrote to P[hilip?] Smith asking him to make inquiries by what right the person who now holds that house claims (*DCC* 19:286).

HUNT, WORNELL, had died some time before March 1728 when Dr. Charles Carroll of Annapolis wrote to Ignatius Leary at Rathnaheen near Menagh, Co. Tipperary, Ireland, stating that Hunt has died leaving several children, and that the eldest is in Annapolis, and is unacquainted with any in those parts, or with his father's or grandfather's Irish affairs. Carroll also wanted to know what kind of an estate Mr. Wornall Hunt's grandfather had and whether he had entailed it on his son. At the same time Carroll also write to Laurence Mitchell at Menagh in the Co. of Tipperary, asking about the Irish estate of the Hunt's (*DCC* 18:325-328).

Notes on the Wornell Hunt Family

1. HARRY [HENRY?] HUNT died about a year ago in the "Warr Time." He was the first to acquire the estate. He made a will and devised the estate in tail to his son *(DCC* 18:325-8): JOHN.

2: Capt. JOHN HUNT, of Carney, Co. Tipperary, Ireland, son of Harry (1), was the father of (*BDML* 1:472-473; *DCC* 18:325-328): WARNELL.

3. WORNELL HUNT, son of John (2), died in the West Indies by 1728/9. He married Caroline [-?-] (*BDML* 427). Warnell Hunt, of Middlesex, "Gent," was admitted to Lincoln's Inn in 1704, and was an office holder in Nevis in 1705. He arrived in MD by c1708, when he was an Alderman in Annapolis. He imported 20 Negroes in 1709. He was elected to the General Assembly and served between 1708 and 1711 (*BDML* 1:472-473).

On 12 Aug 1712 Hezekiah Linthicum and his wife Milcah, for 5 shillings conv. to Wornell Hunt of Annapolis, two tracts: *Margaret's Field*, 280 a., and *Haslin*, 200 a. On 8 Oct 1716, Hunt sold these lots, now reduced to one tract called *Glorious Prospect*, to Richard Colville and wife of London, William Tancred and wife, Mary Carter, Mary Murrell, and Anne Beswisk, all of Great Britain (AALR PK:517, IB#2:308). On 25 Aug 1716 Hunt sold to Charles Carroll of Annapolis all the tenement and lot where Hunt was living, lot 73, and the tenement and lot opposite, lot 66 (AALR IB#2:303).

"Warnett Hunt" [*sic*] was listed on 5 July 1717 as a creditor to the estate of William Talbot of Baltimore Co. (INAC 38A:40).

In March 1728 Dr. Charles Carroll of Annapolis wrote to Ignatius Leary at Rathnaheen near Menagh, Co. Tipperary, Ireland, and to Laurence Mitchell, as described above.

Wornall Hunt married Carolina [-?-]. They were the parents of the following children, born in St. Ann's Parish, Anne Arundel Co., MD (*AACR:* 65, 69, 75; B): WILLIAM, called by Dr. Carroll, the eldest child; HENRIETTA, bur. 17 Sep 1707; JUDITH, b. 17 Oct, bapt. 3 Nov 1707; MARY, b. 27 Jan 1710; FRANCES, b. 17 Dec 1712; and HENRIETTA, d. 4 Feb 1716/7.

4. WILLIAM HUNT, son of Wornell (3), was living in Charleston, SC on 23 June 1730 when he had a letter from Dr. Charles Carroll who advised him that William would have to obtain notarized proofs of his own birth, his parents' marriage, and some statements that William's father Warnell was the son of Capt. John Hunt of Carney, Co. Tipperary. Carroll suggested that Hunt might best obtain these proofs in Nevis (*DCC*: 18:339).

— — 0 — —

LEARY, |-?-|, son of Ignatius Leary at Rathnaheen near Menagh, Co. Tipperary, Ireland, had come to MD some time before March 1728 when Dr. Charles Carroll of Annapolis wrote to the father saying he was sorry he could not give an agreeable account of the son's behavior and conduct. About last Oct the son had run away from here, having stolen a gentleman's horse and some other things (*DCC* 18:325).

PEERMAN, JAMES, married Ann MacCubbin, daughter of John MacCubbin of Anne Arundel Co., MD. They had a son named James who is now living and of full age. His father was entitled to some houses and personal estate as appears by the will of the grandfather of the present James Peerman, and Mr. Benjamin Peerman was the executor. On 28 Oct 1751 Dr. Charles Carroll of Annapolis wrote to William Black, merchant, in London, telling him that Mrs. Ann Peerman had been in London in 1737 to endeavor to obtain some satisfaction for her dower and her son, and left her papers in the hands of a Mr. Cissell (*DCC* 24:264-265).

Notes on the Peerman Family

JAMES PEERMAN married Ann, dau. of John Maccubbin on 14 Feb 1726 in St. Anne's Paris, Anne Arundel Co. (*AACR*: 94). In his will dated 2 Dec 1745, John Maccubbin of Anne Arundel Co. named his dau. Ann Peerman (MWB 20:297).

On 25 April 1760 Nicholas Minskill and John Evits appraised the personal estate of James Pearman of Anne Arundel Co. at £21.8.6. Anne and Sarah Pearman, admins., filed the inventory on 19 June 1760 (MINV 71:39). James Pearman's estate of £21.8.6 was distributed on 19 June 1760 to a child. Ann Pearman, admx. filed the distribution (BFD 4:13).

Ann Pearman died by 19 April 1768 when Thomas Hyde, admin., filed an account of her estate. He cited an inventory of £75.15.6, and listed payments of £79.7.6. He mentioned a payment from the estate of James Pearman, dec., to Ann, granddau. of this Ann Pearman (MDAD 59:243). Another account was filed by Thomas Hyde on 7 March 1770. The balance was paid to Ann Pearman, dau. of the dec., and retained by the said Thomas Hyde as her guardian (MDAD 62:429).

James and Ann (MacCubbin) Pearman were the parents of: JAMES; and ANN (in 1770, a ward of Thomas Hyde).

— — 0 — —

SIMSON, THOMAS, died testate by 9 Nov 1731 when Dr. Charles Carroll of Annapolis wrote to his brother, John Simson in Jamaica, telling him that a bequest of £1000.0.0 had been made to William Pontenay late of MD, but since of Jamaica, dec. Pontenay's widow is entitled to receive the legacy. A Mr. Deays, Scottish, is endeavoring to have the

Commissary General of Maryland declare Simson's will void in favor of one made by Simson at Philadelphia (*DCC* 19:287-288).

Thomas Simson. Gent., of Cecil Co., late of Jamaica, eldest son of Thomas Simson, and residuary legatee of said Thomas Simson, and of Edward James, both merchants of said island, died leaving a will dated 22 Aug 1728 and proved 14 May 1729. He left £10 each to his brothers John, William, James, and Love, and sister Mary. To his divorced wife Ann (dau. of Mary, widow of Jeremiah Pearce, dec., merchant of Bristol), and his mother Ann (at present the wife of Peter Vallete of Jamaica), the sum of £405 each. Joseph, William, George, John, and Valentine Douglas, all of Cecil Co., were to have £200 each. William Pontenay, Gent., of Cecil Co. was to have £1000. Musgrave Yeamand, and Daniel Curtis, executors with the aforesaid. William Pontenay of the estate in Jamaica, were to have £80 each. Joseph, William, and Valentine Douglas were to be executors in Maryland. The poor of Maryland who were not receiving alms were to have the residue of his estate. Dennis Nowland, Ann Ponteny, Mary Douglas and Cornelius Augustine Savin witnessed the will (MWB 19:649).

= = 0 = =

CPSIA information can be obtained at www.ICGtesting.com
Printed in the USA
BVOW011051200513

321169BV00007B/76/P

9 780806 353685